HUMAN
INFORMATION
PROCESSING

PRENTICE-HALL INTERNATIONAL, INC., *London*
PRENTICE-HALL OF AUSTRALIA, PTY. LTD., *Sydney*
PRENTICE-HALL OF CANADA, LTD., *Toronto*
PRENTICE-HALL OF INDIA PRIVATE LTD., *New Delhi*
PRENTICE-HALL OF JAPAN, INC., *Tokyo*

HUMAN INFORMATION PROCESSING

LAWRENCE J. FOGEL

PRESIDENT, DECISION SCIENCE, INC.
SAN DIEGO, CALIFORNIA

PRENTICE-HALL, INC.

ENGLEWOOD CLIFFS, NEW JERSEY

Formerly titled BIOTECHNOLOGY: *Concepts and Applications*

PROLOGUE

The book *Biotechnology: Concepts and Applications*, published in 1963, was an attempt to provide a background of understanding and relevant data to those concerned with the design of man-machine systems. Since then, there has been a growing recognition of this subject and, in particular, of the importance of the human operator because of his control of equipment systems of increasing scope and diversity. The value of including a man in the system rests upon his unique ability to translate sensed data into meaningful command signals. This book contains only those sections of the original text which most directly concern human information processing.

Because this book is a reprint, it opens with Section B, "The Human Information Input Channels" (page 61). This section includes chapters devoted to the visual channel, the auditory channel, the position- and motion-sensing channel, the somatic channel, the taste and smell channels, and concludes with a summary of the sensory channels, taking note of the human ability to sense time and the probability of events.

This section is followed by Section C, "Decision-making." Chapter 9 is devoted to manual tracking wherein the human operator continually attempts to minimize the perceived error through his control system. Chapter 10 of the original text is omitted in that it concerns decision-making by automata. Chapter 11 presents a broader view of human decision-making and the mechanism which embodies this capacity.

Section D, "The Human Information Output Channels," describes various ways in which the results of human decisions may be communicated to the equipment system under control. Chapter 12 is devoted to situations wherein there is overt cooperation on the part of the decision-maker. Chapter 13 describes techniques for sensing and interpreting information concerning the human operator without his overt cooperation.

In view of recent developments, the original Epilogue is included in this book.

v

Section A of the original text concerned the scientific method and mathematical concepts pertinent to Biotechnology. Section E, "Machine and System Design," included chapters devoted to personal equipment design, design of the immediate environment, cockpit design, man-machine task allocation and system design, as well as evaluation and simulation. Section F presented a brief overview of the structure of Biotechnology. Material within these sections is referenced in the index even though these sections do not appear in this reprint. Hopefully, this broader index will lead the reader to relevant applications growing directly out of his interest in human information processing.

L.J.F.

CONTENTS

SECTION C
DECISION-MAKING

SECTION D
THE HUMAN INFORMATION OUTPUT CHANNELS

HUMAN
INFORMATION
PROCESSING

B

THE HUMAN INFORMATION
INPUT CHANNELS

In order that the human operator perform in a purposeful manner, he must both receive and process information in such a way that he can effect control of the presented real world situation. This human functioning may be described in terms of a number of information processing operations:

Reception—the process of accepting an energy stimulus from the real world and translating this signal into a form which can then excite

Perception—the encoding of the received energy into a neural message which is then transferred to the appropriate brain center which can achieve

Cognition—the assimilation of the information contained in the neural message with respect to data extracted from the memory, thus achieving identification based upon some aspect of past experience. This process may or may not be accompanied by

Apperception—the conscious awareness of the result of cognition. The information, once catagorized by cognition, may receive

Mediation—the transformation of the available information from immediate and past cognitive experience and inherent structure into directives which appear in the form of neural messages which must then receive

Implementation—the process of transferring these messages from the mediation center to the action-taking end-organs wherein the neural signal is decoded into a physical energy output of the organism.

It is the purpose of this section to consider only aspects of reception and perception as they may be accomplished in a man-machine context.

The human operator has a wide capability in terms of information accepting sense modalities. Each of these is characterized by sensitivity, type of accepted data, information processing rate, and many other factors. Chapters 3 through 8 will review these and other facets of the sensory channels to provide the reader with an understanding of the essential features and limitations of the human machine in his acceptance of useful information. In many cases, knowledge of the input information dictates the resulting control of the real world.

In the interests of brevity, these chapters can offer only a cursory survey. They generally describe the sensory stimulus, the sensing mechanism, and aspects of both true and false perception. Care is taken to avoid discussion of specific measurement techniques or other material which may best be found in medical and psychophysical literature. Each chapter carries a rather extensive reference bibliography to indicate sources of data in order to allow the reader to enlarge upon the provided discussion. A number of basic references are common to these chapters. These are included in the bibliography which is found at the end of this Introduction.

Inquiry into the mechanism of the human body is the first step toward understanding the manner in which man may be effectively coupled to the real world.

BIBLIOGRAPHY

ALPORT, F. H., *Theories of Perception and the Concept of Structure*. New York: John Wiley & Sons, Inc., 1955.

CHERRY, C., *On Human Communication*. New York: John Wiley & Sons, Inc., 1957.

FULTON, JOHN F. (ed.), *A Textbook of Physiology*. Philadelphia, Pa.: W. B. Saunders Company, 1949.

GELDARD, F. A., *The Human Senses*. New York: John Wiley & Sons, Inc., 1953.

GRANIT, RAGNAR, *Receptors and Sensory Perception*. New Haven, Conn.: Yale. University Press, 1956.

GUILFORD, J. P., *Psychometric Methods*, 2nd edition. New York: McGraw-Hill Book Company, Inc., 1954.

MORGAN, C. T., and ELIOT STELLAR, *Physiological Psychology*, 2nd edition. New York: McGraw-Hill Book Company, Inc., 1950.

OSGOOD, C. E., *Method and Theory in Experimental Psychology*. New York: Oxford University Press, 1953.

PIERON, HENRI, *The Sensations: Their Functions, Processes, and Mechanisms*. New Haven, Conn.: Yale University Press, 1952.

STEVENS, S. S., "Decibels of Light and Sound," *Physics Today*, Vol. 8, No. 10 (1955), 12–17.

STEVENS, S. S. (ed.), *Handbook of Experimental Psychology*. New York: John Wiley & Sons, Inc., 1951.

WOODSON, WESLEY E., *Human Engineering Guide for Equipment Designers*. Berkely–Los Angeles: University of California Press, 1954.

VON BUDDENBROCK, W., *The Senses*. Ann Arbor, Mich.: University of Michigan Press, 1958.

3

THE VISUAL CHANNEL

3.1. THE VISUAL STIMULUS

Vision is probably the most important single sense modality employed by the human operator in his gathering of information concerning his relation to the real world. In particular, it provides knowledge concerning the status of the equipment under his cognizance. The visual sense depends upon the absorption of light energy by the eye and the successive conversion of this energy into neural messages which are mediated by the brain into perceptual patterns. To understand some of the essential properties and limitations of the visual information channel, it is best to consider separately each of the stages in the visual process.

The stimulus energy arrives at the eye in the form of light, that is, electromagnetic radiation at a frequency of almost a billion cycles per second. Such radiation is usually described in terms of its wavelength. The visible spectrum ranges from a wavelength of about 0.7 microns (millionths of a meter) at the red extreme to about 0.4 microns at the violet end of the color spectrum. Wavelength is often expressed in Angstrom units, symbolized by Å, where one Angstrom is equal to 10^{-4} micron. Wavelength, λ, is dependent upon both the frequency, f, and the velocity, v, of the propagating energy according to the relation,

$$v = f\lambda$$

This relationship is useful in cases where light must pass through various media so that the velocity of propagation changes, thus affecting the wavelength with possible modification of the resulting image. The velocity of light is about 186,000 miles per second or 3×10^8 meters per second in passage through a vacuum. The human eye reduces this velocity to different values dependent upon the density of the material in question. The effect will be examined at a more appropriate point below in connection with the resulting index of refraction.

Before vision can occur, the incoming direction of radiant energy must be viewed. The human operator usually has great flexibility in modifying his position in order to view an object. Sometimes, however, the shoulders are restrained as a protective measure. When this is the case, the visual domain is limited by the rotary extremes of the head and eyeballs working together. Head rotation may be expressed in terms of the angle of rotation of the cervical vertebrae, but for the purpose of this discussion it is worth stating only that this rotation of the head can add about ± 70 degrees to the visual angle capability. Reference is made to Chapter 14 for further discussion on the limitation of body movement.

3.2. ASPECTS OF EYE MOVEMENT

On first consideration, it might appear that eyelid movement might interfere with the acceptance of visual information. Involuntary blinking occurs at a varying rate in order to maintain eye lubrication and provides protection from foreign objects. Although a blink might obscure some short duration stimulus, there is presently no evidence that such involuntary blinking interferes to any measurable extent with fixation. As a result, involuntary blinking may be said to have essentially no effect on visual perception.

There is also some coordinated eyelid movement. As the eye tracks a moving target, both the lower and upper lids show motions related to the movement of the cornea (that transparent bulge in the front of the eyeball). Vertical movement of the eye yields the most marked lid motion, especially in the upper lid. As the eye looks progressively downward, the upper lids descend until an observer facing the subject can no longer see the pupil of the subject's eye. When the eye rotates in a horizontal plane, both lids undergo some increased separation near the cornea. These coordinated lid movements are primarily an accommodation.

Each eyeball is moved by six muscles, as shown in Figure 3.1, these being innervated by three cranial nerves. By means of these muscles the eyeballs can execute various rotary movements around different axes. The intersection of these axes is called the center of rotation of the eyeball; this point being about 13.5 millimeters behind the cornea in the normal human male. Specifically, these axes are the horizontal axes, the transverse axes, the vertical axes, and the oblique axes, which include all those axes of rotation making oblique angles with the horizontal plane. Rotation around the oblique axes moves the eyeball obliquely upward and downward. To achieve movement, at least two muscles must act cooperatively, one with increasing tension, and the other relaxing to permit the movement. Obviously, this complex of muscle function cannot be expressed in any simple linear fashion. Any single rotary movement is usually the result of a number of causal factors, each of which is time dependent and directed toward particular muscle couples.

The eyes can be moved with sufficient precision to allow as many as 100,000 different fixation points on objects within a roughly circular range of about 100° around the visual axes (the normal direction of sight). Capability of rotation to the left and to the right is approximately equal, while vertical upward movement is limited to about 40°, and downward movement is usually stopped at 60°. Rotation of the eyeball around the visual axis rarely extends more than 10°.

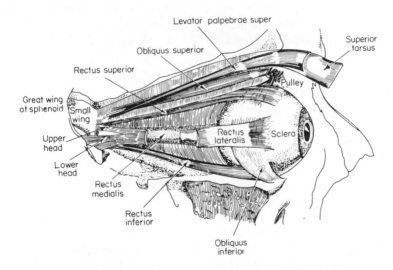

Figure 3.1. Muscles of the right orbit. (From C. M. Goss, *Gray's Anatomy*, 27th edition, Philadelphia: Lea & Febiger, 1959. Reprinted with permission.)

A number of experiments have explored the extent of the visual domain under "standard viewing condition." This condition is defined as a constant fixation on a point at eye level in the mid-saggital plane of the observer (that vertical plane which bisects the subject parallel to the visual axis), with head erect, fixed, and centered on the same plane, with given illumination, contrast, and size of target. As would be expected, it was found that the greater the contrast the broader the visual field, this function being directly dependent upon target size. Breadth of the visual field is also directly dependent upon the level of illumination up to about 0.001 foot lamberts. Above this level the extent of the field observed appears to be limited by other factors. The refraction of incident light also has an effect on the size of visual acceptance angle, the amount being dependent upon the particular shape of the cornea. In this regard, age does not appear to become a serious factor until after about forty years.

As shown in Figure 3.2, the limits of the visual field are constrained by the physical contours of the face. The eyebrow and nose can occlude portions of the domain resulting in the nonsymmetrical patterns shown for the right eye. Only on the temporal side is the visual field limited by the refractive power of the eye. A reversed pattern describes the left eye. Figure 3.3 indicates the associated limits of binocular peripheral vision.

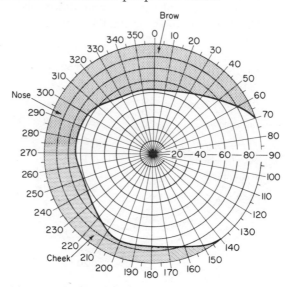

Figure 3.2. Perimetric chart showing the field of vision for an average right eye when the eye looks straight ahead and does not move. (From T. C. Ruch and J. F. Fulton, *Medical Physiology and Biophysics*, 18th edition, Philadelphia: W. B. Saunders Company, 1960. Reprinted with permission.)

The two eyes move together so as to keep the visual axes parallel or to accomplish convergence of these axes upon a common point. Even the simple sequence of fixations of the eyes, along a line of print, requires simultaneous conjugate movement as well as slight convergence-divergence movements. Shift from a far-field point to a near subject requires an intricate set of muscle controls including constriction of the pupil, accommodation of the eye lens, and binocular convergence. Each action directive from the brain is coupled with the required inhibition directive to the antagonist muscles. The result is a smooth configuration of many actions to facilitate the acceptance of visual information. In fact, this binocular interaction can increase the probability of discrimination of small amounts of light over that which would be accomplished by monocular detection alone. Many of the features of binocular vision are deferred to further discussion below.

When the head is moved from side to side while the observer remains fixed in steady attention to a particular object, the eye keeps pointed at that object. This is known as *compensatory* eye movement. The movement is smooth and is adjusted to maintain the retinal image position almost stationary. In a similar manner when the eye follows a moving target there is a smooth eye movement called *pursuit*. Neither compensatory nor pursuit smooth eye motion can be stimulated in the absence of a target upon which to fixate.

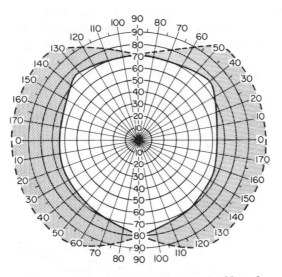

Figure 3.3. Perimetric chart showing the binocular field of view. The fields overlap in the white region. (After W. S. Duke-Elder, *Textbook of Ophthalmology*, St. Louis, Mo.: C. V. Mosby Company, 1934.)

In addition to these gross eye movements, there are other involuntary minor movements. *Tremor* of the eye is a high frequency vibration falling between about 30 and 80 cycles per second. Rotary displacements can occur up to about 30 seconds of arc. Such motion is irregular, occurring in different directions from moment to moment of an angular velocity of about 18 minutes per second, with accelerations up to 20° per second squared. Tremor appears to be independent of outside stimuli and is uncoordinated between the two eyes.

There are particular irregularly occurring short jerky movements of the eye called *flick*. These are identified by a characteristic pattern of initial and terminal movement. The initial motion generally covers from about 1 to 20 minutes of arc lasting for a time duration of about 0.01 seconds. The terminal phase of motion is in approximately the opposite direction, taking about the same time interval, but being of somewhat smaller movement ranging from about 30 seconds to 4 minutes of arc. The velocity of flick is approximately $10°$ per second with accelerations up to the range of $1000°$ per second squared. The time interval between successive flicks ranges from 0.03 seconds to about 5 seconds, averaging around 0.7 seconds. Although flicks are simultaneous for both eyes, their duration and extent are not necessarily the same in both eyes.

The third type of involuntary eye movement is called *drift*. Magnitude of drift is usually less than 6 minutes of arc, but on occasion it may reach 15 minutes. The maximum angular velocity of the eye during drift is about 20 minutes per second. When drift occurs in the vertical plane, the two eyes move together; while in the horizontal plane, the eyes may concur or move in opposite directions (in the latter case convergence is usually the cause).

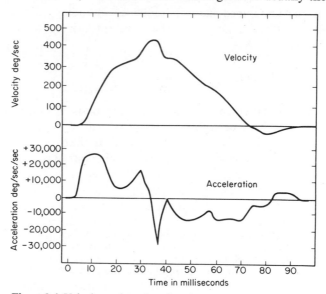

Figure 3.4. Velocity and acceleration changes during a typical $20°$ saccadic movement.

As the eyes roam the visual field, they make jumps from one fixation point to another. These are called *saccadic movements*. The duration of time required for movement ranges along an almost linear scale, from about 30 milliseconds for $5°$ to about 100 milliseconds for $40°$ angular shift of fixation point. The maximum velocity of movement reaches about $350°$ per second for a $10°$ shift and about $550°$ per second for a $30°$ shift in fixation. It is interesting to note the velocity and acceleration patterns for a typical $20°$ saccadic movement. This is shown in Figure 3.4. Note the sudden reversal in acceleration, which bears a resemblance to the action of a switching servo, which corrects the sensed error in a minimum of time by reversing the thrust action at about the halfway point to the intended reference. In each phase of movement, the trajectory equation may be written in the form,

$$A_2 \frac{d^2\theta}{dt^2} + A_1 \frac{d\theta}{dt} + A_0(\theta - \theta_0) = f(t)$$

where A_2 is the moment of inertia of the eyeball, A_1 is the coefficient of friction which the eyeball encounters, and A_0 is the force with which the relaxed muscle opposes the movement, thus introducing a spring force proportional to the displacement from the reference position where both antagonistic muscles are relaxed. This system may be simplified and placed in the standard damped resonance form,

$$\frac{d^2\theta}{dt^2} + 2\zeta\omega_n \frac{d\theta}{dt} + \omega_n^2\theta = K$$

where ω_n is the undamped natural frequency in radians per second, ζ is the damping coefficient, and K is the constant driving force. Algebraic manipulation reveals that

$$\omega_n = \sqrt{\frac{A_0}{A_2}} \quad \text{and} \quad \zeta = \frac{A_1}{2\sqrt{A_0 A_2}}$$

These parameters have been evaluated on the basis of empirical data by G. Westheimer and have been found to approximate $\omega_n = 120$ and $\zeta = 0.7$. This latter value is of interest since it corresponds to the usual design damping ratio rule of thumb for linear tracking servos which intend to provide a good compromise between minimum time to null the error and maximum overshoot. The assumption of a constant driving force appears reasonable since the maximum acceleration of the eyeball showed no significant differences for saccadic movements ranging from 15° to 50°. About 10 milliseconds reaction time delay accompanies each saccadic movement measured from time of initiating nerve stimulation.

Studies have been performed to determine the fixation point, distribution, and pattern corresponding to the view of given geometric displays. Figure 3.5 indicates some typical eye fixation patterns as measured by A. Ford et al. In general, it was found that the eyes were fixated for approximately 85 per cent of the time, the remaining time being spent in moving from one fixation point to another. Obviously this percentage value is severely dependent upon many factors, in addition to the provided geometric pattern. It seems reasonable to assume that the duration of fixations would tend to be longer in those situations where the field being scanned contains much that is unfamiliar or complex.

The amazing thing is that neither the saccadic movement or the other involuntary movements are subjectively observed in normal visual perception, even though such movement causes distinct shift of the image upon the retina.

Figure 3.5. Electro-oculographic patterns of recorded eye movements (a) alternating between 2 dots 30° apart and then back to center, in a horizontal direction (b) alternation for the same amount in the vertical direction (c) eye fixations on 8 spaced dots around the rim of the circular field of search with a diameter requiring a total of 30° of eyeball rotation (d) on the same circular field but without dots, the subject searching for a target in large, random, saccadic jumps between fixations.

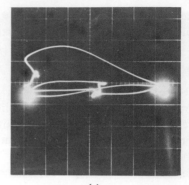

(a)

3.3. OPTICAL PROPERTIES OF THE EYE

The human eyeball is approximately spherical, about 1 inch in diameter, with a pronounced bulge on the forward surface. The outer shell of the eye is composed of three layers of tissue. The outermost of these layers, the sclera, acts as a protective coating for the eyeball. This layer covers about $\frac{5}{6}$ of the surface of the eye and constitutes the "white" of the eye. At the front of the eyeball, it is continuous with the bulging and transparent cornea. The middle layer of the coating of the eye is the uvea, a vascular layer which is the ciliary body and the iris lying at the front of the eye, and the choroid, the lining intimately covered by the retina. The innermost layer is the light-sensitive retina which coats most of the inner surface behind the lens.

There are four light refracting media. The cornea, a tough five-layered membrane through which the light is admitted to the interior of the eye, is generally circular in outline and is almost of uniform thickness throughout—about 1 millimeter. Behind the cornea is a chamber filled with aqueous humor, a salt water solution, which separates the cornea from the crystalline lens. The lens itself is a flattened sphere constructed of a large number of transparent layers of structureless membrane. The frontal surface of the lens is more convex than the rear surface. It is ringed by the ciliary muscle which can distend the periphery of the lens, thereby changing the cross section of the lens and resulting in a corresponding change in the focal length. This muscle accomplishes focus for the eye. Behind the lens there is a larger cavity filled with a fluid called the vitreous humor. This fluid, transparent and somewhat viscous, consists mainly of water (99 per cent), salts, and albumen. It is the pressure transfer of these fluids (about 17 millimeters Hg) which maintains the spherical shape of the eye. Figure 3.6 shows a horizontal section of the human eye showing these media.

The index of refraction is defined as the ratio of the velocity of light in the medium to the velocity of light in vacuum. The ratio of the indices of refraction of contiguous media determines the ratio of the sines of the incident and reflected ray angles of light passing through an interface. The index of re

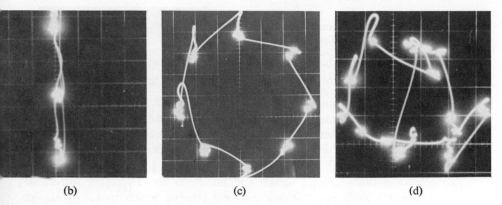

(b)   (c)   (d)

fraction for air is 1.000. The value for both aqueous humor and vitreous
humor is 1.336, for the crystalline lens material it is 1.413. From these values
it becomes apparent that the most significant bending of the incident light
occurs as it enters the eye rather than in its passage through the lens.

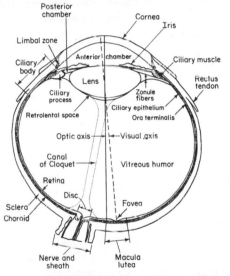

Figure 3.6. Horizontal section of the human eye.
(From J. F. Fulton, *A Textbook of Physiology*, Phila-
delphia: W. B. Saunders Company, 1955. After
F. W. Weymouth from Walls.)

Consideration of the passage of light to stimulate the retina must also
include the stray (entoptic) light. This factor can have an appreciable effect
since even weak stimulation of the entire retinal surface could easily produce
a gross neural message in excess of that corresponding to a specific image
but of much smaller area. There are four sources of such stray light:

(1) the passage of diffused light through the eye wall,

(2) defraction and scattering in the optic media and the interfaces between different refractive indexed media,

(3) reflection from the retinal image, and,

(4) reflection from one portion of the retina to another.

Between the cornea and the lens there is the iris, a pigmented disc with a circular opening called the pupil. The iris rests close upon the lens and is attached to the peripheral muscle around its outer edge which contracts or relaxes to control the amount of light passing into the inner eye. As viewed through the cornea, the iris is magnified by about $\frac{1}{8}$. It is comprised of a complex network of blood vessels and muscle tissue. The inner surface of the iris has a deep purple-black pigment coating which makes it almost impervious to light penetration. The result is an excellent optical diaphragm which can effectively control the amount of light reaching the retina. Further, the location of the iris between cornea and lens is of distinct value, since constriction there occludes the peripheral, the least true, portions of these transparent media. The irises of both eyes are innervated from the same autonomic source, so that light stimulus to either eye should cause a change in the pupil size of both eyes.

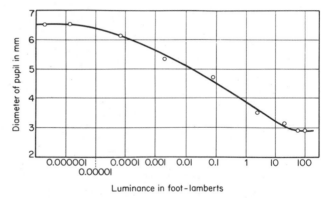

Luminance in foot-lamberts

Figure 3.7. Relation of pupil diameter to illumination. (After F. W. Weymouth from T. C. Ruch and J. F. Fulton, *Medical Physiology and Biophysics*, 18th edition, Philadelphia: W. B. Saunders Company, 1960. Data from Wagman and Nathanson. Reprinted with permission.)

The range of normal pupil diameter is from about 2.9 millimeters to 6.5 millimeters, a five-fold change in area dependent upon incident light intensity (see Figure 3.7). Pupil diameter is a direct function of the adaptation level of the retina, so that a slight decrease in illumination will cause an almost immediate dilation of the pupil, followed by a gradual constriction to the habitual size as the retina adapts to the increased stimulus level. Constriction response time usually takes about 3 or 4 seconds and, as such, offers a safety device for the delicate internal light-sensitive eye structure.

3.4. NEURAL ENCODING OF THE LIGHT ENERGY

After the light has passed through the cornea, aqueous humor, aperture of the iris, lens, and vitreous humor, it impinges upon the retina. The retina is a most complex structure. Light receptor cells are packed closely, one upon another, under a single stratum of brownish pigmented cells which serves as a protection against over-exposure to strong light intensities. The light sensitive retina extends over most of the inner surface of the eyeball and terminates at the rear of the lens. Within this domain, there are approximately 125 million rod cells and 6 million cone cells, the rods and cones being different types of light sensitive receptors. This multitude of cells forms a mosaic which transforms the imposed visual image into a pattern of neural excitation.

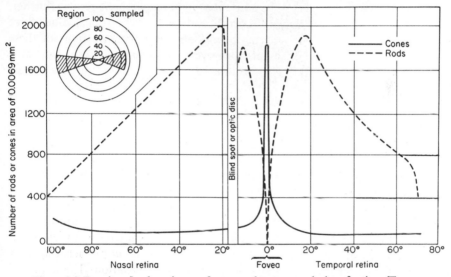

Figure 3.8. Density of rods and cones from nasal to temporal edge of retina. (From "Vision in Military Aviation," *WADC TR 58–399.* Reprinted with permission.)

The density of rod and cone cells is not constant over the retinal surface. (See Figure 3.8.) The indicated break in the curve corresponds to the optic disc, that portion of the retina which is interrupted by the entrance of the optic nerve. It is this area which provides the commonly observed blind spot in vision. Near to the optic disc and directly in line with the visual axis is the most sensitive portion of the retina, the area centralis. The central domain of this area extends over a diameter of about 600 microns. Called the fovea centralis, it contains about 34,000 cones and *no* rod receptors. It is in the region of the fovea that the eye sees with greatest clarity. This seems reasonable since cone cells are connected to fewer individual nerve fibers so that the stimulation of each individual cell calls to action a particular spatial neural energy. This is in contradistinction to rod cells, which are connected in groups so that they respond to a light stimulus over a general area yielding an increase in low level light sensitivity but a decrease in resolution of detail. The result of these differences in structure is a decrease in visual sharpness toward the periphery of the visual field although it is this periphery which offers the greatest sensitivity to light. Very dim light sources can be registered at night on the peripheral part of the retina, when at the same time they would be invisible to the central area.

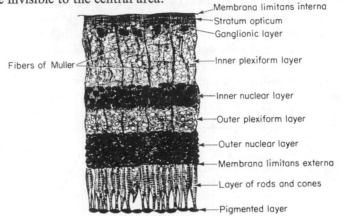

Figure 3.9. Magnified section of the retina. (From C. M. Goss, *Gray's Anatomy*, 27th edition, Philadelphia: Lea & Febiger, 1959. Reprinted with permission.)

Figure 3.9 shows a cross section of the neural structure of the retina, and Figure 3.10 indicates something of its organization. The rod and cone cells appear in just those shapes directly below the topmost protective layer which is composed of a single depth of cells. As light is received, a photochemical reaction occurs which results in an excitation causing an electrical voltage to be produced. This voltage travels to the *axon* of each cell, that extended tail which carries the voltage signal in translation. The axons of these light sensitive neurons end upon the *dendrites* of the middle layer of the retina which is composed of bipolar nerve cells. Dendrites are the input members of neurons, and upon stimulation they can excite the firing of their connected nerve cell through what is called a *synapse* (an electrical connection point). It is at this level that the sharp distinction between rod and cone cell systems breaks down. The majority of rod and cone cells synapse with the diffuse type of bipolar nerve cell due to the multiplicity of dendrites and their apparently random array. There is, however, a second type of bipolar cell which is termed monosynaptic. Since rods never connect electrically with this type of bipolar neuron, the result is an increase in the resolution required for normal visual acceptance of information. In turn, the bipolar cells terminate in axons which synapse with dendrites of the next and lowest layer of neurons called the ganglion cells. These latter neurons also fall into two broadly similar categories. *Diffuse ganglion cells* connect with a great number of bipolar cells and accomplish a general synthesis or averaging, while the

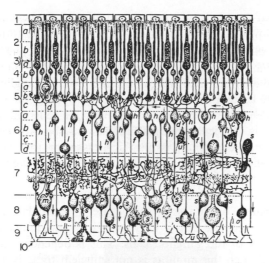

Figure 3.10. Representative structure of primate retina. The numbers and letters at the left indicate elements as follows: (*c*) horizontal cell, (*d*) mop bipolar, (*e*) brush bipolar, (*f*) flat bipolar, (*h*) midget bipolar, (*i*) centrifugal bipolar (amacrine cell), (*m, n,* and *o*) diffuse ganglion cells, (*n*) short ganglion cell, (*s*) midget ganglion cell, (*u*) "radial fibers" of Miller. (From S. S. Stevens, *Handbook of Experimental Psychology*, New York: John Wiley & Sons, Inc., 1959.)

monosynaptic ganglion cells establish synaptic connections with one or two bipolar cells. Thus they are stimulated by only a few cones. The axons of the ganglion cells generally are directed toward the optic disc and are gradually assembled to form bundles which become part of the optic nerve. Figure 3.11

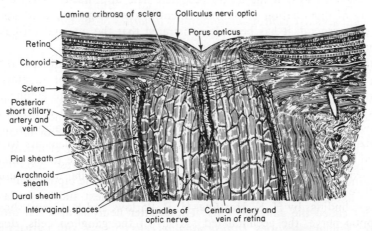

Figure 3.11. Horizontal cross section of the optic nerve and its entrance into the eyeball.

indicates a cross section of the optic disc. All information derived from the optical image must pass through this path in order to reach the brain.

In general, the retina consists of three successive layers. The receptors nearest the light-exposed surface converge onto the bipolar secondary neurons, and these in turn converge onto the layer of ganglion cells. Lateral connections are accomplished within the retina by horizontal cells which lie at the base of the rods and cones and by amacrine cells which lie just above the ganglion cells. Particular midget bipolars may be capable of receiving a signal from a single cone and passing this message on to the optic nerve, but it must be remembered that this link is subject to inhibitive interaction from adjacent nerve cells.

A *receptive field* is defined as that region of the retina within which a change of stimulus brightness would cause a particular ganglion cell to discharge. Each receptive field is surrounded by an annular area which can affect the activity of the ganglion cells. This is dependent upon light level stimulation, although this annulus is not sufficient to activate the ganglion, if it alone receives light stimulus. Three types of receptive fields have thus far been observed. Certain receptive fields may be identified which will cause a sudden increase in the rate of discharge upon the receipt of a small spot of light; others become active only as the light is removed, while still others are excited by either the onset or cessation of the illumination. For all three types of receptive fields the sensitivity decreases toward the periphery.

It is interesting to note that the off-mechanism of field, which are sensitive to the cessation of light stimulus, shows an additive property between the central domain and the peripheral portion of the same field. That is, both of these regions of the off-receptive fields are activated by the termination of the light stimulus. This is in contradistinction to the property of the on-off fields which discriminates between these internal regions. Activation of the peripheral region reduces the signal activity level generated by the central field, and vice versa so that the on-off receptive field appears to measure the inequality of illumination or the movement of the image as placed upon the retina. In general, it has been demonstrated that the on- and off-fields are mutually exclusive at the particular connected ganglion.

The retina is covered with overlapping receptive fields of very different sizes, these being time dependent and related to the level of adaptation. In general, the receptive fields are internally structured so as to emphasize the particular property characteristic of the center of the field and this at the expense of the sensitivity of the peripheral region. The placing of a weak polarizing electric field across the retina causes the on-elements to be inhibited by the anode while off-elements tend to discharge to the anode. In other words, light and the cathode appear to act in a similar manner upon the receptive fields.

These findings by H. K. Hartline, H. B. Barlow, and R. Granit show that the optic nerve, the accumulated axons of the ganglion cells, does not transmit information only about the light intensity at the individual points on the retina. Each nerve fiber actually measures only a single feature of the entire distribution of light in the receptive field area. There are then three distributed channels with a great amount of overlap of individual receptive fields in any one channel. The neural message separately describes the amount and pattern of dimming of the stimulus light through the off-channel, the boundaries of the lighted area and their motion through the on-off channel, and the channel of brightness through the on-channel. A stationary and unchanging imposed visual pattern would gradually allow the optic nerve to return to the quiet level of spontaneous activity and thereby transmit no new information. Body tremor prevents this occurrence.

Definition of the visual image is limited by the size and number of the receptive fields. This is further complicated by the time delay associated with actions of the on- and off-mechanisms. There is certainly a significant amount of redundancy in the complementary on- and off-channel's representation of the imposed light image, and yet it would be difficult to justify the extremely fine mosaic of rod and cone receptor cells if only such gross messages were to be encoded.

As pointed out by J. Lettvin, understanding of the neural encoding of the retina may not come through the relatively simple detailed examination of the effects of activation by a tiny test light stimulus. The essential purpose of the encoding mechanism is to digest gross patterns. The "laboratory" stimulus may be expected to fall outside the capability for retinal translation into a meaningful neural message even if it is applied over a reasonable area. Minute stimulus-response study on individual receptor cells can provide knowledge only of the capability of that cell. This still leaves the complex retinal information transformation as an imposing unknown. The brute force approach of a detailed examination of the entire retinal information transduction must face a prohibitive amount of data. Only the simultaneous monitoring of each of the optic nerve fibers during gross stimulus excitation could provide an indicative measure. Even if such measurement were obtainable, the complexity of structure in terms of interactions and the subjective individual differences would most likely obviate interpretation. To complete the indictment of such an experimental approach, it is only necessary to mention the impossibility of properly separating out the efferent neural signals which come from the brain to the retina as part of the normal closed-loop operation.

In the face of these difficulties to the more classical approach, it appears most reasonable to study the integration of the four distributed transformations which, for example, have been found to exist in the retina of the frog. These operations are independent of the level of general illumination and express the image in terms of

(1) local sharp edges and contrast,
(2) the curvature of edges of a dark object,

(3) the movement of edges, and

(4) the local dimmings produced by movement or rapid general darkening.

These four transformations of the imposed optical image are superimposed in registration within the brain.

Obviously a great portion of the interpretation of the visual field is accomplished directly within the neural encoding mechanism. For example, the second of the four image characteristics for the frog appears to be a means for the rapid identification of bugs, this being independent of the lighting level and motion relative to the background. Evidently many of the characteristics of perception are contained within the essential structure of the retina so that the brain receives partially digested information in a form appropriate to the ensuing decision-making. In truth, the retina is an extended portion of the brain.

A number of different photosensitive substances with individual absorption maxima at different wavelengths may appear in the retina. Since only light which is absorbed can be effective in initiating a stimulus, it is of interest to examine these spectra and the corresponding substances.

Visual purple was discovered in the eye of the frog by Boll in 1876. The visual purple which is found in the human eye has been shown to possess an absorption characteristic which closely approximates the spectral response of the dark-adapted observer. This agreement is only on an average basis and therefore does not necessarily imply that each of the optic nerves may carry only such a spectral response message. The total perceived brightness is certainly not based upon events corresponding to a single nerve factor. Indeed, aspects of averaging, which takes place within the psychophysical functioning, have been demonstrated to show that the individual variability produced through the light sensitivity of various substances results in an over-all spectral response corresponding to scotopic vision.

It is well known that vision after light adaptation is the result of cone action and that this over-all spectral response is different from that which is obtained through the action of the rods operating through visual purple on the dark-adapted field. More particularly, the photopic response reaches its peak around 5600 Å, which is about 600 Å above the scotopic spectral sensitivity curve maxima. These data are shown in Figure 3.12, expressed in terms of wavelength and the corresponding visibility coefficient. This shift in the frequency of maximum sensitivity is called the *Purkinje shift* after its original discoverer.

As indicated above, several receptors may converge upon a single optic nerve fiber so that this fiber may respond in both the dark-adapted and light-adapted eye. Now the minimum latency of response in the visual cortex for optic neural stimulation is known to be in the order of 2 milliseconds so that the encoded message would appear to be conducted by some of the largest and fastest conducting fibers available (those with an average conduction velocity of about 34 meters per second and a maximum of 70 meters per second). Since both scotopic and photopic vision actuates the same fiber, the amount depending upon stimulus strength and state of adaptation, it is reasonable to suspect that this fiber may deal with the general brightness distribution. The same fibers must serve as a basis for achromatic vision. They would not be expected to represent any wavelength discrimination correspondence to color, except by frequency of neural stimulation or time modulation. This problem remains unresolved.

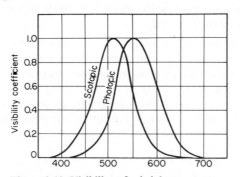

Figure 3.12. Visibility of a bright spectrum as seen by cones (photopic) and of a dim spectrum as seen by rods (scotopic). The visibility coefficient is the reciprocal of the energy which is just visible for each wavelength of light (scotopic), or which matches a moderately bright standard light (photopic). Although cones are much less sensitive than rods, the curves are plotted so that the maximum visibility coefficient is unity. (From Rawdon-Smith, *Theories of Sensation*, New York: Cambridge University Press, 1938. After Hecht and Williams, *J. Gen. Physiology*, 1922, 5: 1–34.)

If it is reasonable to assume that the perception of color is the result of spectral analysis within the retina, then it is equally reasonable to assume that these different sensed characteristics, such as frequency bands, might be transmitted along independent sets of optic nerve fibers to terminate in separate points in the brain. Experimental evidence has shown that the time interval difference between stimulus presentation and perception is dependent upon the exciting wavelength of the light energy. Very short-time duration flashes of different monochromatic light (in the order of a few microseconds) were presented in pairs to a rod-free area of the subject's retina. The subjective decision as to which color flash came first was found to be quite repeatable even when the time between flashes was reduced to a few milliseconds. In almost all cases it was found necessary to place a time interval between flashes of different color in order to obtain a subjective decision of simultaneity. This time interval then becomes a measure of the latency differ-ence in the neural system. For example, simultaneous red and blue flashes were perceived with red first, there being a tend to fifteen millisecond latency measured for normal subjects.

The velocity of propagation of a nerve impulse is dependent upon a number of factors, including a strong dependence upon the diameter of the nerve fiber as mentioned above (reference a related discussion in Chapter 11). In this manner, it is possible that the encoded message may contain a temporal distribution serving to identify the particular color of the stimulus. P. Scott and K. G. Williams suggest that,

> The fibers of the optic nerve might be in contact with the retinal layers in such a way that a given spectral distribution of input gives rise to nerve impulse transmission predominantly along nerve fibers that can be related to the input spectrum, the degree of activity of the fiber being functionally dependent on its associated conduction velocity as compared to the stimulus wavelength. At the brain, the over-all effect of impulsive stimulation would be a temporal pattern with an outline that could be related to the spectral characteristics of the visual stimulus.
>
> If such a mechanism forms the basis of normal color perception further apparatus would be necessary to generate discrete stimulation of the retinal receptor cells, otherwise the temporal coding would be lost in continuous stimulation. It could be suggested that the continuous, involuntary tremor of the eyeball, which has been shown to be necessary for visual discrimination and color perception, may transform continuous visual inputs into sets of dis-crete stimuli in the sweep from one receptor to the next.

More recently, O. Myers states:[1]

> If, as seems inescapable, spectral information is superposed upon spatial infor-mation in the over-all temporal pattern of nerve activity on arrival at the cortex, a time reference is required. Otherwise, the two patterns could not be separated unambiguously. It is suggested that this reference may be from the saccadic eye movements. Visibility is reduced by more than 10 db during a saccade. According to this notion, a spatial pattern is perceived primarily through the agency of cones with maximum response near the peak of the photopic visibility function, supplemented by rod activity. Interfering information which arrives earlier or later is perceived as red or blue, with hue difference proportional to time difference. This process is repeated with each saccadic movement, or other interruption of vision. The time reference is maintained even for mono-chromatic illumination by means of the rods. Because no mechanism for spec-tral to temporal transformation is available to them, their contribution (at constant sensitivity) to the spatial to temporal transformation will be indepen-dent of wavelength.

It is recognized that the comments made above are of a conjectural nature. However, they appear to offer sufficient merit to be worthy of more detailed neurological investigation in the future.

[1] From personal communication dated March 2, 1962.

The sensory nerve fibers from the retina of each eye form the optic nerve which passes through the interbrain and stimulate relay nerve fibers which carry the neural message on to the occipital lobe of the brain. Each optic nerve is comprised of at least one million individual fibers. These two nerves come together at the optic chiasm where some of the fibers of each nerve cross over in accordance with the pattern as shown in Figure 3.13. The fibers

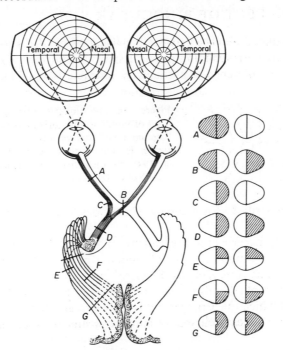

Figure 3.13. Diagram of central visual pathways passing to left hemisphere. Shaded areas in inserts indicate visual defects resulting from lesions at point indicated by corresponding letter on left hand figure. For convenience, visual fields for two eyes are shown separated, but actually they superimpose so that vertical meridians coincide. (From John Homans, *A Textbook of Surgery*, 6th ed., 1945. Courtesy of Charles C. Thomas, Publisher, Springfield, Illinois.)

from the inner half of the retina (corresponding to the temporal fields of view) cross over while those in the outer half of the retina (corresponding to the nasal visual field) do not. This crossover follows the general rule that each half of the brain is primarily concerned with the opposite side of the body.

It is curious that this division of the visual field into two related occipital lobes produces no subjective discontinuity in the perceived field of view. A single stimulus impinging on corresponding points of the two eyes releases optic nerve impulses that would appear to find a final common path within the brain in order to achieve proper registration. Evidently there must be considerable interconnection between the halves of the brain in order to account for this. It may be that the crossover pattern permits much greater reliability of the visual system through the contributed redundancy.

3.5. THE EFFECT OF BINOCULAR VISION

There is a distinct difference between the visual space that is perceived by the subject and the corresponding physical space of the real world under observation. This difference is particularly characteristic of binocular vision

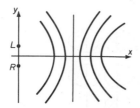

Figure 3.14. The subjective arrangement of a set of points in the horizontal plane into "straight lines" transverse to the visual axis. (From R. Luneburg, *Studies and Essays*, © 1948 by Interscience Publishers, Inc., New York. Reprinted with permission.)

and may be described as a mapping of the objective space into a subjective space.

Several early experiments are worthy of review. H. Helmholz required that the subject arrange a number of luminous points in the horizontal plane into a straight line transverse to the visual axis. The resulting arrangements formed members of a family of curves as shown in Figure 3.14. There is some distance x_0 at which the arrangement is truly straight, but for x less than x_0 the points trace concave curves while for x greater than x_0 the points trace

Figure 3.15. The subjective arrangement of points to form an alley of equidistant walls. (From R. Luneburg, *Studies and Essays*, © 1948 by Interscience Publishers, Inc., New York. Reprinted with permission.)

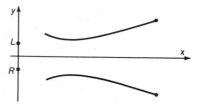

convex curves; the degree of distortion is directly dependent upon the radial distance of the points from the distance x_0. This family of curves is called the *frontal plane horopters*.

Another experiment was carried out by F. Hillebrand which asked the subject to arrange luminous points into two receding lines to form an alley where the distance between the walls remains fixed. The resulting physical arrangement is shown in Figure 3.15. Later, W. Blumenfeld repeated and confirmed this finding. However, if the instruction to the subject was modified to arrange the points along parallel straight lines, then these "parallel alleys" were consistently located inside the "equidistant alley."

Let it be assumed that the physical space under observation is Euclidean and that the right eye, R, and the left eye, L, are placed respectively at centers of rotation $x = z = 0$, $y = \pm 1$ of a Cartesian coordinate system. If these eyes are fixated at point, P', then the optical axes of the eyes converge forming RP' and LP' as shown in Figure 3.16. This geometry is characterized by the angles α, β, and θ. The physical point P' is seen as the observed point P in the visual space which can be referenced with respect to the physical coordinate system to form a Euclidean map of the visual space.

Figure 3.16. Geometry of binocular sighting on a point P'. (From R. Luneburg, *Studies and Essays*, © 1948 by Interscience Publishers, Inc., New York. Reprinted with permission.)

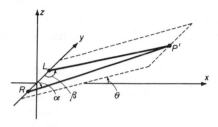

The experiments described above demonstrate that the visual field contains a separate and distinct metric, that of distance between points. If the distance measure were the same in physical and visual space, then the straight lines of the physical space must represent the straight lines, the geodesics, of the visual space. These same experiments show that this is not the case. This is further evidenced by everyday experience. The visually sensed distance of

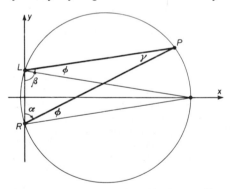

Figure 3.17. Geometry of the bipolar parallax angle. (From R. Luneburg, *Studies and Essays*, © 1948 by Interscience Publishers, Inc., New York. Reprinted with permission.)

distant objects is certainly not proportional to its physical distance, nor is its sensed size proportional to physical size. The greater the distance the more obvious this distortion becomes. If the metric of visual space were Euclidean, then the "parallel alleys" and "equidistant alleys" would be identical, but this is not the case. The only conclusion is that the visual space is non-Euclidean.

The angles α, β, and θ deserve further attention since these furnish the set of physiological cues necessary for binocular vision. Following the excellent analysis of R. Luneburg, two physically significant angles may be introduced. As shown in Figure 3.17 the bipolar parallax angle is designated as γ where

$$\gamma = \pi - \alpha - \beta$$

and the bipolar latitude angle is called ϕ where,

$$\phi = \tfrac{1}{2}(\beta - \alpha)$$

If the angle γ is fixed, then there results a curved surface as shown in Figure 3.18. The horizontal latitude lines correspond to fixed ϕ while the vertical

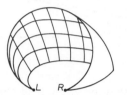

Figure 3.18. The surface segment of a torus for fixed bipolar parallax angle. (From R. Luneburg, *Studies and Essays*, © 1948 by Interscience Publishers, Inc., New York. Reprinted with permission.)

meridians result if θ is invariant. The coordinate γ determines the apparent distance of the sensed point from the apparent center of observation.

In general form, then, let the following three coordinates be defined by

$$\xi = f(\gamma) \cos \phi \cos \theta$$
$$\eta = f(\gamma) \sin \phi$$
$$\zeta = f(\gamma) \cos \phi \sin \theta$$

Figure 3.19. The geometric relation between the visual space and physical space in cross section. (From R. Luneburg, *Studies and Essays*, © 1948 by Interscience Publishers, Inc., New York. Reprinted with permission.)

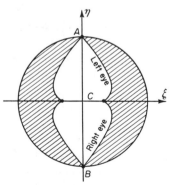

Leaving justification to a later and more appropriate point let the arbitrary function, $f(\gamma)$, be specified to be

$$f(\gamma) = 2e^{-\sigma \gamma}$$

where $\sigma > 0$. These three coordinates can be represented in a three-dimensional Euclidean space to yield a map of the visual space. The relation of this map to the former physical map is shown in Figure 3.19. The physical space is imaged onto the interior of the surface of revolution obtained by rotating the shaded domain around the η-axis. This domain is bounded by a circle of radius 2 and two sections of the logarithmic spirals

$$\rho = 2e^{-\sigma\pi}\, e^{\pm 2\sigma\phi}$$

The outer boundary $\rho = 2$ corresponds to the infinity of physical space, while the inner boundary corresponds to the two eyes. The points A and B represent the two portions of the y axis where $y > 1$ and $y < -1$; the circle represented by the rotation of C about the y axis corresponds to that remaining segment, $-1 < y < 1$, of the y axis. Both the direction and distance of the sensed point are preserved in this mapped space. It may be assumed that there exists some constant, σ, for each observer such that the above Euclidean map becomes a conformal image of the visual space.

To describe the binocular mapping completely, it is necessary to determine the psychometric distance function, $D(P, Q)$, which associates a real number, D, with the apparent distance between the two points P and Q. Such a function must satisfy the following constraints:

$$D(P, Q) = D(Q, P) > 0$$

for all P and Q which are sensed as being different.

$$D(P, Q) = 0$$

if such difference discrimination is not achieved.

$$D(P, Q) \leqq D(P, R) + D(R, Q)$$

for any three points located in the visual space. This last constraint is the triangle inequality.

The definition of a psychometric distance function requires only a rank-order relation. That is, if some distance between two points, P and Q, is sensed as S and there are two other points, P' and Q', sensed as being separate by S', then if $S > S'$, then $D(P, Q) > D(P', Q')$, and vice versa. Further, such a rank order psychometric function should obey the triangle law; thus only an unscaled $D(P, Q)$ function satisfies the requirement. Multiplication by any constant does not remove any essential determinacy.

In order to ensure such uniqueness for visual sensations, it is necessary to add the following two axioms to the above-listed constraints:

The visual space is finitely compact, that is, if $P_1, P_2 \ldots$ is a sequence of points for which the numbers $D(P_1, P_v)$, $v = 1, 2, 3, \ldots$ are bounded, then a point P and a sequence P_{n_v} of P_n exist with $D(P, P_{n_v})$ approaching zero, and the visual space is convex; that is, for any two different points, P, Q there is a point R, different from P and Q such that,

$$D(P, R) = D(R, Q) + D(P, Q)$$

Now, it is recognized that these last two axioms are not directly observable since they relate to properties of infinitely many points. Still the validity appears reasonable in view of the postulated continuum of the perceptual space as well as the imposed rationale superimposed upon sensed point patterns.

One of the important features of visual space is *free movability*, that is, there exists a motion of the space which can move any object-configuration into any other congruent configuration. Under certain quite general restrictions, only the homogenous space (Reimannian spaces of constant curvature) possess free movability. Free movability of the visual space is an expression of the subjective independence of metric form and localization. That is to say, it is possible to construct a congruent configuration to any given object at any desired point in the visual space. This is the tacit assumption upon which a realistic painter realizes his goal. Further, it can be shown that it is possible to construct an infinite set of physically curved rooms which are visually equivalent to and, indeed, which are visually identical with a given rectangular room. In two dimensions such illusory configurations are members of the set shown in Figure 3.20. These illusions will be discussed below.

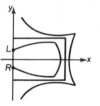

Figure 3.20. Congruent transformations of a rectilinear figure. (From R. Luneburg, *Studies and Essays*, © 1948 by Interscience Publishers, Inc., New York. Reprinted with permission.)

As a consequence of the assumption of free movability, it is permissible to confine further attention to the distance functions of Riemannian spaces of constant curvature. Such distance functions are found by integrating Riemann's general line element,

$$ds^2 = \frac{d\xi^2 + d\eta^2 + d\zeta^2}{[1 + \frac{1}{4}K(\xi^2 + \eta^2 + \zeta^2)]^2}$$

along the associated geodesics, where K is the constant Riemannian curvature of the space. It may also be said that the coordinate system ξ, η, and ζ exists in the visual space in which the distance element, ds, is given by this last equation. In fact, it may be interpreted as the psychometric distance between two sensed neighboring points ξ, η, ζ and $\xi + d\xi$, $\eta + d\eta$, $\zeta + d\zeta$. The constant K may be viewed as a characteristic parameter for each observer. It now remains to relate the distance function in the as yet unknown coordinates ξ, η, and ζ to the physical distance of points P and Q.

If there is presumed to be a one-to-one correspondence of sensed points to physical points, then it is possible to relate the sensory coordinates ξ, η, ζ to the angular coordinates γ, ϕ, θ of the corresponding physical point. Interpret the sensory coordinates ξ, η, ζ as being Cartesian coordinates in a Euclidean space thus yielding a conformal map of the visual space wherein the Euclidean angles on the map are equal to the apparent angles of visual observation. Let the metric of the map be spherically symmetrical to the origin, $\xi = \eta = \zeta = 0$, the center of observation. Place the observer in spherical coordinates ρ, φ, ϑ where constant ρ is the distance to apparent spheres around the observer, and φ and ϑ are the apparent direction of sensed points. Then, in general

$$\xi = \rho \cos \varphi \cos \vartheta$$

$$\eta = \rho \sin \varphi$$

$$\zeta = \rho \cos \varphi \sin \vartheta$$

From the experimental work described above the spherical coordinates must be related to the bipolar angles by

$$\rho = f(\gamma)$$

$$\varphi = \phi$$

$$\vartheta = \theta$$

where $f(\gamma)$ is as yet unknown. The line element becomes

$$ds^2 = \frac{f^2(\gamma)}{(1+\tfrac{1}{4}Kf^2)^2} \left(\frac{f'^2}{f^2} \, d\gamma^2 + d\phi^2 + \cos^2 \phi \; d\theta^2 \right)$$

If the physical space is submitted to the transformation

$$\gamma' = \gamma + \tau$$

$$\phi' = \phi$$

$$\theta' = \theta$$

where τ is a constant, then any particular configuration will be observed as the same sequence of retinal images before and after the transformation. Indeed, the differences $\Delta\gamma$, $\Delta\phi$, $\Delta\theta$ remain unchanged. Such transformation may be termed *iseikonic* and requires that corresponding angles be preserved. This transformation is therefore a conformal mapping of the visual space.

Noting the result of such a transformation, it is necessary that the expression

$$\frac{f'^2}{f^2}$$

in the expression for the line element, must be a constant σ^2. It therefore follows that

$$f(\gamma) = Ce^{-\sigma\gamma}$$

C being some other constant. Since any psychometric coordinate contains an undetermined constant coefficient, this C can be taken to equal 2 without loss of generality. Thus

$$ds^2 = \frac{4}{(e^{\sigma\gamma}+K\,e^{-\sigma\gamma})^2}\,(\sigma^2\,d\gamma^2 + d\phi^2 + \cos^2\phi\,d\theta^2)$$

and

$$\xi = 2e^{-\sigma\gamma}\cos\phi\cos\theta$$

$$\eta = 2e^{-\sigma\gamma}\sin\phi$$

$$\zeta = 2e^{-\sigma\gamma}\cos\phi\sin\theta$$

is the relation between the sensory and physical coordinates.

The same distance element, as described above, can be obtained without the hypothesis of free movability. An alternate base rests upon an analysis of certain phenomena observed on Vieth-Müller circles; in a single convergence state only points which lie upon a circle will simultaneously fall upon corresponding points on the retinas of both eyes. Reference is made to Figure 3.21 which indicates the geometry of similar triangles which make this evident. This independent derivation indicates that K must be negative so that the visual space geometry is hyperbolic.

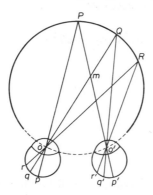

Figure 3.21. The geometry for binocular vision wherein the image of points will fall upon corresponding points on the two retinas. (From *Sensation and Perception in the History of Experimental Psychology*, by Edwin C. Boring. Copyright 1942 Appleton-Century Co., Inc. Reproduced by permission of Appleton-Century-Crofts.)

Both parameters σ and K are peculiar to the observing individual. σ determines the sensitivity of depth perception as compared with perception of lateral size and is thus a function of the interpupillary distance of the eyes. Since the just noticeable difference[2] (jnd) of depth perception is considerably smaller than that for size perception, it is expected to find $\sigma \gg 1$. The constant K describes the relation of sensory judgment of size to physical size. Minimum error is achieved if $K = -1$ where the visual space recedes to match the infinite physical space. The better the visual field judgment of size, the nearer the observer's K parameter value approaches to -1. It would be expected the K would be a more sensitive personal measure than σ.

[2] The value at which discrimination takes place with probability of 0.5.

The geodesics of the visual space (Helmholz's horopters) lie symmetric to the x-axis in the horizontal plane in circles

$$K(\xi^2 + \eta^2) = 4(1 - C\xi)$$

of the ξ, η-plane, C being an arbitrary constant. These circles pass through the points

$$\xi = 0, \quad \text{and} \quad \eta = \pm \frac{2}{\sqrt{K}} \quad \text{if } K > 0$$

They are normal to the circle

$$\xi^2 + \eta^2 = -\frac{4}{K} \quad \text{if } K < 0$$

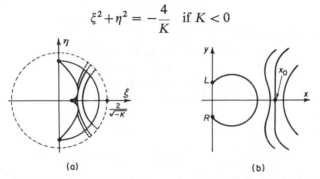

(a)   (b)

Figure 3.22. Geometry relating to the intersection of the visual space geodesics with the logarithmic spirals yielding agreement with Helmholtz's observation. (From R. Luneburg, *Studies and Essays*, © 1948 by Interscience Publishers, Inc., New York. Reprinted with permission.)

They may or may not intersect the two logarithmic spirals which represent the eyes as shown in Figure 3.22, thus the corresponding curves in the physical space must have precisely the form observed by Helmholtz. The point X_0 can be used to determine K and σ and vice versa.

The distance alleys are formed of points which have a constant geodesic distance from the x-axis. These are given by the circles

$$K(\xi^2 + \eta^2) = -4(1 - C\eta)$$

of the (ξ, η)-plane, symmetric to the η-axis. They pass through the points $\xi = \pm 2/\sqrt{-K}$, $\eta = 0$ for $K < 0$ or are normal to the circle $\xi^2 + \eta^2 = 4/K$ for $K > 0$. As shown in Figure 3.23, the empirical results obtained by F. Hillebrand are as would be expected.

Parallel alleys are defined by geodesics which are normal to the η-axis, the equation being

$$K(\xi^2 + \eta^2) = 4(1 - C\eta)$$

These are similar to the distance alleys, and, since $K < 0$, the parallel alleys lie inside of the distance alleys, being asymptotic at the infinity point. This agrees with Blumenfeld's empirical evidence and further confirms that the visual space is hyperbolic. It is the asymptotic behavior of the distance and parallel alleys at infinity which affords a second opportunity to evaluate K and σ. The asymptotes satisfy the equation,

$$y = \tan \varphi_0(x+b)$$

where

$$b_D = 2\sigma\frac{1-K}{1+K}$$

for distance curves, and

$$b_P = 2\sigma\frac{1+K}{1-K}$$

for parallel curves. Then,

$$4\sigma^2 = b_P b_D$$

and

$$\left(\frac{1-K}{1+K}\right)^2 = \frac{b_D}{b_P}$$

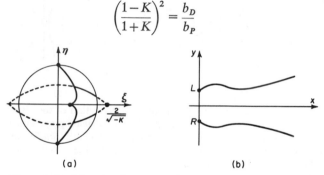

(a)

(b)

Figure 3.23. The visual space and physical space relating to Hillebrand's observation. (From R. Luneburg, *Studies and Essays*, © 1948 by Interscience Publishers, Inc., New York. Reprinted with permission.)

On this basis Blumenfeld's results approximate $K = -0.095$ and $\sigma = 14.6$.

It must be clearly understood that this analysis of the mapping of binocular visual space relates only to macroscopic perception, that is, under the constraint that two close but distinct physical points will remain separate in visual perception. Further, the viewed field must be "clueless"; that is, all interreference in terms of objects, space, size, color, and so on, is lacking. Reference cues destroy the free perception and offer a preconceived basis for the observed data.

Many human activities depend upon perceptive ability in such a clueless visual space. For example, consider the use of stereoscopic optical instruments. The binocular microscope requires perceptive determination of physical shape (contour definition) and localization of unknown objects by their apparent shape and locale in the visual space which is generally clueless. High altitude and submarine visual exploration present similar problems.

The results of such perceptive activity can be trusted only if the relation of visual binocular perception to physical reality is known in a quantitative manner.

3.6. THE PSYCHOVISUAL CAPABILITY

The psychovisual capability concerns light, space, and time. Light discrimination capability includes *brightness sensitivity*, the ability to detect a very dim light, *brightness discrimination*, the ability to detect a difference in brightness, and *color discrimination*, the ability to discern color.

The human eye is extremely sensitive to light as a stimulus. Even a few quanta of light energy may prove sufficient to stimulate the visual response under ideal conditions. Such conditions, however, are far from usual. More often than not, the observer is found in some degree of light-dark adaptation, and it is this degree which determines his brightness sensitivity. Ambient light conditions, the nature of the prestimulus object and field, its duration, spectral components, and so on, can greatly influence the ability of the observer to notice a faint signal.

Maximum brightness sensitivity can only be achieved after dark-adaptation has gone to completion. Figure 3.24 indicates the time dependency of adaptation. Note that this curve has two distinct parts. First, there is a rapid decrease of threshold leveling off at about 10 minutes. The value at this point corresponds to the lowest cone threshold, that is, the dimmest light which can be seen by cones when they have fully adapted. Cones normally respond to brightness over the range from 0.004 millilambert to about 10,000 millilamberts. The second section of the curve reaches its asymptotic value about 40 minutes after adaptation has begun. At that time, the sensitivity is defined by the lowest rod threshold. Rods normally respond to light in the brightness range from about 0.004 millilambert to about 0.00001 millilambert. Color discrimination will remain only during the first portion of the adaptation.

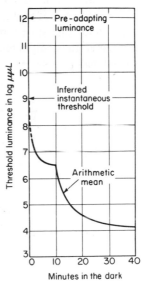

Figure 3.24. Dark-adaptation curve as a function of time in darkness. (From *WADC TR 58–399.* Reprinted with permission.)

Brightness sensitivity is greatest for colors near the center of the visible spectrum, as indicated in Figure 3.12. Because of spectral dependence, there is no one-to-one correspondence between energy output of a source and the observer's perception of its brightness. A more detailed discussion in Chapter 15 considers the practical problems associated with visual tasks under dimly lighted environments.

Brightness discrimination becomes of interest once the visual intensity threshold has been exceeded. The minimum difference in luminance between a controlled light source and that of a test light, which will be noted by the observer, defines the *difference threshold*. An object of the same hue as the background will not be seen unless its brightness exceeds the difference threshold. The relationship between these brightnesses is called the *brightness contrast*. More specifically, contrast may be expressed as a percent by taking $\Delta B/B \times 100$, where ΔB is the difference in luminance between object and background and B is the luminance of the background. Figure 3.25 indicates the threshold contrast to be an inverse function of the luminance, reaching an asymptotic value for high illuminations in the order of 100 millilamberts. As would be expected, the ability to detect differences in brightness increases with increased illumination and object size. Once again a breakpoint in the curve corresponds to the shift from rod to cone vision. To reach full generality other factors must be considered, including shape of the object under observation, spectral components of the illumination, region of the retina which is stimulated, and so on.

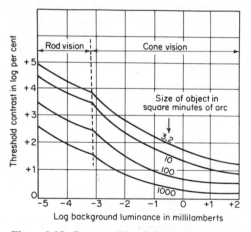

Figure 3.25. Contrast Discrimination Curve as a function of background luminance. (After W. S. Duke-Elder, *Textbook of Ophthalmology*, St. Louis, Mo.: C. V. Mosby Company, 1934.)

Three components, related in a complex manner to the physical characteristics of stimuli, can elicit the sensation of color. These are hue, saturation, and brightness. Hue is a measure of the particular spectral properties of the impinging light energy. For instance, the sensation of red, green, violet, yellow, and so on, depends upon the dominant wavelength present. Saturation relates to the purity of color as measured by the amount of white light which is mixed with the color. In general brightness relates to the rate of energy transfer within the visual spectrum. Hue discrimination is usually measured in terms of the minimum difference in wavelength which will be perceived as a different hue. Under good conditions of illumination and saturation, about 128 different hues can be distinguished over the visible spectrum, these being unevenly distributed. In the blue-green and yellow portions of the spectrum, hue discrimination can take place with as little change of wavelength as a millimicron, while at the red (long wavelength) end of the spectrum hue distinction may require 20 millimicrons.

Color discrimination encompasses the perception of hue, saturation, and brightness, which are always relative to the surroundings and the temporal sequence of exposures. Specification of a color is not the same as specification of the color of an object or the light under which that object is viewed. Rather it is a description of a particular light-object-observer situation.

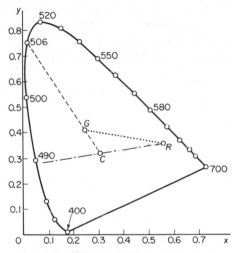

Figure 3.26. Chromaticity Diagram G represents the color of a green paint sample. R is a red sample, and C is one of the three standard illuminates. (From *WADC TR 58–399*. Reprinted with permission.)

The tristimulus method for colorimetry is based upon the matching of a given color to a particular combination of three primary colors by a normal observer (as represented by a statistical average over a sample of the population). The International Commission on Illumination (ICI) set up arbitrary standards to facilitate and standardize the description of color. Under a known light, the spectrophotometer is used to determine the reflectance factor as a function of wavelength over the visible spectrum. This function is multiplied by each of the ICI tristimulus values for that wavelength. The resulting values are summed over all wavelengths separately for each primary, yielding three values, X, Y, and Z which represent the total contribution of each of the three primaries to the color of the sample.

The tristimulus values are transformed into "trichromatic coefficients" x and y by

$$x = \frac{X}{X+Y+Z} \quad \text{and} \quad y = \frac{Y}{X+Y+Z}$$

which are plotted on Cartesian coordinates. The value for z is determined since

$$x+y+z = 1$$

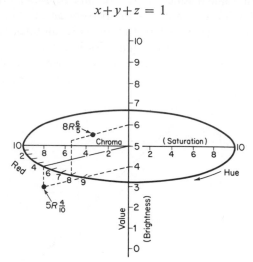

Figure 3.27. The coordinates of the Munsell color solid. (After *WADC TR 58–399* from the *Munsell Book of Color*, Munsell Color Company, Inc., Baltimore, Md. Reprinted with permission.)

Reference is made to Figure 3.26 which indicates the visible range of colors in a chromaticity diagram. From this diagram, it is possible to describe a color with respect to *dominant wavelength*, the psychophysical equivalent of hue, *purity*, the psychophysical equivalent of saturation, *complementary wavelength*, that color which if mixed together with the original color will appear achromatic, and *brightness*, as given by the ratio between the total amount of primary contribution and that of a perfectly reflecting sample viewed under the same illumination.

Another interesting and useful method for specifying color is the Munsell System. Here colors are also considered with respect to hue, saturation (called "chroma"), and brightness (called "value"). A dual cone is erected representing these psychological properties as shown in Figure 3.27. Hues are arranged to form a continuous ring by joining the extremes of dominant wavelength. Saturation increases radially in a horizontal plane, so that colors on the vertical axis are achromatic. Completely saturated colors appear on the rim. Complementary colors are diagrammatically opposed. Brightness runs from extreme dark at zero value to extreme light at a value of ten.

Colors can be combined through either an additive or subtractive process. Addition is more frequent, occurring when lights of different wavelengths are simultaneously reflected or transmitted to the eye from the same source. Color vision is non-analytic so that the mixture of, say, two colors seen as a third color falls somewhere along the line connecting the original two colors on the chromaticity diagram. The superposition of red and green on a single screen yields an intermediate hue in the yellow range. The blend of green and blue in the same manner will yield green-blue.

The subtractive color process is less common; it occurs when light travels through or is reflected by two or more filtering media. Each medium absorbs a greater amount at certain wavelengths so that a residue of light reaches the observer. It is this process which occurs in the mixing of paints. In water colors, for example, green can be produced by a suitable mixture of yellow and blue; as a result green is not considered to be a "primary" color in art. But examine the process more closely. The yellow pigment absorbs all but yellow and green light, reflecting these. In a similar manner, the blue pigment

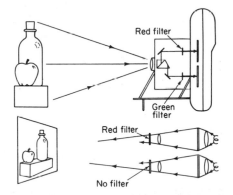

Figure 3.28. Diagram of photography and projection arrangement.

reflects blue and green, absorbing all light of other wavelengths. A double subtraction has been imposed upon the incident white light, leaving only green. Thus, green is considered as one of the primary colors in visual science. This same subtractive residue results through the use of colored optical filters. The results of color combination, either by addition or subtraction, are well known and highly predictable.

There still remains much to be explored and explained with respect to the phenomena of color vision. E. H. Land (1959) reports that total contextual color images can be produced which are unlike those which would be predicted on the basis of the above-described classical theory. He describes a series of rather remarkable experiments which utilize the superposition of two black-and-white images presented through the same color filters used in taking these images by photographic means, as shown in Figure 3.28. The resulting image is seen *in full color*—this regardless of whether ambient illumination is present or not. As a result of these experiments, Land developed a new coordinate system for the description of color in images (including the achromatic range). This system is physically dimensionless, involving a ratio of ratios, holding constant only a pair of wavelengths. The percentage of available short-wavelength stimulus is plotted against the percentage of long-wavelength stimulus. That is to say, if the brightness on the screen at the brightest point for the long-wavelength image is taken as 100, then the brightness for this same image at any other point can be expressed as a percentage. This percentage is plotted against the percentage of available light for the short-wavelength image taken alone at the same point on the screen.

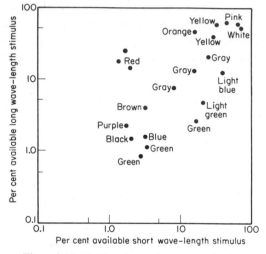

Figure 3.29. The Land color-image coordinate system.

The ratio of these two percentages describes the color at that point. Figure 3.29 illustrates empirical results. Grays fall on a straight line at an angle of 45°, while warm colors fall on one side and cool colors fall on the other side. Various interesting effects can be obtained through choice of filter wavelength and the adjustment of other parameters of the experiment.

Spatial discrimination is a result of the perception induced by a patterned stimulation of the retina which includes four categories of visual performance: *visual acuity*, *depth discrimination*, *form discrimination*, and *movement discrimination*.

Visual acuity is a description of the ability of the eye to see fine details, that is, the resolving power of the retina for various kinds of detail in the image. Visual acuity can be measured in terms of the ability to see a point source of light. Here intensity of that source is the determining parameter. Minimum perceptible acuity is a measure of ability to see a small object against a plain background. Most often the "object" chosen is fine black wires or small black dots against an illuminated white background. Minimum separable acuity defines the ability to see objects as being separate when they are placed close together. Various object configurations can be used with the measure being the visual angle corresponding to the minimum discernible gap.

Minimum distinguishable acuity is the ability to recognize irregularities and discontinuities in the contours of an object. Standard configurations are used, such as the Landolt "C" figures or Snellen letters. The Snellen eye chart is used to compare the vision of a subject to that of a normal observer. Vision rated at, say, 20/200 indicates that the observer can distinguish at 20 feet that which a normal observer can see at a distance of 200 feet (threshold size for this subject is ten times normal, this being "legally blind" in a number of countries). Figure 3.30 indicates a three-dimensional surface which separates acceptable from unacceptable combinations of visual angle, contrast, and background brightness for a common visual task.

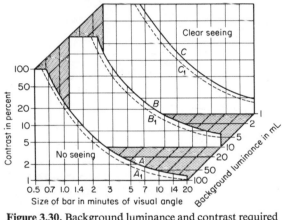

Figure 3.30. Background luminance and contrast required for bars subtending various visual angles as seen under daylight conditions.

Depth discrimination or distance judgment is the ability of an observer to estimate the distance of an object or the relative distance of two or more objects. Ten well-defined cues are brought to bear in reaching such a judgment. Binocular vision allows two different images to be formed with a single observance. This includes the difference due to the viewing angle as well as the fact that objects, nearer to the observer than the fixated object, form crossed images, while objects farther away form uncrossed images, as shown in Figure 3.31. The second cue relates to the muscle tension required to accomplish convergence upon the point of fixation. The remaining cues are monocular. These include sensing

(1) the angle subtended by an object of *known* size, this angle being interpreted in terms of distance,

(2) the decrement in color contrast or the difference from the known contrast, this being interpreted in terms of the scattering of light by air which in turn relates to distance,

(3) linear perspective, this revealing an angle of convergence which relates to distance,

(4) the relation of lights and shadows, this describing the relation of objects to the light source and other objects thereby relating to distance,

(5) the determination of overlapping contours relates to relative distance,

(6) motion parallax in terms of the relative movement of objects within the visual field while the observer is moving, the less the relative movement the greater the distance from the observer to the object,

(7) accommodation within the eye, this being a significant cue only for very short distances,

(8) association within context, this being highly dependent upon the particular situation as indicative of distance.

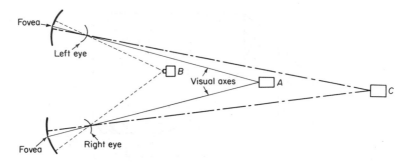

Figure 3.31. In stereoscopic vision focused on object *A*, the images of object *B* appear crossed while those of object *C* appear uncrossed. (After W. S. Duke-Elder, *Textbook of Ophthalmology*, St. Louis, Mo.: C. V. Mosby Company, 1934.)

Form discrimination requires visual acuity together with stored information which can be referenced to allow the classification of shapes, objects, or even particular items. The discrimination of three-dimensional form also requires depth perception. This task is essentially one of information retrieval and comparison. It can be studied in terms of reaction time under a known ensemble of possible stimuli-objects governed by a known probability distribution. In general, there appears to be little dependence of form discrimination ability on the shape, contour, or complexity of the stimulus.

A study was conducted to measure the recognizability of imperfect images as a function of visual angle and the degree of imperfection. Test objects were artificial "photographs" of semicircles and isosceles triangles. The "grain" was a grid of squares upon which the semicircles and triangles were superimposed, such that those squares more than half enclosed by the object were painted black and the rest left white. By using different size squares, varying object-area square-area (O/S) ratios were obtained. Visual angle was altered by varying the distance between the subject and the stimulus. The subject was asked to judge whether each stimulus was a semicircle or a triangle. For visual angles in the range 25 to 159 minutes, the number of correct responses increased as the O/S ratio increased. At visual angles less than 25 minutes an increase in recognition was obtained for all O/S ratios that had not previously yielded 100 per cent recognition.

Movement discrimination is the ability to detect a change of position of an object within the visual field. This movement may be due to a change in position of the object, the observer, or both. The perception of movement is the result of a change in the position of the retinal image in relation to the periphery of the visual field, or a change in object position relative to other objects within the visual field. These cues can be aided by physical eye tracking of the movement with a resultant muscular sensation; however, even the stationary eye can accomplish movement discrimination.

Temporal discrimination is limited by the response time lag of visual channel stimulation, this being anywhere from 0.05 to 0.4 seconds dependent upon the color and intensity of the stimulus. If a pulsing light is presented with increasing pulse repetition rate, a point will be reached where the observed flicker disappears so that the light stimulus appears to be of constant intensity. The fundamental frequency at which this transition takes place is called the *critical flicker frequency* or the *flicker-fusion frequency*. Light adaptation is normally much more rapid than dark adaptation. As a result, changes in intensity of the light are smoothed to an increasing degree as the pulse repetition rate is increased until it becomes too small to cause a sensation. It is interesting to note that the perceived brightness level is also a function of the pulse repetition rate. This brightness can reach as much as twice the steady-state brightness for a light-dark ratio of one-to-one at a frequency just below 10 cycles per second (coinciding with the alpha rhythm of the brain). The critical flicker frequency can be used as an indicator of the state of fatigue of the observer.

3.7. VISUAL ILLUSIONS

An illusion exists when the perception of an object fails to represent that object truly in some regard. The simplest illusions utilize context to yield a perceptual distortion. For example, Figures 3.32a, b, and c illustrate apparent curvature imposed on straight lines and "distortion" of a circle. Length can also be distorted as seen in Figures 3.33a and b. Broken lines can produce interesting effects as seen in Figures 3.34a and b. The context can affect the apparent brightness as shown in Figure 3.35. Similar illusions can be developed using colors.

Two-dimensional figures can be used to represent three-dimensional objects. The dimension of "depth" is inferred from the various cues such as precedence and relative size of known objects. Figure 3.36a and b presents the famous ambiguous depth figures. Such figures do not directly misrepresent; rather they furnish sufficient information to identify the three-dimensional nature of the object and yet insufficient data to allow resolution of the depth

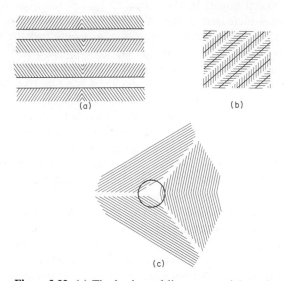

Figure 3.32. (a) The horizontal lines are straight and parallel. (From M. Luckiesch, *Light, Vision and Seeing*, Copyright 1944. D. Van Nostrand Company, Inc., Princeton, N.J. Reprinted with permission.) (b) the long lines are parallel. (By permission from *Psychology* by R. Stagner and T. F. Karwoski, Copyright 1952, McGraw-Hill Book Company, Inc.) (c) the angular lines distort the shape of the circle.

ambiguity. Either way of perceiving the object is equally correct, and the observer can change from one to the other almost at will. Shift of the point of visual center can aid this reversal of the depth dimension.

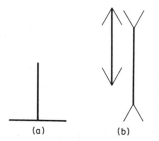

Figure 3.33. (a) Although the lines are of equal length, the vertical seems longer (b) the Müller-Lyer illusion (1896). The heavy lines are of equal length. (By permission from *Psychology*, by R. Stagner and T. F. Karwoski, Copyright 1952, McGraw-Hill Book Company, Inc.)

The depth dimension can be distorted through contextual ambiguity. Use of the mathematical representation for the mapping of the binocular visual space described above permits the construction of visually congruent configurations to any given object. For example, a rectangular room may be used to generate an infinite set of physically warped rooms which would result in a view equal to that of the rectangular room. The general expectation

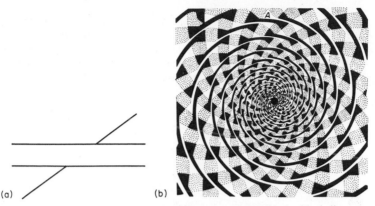

(a)   (b)

Figure 3.34. (a) The broken line segments are colinear (b) the black lines are parts of circles. (By permission from *Psychology*, by T. Stagner and T. F. Karwoski, Copyright 1952, McGraw-Hill Book Company, Inc. Adapted from Fraser, 1908.)

that a room is rectangular would then dominate the interpretation and result in a direct illusion.

Motions in the hyperbolic visual space are conformal transformations which transform the sphere

$$\xi^2 + \eta^2 + \zeta^2 \leqq -\frac{4}{K}$$

onto itself. Of special interest are those motions which do not change the position of the $x, y,$ and of the x, z plane. These are given by the transformations

$$\xi' = -a - \left(a^2 + \frac{4}{K}\right)\frac{\xi - a}{(\xi - a)^2 + \eta^2 + \zeta^2}$$

$$\eta' = \left(a^2 + \frac{4}{K}\right)\frac{\eta}{(\xi - a)^2 + \eta^2 + \zeta^2}$$

$$\zeta' = \left(a^2 + \frac{4}{K}\right)\frac{\zeta}{(\xi - a)^2 + \eta^2 + \zeta^2}$$

where a is an arbitrary parameter. Such transformations will yield a set of patterns as shown in Figure 3.20. Figure 3.37 shows an illusion room which achieves the deceptive result of appearing to be rectangular.

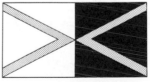

Figure 3.35. The "V" on the left is of the same brightness as that on the right. (From M. Luckiesch, *Light, Vision and Seeing*, Copyright 1944, D. Van Nostrand Company, Inc., Princeton, N.J. Reprinted with permission.)

It is of special interest to consider those configurations congruent to objects at physical infinity. A landscape is usually far enough away from the observer

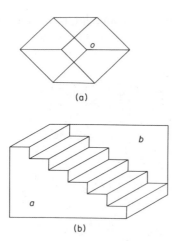

(a)

(b)

Figure 3.36. (a) Necker's Cube (1832) where point *o* may appear to be either the near or the far corner of the cube; (b) Schröder's staircase (1858) where either side *a* or side *b* may appear to be nearer the observer.

Figure 3.37. Misconceptions induced by the Ames room. The camera is placed in a high position so that light rays reflected from the left wall and the right wall impose equal images on the film. Under this condition reference to past experience indicates that the two walls are almost sure to be equal in size. But if the walls are equal, then the two women must be of quite unequal height (physically they are both 5′ 8″ tall). Once the room is perceived to be rectangular, the viewer is almost forced into misjudging the height of the enclosed personnel. (From Julian Huxley, *Evolution in Action*, New York: Harper and Brothers, Publishers, 1953. Reprinted with permission.)

to be considered at infinity. Pictorial representation of such a landscape can be created on a flat surface such that the image is congruent to the true scene at infinity. A point at infinity is given by the coordinates

$$\xi = 2 \cos \phi \cos \theta$$

$$\eta = 2 \sin \phi$$

$$\zeta = 2 \cos \phi \sin \theta$$

A motion translated by the transformation above yields the associated image point

$$\xi' = -a - \left(a^2 + \frac{4}{K}\right)\frac{\xi - a}{4 + a^2 - 2a\xi}$$

$$\eta' = \left(a^2 + \frac{4}{K}\right)\frac{\eta}{4 + a^2 - 2a\xi}$$

$$\zeta' = \left(a^2 + \frac{4}{K}\right)\frac{\zeta}{4 + a^2 - 2a\xi}$$

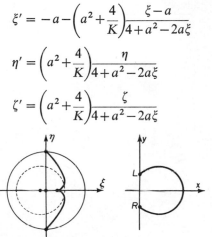

Figure 3.38. The perceptual correspondence of distant points in physical space. (From R. Luneburg, *Studies and Essays,* © 1948 by Interscience Publishers, Inc., New York. Reprinted with permission.)

All infinity image points lie on the sphere which intersects the ξ-axis at points

$$\xi_1 = \frac{2a + \frac{4}{K}}{a - 2}$$

and

$$\xi_2 = \frac{\frac{4}{K} - 2a}{a + 2}$$

The corresponding surface in the physical space has the form illustrated in Figure 3.38.

It is interesting to note that the direction of the image points, relative to the observer, is not identical with the direction of the original points. Thus reproduction based upon central projection cannot give a psychometrically true image of the original sensation. It is this very fact which explains why in a photograph of a landscape, objects such as houses, mountains, and so on, appear to be too small. It is evident that greater depth and apparent validity can be achieved through the projection upon a curved screen. This technique has come into use in certain commercial motion pictures and has been demonstrated by A. Ames, Jr., in his use of a curved screen which is part of the Vieth-Müller surface.

Figure 3.39. An artistic ambiguous picture entitled "All is Vanity."
(Copyright by Art Lore, Inc. Reprinted with permission.)

Ambiguity may be employed to portray two different pictures with the same image. Figure 3.39 is an artistic achievement of two pictures in one. The particular perception is to some extent dependent upon the included visual angle and to a lesser extent upon the observer's knowledge of the nature of the more detailed image. It is suggested that initial observation be from at least four feet, followed by closer inspection.

Figural after-effects can be illusory. As a curved line is steadily viewed it becomes progressively less curved. Further, a straight line, viewed after a curved line, will appear to curve in a direction opposite to the original curvature. A similar effect can be demonstrated when a straight line appears as two straight line segments joined at an obtuse angle of opposite direction to a previous stimulus of an obtuse angle. Many other predictable time sequence illusions can be demonstrated.

Apparent movement can be induced if a fixed image is presented to the observer for a brief duration, greater than a few milliseconds but less than about 400 milliseconds, followed by another fixed image which is similar to, but in some way slightly different from, the former image. The adequacy of the movement illusion depends upon the relation between the duration of each of the sequence of images, the duration of the pause between image presentations, the intensities of the images, the visual angle corresponding to the displacement of the altered part of the image, and other factors including the nature of the context and the instructions given the viewer. This effect has proved to be of distinct value in motion pictures, television, and various electrical advertising displays.

3.8. CONCLUSION

The visual channel is truly remarkable in a number of ways. The physical mechanism of the eye requires only about 0.005 seconds in addition to the reaction time of about 15 seconds to move to a new steady-state position. This is accomplished with a control torque to moment of inertia ratio of about 436 radian per second squared. (As a matter of interest this same ratio is about 0.0095 for a submarine, 0.02 for an airship, 1.0 for a helicopter, 4.0 for aircraft, and 13 for an automobile.) The moment of inertia for the eye is only about 3×10^{-7} slug-feet squared.

At any instant of time each fiber of the optic nerve may be excited or quiescent. Thus, the message to the brain may be in any one of $2^{1,000,000}$ different states. That is to say, about $10^{300,000}$ different visual configurations might conceivably be seen. To appreciate the size of this figure, it is only necessary to note that about 10^{54} neurons could be packed into a cubic light year.

It has been estimated that the eye is capable of transmitting information to the brain at about 5 bits per second per nerve fiber.

It is well known, however, that there is a great reduction in the amount of information which is separately processed. In cases where a visual display presents an excessive amount of data, the observer accepts only an abstraction of the display by selecting those features which represent redundant groups of data. If a highly detailed surface field is presented, the subject notes the "texture" rather than each of the minutia. The process of perception is characterized by classification which best codes the amount of redundancy of the display. The resulting perception captures a comparatively small amount of information, but maintains the essential character or "meaning" by selectively eliminating most of the redundancy. There results parameters such as texture, form, gross color, gross location, symmetry, and many others.

Surprisingly enough a major portion of this data reduction occurs in the retina and optical nerve. This is accomplished by a neural structure of interconnections. The essential genetic organization could conceivably limit the capability of an organism to achieve an internal isomorphic representation of the outside world. Evidently such a limit has not been met by man. The human operator can perceive as many as 30,000 different colors and visually accept information far in excess of the rate at which the brain can assimilate these data. There is extremely small probability that two identical images will fall upon a retina during the human life span, and yet complex objects and contours are readily recognizable. There appears to be a highly efficient coding process which couples to the information storage in such a way as to allow retrieval of a transformed image (as the same object would be seen from a different viewing position). Much remains to be learned about the visual sensory system at all levels: gross behavioral, neural interconnection, electro-chemical, and data reduction.

BIBLIOGRAPHY

ADAMS, O. S., D. J. CHAMBLISS, and A. J. RIOPELLE, "Stimulus Area, Stimulus Dispersion, Flash Duration, and the Scotopic Threshold," *Journal of Experimental Psychology*, Vol. 49 (1955), 428–430.

ALLUISI, E. A., "Measured Visual Acuity as a Function of Phenomenal Size," *USAF WADC TR 55–384* (October 1955).

ANDREW, A. M., "Action Potentials from the Frog Colliculus," *Journal of Physiology*, Vol. 130 (September 23–24, 1955), p. 25p.

ARCHER, E. J., "Identification of Visual Patterns as a Function of Information Load," *Journal of Experimental Psychology*, Vol. 48 (1954), 313–317.

ARDEN, G. B., "A Narrow-Band Pigment Present in Visual Cell Suspensions," *Journal of Physiology*, Vol. 123 (1954), 396–408.

ARMINGTON, J. C., "Electrical Responses of the Light-Adapted Eye," *Journal of the Optical Society of America*, Vol. 43 (1953), 450–456.

ATTNEAVE, FRED, "Some Informational Aspects of Visual Perception," *Psychological Review*, Vol. 61, No. 3 (May 1954), 183–193.

BAKER, C. A., and W. F. GRETHER, "Visual Presentation of Information," *USAF WADC TR 54–160* (August 1954).

BARLOW, H. B., "Eye Movements During Fixation," *Journal of Physiology*, Vol. 232 (1952), 290–306.

———. "Summation and Inhibition in the Frog's Retina," *Journal of Physiology*, Vol. 119 (January 1953), 69–88.

BARLOW, H. B., R. FITZHUGH, and S. W. KUFFLER, "Change of Organization in the Receptive Fields of the Cat's Retina During Dark Adaptation," *Journal of Physiology*, Vol. 137 (August 1957), 338–354.

BARTLEY, S. H., *Vision*. Princeton, N.J.: D. Van Nostrand Company, Inc., 1941.

BERNARD, C. G., "Isolation of Retinal and Optic Ganglion Response in the Eye of Dytiscus," *Journal of Neurophysiology*, Vol. 5 (1942), 32–48.

BIRREN, F., "The Specifications of Illumination and Color in Industry," *Transactions of the American Academy of Ophthalmology and Otolaryngology* (1947), 242–251.

BLACKWELL, H. RICHARD, "Evaluation of the Neural Quantum Theory in Vision," *American Journal of Psychology*, Vol. 66 (July 1953), 397–408.

BOUMAN, M. A., and H. A. VAN DER VELDEN, "The Two-Quanta Explanation of the Threshold Values and Visual Acuity on the Visual Angle and the Time of Observation," *Journal of the Optical Society of America*, Vol. 37 (1947), 908–919.

BOYNTON, R. M., and L. A. RIGGS, "The Effect of Stimulus Area and Intensity Upon the Human Retinal Response," *Journal of Experimental Psychology*, Vol. 42 (1951), 217–226.

BRANDT, H. F., *The Psychology of Seeing*. Philosophical Library, 1945.

BRENNAN, J. G., R. A. BURNHAM, and S. M. NEWHALL, "Color Terms and Definitions," *Psychology Bulletin*, Vol. 45 (1948), 207, 230.

BROWN, R. H., "The Visual Discrimination of Velocity as a Function of the Rate of Movement and Other Factors," *Naval Research Laboratory Report 4299*, 1954.

———. "Velocity Discrimination and the Intensity-Time Relation," *Journal of the Optical Society of America*, Vol. 45 (1955), 189–192.

———. "The Effect of Extent on the Intensity-Time Relations for the Visual Discrimination of Movement," *Journal of Comparative Psychology*, Vol. 50 (1957), 109–114.

BROWN, W. R. J., "The Influence of Luminance Level on Visual Sensitivity to Color Difference," *Journal of the Optical Society of America*, Vol. 41 (1951), 684–688.

CHALMERS, E. L., JR., "Monocular and Binocular Cues in the Perception of Size and Distance," *American Journal of Psychology*, Vol. 65 (1952), 415–423.

CHAPANIS, A., and R. A. McCLEARY, "Interposition as a Cue for the Perception of Relative Distance," *Journal of General Psychology*, Vol. 48 (1953), 113–132.

COCQUYT, P., "Sensory Illusions," *Flight Safety Foundation, Inc.*, 1952, *Shell Aviation News* No. 178 (April 1953).

COMMITTEE ON COLORIMETRY, *The Science of Color*, Optical Society of America. New York: Thomas Y. Crowell Company, 1953.

CRAIK, K. J. W., and M. D. VERNON, "The Nature of Dark Adaptation," *Britain Journal of Psychology*, Vol. 32 (1941), 62–81.

CRAWFORD, B. H., "The Scotopic Visibility Function," *Proceedings of the Psychology Society of London*, Vol. 62 (1949), 321–334.

110 THE VISUAL CHANNEL

DALLENBACK, K. M., "The Elastic Effect: An Optical Illusion of Expansion," *American Journal of Psychology*, Vol. 66 (1953), 634–636.

DARTNALL, H. J. A., "Evidence for a Visual Pigment Having Modulator-Like Properties," *Journal of Physiology*, Vol. 122 (1953), 12–31.

DIAMOND, S., "Time, Space and Stereoscopic Vision," *Aerospace Medicine*, Vol. 30 No. 9 (September 1959), 650–663.

DITCHBURN, R. W., "Eye Movements and Visual Perception," *Research* (London) Vol. 9 (1956), 466–471.

DONNER, K. O., and R. GRANIT, "Scotopic Dominator and State of Visual Purple in the Retina," *Acta Physiologica Scandinavica*, Vol. 17 (1949), 161–169.

DUMAS, F. M., "A New Visual Illusion," *American Journal of Psychology*, Vol. 66 (1953), 142–143.

EVANS, R. M., *An Introduction to Color*. New York: John Wiley & Sons, Inc., 1948.

EKMAN, G., "Dimensions of Color Vision," *Journal of Psychology*, Vol. 38 (1954), 467–474.

FITTS, P. M., M. WEINSTEIN, M. RAPPAPORT, N. ANDERSON, and J. A. LEONARD, "Stimulus Correlates of Visual Pattern Recognition: A Probability Approach," *Journal of Experimental Psychology*, Vol. 51 No. 1 (January 1956), 1–11.

FORD, A., C. T. WHITE, and M. LICHTENSTEIN, "Analysis of Eye Movements during Free Search," *Journal of the Optical Society of America*, Vol. 49 No. 3 (March 1959), 287–292.

FRY, G. A., and M. ALPERN, "The Effect of a Peripheral Glare Source Upon the Apparent Brightness of an Object," *Journal of the Optical Society of America*, Vol. 43 (March 1953), 189–195.

GERATHEWOHL, S. J., and H. STRUGHOLD, "Time Consumption of Eye Movements and High-Speed Flying," *Journal of Aviation Medicine*, Vol. 25 (1) (1954), 38–45.

GIBSON, J. J., "The Perception of Visual Surfaces," *American Journal of Psychology*, Vol. 63 (1950), 367–384.

GOGEL, W. C., and G. S. HARKER, "The Effectiveness of Size Cues to Relative Distance as a Function of Lateral Visual Separation," *Journal of Experimental Psychology*," Vol. 50 (1955), 309–315.

GOODLAW, I. E., "Visual Discomfort Caused by Fluorescent Lighting," *American Journal of Optometry*, Vol. 22 (1945), 406–424.

GRAHAM, C. H., and W. S. HUNTER, "Thresholds of Illumination for the Visual Discrimination of Direction of Movement and for the Discrimination of Discreteness," *Journal of General Psychology*, Vol. 5 (1931), 178–190.

GRANIT, R., "A Physiological Theory of Colour Perception," *Nature*, Vol. 151 (1943), 11–14.

———. *Sensory Mechanisms of the Retina*. London: Oxford University Press, 1947.

GRANIT, R., "The Colour Receptors of the Mammalian Retina," *Journal of Neurophysiology*, Vol. 8 (1945), 195–210.

GRUBER, H. E., "The Relation of Perceived Size to Perceived Distance," *American Journal of Psychology*, Vol. 67 (1954), 411–426.

HARDY, L. H., G. RAND, and M. C. RITTLER, "Investigation of Visual Space: The Blumenfeld Alleys," *A.M.A. Archives of Ophthalmology*, Vol. 45 (January 1951).

HARTLINE, H. K., and C. H. GRAHAM, "Nerve Impulses from Single Receptors in the Eye," *Journal of Cellular and Comparative Physiology*, Vol. 1 (1932), 277–296.

HARTLINE, H. K., "The Modification of Sensory Information by Neural Interaction in the Eye, and Its Relation to Vision," *IRE Transactions on Medical Electronics*, Vol. ME-6 No. 2 (June 1959).

————. "The Receptive Fields of the Optic Nerve Fibers," *American Journal of Physiology*, Vol. 130 (October 1940), 690–699.

————. "The Response of Single Optic Nerve Fibers of the Vertebrate Eye to Illumination of the Retina," *American Journal of Physiology*, Vol. 121 (February 1938), 400–415.

HARTRIDGE, H., *Recent Advances in the Physiology of Vision*. New York: Blakiston Company, 1950.

HELSON, H., "Vision," *Annual Review of Psychology*, Vol. 3 (1952), 55–84.

HOUSTON, R. A., "Theory of Color Vision," *Journal of the Optical Society of America*, Vol. 45 No. 8 (August 1955).

HUNT, R. W. G., "The Perception of Color in One Degree Fields for Different States of Adaptation," *Journal of the Optical Society of America*, Vol. 43 (1953), 479–484.

————. "Light and Dark Adaptation and the Perception of Color," *Journal of the Optical Society of America*, Vol. 42 (1952), 190–199.

IES Lighting Handbook, 2nd ed. New York: Illuminating Engineering Society, 1952.

Industrial Lighting. New York: American Standard Practice, Illuminating Engineering Society, 1952.

ISHAK, I. G. H., I. M. H. HEFZALLA, and Y. K. M. BADAWY, "Role of Convergence in Stereoscopic Vision," *Journal of the Optical Society of America*, Vol. 46 (1956), 303.

JACOBSON, H., "The Informational Capacity of the Human Eye," *Science*, Vol. 113 (1951), 292–293.

KLEMMER, E. T., and F. C. FRICK, "Assimilation of Information from Dot and Matrix Patterns," *Journal of Experimental Psychology*, Vol. 45 No. 1 (1953), 15–19.

KOHLER, WOLFGANG, "Relational Determination in Perception," in *Cerebral Mechanisms in Behavior*, ed. by Lloyd A. Jeffress. New York: John Wiley & Sons, Inc. (1951), 200–229.

KUFFLER, S. W., "Discharge Patterns and Functional Organization of Mammalian Retina," *Journal of Neurophysiology*, Vol. 16 (January 1953), 37–68.

LAND, E. H., "Color Vision and the Natural Image," Part I and Part II, *Proceedings of the National Academy of Sciences*, Vol. 45 No. 1 (January 1959), 115–129.

LANDIS, C., *An Annotated Bibliography of Flicker Fusion Phenomena*. Armed Forces-National Research Council Vision Committee Secretariat, University of Michigan, June 1953.

LENNOX, M. A., and A. MADSEN, "Cortical and Retinal Responses to Colored Light Flash in Anesthetized Cat," *Journal of Neurophysiology*, Vol. 18 (1955), 412–424.

LETTVIN, J. Y., H. R. MATURANA, W. S. McCULLOCH, and W. H. PITTS, "What the Frog's Eye Tells the Frog's Brain," *Proceedings of the IRE* (November 1959), 1940–1951.

LEYZOREK, M., "Two-Point Discrimination in Visual Space as a Function of the Temporal Interval Between the Stimuli," *Journal of Experimental Psychology*, Vol. 41 (1951), 364–375.

LINFOOT, E. H., "Information Theory and Optical Images," *Journal of the Optical Society of America*, Vol. 45 (1955), 808–819.

LINKSZ, A., *Physiology of the Eye*, Vol. 2, *Vision*. New York: Grune & Stratton, Inc., 1952.

LUDVIGH, E. J., "Direction Sense of the Eye," *American Journal of Ophthalmology*, Vol. 36 No. 6, Part II (June 1953).

——— *Visual and Stereoscopic Acuity for Moving Objects*, Proceedings of the Symposium on Physiological Psychology, Washington, D.C.: Office of Naval Research, 1955.

LUNEBERG, R., "Metric Methods in Binocular Visual Perception," in *Studies and Essays*, presented to R. Courant on January 8, 1948, New York: Interscience Publishers, Inc., 215–240.

LUNEBERG, R. K., "The Metric of Binocular Visual Space," *Journal of the Optical Society of America*, Vol. 40 (1950), 627–642.

MAERZ, A., and M. R. PAUL, *Dictionary of Color*, 2nd ed. New York: McGraw-Hill Book Company, Inc., 1950.

MANDELBAUM, J., and L. SLOAN, "Peripheral Visual Acuity: With Special Reference to Scotopic Illumination," *American Journal of Ophthalmology*, Vol. 30 (1947), 581–588.

McCULLOCH, W. S., and W. H. PITTS, "How We Know Universals. The Perception of Auditory and Visual Forms," *Bulletin of Mathematical Biophysics*, Vol. 9 (June 1947), 127–147.

MILES, W. R., "Effectiveness of Red Light on Dark Adaptation," *Journal of the Optical Society of America*, Vol. 43 (1953), 435–441.

MILLER, J. W., and S. H. BARTLEY, "A Study of Object Shape as Influenced by Instrumental Magnification," *Journal of General Psychology*, Vol. 50 (1954), 141–146.

MOTE, F. A., and G. E. BRIGGS, "The Reliability of Measurements of Human Dark Adaptation," *Journal of Experimental Psychology*, Vol. 48 (1954), 69–74.

MOTOKAWA, K., and M. EBE, "The Physiological Mechanism of Apparent Movement," *Journal of Experimental Psychology*, Vol. 45 (1953), 378–386.

Munsell Book of Color. Baltimore: Munsell Color Company, 1929.

O'BRIEN, B., "A Study of Night Myopia," *USAF WADC TR 53-206* (May 1953).

OGLE, K. N., "On the Limits of Stereoscopic Vision," *Journal of Experimental Psychology*, Vol. 44 (1952), 253–259.

———. "Basis of Stereoscopic Vision," *A.M.A. Archives of Ophthalmology*, Vol. 52 (1954), 197–210.

———. "On the Resolving Power of the Human Eye," *Journal of the Optical Society of America*, Vol. 41 (1951), 517–520.

PICKFORD, R. W., *Individual Differences in Colour Vision*. London: Routledge & Kegan Paul, Ltd., 1951.

PIERCE, J. R., and J. E. KARLIN, "Reading Rates and the Information Rate of a Human Channel," *Bell System Technical Journal*, Vol. 36 (March 1957), 497–516.

PIRENNE, M. H., "The Absolute Sensitivity of the Eye and the Variation of Visual Acuity with Intensity," *British Medical Bulletin*, Vol. 9 (1953), 61–67.

———. *Vision and the Eye*. London: Pilot Press, Ltd., 1948.

POLLOCK, W. T., and A. CHAPANIS, "The Apparent Length of a Line as a Function of its Inclination," *Journal of Experimental Psychology*, Vol. 4 (1952), 170–178.

POLLOCK, W. T., "The Visibility of a Target as a Function of its Speed of Movement," *Journal of Experimental Psychology*, Vol. 45 (June 1953), 449–454.

POLYAK, S., H. KLÜVER (ed.), *The Vertebrate Visual System*. University of Chicago Press, 1958.

POULTON, E. C., and R. L. GREGORY, "Blinking During Visual Tracking," *Great Britain*, A.P.U. 152.51. Medical Research Council, Applied Psychology Research Unit, Psychological Laboratory, Cambridge, June 1951.

RIGGS, L. A., R. N. BERRY, and M. WAYNER, "A Comparison of Electrical and Psychophysical Determinations of the Spectral Sensitivity of the Human Eye," *Journal of the Optical Society of America*, Vol. 39 (1949), 427–436.

ROUSE, R. O., "Color and the Intensity Time Relation," *Journal of the Optical Society of America*, Vol. 42 (1952), 626–630.

RUSHTON, W. A. H., and R. D. COHEN, "Visual Purple Level and the Course of Dark Adaptation," *Nature*, Vol. 173 (1954), 301–302.

SCOTT, P., and K. G. WILLIAMS, "A Note on Temporal Coding as a Mechanism in Sensory Perception," *Information and Control*, Vol. 2 No. 4 (December 1959), 380–385.

SENDERS, V. L., "The Physiological Basis of Visual Acuity," *Psychological Bulletin*, Vol. 45 (1948), 465–490.

SLOAN, L. L., "The Threshold Gradient of the Rods and the Cones: In the Dark-Adapted and in the Partially Light-Adapted Eye," *American Journal of Ophthalmology*, Vol. 33 (1950), 1077–1089.

SMITH, W. M., "Effect of Monocular and Binocular Vision, Brightness, and Apparent Size on the Sensitivity to Apparent Movement in Depth," *Journal of Experimental Psychology*, Vol. 49 (1955), 357–362.

STARK, L., "Stability, Oscillations, and Noise in the Human Pupil Servomechanism," *Proceedings of the IRE*, Vol. 47 No. 11 (1939), 1925–1939.

SVAETICHIN, G., and E. F. McNICHOL, JR., "Retinal Mechanisms for Chromatic and Achromatic Vision," *Annals of the New York Academy of Science*, Vol. 74 (November 1958), 385–404.

SZIKLAI, G. C., "Some Studies in the Speed of Visual Perception," *Transactions of the IRE* PGIT-2 (September 1956), 125–128.

TIFFIN, J., *Industrial Psychology*, 3rd ed. Englewood Cliffs, N.J.: Prentice-Hall, Inc., 1952.

VOS, J. J., A. LAZET, and M. A. BOUMAN, "Visual Contrast Thresholds in Practical Problems," *Journal of the Optical Society of America*, Vol. 46 No. 12 (December 1956), 1065–1068.

WESTHEIMER, G., and D. W. CONOVER, "Smooth Eye Movements in the Absence of a Moving Visual Stimulus," *Journal of Experimental Psychology*, Vol. 47 No. 4 (April 1954), 283–284.

WESTHEIMER, G., "Mechanism of Saccadic Eye Movements," *A.M.A. Archives of Ophthalmology*, Vol. 52 (November 1954), 710–724.

———. "Eye Movement Responses to a Horizontally Moving Visual Stimulus," *A.M.A. Archives of Ophthalmology*, Vol. 52 (December 1954), 932–941.

WHITESIDE, T. C. D., *The Problems of Vision in Flight at High Altitude*. London: Butterworth Scientific Publications, 1957.

WULFECK, J. W., A. WEISZ, and M. W. RABEN, "Vision in Military Aviation," *USAF WADC TR 58–399* (November 1958).

4

THE AUDITORY CHANNEL

4.1. THE AUDITORY STIMULUS

The human operator probably receives the second greatest amount of information through hearing. Complex mechanical vibrations of air molecules can transmit energy to the human ear and stimulate a sensation related to the physical sound. These vibrations are longitudinal; that is, the particles move in a direction parallel to the direction of propagation of the energy wavefront causing successive condensation and rarefaction at each point in the medium. Although such vibrations may be described in a great number of ways, it is particularly useful to consider them with respect to their sinusoidal harmonic content (those sinusoidal frequencies which could be linearly combined to synthesize the complex waveform).

The simplest sound, a "pure tone," consists of a single frequency of sinusoidal vibration. It may be fully described by three parameters: frequency, amplitude, and phase. The frequency, which is determined by the generating sound source, is the number of condensation-rarefaction cycles which occur per unit time. When the wavefront spreads as a result of mechanical contact of molecules, the frequency remains unchanged. The velocity of propagation is dependent upon the physical properties of the medium; for air at sea level pressure (29.92 inch of Hg) and standard temperature (68° F) this velocity is about 1,127 feet per second. Even though a wide range of sound frequencies can be established in air, the human auditory channel can be stimulated only by those frequencies within the range of 16 to 20,000 cycles per second.

The amplitude of the sinusoid is a measure of the physical displacement of the individual air molecules. This amplitude corresponds to the amount of propagating energy and relates to perceived intensity of the sound wave. In air the mean displacement of molecules in their random motion is very small, about 10^{-9} centimeters; but this is not far beyond the sensitivity of the normal human ear. In fact, this sensitivity approaches that required to sense the Brownian movement of air particles resulting from molecular motion, or the vibration due to the flow of blood through the capillaries within the ear.

The physical magnitude of a sound at a point may be measured in terms of the sound pressure of the impinging wavefront (dynes per square centimeter) or in terms of the sound energy imposed upon a given area (watts per square centimeter). The sound pressure, p, is conventionally described by the rms (root-mean-square) value of the pressure difference between the high and low extremes of pressure during a single cycle. Since the acoustic impedance of air is almost purely resistive (very small compliance and low inertia), the volume velocity is proportional to the pressure, p. The sound power, P, is then given by

$$P = gp^2 A$$

where g is the reciprocal of the acoustical resistance of air, and A is the frontal area of the wavefront. Sound power per unit area is proportional to the square of the pressure.

In order to express this power over a very wide range of values, a logarithmic unit called the *bel* was chosen, and defined as

$$\text{bel} = \log_{10} \frac{P_1}{P_0}$$

where P_1 is the sound power of the acoustic energy being described, and P_0 is an arbitrary reference value chosen to correspond to the lowest value of power which is audible to a normal person. Thus the lowest sound pressure level is heard at about zero bels.

A convenient size unit for usual measurements of power level is one tenth of a bel, called the *decibel*, abbreviated db. Then the sound power level, PWL, may be expressed in db as

$$\text{PWL} = 10 \log_{10} \frac{P_1}{P_0}$$

The second degree relation indicated above may be used to translate this db sound power level into a measure of relative waveform amplitude or sound pressure level, SPL,

$$\text{SPL} = 20 \log_{10} \frac{p_1}{p_0}$$

The human auditory channel ranges from a threshold defined as zero db to a maximum near 160 db. Refer to Figure 4.1 for an indication of the usual sound levels in common situations. Note that the threshold of discomfort is at an energy level 1,000,000,000,000 times that of the threshold of perception. As the spherical wavefront of sound energy propagates in a free field, the intensity (the sound pressure level) diminishes according to the inverse square of the distance; thus doubling the distance results in a loss of 6 db.

According to the basic relation, $v = f\lambda$, the wavelength of sound waves ranges from about 0.6 inches at the high frequency extreme to about 70 feet at the low frequency end of the audible spectrum. Obviously the human dimensions become insignificant in comparison to the wavelength for lower frequency sounds, whereas this is certainly not the case at the high frequency

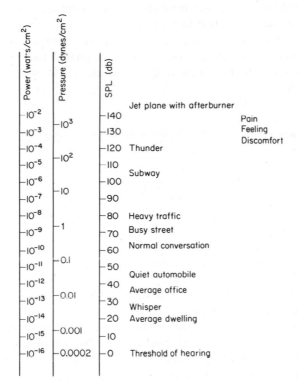

Figure 4.1. The range of auditory sound levels.

end of the spectrum. Displacement by a portion of a wavelength corresponds to a proportionate phase shift. This phase property aids in the subjective localization of the direction of arrival of the received sounds. This capability will be described more fully at an appropriate point below.

A true sinusoidal waveform is a steady state representation extending over all time. Since such a model cannot be found in the real world, it is important to state not only the frequency, amplitude, and phase of a sound stimulus but also the time duration over which it exists. Further, the initial and final transients, being described by some rise-time and damping characteristic, may be expected to be indigenous to the particular sound generator. Such nonsinusoidal waveforms may be synthesized through the additive combination of a spectrum comprised of many sinusoids of frequencies higher than that of the "steady state" fundamental waveform.

Simple sounds of sinusoidal waveform almost never occur outside the acoustic laboratory. The sound pressure waveform of speech, music, or noise is a single-valued function of time which could only be synthesized if a very large number of sinusoids were additively superimposed. Those higher frequency components which are integral multiples of a lower frequency are called *harmonics* of that lower frequency. The lowest frequency component in the analyzed waveform is called the *fundamental*.

The *quality* of a sound is a subjective description of the particular waveform. In terms of spectral analysis, it is characterized by the number and amplitude of each of the higher frequency components which are present. The discrete summation of sinusoids of any frequency yields only a periodic waveform of infinite time extent. Finite time duration signals would require a continuous spectrum of sinusoids for exact synthesis. Thus it is usual to describe auditory stimuli by their spectral content over some continuous range of frequencies.

Speech is a most important class of auditory stimuli. The sounds encountered in speech lie in the frequency range roughly from 100 to 10,000 cycles per second. The fundamental frequency of male vocal chords is about 125 cycles per second and about twice this frequency for the female voice. The lowest frequency varies during speech, and there appears to be a distinct tendency to increase the frequency with increase of intensity. It is this characteristic which allows estimation of the original speech intensity, based only upon the pitch of a perceived speech.

The various sounds within speech differ in the way energy is distributed over the spectrum. In particular, vowels are predominantly sinusoidal with most of the energy concentrated in the lower frequency portion of the spectrum. The various vowels are produced by the positioning of the vocal cavities, including the lips and the tongue, so that certain harmonics are resonated while others are suppressed. The consonant sounds, characteristically of higher frequency content, are the result of manipulated unvoiced sounds. Figure 4.2 indicates the power level versus frequency for the phonetic sounds of speech.

There is a wide variation in the power of average conversational speech, but typical speech is usually at about 10 microwatts. Excluding the silent intervals during conversation, this average is increased to approximately 15 microwatts, an extremely small amount of energy. To realize this better, note that the total average power of all the inhabitants of the earth talking simultaneously would be less than the power radiated from a single large radio broadcasting station. A loud shout increases the average power to about 100 times that of normal speech, while a low whisper reduces the average power to approximately 1/100th of the average value. Minimum

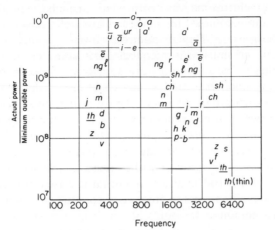

Frequency

Figure 4.2. The intensities and regions for most important frequency components of fundamental speech sounds. When a sound has several principal components, the intensity and frequency of each are indicated. (By permission from *Radio Engineering*, by F. E. Terman, copyright 1955. McGraw-Hill Book Company, Inc.)

and maximum powers encountered in speech range from about 0.01 microwatts to 5,000 microwatts. This corresponds to an intensity range of 500,000 to 1. Figure 4.3 indicates the relative power of speech versus frequency.

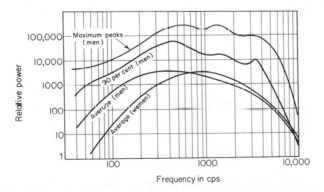

Frequency in cps

Figure 4.3. Distribution of average speech energy over the frequency spectrum. When the speech is divided into time intervals of ⅛ second duration, the peak intensity in 90 per cent of these intervals does not exceed the value given by the curve marked "90 per cent." (By permission from *Radio Engineering*, by F. E. Terman, copyright 1955. McGraw-Hill Book Company, Inc.)

Music generally covers a much wider spectrum than does speech, since it ranges from approximately 60 cycles per second and even less, to important harmonics occurring near 15,000 cycles. Each musical instrument has a particular characteristic sound waveform which may be viewed as a spectral intensity distribution. These characteristics are well known and in fact may be used for the programming of electronic organs in such a way that they synthesize particular musical instruments quite well.

A large orchestra may reach a peak sound power of approximately 100 watts, depending upon the number and character of the instruments being played as well as the programming of the musical composition. The greatest single sound power source in the orchestra is produced by the bass drum which generates peaks reaching to approximately 25 watts. Compare this to the piano with a peak power of 0.267 watt and to the piccolo with a peak power of 0.084 watt. A section of violins playing together does not produce a sound intensity which is the direct sum of the intensity of each of the instruments, since the emitted sounds of the various instruments do not generally remain in phase correspondence.

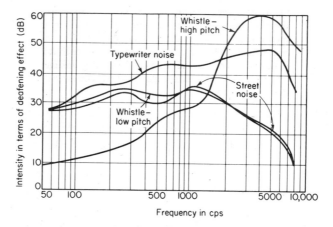

Figure 4.4. Energy distribution of typical noises expressed in terms of the deafening (or masking) effect. The distinguishing feature of noises is the more or less continuous energy distribution over a wide frequency range. (By permission from *Radio Engineering*, by F. E. Terman, copyright 1955. McGraw-Hill Book Company, Inc.)

Noise stimuli can cover the entire auditory spectrum, as shown in Figure 4.4. The total sound level of several noise sources acting simultaneously can be found by combining them on an energy basis. The procedure for doing this is to convert the decibel quantities into relative powers, to add or subtract them, as the situation may require, and then to convert back to the corresponding db level. Thus the combining of two 80 db noise sources yields a total level of 83 db and *not* 160 db. Figure 4.5 provides a graphic reference for adding two sound levels. This chart may be used repetitively to find the total intensity for any number of combined sources.

The sound which reaches the listener is generally quite different from the sound which is being generated, this difference being due to the acoustic characteristics of the environment. Walls and specific objects reflect and absorb sound energy and thus modify both spectral and intensity characteristics of the sound. Some spatial volumes of increased intensity may be created while other null regions may be found. Sound absorbing material in the environment can grossly change the amount of sound energy which reaches the listener. The absorbing property of material may also be frequency sensitive so that certain harmonics may be removed from the reflected energy thus changing the quality of the sound as heard by the listener.

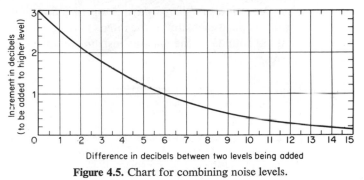

Difference in decibels between two levels being added

Figure 4.5. Chart for combining noise levels.

Rooms have a reverberant quality, especially when they are of small volume and have sound-reflecting wall surfaces. In large theaters and auditoriums the reverberation time (that time required for the sound intensity to drop 60 db) is generally in the order of several seconds. In the ordinary living room the sound has the opportunity to travel only a short distance between absorptive reflections. Hence the reverberation time is usually very short. The "sound" of the living room is usually quite different from that of the kitchen or the bathroom. A certain amount of reverberation is normally desired in that it aids the speaker or musical performer in attaining a "full" tone quality.

Recently devices have been marketed which create artificial electronic reverberation so that a radio or electric organ can be made to sound as if it were being played in a large auditorium even though it is actually in a normal sized living room. For the reverberant sound to seem "natural," the reverberation time should rise about 50 per cent at 128 cycles per second and be constant above about 500 cycles per second. It is possible to treat a performance studio in such a way as to produce the desired reverberation, in fact, it is possible even to create variable reverberation should this be desired.

The listener often receives a limited spectrum reproduction of the original sounds. AM broadcast radio, for example, produces sound of from 100 to 5,000 cycles per second, whereas FM radio realizes from 50 to 15,000 cycles per second. It is also important to evaluate the distortion introduced into the reproduction by nonlinearities of the reproducing system. This subject lies well within the domain of audio engineering.

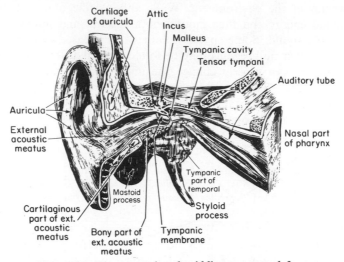

Figure 4.6. The external and middle ear, opened from the front. Right side. (From C. M. Goss, *Gray's Anatomy*, 27th edition, Philadelphia: Lea & Febiger, 1959.)

4.2. THE SENSING MECHANISM

Figure 4.6 shows a cross section of the human ear. Incident sound energy is directed by the external ear, the auricular, to travel inward through an oval

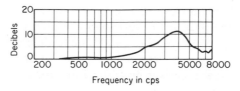

Figure 4.7. Effects of resonance on the external ear. The ordinate shows the ratio in decibels between the sound pressure at the eardrum and the sound pressure at the entrance to the auditory canal. (From S. S. Stevens, *Handbook of Experimental Psychology*, New York: John Wiley & Sons, Inc., 1951.)

cylindrical canal to arrive at the tympanic membrane, the eardrum. Figure 4.7 describes the effects of resonance of the external ear. The ordinate shows the ratio in db between the sound pressure at the eardrum and the sound pressure

at the entrance to the auditory canal. The external ear is acoustically ineffective for directing low frequency sounds where the wavelength is in the order

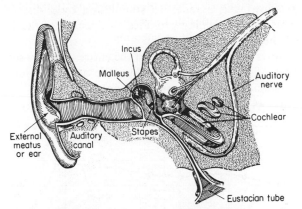

Figure 4.8. A simplified sketch of the auditory sensing
mechanism. (After D. C. Kimber, C. E. Gray, C. E. Stack-
pole, and L. C. Leaville, *Textbook of Anatomy and Physiology*,
13th edition, New York: Macmillan Company, 1955.
Reprinted with permission.)

of magnitude of several feet. It does, however, offer protection against foreign
bodies and aids in maintaining the temperature and lack of humidity at and
near the eardrum. The tympanic membrane partitions an otherwise con-

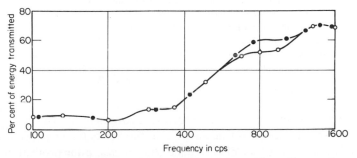

Figure 4.9. Transmission of energy at the eardrum. The ordinate values
were computed from impedance measurements. They indicate the percentage of the incident sound energy transmitted to the middle ear.
The open circles refer to the left and the dots refer to the right ear of the
subject. The difference between the ordinate values and 100 per cent is
the amount of energy reflected at the eardrum. (From S. S. Stevens,
Handbook of Experimental Psychology, New York: John Wiley & Sons,
Inc., 1951. After Waltzman and Keibs. Reprinted with permission.)

tinuous tube going from the external ear to the nasal part of the pharynx.
The inner portion of this canal is called the Eustacian tube. It is this tube which
serves the valuable purpose of maintaining equality of pressure on both sides
of the eardrum. If it were not for the Eustacian tube, the air trapped in the

middle ear would be partly absorbed and cause the tympanum to bulge inward with resulting discomfort and interference with hearing sensitivity. The act of swallowing is a reflex to stimulation by a distended tympanic membrane. This act or yawning provides an opening of the Eustacian tube to the cavity behind the nose.

Figure 4.8 shows a simplified sketch of the entire auditory sensing mechanism. Movement of the eardrum translates the arriving sound energy into mechanical movements of three small bones which span the middle ear. Figure 4.9 indicates the percentage of incident sound energy which is trans-

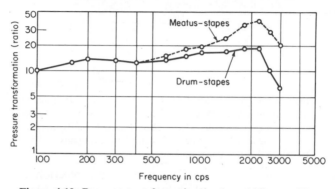

Figure 4.10. Pressure transformation in the middle ear. The pressure at the stapes is increased over the pressure at the meatus (and at the drum) by the ratio shown. This pressure transformation serves toward matching the impedance of the air to the impedance of the cochlea. At the higher frequencies, the ratio of transformation between stapes and meatus is enhanced by the resonance of the meatus. (From S. S. Stevens, *Handbook of Experimental Psychology*, New York: John Wiley & Sons, Inc., 1951. After Békésy. Reprinted with permission.)

mitted to the inner ear by the eardrum. Movement of the *malleus* (the hammer) displaces the *incus* (the anvil), and this rocks the *stapes* (the stirrup) about a fulcrum. These members, called the *ossicles*, offer protection for the sensitive inner ear against damage from high-intensity low-frequency sounds. In the usual frequency range, they effectively amplify the pressure at the eardrum into larger movements of the labyrinthic wall, as shown in Figure 4.10.

The inner ear contains both the vestibular position and motion sensing mechanism (discussed in Chapter 5) and the *cochlea*. This latter apparatus translates the pressure-sensed incident movements into neural messages which result in the subjective sensation of hearing. The inner ear is entirely filled with liquid. The cochlea is a tube about 35 millimeters long which is coiled in a spiral as shown in Figure 5.1. It is subdivided into two principal channels by means of an elastic partition which contains the auditory nerve endings and many other structures which relate to the neural translation of the mechanical vibrations. These channels are interconnected at the far end by the *helicotrema* to protect the neural membrane against damage from single-sided static pressures. When the stapes moves inward, a high pressure wave-front is set up along the upper channel. This increased pressure wave deforms the partition wall, the *basilar membrane*. The displacement of this membrane is almost proportional to the causal movement of the stapes, as shown in Figure 4.11.

Figure 4.12 shows a typical cross section of a cochlear canal. The basilar membrane supports a rather complex structure known as the organ of Corti.

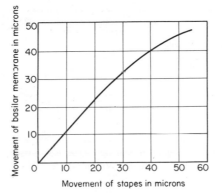

Movement of stapes in microns

Figure 4.11. Amplitude of vibration of the basilar membrane as a function of the amplitude of the stapes. At values far above the threshold of feeling, the movement of the basilar membrane ceases to be proportional to the movement of the stapes. (From S. S. Stevens, *Handbook of Experimental Psychology*, New York: John Wiley & Sons, Inc., 1951. After Békésy. Reprinted with permission.)

It is this organ which contains the sensory cells which result in audition. Figure 4.13 shows an expanded view of just this portion of the auditory mechanism. The hair cells of the organ of Corti form a long and narrow sensory surface about four or five cells in width, running the length of the basilar membrane. These hair cells are about 10 microns in diameter, numbering about 23,500.

The auditory nerve stems from the cochlea, leaving by way of the center of the spiral cord. There are about 27,000 ganglion nerve cells which trace an uninterrupted path between the hair cells on the organ of Corti and nerve cells inside the central nervous system. The inner hair cells are connected to one or two nerve fibers, but the connection of external hair cells is more complicated. The fibers of the auditory nerve are arranged in an orderly but complicated fashion, twisted like strands of a rope around the central core.

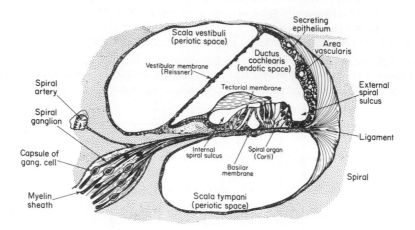

Figure 4.12. Vertical cross section of a choclea canal showing the organ of Corti with its hair cells, the end organs of hearing. (After Rasmussen, *Outlines of Neuro-anatomy*, 3rd edition, Dubuque, Iowa: William C. Brown Company, 1943.)

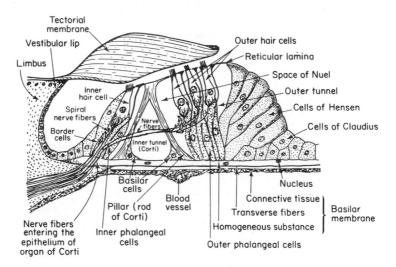

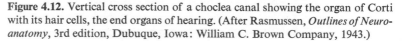

Figure 4.13. Vertical cross section of the organ of Corti (named after Alfonso Corti, its discoverer). The outer hair cells are supported by their respective phalangeal cells which rest in turn on the moveable basilar membrane. Motion of the basilar membrane presumably distorts the hair cells. (After Rasmussen, *Outlines of Neuro-anatomy*, 3rd edition, Dubuque, Iowa: William C. Brown Company, 1943.)

These central fibers originate at about the middle of the basilar turn. The auditory nerve is short, entering the lower brain stem (*medulla oblongata*) where the fibers divide. At this point the first synapses occur in the auditory system, and maintain the general orderly pattern.

4.3. THEORIES OF AUDITION

Over the years a number of theories have been advanced to explain the observed characteristics of the auditory channel. Helmholtz (1857) advanced one of the first of these. He proposed a linear resonance concept in order to explain pitch discrimination. More specifically, he considered the basilar membrane to be composed of a series of individual resonators which could sympathetically respond to the sinusoidal spectral components of the waveform of the impinging energy in accordance with its Fourier analysis. This theory permitted the explanation of beats in terms of the excitation of a single resonating element by two audio tones of almost the same frequency.

Lack of anatomical evidence supporting the tuned resonance theory made a traveling wave theory more acceptable. G. von Békésy, its originator, indicated that the long curved channel could yield standing waves resulting from the coupling of energy in the form of incoming and reflected pressure waves. The position of maximum amplitude of the standing wave would be determined by the frequency so that only a position related neural mechanism would be excited. The anomaly remains, however, in that human ability in pitch discrimination is far better than what would be offered by the broad tuning of the basilar membrane. Evidently if this were the basic mechanism there would have to be additional discrimination achieved in the neural encoding or transition of the message to the cortex. In general, "place theories" are those which presume that the position of maximum stimulation along the basilar membrane determines pitch.

J. F. Schouten noted the sensation of a low frequency tone in the presentation of periodic stimulus consisting only of a number of higher harmonics. The empirical evidence demonstrated that auditory phenomena do not obey Ohm's acoustic law (1843).[1] Further, the controlled experiment prevented nonlinear distortion from producing spurious harmonics. It was thus found necessary to advance the "residue theory" in an effort to explain the perception of a nonexistent auditory tone. The residue theory hypothesized that complex stimuli contained two components which give rise to the same pitch sensation. The high harmonics stimulating the high frequency region of the basilar membrane were presumed to be collectively observed. It is the periodicity of the collective summation of these higher harmonics which is called the "residue" resulting in the sharp low frequency perception. In fact, it was subsequently demonstrated that the low frequency sensation could be excited by a physical stimulus which contained no low frequency components.

[1] That complex sounds are perceptually resolved into a series of simple component pendular waves.

J. C. R. Licklider extended study of the relation between relative phase of stimulus components and the pitch judgment of complex stimuli. Using a number of independent oscillators, he found it possible to adjust the relative phases so that the low "residue" pitch was consistently and clearly heard. If, however, the phases were randomly arranged, it often happened that no pronounced peaks and valleys of waveform were produced, and in such cases the low frequency component was missing.

Schouten's hypothesis, that frequency components which do not maximally stimulate the apical (low frequency) end of the basilar membrane can produce judgments of low pitch, was further strengthened by experimental observations of S. S. Stevens who employed repeatable pulses generated by resonant circuits of different frequencies. All of these circuits used the same damping constant, and the stimuli were judged to have a definite low pitch signal of about 125 cycles per second, even though the relative level of this component of the actual stimulus was very small. Several experiments were carried out to further substantiate the generation of the low frequency pitch sensation. E. deBoer asked subjects to match the pitch of two complex stimuli, one of which was composed of frequency components which were harmonically related. It was found that the residue pitch of amplitude modulated samples is not simply a function of the envelope repetition rate, but is determined in part by the approximate period of the signals.

Additional experiments were carried out by G. A. Miller and W. G. Taylor using repeated bursts of wide-band noise. These experiments formed an additional challenge to the place theory of pitch discrimination, and showed that the ability of the mechanism to distinguish small changes of burst rate is a contradiction of Ohm's acoustic law. It was found that if the burst rate was made sufficiently great, then repeated bursts of noise can no longer be distinguished from a continuous noise. This viewpoint is dependent upon the sound-time fraction, that is, the ratio of time duration of a burst to the period of repetition, as well as upon the stimulus intensity.

The experiments referred to above have a bearing upon the theoretical approach to pitch discrimination. Stimuli which excited the basal end of the cochlea are judged as having a low pitched quality. Further, there is the ability to distinguish changes in the burst rate of modulated noise, even though such change leaves the spectral characteristic of the stimulus virtually unchanged In both cases experimental results are difficult to explain on the basis of a pure place theory for discrimination.

Two recent theories of pitch discrimination represent extensions of the place theory. One is the "volley theory" advanced by E. G. Wever, and the other is the "duplex" or "triplex theory" of Licklider. The volley theory is based on the demonstration that a group of nerve fibers can respond synchronously to repetitive stimulation yielding a much higher repetition rate than would a single fiber. Members of a compound nerve may be said to fire in rotation so that the composite response may be synchronous, even though the individual fibers do not fire with each cycle of excitation. Wever states:

> In the volley theory, the place and frequency principles are accepted, not in their most inclusive form of operation as conceived in the classical hypotheses where they arose, but subject to certain restrictions. In the first instance, the roles to which they are assigned in pitch perception vary according to the tonal region. Frequency serves for the low tones, and both perform in the broader ground between. This allocation follows the evidence that volley action is faithfully representative for low and intermediate frequencies but becomes inaccurate and fails for the high frequencies; and on the other hand that place representation is discriminatory in the upper and middle portions of the auditory scale but on account of spread of response is decidedly less so at the lower end. The two variables thus are in part auxiliary and in part complementary in their determination of pitch.

Thus pitch is given a dual representation in terms of both place on the basilar membrane as well as a composite impulse frequency in the neurological translation which causes the psychological response. The frequency ranges suggested were from 15 to 400 cycles per second for the low region where there remains synchronism of neural response with the stimulus repetition, 400 to 5,000 cycles per second where both frequency and place encoding are operative, and 5,000 to 24,000 cycles per second where pitch is entirely dependent upon place. This theory is primarily based upon physiological evidence related to the response to pure tone stimuli.

In contrast, Licklider specified both frequency analysis and autocorrelation analysis as required to yield pitch discrimination. He states:

> The essence of the duplex theory of pitch perception is that the auditory system employs both frequency analysis and autocorrelational analysis. The frequency analysis is performed by the cochlea, the autocorrelational analysis by the neural part of the system. The latter is therefore an analysis not of the acoustic stimulus itself but of the trains of nerve impulses into which the action of the cochlea transforms the stimulus. This point is important because the highly nonlinear process of neural excitation intervenes between the two analyses.

More specifically the suggestion is made that the cochlea analysis resolves the stimulation into a function of time, t, and position, x, along the cochlea. A running autocorrelation is accomplished by the neural mechanism associated with each position along the cochlea. There results a two-dimensional function; x position along the nervous tissue into which the lengthwise dimension of the cochlea projects and the τ dimension, correspondent to the delay, this being functionally orthogonal as shown in Figure 4.14. The stimulus $f(t)$ is represented in terms of the autocorrelation function, $\phi(t; \tau, x)$. By adding a third orthogonal dimension, it was possible to include a representation for the binaural mechanism in terms of a crosscorrelation operator which precedes autocorrelation.

M. H. Goldstein carried out neurophysiological experiments, which tend to validate Wever's volley principle, in that neural impulses followed repetitive stimuli. Further studies of the tonotopic organization of the cortex indicated that the linear tuning is probably related to a place mechanism at the cochlea as observed at low and middle frequencies as well as high fre-

Figure 4.14. Schematic illustrations of duplex analysis. (a) represents the analysis of a 100 cps sinusoid, (b) of white noise interrupted 100 times per second, (c) of a set of high-frequency harmonics of 100 cps, and (d) of a 200 cps sinusoid. At the left in each plot are shown the stimulus waveform $f(t)$, the waveform $F(t, x_i)$ of the signal carried by the first-order neurons (acting as a group) at x_i, and the autocorrelation function $\varphi(\tau, x_i)$ of $F(t, x_i)$. At the top of each plot is the distribution of activity along the length of the cochlea: $\overline{A(x, t)}$ is the root-mean-square of the instantaneous amplitudes of oscillation $A(x, t)$ at various positions along the cochlear partition. $F(t, x)$ results from the rectification and smoothing of $A(x, t)$. The density of stippling in the rectangle represents $\varphi(\tau, x)$, the autocorrelation functions of the signals to the various x-channels. (Since the signals are in steady state, the t dimension is omitted here.) Note that the first three (x, τ)-plots are similar in the τ- but not in the x-dimension. This corresponds to the fact that they are subjectively similar in one pitch-like attribute but not in another. (d) is somewhat similar to (a) in the τ-dimension; the odd-numbered maxima of $\varphi(\tau, x)$ in (d) coincide with the maxima in (a). This corresponds to the subjective uniqueness of the octave relation.

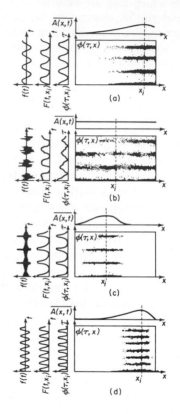

quencies. This study appears to confirm that there is dual representation for low tones in both place and temporal pattern.

It has been suggested that the spectral distribution of energy and the envelope waveform are the characteristics of the acoustic signal which are discriminable in audition. It is concluded that frequency analysis is performed primarily through the mechanical filtering of the basilar membrane. Throughout the low and moderate frequency ranges, this filtering is essentially linear and represents a "place" analysis which is then directly encoded into a physical pattern of neural fibers which correspond in an analogic manner to the spectrum of the signal. The nonlinearity of the read-out process between the cochlea and the cortex accomplishes a considerable sharpening of the spectral analysis.

There is, indeed, a further type of neural nonlinearity which operates with respect to envelope-waveform discrimination. A synchrony of neural activity level at the cochlea has been observed in correspondence with the low intensity stimulus envelope. This synchrony disappears near repetition rates at which the observer is unable to judge the presence of envelope modulation. Synchrony at the cortex disappears near the repetition rate at which discriminability of changes in the repetition rate of repeated bursts of noise decreases sharply in psychophysical tests. Goldstein suggests that stimulus-signal properties of spectral distribution and envelope-waveshape are probably represented at the cortical level by spatial and temporal patterns of responses.

4.4. THE PSYCHOACOUSTIC CAPABILITY

The purpose of the auditory channel is to receive and transform sounds into neural codes capable of conveying intelligence to the human operator. Direct perception furnishes a representation of the sound itself. It is usually necessary to operate further on this perception or set of perceptions in order to furnish a representation of the message content or other inference about the sound, the sound source, and/or the listener's environment.

The perception-response domain may be looked upon as a hyperspace characterized by a number of variables including pitch, loudness, duration, and spatial localization. Thus space is in rough correspondence to the physical space in which the sound-stimulus can be described in terms of frequency, intensity, duration, and relative position to the observer. It is of interest to examine the relation between these hyperspaces.

Pitch is a single-valued subjective summary of the sensed spectral properties of the sound-stimulus. The listener describes a sound as being "high" or "low." Generally, the pitch of a note roughly corresponds to the frequency of the predominant sinusoidal components which might be used to synthesize the pressure amplitude waveform. Pitch can run the gamut of sensed sound frequencies from about 20 cycles per second to an upper limit of about 16,000 to 20,000 cycles per second, dependent upon the listener.

As the spectral property of a sound-signal is made more diffuse over a band of frequencies, it becomes more difficult for the listener to distinguish pitch. He hears the note clearly but is unable to offer a singular representation for the spectrum. Some sounds, such as white noise (equal amplitude components over a wide frequency range) and a very short sinusoid (where there is insufficient time to establish a spectral identity), can have *no pitch at all*. Sounds as low as 5 cycles per second or as high as 100,000 cycles per second have been heard due to the nonlinearity of the auditory channel which serves to convert portions of the impinging sound energy into frequencies within the normal auditory range. The reported cases are without specific sensation of pitch.

Pitch appears as a two-dimensional attribute. First, there is the pitch itself, and second, there is the intensity of the pitch sensation as measured by the ease with which the listener is able to distinguish it. Timbre, brightness, fullness, and so on, are other spectral-dependent perception attributes. However, these are considered to be of secondary importance.

The perceived pitch of a sound is related to other aspects of the physical stimulus. Pitch is lowered by an increase in intensity of pure tones in the range below 500 cycles per second. That is, low notes appear lower when they are stronger. In a similar manner, high tones above 4,000 cycles per

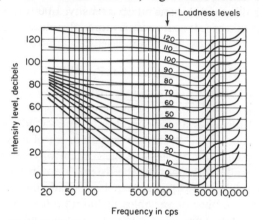

Figure 4.15. Contours of equal loudness. (From *WADC TR 52-204*. Reprinted with permission.)

second appear higher upon increase of the stimulus intensity. The octave (the range between tones which are related by a frequency factor of two) is the common unit of measure in music. Pitch, however, is nonlinearly related to frequency in such a way that octaves toward the ends of the musical scale appear to be of shorter range than octaves in the middle range. To overcome this difficulty, a scale has been developed using the unit of mel, this being defined as the unit of equal pitch as judged by an average listener. Arbitrary reference has been established as a 1,000 cycle per second sinusoidal tone stimulus heard at 40 db above the threshold of audition. This is said to correspond to the 1,000 mel point. Pitch of a given signal might be judged to be one-half that of the reference, in which case it would be described as being of 500 mels. Such a scale is particularly useful in efforts to determine a set of signals which would have maximum "separation" to the human observer, thereby increasing ease of identification and the communication of certain forms of coded intelligence.

Loudness is the subjective judgment of the intensity of the observed sound-stimulus. This judgment can be achieved over an extremely wide range of physical sound intensities. The normal ear responds above zero db as shown in Figure 4.15, which corresponds to 0.0002 dynes per square centimeter. The auditory channel can respond to sound pressure levels which produce a force as small as a three millionth of a gram. At the other extreme discomfort is sensed at about 120 db, feeling occurs at about 130 db, and pain is induced at about 140 db. The usable sound intensities extend over a range of several million times the smallest pressure.

It has been found useful to develop several different scales for the description of perceived intensity. The *phon* is the unit defining the equal-loudness-level scale. A 1,000 cycle per second tone taken as reference is measured in terms of the db level of the physical sound stimulus. Any sound which is judged to be equal in loudness to a 50 db intensity, 1,000 cycle per second tone is called a 50 phon sound. It is, however, more often necessary, to estimate the relative intensity of sounds. In such a case, it is appropriate to use the *sone*

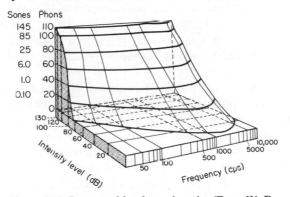

Figure 4.16. Perceptual loudness domain. (From W. E. Woodson, *Human Engineering Guide for Equipment Designers*, 1954, Berkeley, Calif.: University of California Press. Reprinted with permission.)

scale wherein one sone is taken to be the perceived loudness of a 1,000 cycles per second pure tone, 40 db above auditory threshold at that frequency. If a given sound is judged to be twice as loud as the reference, it is called a two sone sound. Figure 4.16 indicates the extent of the audible domain in terms of the phon and sone scales. A third useful scale relates to the *sensation level* as measured in db above the intensity of the just-audible sound. Sensation level is not linearly related to the physical amplitude of the sound stimulus, as was shown in Figure 4.15.

The precision of perception can be stated in terms of the size of the just-noticeable difference (jnd), that minimum amount of change in the stimulus which will be detected with a probability of 0.5. The frequency jnd is smaller for tones toward the low end of the frequency spectrum, the actual amount being dependent upon the sensation level. Below 20 db sensation level, the average human loses his ability to perceive change of frequency. Above that intensity level a frequency difference of three cycles is significant for tones below 1,000 cycles per second. Above that frequency the jnd is approximately three tenths of one per cent of the tone's frequency. In the loudness range

below 20 db, the detectable difference is from 2 to 6 db dependent on frequency of the sound, while in the range above 20 db ½ to 1 db is sufficient.
At extremely high frequencies a larger increment is required to assure detection of the change. The auditory channel is most sensitive to change in the
signal intensity over the frequency range between 500 and 10,000 cycles per
second.

There appears to be greater correspondence between the physical duration
of a sound-signal and the extent of time over which that sound is perceived.
The perception of extremely short tones depends upon the transmission of
sufficient energy into the auditory channel to stimulate a significant neural
response with respect to the ambient neural-noise level. For very short tones
the perceived intensity is inversely proportional to duration. At the other
extreme, it is possible to have an auditory after-image. Listening to a train
of sharp pulses for some seconds may result in a subjective modulation of
normal sound perception which immediately follows causing an unusual
"jangled" or "twangy" effect.

Physical tones which appear for less than 0.01 second are of insufficient
duration to yield a pitch. These are more properly described as "clicks."
The pitch is heard to rise as the duration is increased until pitch-saturation
is reached at about 0.1 second. Duration also affects the loudness of the
perceived sound. There is a sudden rise in loudness as the duration is increased
to about 0.2 second. A maximum loudness is reached at about 0.5 second
followed by a decrease in the intensity of perception for longer durations.
For the same duration and amplitude, low frequency tones are less loud than
high frequency tones.

Spectral analysis of short tones aids an understanding of the observed
perceptions. In 1822, Fourier demonstrated that any complex waveform can
be analyzed into, or synthesized from, a sufficient number of sinusoids. If
the waveform is repetitive and extends over all time, then only a discrete set
of infinite-time-extent sinusoids is required; however, if the waveform is of
finite duration, a continuous spectrum of frequency components is required
to specify the original waveform exactly. Figure 4.17a indicates the correspondence of the infinite-time-duration sinusoid to the spectral representation.
Figure 4.17b presents a sinusoid of the same amplitude but of short duration,
together with its spectral equivalent. (Note that it is also necessary to include
a statement of the phase of each spectral component.) If the sinusoidal pulse
were made shorter, the spectrum would still range over all frequencies, but
would become more concentrated at the frequency of the sinusoid used to
generate the given waveform. Therefore, the longer the duration of a pure
tone, the more obvious becomes its pitch.

There is a further essential limitation upon the precision with which the
initiation or termination time of occurrence of a sound-signal may be judged.
Heisenberg's Uncertainty Principle (1927) is one of the primary concepts
upon which Quantum Mechanics has been developed. It states that there is

an essential relation between the position of a physical particle and its momentum, such that the precision of measuring either of these parameters limits the precision with which the other can be determined. Such variables are called *canonical* and express what might well be viewed as different measures of the same physical property. A measurement is always the result of an interaction of the observer and the observed. The Uncertainty Principle has been generalized to other phenomena including time-energy and time-frequency statements. In the latter regard,

$$\Delta t \, \Delta f \geq 1$$

where Δt is the uncertainty interval of the time point in question, and Δf is the uncertainty interval surrounding the actual frequency. Both time and frequency affect the perceptual image of physical reality. The precision of perception can certainly be no better than the uncertainty limit permits.

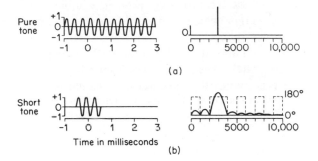

Figure 4.17. Waveform and spectra (a) for a pure tone sinusoid over all time and (b) for a short tone of the same frequency sinusoid. The spectral representation of amplitude, frequency distribution, and phase is an exact representation for the signal as first expressed in the time domain. (From S. S. Stevens, *Handbook of Experimental Psychology*, New York: John Wiley & Sons, Inc., 1951. Reprinted with permission.)

Localization of a sound refers to the ability of the subject to perceive the direction from which a sound arrives. Although each ear has a non-uniform directional sensitivity, localization information is primarily a result of the comparison of stimuli separately sensed by the ears. Symmetry of car location on the head results in minimum localization sensitivity in the median plane. "Cones of confusion" define the domain of ambiguity for sounds perceived to arrive from other than the median plane.

The ability to sense direction is a function of the time and intensity comparison of the signal as "seen" by each of the ears. At frequencies below about 1,000 cycles per second, the time difference is the predominant source of directional information, while above that frequency, loudness difference becomes significant for the discrimination of direction.

Sound which arrives from other than the median plane must travel a greater distance to reach one ear than the other. Figure 4.18a indicates the situation for a near sound source, considering the human head to be approximated by a sphere of radius, r equal to about 8.75 centimeters. The angle θ is measured with respect to the median plane. The sound travels through an angle of $90° - \theta$ to reach the near ear and $90° + \theta$ to reach the farther ear. Thus the difference angle is 2θ and the distance difference is $2\theta r$, θ being expressed in radian measure. The situation for sound sources more distant than several feet is indicated in Figure 4.18b, where the rays of arrival of the wavefront are

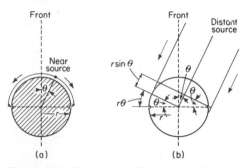

Figure 4.18. Geometry indicating the distance difference for sound wave reaching the ears. (From R. S. Woodworth and H. Schlosberg, *Experimental Psychology*, New York: Holt, Rinehart & Winston, Inc. Reprinted with permission.)

essentially parallel. In this case the distance difference is $r(\theta + \sin\theta)$. Sound travels about 0.029 millisecond per centimeter in air so that the time differences become those shown in Table 4.1.

If a click is heard in one ear less than about 0.03 millisecond before the other, then there is no significant localization capability. If the time difference reaches 0.65 millisecond, complete localization due to time difference is achieved.

Loudness difference between the ears is the result of a shadow-effect, which becomes more significant for high frequencies where the wavelengths are shorter. To illustrate, the intensity ratio of the sound at the ears is shown in Table 4.2 for an arrival angle of 15°.

The use of two binaural aspects (time difference and relative loudness) facilitates localization of signals at either extreme of the auditory frequency range. It is easiest to locate the sound source of pure tones in the 500 to 700 cycle per second range. Greatest error is found for signals around 2,000 cycles per second. Distance of the sound source from the observer cannot be judged without the existence of prior knowledge concerning the nature of the sound source.

The auditory channel is analytic. A single-valued function of time, such as is produced by the movement of the diaphragm of a loudspeaker, can be

Table 4.1. BINAURAL TIME DIFFERENCE ACCORDING
TO DIRECTION (AND DISTANCE) OF SOURCE OF SOUND

Direction Angle	Time difference in milliseconds	
	Source* Close to Head	Source Distant
0°	0	0
1°	0.009	0.009
2°	0.018	0.018
3°	0.027	0.027
4°	0.036	0.036
5°	0.044	0.044
10°	0.089	0.088
15°	0.133	0.132
20°	0.178	0.176
25°	0.222	0.218
30°	0.266	0.260
35°	0.311	0.301
40°	0.355	0.341
45°	0.400	0.379
50°	0.444	0.416
55°	0.488	0.452
60°	0.533	0.486
65°	0.577	0.518
70°	0.622	0.549
75°	0.666	0.578
80°	0.710	0.605
85°	0.755	0.630
90°	0.799	0.653

* When the source lies behind the aural axis, reckon its direction angle from the rear; so for $\theta = 100°$, use $180° - 100° = 80°$.

From R. S. Woodworth and H. Schlosberg, *Experimental Psychology*. New York: Holt, Rinehart & Winston, Inc., 1954, p. 353. Reprinted with permission.

Table 4.2. BINAURAL INTENSITY DIFFERENCE

Frequency (in cycles per second)	Intensity Ratio (in decibels)
300	1
1,100	4
4,200	5
10,000	6
15,000	10

heard as a simultaneous array of separate tones. Fourier analysis specifies the spectral content, and yet this may or may not correspond to the particular separation which is subjectively observed. The listener may hear an orchestra as a grouping of separately identifiable instruments with individual tone quality associated with each instrument. This perception is a composite result of the analytic audition coupled with stored information derived from the previous cultural experience, a far cry from the summation of individual perceptual response to the components of the present stimuli.

When two pure tones are simultaneously presented, the subject may be aware of a beat frequency which corresponds to the difference between the original frequencies. If the original tones are very close in frequency, say less than about six beats per second, a single tone is perceived to be intensity modulated at the difference frequency. If the original tones are made more disparate with a difference of greater than eight cycles per second, then two tones are heard within a throbbing at the difference frequency. When the original tones are of greater separation than twenty cycles per second it is possible to distinguish three separate tones, the original two, together with the intertone which first appears as a buzz and then fades in intensity when its frequency increases as the two tones are further separated.

In a similar manner, the nonlinearity of the auditory channel often creates a perceived summation tone, provided this frequency falls within the frequency band of auditory sensation. Further, the difference frequency tones may appear in summation form with the original tones and yield a complex tone of higher pitch. Thus a pitch can be heard which has no counterpart in the original signal. A low pitch can even be observed in listening to an audio system which is known to be physically incapable of producing such a low frequency tone. Figure 4.19 indicates the various sensations produced by two simultaneous tones.

The transmission of intelligence may be hampered through the occurrence of unwanted sounds. It is, therefore, of interest to quantify the effect of masking which may be produced by various noises upon different types of signals. To illustrate, Figure 4.20 presents a summary of measured data indicating the effect of an 800 cycle per second masking tone on the auditory threshold of various frequency pure tone signals. In general, the range of signal frequency which is affected increases with the intensity of the masking tone. Further, the effect of masking appears to be greatest on signals of frequency in the immediate vicinity of the masking tone frequency. The masking effect is greater on higher frequencies than the masking signal, with diminished masking at those frequencies which correspond to harmonics of the masking frequency. This latter effect is due to the appearance of beat frequencies which facilitate identification of the existence of a signal. A lower frequency masking sound masks over a wider range of frequencies. Reference is made to Chapter 12 for further discussion relating to the perception of speech and some other codes for the transmission of intelligence under the disturbance of noise.

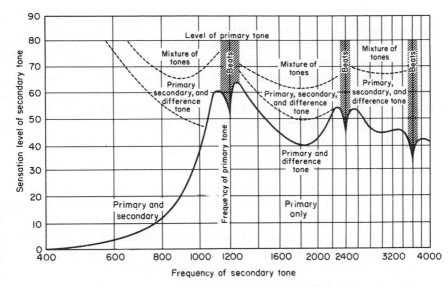

Figure 4.19. The various sensations produced by a two-component tone. The primary component is a sinusoid of 1200 cycles per second, 80 decibels above threshold. The secondary component is a sinusoid of the frequency and sensation level indicated by the coordinates. When the secondary component is above its masked threshold, however, the auditory sensation may be quite complex as indicated by the descriptions in the several regions of the graph. (After R. L. Wegel and C. B. Lane, "The Auditory Masking of One Pure Tone by Another and Its Probable Relation to the Dynamics of the Inner Ear," Phys. Rev., Vol. 23 (1924), 266–285.)

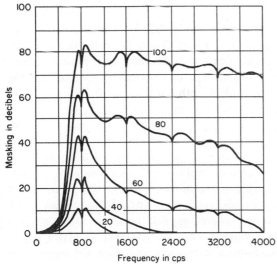

Figure 4.20. The masking of a tone by a primary tone of frequency 800 cycles per second. The parameter is the sensation level of the primary tone in decibels. The masking in decibels is plotted as a function of the frequency of the secondary tones. (After R. L. Wegel and C. B. Lane.)

Perceptual space is extremely complex. The chosen coordinates are inter-dependent and do not define the entire space. In recent years, considerable experimental evidence has accrued as a result of the numerous attempts to describe particular aspects of auditory perception. Unfortunately, a large portion of this work was based upon the use of simple stimuli such as pure tones and clicks. The nonlinearity of the auditory channel makes it necessary to question whether exploration of the perceptual-space of simple stimuli offers significant information relative to the perceptual space for the types of complex stimuli which are useful for the transmission of intelligence. It is certainly unwise to estimate specific perceptual response to nonsense syllables, orchestral sounds, and speech within context from only a summary know-ledge of the response-perception of simple stimuli which could be used to synthesize these same complex stimuli. Furthermore, real world audition is even more difficult to understand because it is confounded by the presence of fluctuating and unpredictable ambient noise. The recognition that a particular sound corresponds to the breaking of a twig, requires a great amount of unique perceptual sensation and subsequent mediation.

4.5. CONCLUSION

The human operator usually derives a significant amount of information from his surround by means of his auditory channel. Sound energy may be simultaneously received directly from a number of separate sources and their reflections, thus furnishing an integrated "view" of the environment.

The dual auditory sensing system provides for redundant data collection with regard to such parameters as pitch, loudness, time duration, and others, furnishing greater reliability over the non-repairable life. At the same time, this redundancy provides additional capability with respect to spatial localiza-tion through binaural comparison of intensity difference and time interval between the signal arrival at each of the ears. There appears to be further redundancy in the auditory channel. The acoustic center of the brain has been associated with the temporal lobes of the cerebrum. This would appear substantiated by the fact that removal of both temporal lobes is followed by complete deafness, while removal of one temporal lobe is followed by impairment of hearing. As a result, it is thought that some auditory nerve fibers from each ear cross to the opposite side of the cerebrum, and some end on the same side, this in a manner similar to the scheme of the optic chiasma.

Other features of the auditory channel appear well suited to serve as pro-tection against damage. The inertia of the bone chain of ossicles may limit the response to high frequency sounds, yet it provides assurance against the onslaught of shock waves or other sudden impact. The ear drum separates the inner mechanism from the physical and disease hazards of the outer world. The delicate sensing mechanism is found deep inside the bony mass of the skull.

The information rate through the auditory channel would appear to be far in excess of the measured information rate as related to the discrimination of laboratory auditory displays. Through the use of several perceptual dimensions per stimulus, I. Pollack found it possible to reach 3.1 bits per stimulus, nearly equalling the 3.5 bits which would correspond to the linear sum of the information contributed by separate discrimination along each of the dimensions which were used. The interdependence of perceptual parameters should limit the possibilities of displays intended for maximum information rate transmission. Although there has been considerable advance in recent years toward an adequate theory of hearing, there remains much to be accomplished before the empirical evidence of perception can be accounted for in terms of the auditory mechanism and neural coding.

BIBLIOGRAPHY

BLACK, J. W., "The Information of Sounds and Phonetic Diagrams of One- and Two-Syllable Words," *Journal of Speech Disorders*, Vol. 19 (1954), 397–411.

BOLT, R. H., *et al.*, *Handbook of Acoustic Noise Control: Vol. 1, Physical Acoustics, USAF WADC TR 52–204* (December 1952).

CHERRY, E. C., and W. K. TAYLOR, "Some Further Experiments Upon the Recognition of Speech with One and with Two Ears," *Journal of the Acoustical Society of America*, Vol. 26 No. 4 (July 1954), 554–559.

CHERRY, C., ed., *On Human Communication*. New York: John Wiley & Sons, Inc., 1957.

CHRISTMAN, R. J., "The Perception of Direction as a Function of Binaural Temporal and Amplitude Disparity," *IRE Convention Record*, Part 9 Vol. 4 (1956), 3–7.

DAVIS, H., "Energy Into Nerve Impulses: Hearing," *Medical Bulletin*, St. Louis University, Vol. 5 (1953), 43–48.

DEBOER, E., "Pitch of Inharmonic Signals," *Nature*, Vol. 178 (1956), 535–536.

EHMER, R. H., "Masking by Tones vs. Noise Bands," *Journal of the Acoustical Society of America*, Vol. 31 No. 9 (1959), 1253–1255.

FLETCHER, H., *Speech and Hearing in Communication*. New York: Van Nostrand, Inc., 1953.

GALAMBOS, R., and A. RUPERT, "Action of the Middle Ear Muscles in Normal Cats," *Journal of the Acoustical Society of America*, Vol. 31 No. 3 (March 1959), 349–355.

GALAMBOS, R., "Neurophysiology of the Auditory System," *Journal of the Acoustical Society of America*, Vol. 22 No. 6 (November 1950), 785–792.

GARNER, W. R., "Hearing," *Annual Review of Psychology*, Vol. 3 (1952), 85–104.

———. "An Equal Discriminability Scale for Loudness Judgments," *Journal of Experimental Psychology*, Vol. 43 (1952), 232–238.

GARNER, W. R., "An Information Analysis of Absolute Judgments of Loudness," *Journal of Experimental Psychology*, Vol. 46 (1953), 373–380.

GOLDSTEIN, M. H., *et al.*, "Responses of the Auditory Cortex to Repetitive Acoustic Stimuli," *Journal of the Acoustical Society of America*, Vol. 31 No. 3 (1959), 356–364.

GOLDSTEIN, M. H., and N. S. KIANG, "Synchrony of Neural Activity in Electric Responses Evoked by Transient Acoustic Stimuli," *Journal of the Acoustical Society of America*, Vol. 30 No. 2 (February 1958), 107–117.

GOLDSTEIN, M. H., *Neurophysiological Representation of Complex Auditory Stimuli*, MIT TR 323, February 19, 1957.

GREEN, D. M., "Psychoacoustics and Detection Theory," *Journal of the Acoustical Society of America*, Vol. 32 No. 10 (October 1960), 1189–1202.

HARRIS, J. D., "Pitch Discrimination," *Journal of the Acoustical Society of America*, Vol. 24 (1952), 750–755.

HARRIS, J. D., and C. K. MYERS, "Experiments on Fluctuation of Auditory Acuity," *Journal of General Psychology*, Vol. 50 (1954), 87–109.

HEISE, G. A., and G. A. MILLER, "An Experimental Study of Auditory Patterns," *American Journal of Psychology*, Vol. 64 (1951), 68–77.

HIRSH, I. J., "Binaural Summation and Interaural Inhibition as a Function of the Level of Masking Noise," *American Journal of Psychology*, Vol. 45 (1948), 205–213.

———. "Binaural Summation: A Century of Investigation," *Psychology Bulletin*, Vol. 45 (1948), 193–206.

———. *The Measurement of Hearing*. New York: McGraw-Hill Book Company, Inc., 1952.

HIRSH, I. J., and W. D. BOWMAN, "Masking of Speech by Bands of Noise," *Journal of the Acoustical Society of America*, Vol. 25 No. 6 (November 1953), 1175–1180.

HIRSH, I. J., *et al.*, "Intelligibility of Different Speech Materials," *Journal of the Acoustical Society of America*, Vol. 26 No. 4 (July 1954), 530–539.

HUGGINS, W. H., and J. C. R. LICKLIDER, "Place Mechanisms of Auditory Frequency Analysis," *Journal of the Acoustical Society of America*, Vol. 23 (1951), 290–299.

JACOBSON, H., "The Informational Capacity of the Human Ear," *Science*, Vol. 114 (1950), 143–144.

———. "Information and the Human Ear," *Journal of the Acoustical Society of America*, Vol. 23 (1951), 464–471.

JENKINS, R. A., "Perception of Pitch, Timbre, and Loudness," *Journal of the Acoustical Society of America*, Vol. 33 No. 11 (November 1961), 1550–1557.

KIANG, S., M. H. GOLDSTEIN, and W. T. PEAKE, "Temporal Coding of Neural Responses to Acoustic Stimuli," *IRE Transactions on Information Theory*, Vol. IT-8 No. 2 (February 1962), 113–119.

KOCK, W. E., "Binaural Localization and Masking," *Journal of the Acoustical Society of America*, Vol. 22 No. 6 (November 1950), 801–804.

KRYTER, K. D., "On Predicting the Intelligibility of Speech from Acoustical Measures," *Journal of the Acoustical Society of America*, Vol. 28 No. 4 (July 1956), 590–591.

LICKLIDER, J. C. R., "A Duplex Theory of Pitch Perception," *Experientia*, Vol. 7 (1951), 128–133.

MEYER, M. F., "Neurological Theory of Beat Tones," *Journal of the Acoustical Society of America*, Vol. 28 No. 5 (September 1956), 877–881.

MILLER, I., "Perception of Nonsense Passage in Relation to Amount of Information and Speech-to-Noise Ratio," *Journal of Experimental Psychology*, Vol. 53 (1957), 388–393.

MUNSON, W. A., and J. E. KARLIN, "Measurement of Human Channel Transmission Characteristics," *Journal of the Acoustical Society of America*, Vol. 26 (1954), 542–553.

NEU, D. M., "A Critical Review of the Literature on 'Absolute Pitch'," *Psychology Bulletin*, Vol. 44 (1947), 249–266.

POLLACK, I., "Method of Reproduction and the Identification of Elementary Auditory Displays," *Journal of the Acoustical Society of America*, Vol. 26 No. 6 (November 1954), 1060–1063.

————. "Intensity Discrimination Thresholds Under Several Psychophysical Procedures," *Journal of the Acoustical Society of America*, Vol. 26 No. 6 (November 1954), 1056–1059.

————. "The Information of Elementary Auditory Displays," *Journal of the Acoustical Society of America*, Vol. 24 (1952), 745–749.

————. "The Information of Auditory Displays. II," *Journal of the Acoustical Society of America*, Vol. 25 (1953), 765–769.

POLLACK, I., and L. FICKS, "Information of Elementary Multidimensional Auditory Displays," *Journal of the Acoustical Society of America*, Vol. 26 (1954), 155–158.

POLLACK, I., and W. J. TRITTIPOE, "Binaural Listening and Interaural Noise Cross Correlation," *Journal of the Acoustical Society of America*, Vol. 31 No. 9 (September 1959), 1250–1252.

RANKE, O. F., "Theory of Operation of the Cochlea: A Contribution to the Hydrodynamics of the Cochlea," *Journal of the Acoustical Society of America*, Vol. 22 No. 6 (November 1950), 772–778.

ROSENBLITH, W. A., "Auditory Masking and Fatigue," *Journal of the Acoustical Society of America*, Vol. 22 No. 6 (November 1950), 792–801.

ROSENBLITH, W. A., and K. N. STEVENS, "Handbook of Acoustic Noise Control. V. 2. Noise and Man," *USAF WADC TR 52-204* (June 1953).

SAYERS, McA. B., and E. C. CHERRY, "Mechanism of Binaural Fusion in the Hearing of Speech," *Journal of the Acoustical Society of America*, Vol. 29 No. 9 (September 1957), 973–987.

SNOW, W. B., "Effect of Arrival Time on Stereophonic Localization," *Journal of the Acoustical Society of America*, Vol. 26 (1954), 1071–1074.

STEVENS, S. S., "Pitch Discrimination, Mels, and Kock's Contention," *Journal of the Acoustical Society of America*, Vol. 26 (1954), 1075–1077.

VAN KREVELEN, A., "The Ability to Make Absolute Judgments of Pitch," *Journal of Experimental Psychology*, Vol. 42 (1951), 207–215.

VON BÉKÉSY, G., "Neural Funneling Along the Skin and Between the Inner and Outer Hair Cells of the Cochlea," *Journal of the Acoustical Society of America*, Vol. 31 No. 9 (September 1959), 1236–1249.

————. "Paradoxical Direction of Wave Travel along the Cochlear Partition," *Journal of the Acoustical Society of America*, Vol. 27 No. 1 (January 1955), 137–145.

WEBSTER, J. C., M. LICHTENSTEIN, and R. S. GALES, "Individual Difference in Noise Masked Thresholds," *Journal of the Acoustical Society of America*, Vol. 22 (1950), 483–490.

WEVER, E. G., M. LAWRENCE, and G. VON BÉKÉSY, "A Note on Recent Developments in Auditory Theory," *Proceedings of the National Academy of Science*, Vol. 40 (1954), 508–512.

WEVER, E., and M. LAWRENCE, "Patterns of Injury Produced by Overstimulation of the Ear," *Journal of the Acoustical Society of America*, Vol. 27 No. 5 (September 1955), 853–858.

YANTIS, P. A., and M. LAWRENCE, "Overstimulation, Fatigue, and Onset of Overload in the Normal Human Ear," *Journal of the Acoustical Society of America*, Vol. 29 No. 2 (February 1957), 265–275.

ZWISLOCKI, J., "Theory of the Acoustical Action of the Cochlea," *Journal of the Acoustical Society of America*, Vol. 22 No. 6 (November 1950), 778–785.

5

THE POSITION- AND MOTION-
SENSING CHANNEL

5.1. THE SENSING MECHANISM

Man orients himself with respect to his environment by means of his sense organs. Vision, hearing, touch, taste, and smell all provide cues regarding the nature of objects in his immediate surround. The brain integrates these cues and makes appropriate inference with respect to body attitude. But there is a more direct source of orientation information—that supplied by the labyrinthian and kinesthetic sensors which furnish direct data with respect to the local "vertical."

Figure 5.1 shows the structural members of the human labyrinth within the inner ear. This consists of the cochlear apparatus as described in Chapter 4 and the vestibular sensing mechanism. The vestibular mechanism consists of two functionally different parts, the semicircular canals and the vestibule. Figure 5.2 shows an open section of this structure. The semicircular canals are filled with a saline solution called the *endolymph fluid*. At the end of each canal there is an enlarged region called the *ampulla*. Each ampulla contains a gelatinous mass containing hair tufts which are called the *cristae*. Tilt of the head changes the fluid pressure distribution on these hair cells and thus excites a particular neural message corresponding to that position.

The semicircular canals of each ear are connected to the vestibule as a common base. The vestibule contains the *utricle* and the *saccule* which are also filled with the endolymph fluid. These sacs enclose the otolith sensing

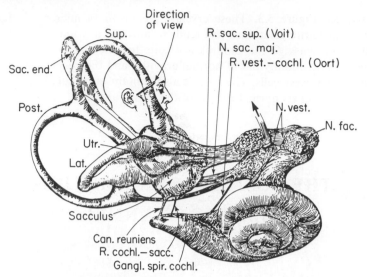

Figure 5.1. The vestibular apparatus, cochlea, and structural relations of innervation of human labyrinth.

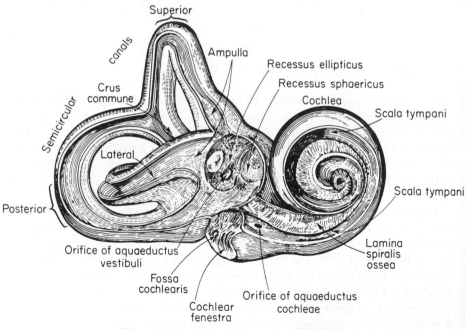

Figure 5.2. Interior of right osseous labyrinth.

system. The utricle receptor is the *macula*, which is an oval-shaped, flat thickening of the vestibular wall. The ciliated hair cells reside on this surface and are connected to nerve cells. These hair cells are surrounded by a gelatinous pad which also contains the *otoliths*, many small calcium carbonate crystals; see Figure 5.3. These crystals are up to 14 microns in diameter in man. The entire gelatinous pad tends to move as a whole due to its semi-rigidity. The mass of the otoliths accounts for their response to imposed acceleration (including that of normal gravity), and this displacement excites the connected nerve cells. The saccule also contains a macula like that of the utricle but with axis normal to that of the sensor above.

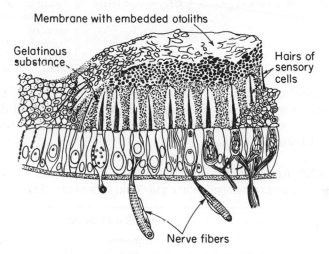

Membrane with embedded otoliths

Gelatinous substance

Hairs of sensory cells

Nerve fibers

Figure 5.3. Sensory cells involved in equilibrium sense. A highly magnified cross section of a membrane in the vestibule.

The semicircular canals lie in three planes which are roughly at right angles to one another. This makes it possible for the subject to "read" the orientation with respect to the local gravity (g) force regardless of its direction. The right and left horizontal canals are in the same plane, which is brought to the horizontal if the head is tilted about 25° or 30° forward. About 19,000 nerve fibers, connected to each vestibular sensor, are directed toward the brain. Unfortunately, the particular area at which these terminate on the cerebral cortex has not as yet been determined. Table 5.1 lists the specified non-auditory receptors of the inner ear together with location, affective stimuli, and function.

O. Löwenstein and A. Sand have made a fundamental discovery about neural message coding of the vestibular canals. Although the labyrinth from the thornback ray (fish) was utilized in the experimental investigation, the results are in essential agreement with those obtained on other animals, including mammals. Specifically, highly sensitive mechanoreceptors, such as those of the vestibular canals, exhibit spontaneous discharge activity. Rotation in one way caused an increase of spontaneous discharge activity, while rotation in the opposite direction suppressed it. It seems reasonable to find

Table 5.1. RECEPTORS FOR INNER EAR SENSES AND AFFECTIVE STIMULI

Receptor	Location	Stimulus	Function
Cristae and Ampullaris	Semicircular canals	Angular acceleration	Perception of rotary motion
Otoliths and Maculae	Utricle and Saccule	Gravity and linear acceleration	Perception of change in direction with respect to gravity Perception of change in linear velocity

that the neural message is encoded in terms of combinations of the activity level of the six semicircular canals as indicated by the observed data shown in Table 5.2. Note that this pattern of activity is subconsciously resolved at a low level of brain functioning.

Table 5.2.* RESPONSES OF THE SIX SEMICIRCULAR CANALS TO ANGULAR DISPLACEMENTS ABOUT THE THREE PRIMARY AXES

Semicircular Canal	Rotation about the					
	Longitudinal Axis		Transverse Axis		Vertical Axis	
	Right	Left	Forward	Backward	Clockwise	Counter-clockwise
Right ant. vert.	●	⊗	●	⊗	⊗	●
Left ant. vert.	⊗	●	●	⊗	●	⊗
Right post. vert.	●	⊗	⊗	●	●	⊗
Left post. vert.	⊗	●	⊗	●	⊗	●
Right horizontal	○	○	○	○	●	⊗
Left horizontal	○	○	○	○	⊗	●

● excited; ⊗ inhibited; ○ unaffected; ant. vert. = anterior vertical; post. vert. = posterior vertical.
* From O. Löwenstein and A. Sand, *Journal of Physiology* (1940).

There is a direct connection between the vestibular sensing of head movement and the *compensatory eye movement*—that movement which allows continuous fixation on the same point during head movement. Experimental evidence demonstrates that this coordinated reflex is almost instantaneous in response, yet the narrow (about 1.4 millimeter in diameter) semicircular canals operate with considerable fluid frictional resistance, which produces a relatively large lag in response. Evidently there is some other active position sensing mechanism which operates with great rapidity.

There are *proprioceptors* distributed throughout the body which indicate the effect of movement and relative position. These sensing receptors are located in the muscles, joints, and tendons and are activated by stretching or movement. The resulting neural message is sent by a multitude of nerve paths to the somesthetic area of the brain where this information is correlated. The subject is thus furnished with a sensed position for the various parts of his body. This is called the *kinesthetic sensation*. Together with the vestibular sense, it forms total information as to body position and movement. Most likely, the proprioceptors in the neck and shoulders provide the rapid response information reflected in the compensatory ocular reflex. Proprioceptors yield continual and precise knowledge regarding position and movement for every external part of the body. It is because of these that a man can scratch his back accurately without the aid of a mirror. The kinesthetic sense offers a prime factor in the maintenance of balance.

5.2. THE SENSING OF POSITION

Much experimental data has been gathered in the laboratory on position sensing of the human operator. The observer is typically required to set some object to the vertical or horizontal. The object might be a visible line, the chair on which the observer sat, or his own body. The subject's errors are taken to be the deviation of the object from the "true" vertical. It should be borne in mind that in those cases where the observer aligns the chair in which he is sitting to the vertical, the measurements are made from the chair. There is, in the interpretation of these experiments, the tacit assumption that the observer is perfectly oriented to the chair—that his "body position image" includes the chair. Consider the following summary data in the light of these comments.

Perception of Body Position on the Basis of Postural Data Alone

A series of directly relevant experiments were performed by H. A. Witkin and others. The subject was seated in a chair and then tilted. He was required either to bring the chair back to vertical from the tilted position or report when the chair reached vertical. The subject was either blindfolded or the experiments were run in a dark room. There was no visual data. When the subject manipulated the chair himself, there was no constant error bias but there was an error variance of about 1.9°. If the subject verbally reported, the constant error was about 2.4° and variance error of about 3.2°. Return from lateral tilt yielded smaller errors than return from medial tilt ("roll" better than "pitch"). There was no improvement found with practice or knowledge of results, nor was there a significant difference between experienced aircraft pilot subjects and naive college students. When the chair and subject were immersed in water, there was no change in the constant error, but an increase in variability resulted. When the chair was padded with foam rubber, no change in constant error resulted, but there was again an increase in variability. When the subject's head was fixed to the chair by a head clamp, the errors were slightly less than if the head were free to move about. Adaptation to tilt becomes apparent in about 10 seconds and reaches its asymptotic value within about 60 seconds. Thus, the longer a subject remains tilted the more likely it is that an error will be made when he is required to return to level.

Perception of Body Position when Postural and Visual Data are in Conflict

The subject was seated in a chair, tilted, and required to bring the chair back to vertical. In these cases the visual field, a small room, was tilted with respect to the vertical. When the room and chair tilted in the same direction, it was found that the constant error was about 2.0° with a variance of about 9.4°. When the room and chair were tilted in opposite directions, the constant error was about 1.0° with a variance of about 5.9°.

Perception of the Verticality of a Visible Object

Under normal conditions, observers set a line to the vertical or horizontal within a constant error of from 0.2° to 0.4°, but when the line was embedded visually in a large framework tilted to, say, 22.0°, error increased to about 8.0°. When the body was tilted, the error increased. When the observer was whirled in a centrifuge containing a non-swinging blacked-out car and a single luminous line, the line appeared vertical. When it was colinear with the resultant g, there was a considerable time lag evidenced. (This is equivalent to tilting the subject.) Once again in the centrifuge, the luminous line was surrounded by a luminous square normal to the car, and was set to the following values: with the resultant g at 23.6°, the line was set to 9.4°; with the resultant g at 44.5°, the line was set to 16.5°.

There is only one perceived vertical. There is no separate experience of the postural vertical and another for the visual vertical. As is evident from the data above, when both the postural and visual data are coincident, perception of the vertical is accurate to within a degree. The same order of accuracy is obtained in the absence of visual data. It has, to date, been impossible to eliminate postural data for any significant length of time, for example, to achieve a steady state of weightlessness. When postural and visual data are in conflict, a compromise is reached under imposed stress.

5.3. THE SENSING OF ACCELERATION

The angular acceleration sensitivity of the semicircular canals is very great. For example, in the rabbit, accelerations as small as 0.09° per second per second can stimulate a response with an average latency of 2.9 seconds. At an acceleration of 0.5° per second per second the latency is decreased to about 1.1 seconds. The lowest acceleration threshold reported on a human subject is 0.2° per second per second. It is generally found that this threshold increases with age in adults. The threshold for sensing angular acceleration is an inverse function of the time of stimulus duration. Typical findings are shown in Figure 5.4. Linear acceleration in the vertical direction can normally be sensed from approximately 4 to 12 centimeters per second per second and in the horizontal direction from approximately 12 to 20 centimeters per second per second.

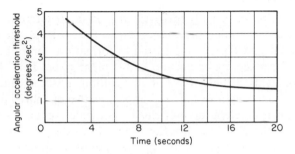

Figure 5.4. Angular acceleration threshold vs. time.

Accelerative forces can have distinct effects upon the human operator with respect to both his physiological and psychological functioning. Reference the more complete discussion in Chapter 15 relating to this subject.

5.4. ILLUSORY EFFECT DUE TO ACCELERATION

As a result of evolution the sense organs function best in their natural environment. This environment is the two-dimensional, slow-tempo world of everyday life. During high-speed flight maneuvers in the three-dimensional world above the earth's surface, the usual cues by which orientation is normally accomplished can be missing or may appear severely distorted. Either of two things may happen: (1) sense receptors may provide erroneous data which the pilot accepts as fact, or (2) the pilot may misinterpret correct data. Either case results in mistaken perception, and that is what is meant by the term *illusion*. Mistaken perception may also be accompanied by other psychological factors. The knowledge that "something is wrong" may cause cognitive and emotional reactions which further confuse the pilot.

During flight, many kinds of illusions occur because of sudden changes in linear acceleration or departure of the aircraft from a straight path. These may be compounded by adverse weather or night flight conditions which restrict visibility. They may result when sensory cues conflict or the subject is under psychic stress (primarily fear).

Visual cues ordinarily predominate over kinesthetic cues. We depend upon what we see. In a normal environment there is seldom conflict between visual and nonvisual cues because each sense organ normally returns valid information; hence a consistent "view" results. However, in an aircraft many conditions develop which reduce, distort, or blank-out visual cues. When this happens, erroneous information from nonvisual sense organs may not be contested in the brain. Total perception may be wrong. The simple definition of an illusion as "a mistaken perception" includes many kinds of illusions which are potentially dangerous to the pilot.

The Visual—g Illusion

This type of illusion usually involves error in interpreting the meaning of lights. Lights give the pilot information about the horizon, altitude, location of other aircraft and obstacles, position in formation, aircraft attitude, and so on. They form the major portion of his night visual field. Errors in the perception of lights include those of recognition, position, and movement. Fatigue may cause a light to split and appear as two or more lights. Stimulation from angular acceleration may cause nystagmic eye movements in which slow sweeps of the eye (in a direction opposite to the rotation) accompany positive acceleration. Eye-sweeps in the opposite direction accompany deceleration. When eye-sweeps subside, a series of eye-sweeps in the opposite direction (inverse nystagmus) may occur and develop rapidly, attaining a velocity of perhaps $5°$ per second before gradually declining. Interaction with voluntary eye movements and ocular reflexes, when nystagmus is present, may cause serious difficulty in reading instruments.

The Autokinetic Illusion

A single fixed point of light may appear to move in random fashion when viewed steadily against a dark background. This can be demonstrated by staring fixedly at a fairly bright, isolated star. A subject asked to localize such a light usually reports this to be impossible, because of the (apparent) movement of the star. W. E. Vinacke reports that the illusion is probably experienced by all normal persons. After a short delay before onset, movement is reported about half the time in any direction. Median duration of the movement is about 10 seconds, and voluntary control over it is slight. The effect is abolished only with difficulty. Figure 5.5 illustrates how the apparent random movement of an exterior light might appear to a pilot. The alternately blinking lights used on current aircraft tend to destroy the illusion. Moving the eyes and avoiding steady fixation also tends to prevent it.

The Oculogyral Illusion

This visual illusion may result when a pilot is subjected to rotary motion. It is caused by a reflex response consisting of movements of the eyeball following semicircular canal stimulation. The direction of apparent motion is in accord with the sensation of rotation during acceleration. If the subject is rotated to the right, a visual target fixed in relation to the subject appears to move in that direction. Movement gradually comes to a standstill after which it may appear to shift slowly to the left. When rotation is stabilized, apparent motion ceases. Sudden deceleration causes the visual target to have

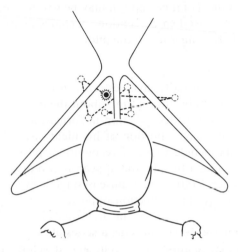

Figure 5.5. Apparent movement of exterior light source due to autokinetic effect.

rapid apparent motion to the left, with a successive stage in which apparent motion is to the right. The pilot may interpret this as motion of the aircraft. R. G. F. Epple says:

> After recovering from a spin to the left which involves large accelerations, a pilot will sense a turning to the right, and if he attempts to correct for this illusory turning, he will cause the airplane to spin to the left again. This reflex response of the eyeballs cannot be eliminated, and the only remedy is to train the pilot to ignore the sensations it produces.

Figure 5.6 illustrates how the oculogyral illusion might affect the pilot's perception following spin to the left. While the actual line of flight is toward point *A*, the apparent movement of the light toward the right gives the sensation of flight toward point *B*. The unreliability of judgment values based on the body's indicators stresses one point—the pilot must depend on his instruments.

The Oculogravic Illusion

Conflicting sensory information supplied by the eye and vestibular sense organs can cause an illusion consisting of the apparent displacement of objects in space as well as body displacement. R. McFarland reports experi-

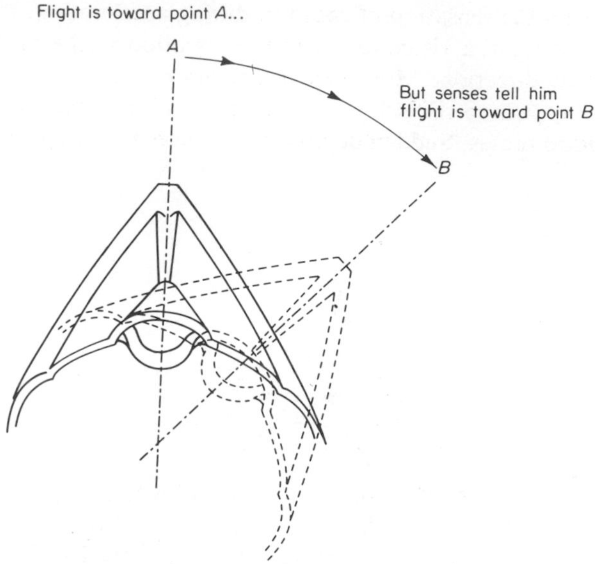

Flight is toward point A...

A

But senses tell him
flight is toward point B

B

Figure 5.6. Oculogyral illusion following spin to left.

ments using a fixed light in an aircraft under exterior dark conditions which produced the illusion. Sensations of motion and displacement of the light occurred between 10° and 60° of bank and increased with increasing bank. The illusion "always occurs during banks of 40° and more."

W. J. White describes an experiment which demonstrates the full oculogravic effect. The subject faces the center of a centrifuge while viewing a fixed light during exposure to acceleration which attain 3.0 g within three seconds. With onset of rotation, the subject feels he is changing position and the light is rising. The apparent change is described as a sensation of being slowly tilted backward along with the chair and centrifuge platform, thus the illusion includes both apparent exterior motion and body displacement. When radial velocity reaches 1.5 g, the subject reports a sensation of being on his back in a horizontally placed chair fixed to a vertical platform with walls of the centrifuge rotating around him. The opposite sensation occurs when the centrifuge is stopped. Figure 5.7 illustrates how this illusion might affect a pilot during normal spin. The pilot feels he is being forced slowly forward. He identifies the apparent displacement of his body with changing attitude of aircraft through sensory contact (body pressure senses) with the airplane. The shadow airplane in Figure 5.7 shows the pilot's sensed attitude during height of illusory effect.

During inverted spin, the opposite effect would occur due to changed axis of rotation and body position. Figure 5.8 illustrates the oculogravic effect on a pilot during inverted spin. Force lines indicate sensed changing attitude of aircraft as the illusion becomes more intense.

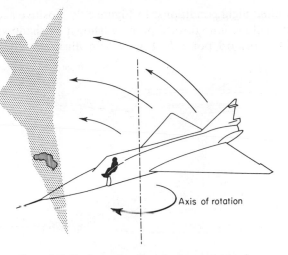

Figure 5.7. Oculogravic effect during upright spin.

Blindfolded subjects perceive rapid positive acceleration as backward tilt and rapid deceleration as forward tilt. These sensations are interpreted as changing altitude, climbing in the case of positive acceleration and diving in

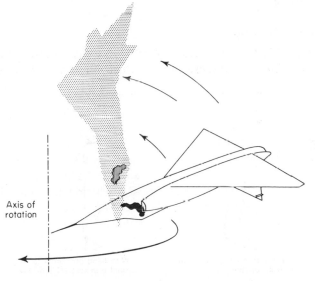

Figure 5.8. Oculogravic effect during inverted spin.

the case of negative acceleration. An acceleration increment of about 0.1 g was interpreted as a climb at a 20° to 25° angle. A deceleration of about the same magnitude was interpreted as a dive at a 15° angle below horizontal. Figure 5.9 illustrates how accelerative changes may affect perception under minimal or blind flight conditions. In Figure 5.9a, positive acceleration gives the effect of shallow climb toward point *A* (shown by shadow aircraft), when actual flight is toward point *B*. Figure 5.9b illustrates the opposite effect

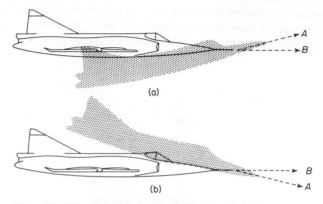

(a)

(b)

Figure 5.9. Perceptual illusions resulting from sudden changes in acceleration when visual cues are reduced or absent.

during sudden deceleration. Actual flight is toward point *A*, perceived flight toward point *B*. Under blind flying conditions, body senses alone may be highly unreliable.

The Non-Visual Illusion

Illusions of this type may result solely from accelerative stimulation of vestibular and kinesthetic sense organs. Such illusions are marked by per-

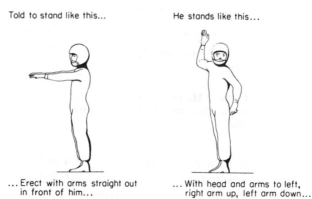

Told to stand like this...   He stands like this...

...Erect with arms straight out   ...With head and arms to left,
in front of him...   right arm up, left arm down...

Figure 5.10. Rotatory illusion following rapid spin to left with sudden deceleration.

ceived rotation during and following actual rotation and by changes in linear acceleration. White reports that a subject may sense the onset of rotation but lose the sensation when rotation becomes constant. After a momentary lag or during deceleration, an illusion of turning in the opposite direction occurs. According to F. A. Geldard, rotation evokes a number of responses in the neck, limbs, and trunk. The head may show slow sweeping motions in a direction opposite rotation during positive acceleration. Sudden deceleration brings compensatory movements in head and limbs. If a blindfolded subject in a counterclockwise rotating chair is told to stand with his arms raised

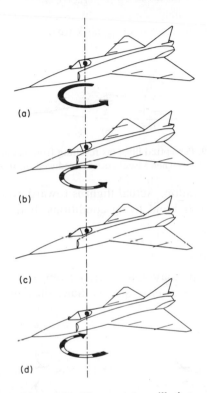

(a)

(b)

(c)

(d)

Figure 5.11. How rotatory illusion might affect pilot in reduced visual field.

straight out in front of him, he may stand with his head and arms to the left, right arm up, left arm down, as shown in Figure 5.10. A radical change in head position at this time may endanger his balance.

Rotating chair experiments may be used to illustrate how deceleration while in spin, with reduced visual field, might affect pilot judgment. This is shown in Figure 5.11. The pilot quickly senses onset of spin (Figure 5.11a), but sensation fades (Figure 5.11b) and vanishes as speed becomes constant (Figure 5.11c). During deceleration, the pilot feels he is turning in a direction opposite the actual turn (Figure 5.11d).

The Audiogyral Illusion

The ears also return faulty information as a result of rotary deceleration. A sound source in front of the subject was reported as arising from left of center following left spin. Figure 5.12 illustrates how audiogyral illusion might affect a pilot who has become oriented to the afterburner sound. Following spin to left, the pilot might perceive afterburner sound as coming from right of rear. Similarly, spin to right would dislocate the sound to left of rear. Although the illusion is not well known in current aviation, it may

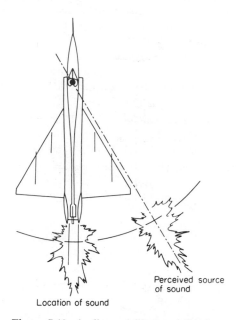

Location of sound

Perceived source of sound

Figure 5.12. Audiogyral illusion following spin to left.

have effects detrimental to performance. The presence of the illusion would cause conflict between information from the ears and that from other senses. This alone is sufficient to cause confusion.

Vertigo

Vertigo may be defined as the subjective loss of orientation with respect to the direction of "up." The human being is primarily a forward moving animal whose personal reference coordinates have been established through many centuries of evolution. As a result, primary reference is the difference between body vertical and the real world "up," and secondary reference is the lateral angle from "dead ahead." Vertigo may be induced by certain physiological and/or psychological factors. The physiological causes have been presented in an excellent summary by N. D. Van Sickle:

Sensation of Climbing While Turning. In a properly banked turn, acceleration tends to force the body firmly into the seat in the same manner as when the aircraft is entering a climb or pulling out of a dive. Without visual references, an aircraft making a banked turn may be interpreted as being in a climbing attitude, and the pilot may react inappropriately by pushing forward on the control column.

Sensation of Diving While Recovering from a Turn. The positive g-forces sustained in a banked turn are reduced as the turn is completed. This reduction in pressure gives the flyer the same sensation as going into a dive and may be interpreted in this way. He may overcorrect by pulling back on the control column and cause the aircraft to stall.

Sensation of Diving Following Pull-out from a Dive. The accelerative forces on the body during the pull-out from a dive are reduced after recovery is complete. This reduction in g-forces may be falsely identified as originating from another dive.

Sensation of Opposite Tilt While Skidding. If skidding of the aircraft takes place during a turn, the body is pressed away from the direction of turning. This may be falsely perceived as a tilt in the opposite direction.

The Coriolis Phenomenon. This is a severe loss of equilibrium in which vertigo results. When the pilot is rotating with the aircraft and then moves his head out of the plane of rotation, there is a differential stimulation of two sets of semi-circular canals. For example, if during a spin the pilot moves his head forward or backward, an additional pair of semi-circular canals is stimulated and extreme dizziness and nausea (can be) suddenly produced. The consequence of such an unusual reaction in flight is apparent.

Sensation of Reversed Rotation. If a rotary motion persists for a short period and is then discontinued, there is a sensation of rotation in the opposite direction. This occurs in a spinning aircraft when the pilot has poor visual reference to the earth. After recovery from a spin to the left, there is a sensation of turning to the right. In attempting to correct for this, the pilot puts the aircraft back into the spin to the left. Flyers have given this illusion the sinister name of "graveyard spin."

The most important psychological factor results from the presentation to the pilot of two different vertical indications. This requires his decision with respect to which of these is "correct," and this decision in itself may result in a loss of orientation. Such a situation often develops when the body-sensed vertical is in disagreement with the vertical indicated by the attitude instrument.

There are many degrees of vertigo. They range all the way from what is commonly called the "leans" (wherein the pilot feels that he is slightly tilted with respect to the instrument-indicated vertical), to the outright situation where the pilot can even be flying upside down without knowledge that such is the case.

As would be expected, flight which imposes higher accelerations and requires more attention to the tracking of orientation is more conducive to vertigo. The illusion can occur for various lengths of time—all the way from a few seconds to one flight on record which lasted one hour and forty-five minutes during which time the pilot reported a continual experience of feeling that he was on his right side. Vertigo effects resulting from severe g stress have been known to last for days.

The seriousness of the vertigo problem can best be realized by reading vertigo accident reports. Records of pilots' radio conversations just prior to impact has in some cases left no doubt that vertigo was the primary cause. A large number of "near-miss" accidents testify to the increasing importance of this problem. An even greater number of unexplained incidents implicate vertigo either directly or indirectly. A recent newspaper reported:

> The fighters . . . were on a night navigational and air refueling training mission. The air base said the three planes were observed hurtling toward the ocean and that there apparently had been no collision. None of the three pilots was seen to parachute.

A study of spatial disorientation in operational flying was conducted by J. B. Nuttall and W. G. Sanford in which information was obtained disclosing a high incidence of vertigo among pilots. It was generally learned that spatial disorientation of varying degrees was experienced by *all* pilots ranging all the way from the "leans" to complete loss of the sense of the vertical. Almost all of the reported disorientation cases were of the "attitude and motion" type with the related visual illusions being rarely reported. Severe vertigo was reported to be five times as prevalent among jet pilots as among non-jet pilots, presumably because of the higher performance factors. This is in conflict with a recent report by Y. Yuganov and D. M. Zakhmatov:

> The illusions are less common in flights in jet aircraft, which is explained by a number of reasons. In connection with the increase in the speed of flight of the jet aircraft, the magnitudes of the rectilinear and angular accelerations acting on the flier during flight are considerably decreased. This is important but is not the only cause for the decrease in frequency of degree of illusory perceptions.

Only recently has vertigo come to be recognized as a significant cause of aircraft accidents. During one report period of time 14 per cent of the fatal accidents were attributed to vertigo as a primary cause. It is difficult to identify a specific cause for the onset of vertigo; however, it has been found that switching of the orientation frame of reference has been a usual factor. Pilot instructions, strong in this regard, emphasize the necessity of remaining on instruments even during weather which might permit intermittent contact flight. Pilot training insists that the pilot learn to disregard his body sensations and only concern himself with the indicated vertical on the instrument panel. Such instruction is considered to be unnatural; however, in the past it was certainly the only reasonable course of action. Reference is made to Chapter 17 which discusses one positive approach toward inhibition of the onset of vertigo.

5.5. MOTION SICKNESS

Motion sickness appears to be one of the unfortunate results of the vestibular sensations. Imposed gross reciprocating motion can in time induce cold sweat, nausea, and vomiting. The term *cold sweat* is used to distinguish this particular reaction from the ordinary sweat accompanying the feeling of warmth. When it occurs, the subject is reacting through autonomic nervous response, and the feeling is a precursor to the onset of nausea. The fact that it is the vestibular organ which is a primary cause for motion sickness has been demonstrated by the fact that deaf people with no vestibular sensitivity do not have motion sickness reaction. This is not to say that psychic factors are not contributory. For example, fear or the feeling of uneasiness can set the stage for motion sickness; unpleasant odors or high temperature may intensify it; or the sickness can result from a complex of contributory factors.

It has been demonstrated that vertical reciprocating movement excites motion sickness more than similar motion in other directions. The subject does well to recline so as to change the head orientation in order to prevent completion of the syndrome. It appears that certain frequencies are particularly conducive to motion sickness. Frequencies in the range of 22 cycles per minute are notably effective in this regard, while in contrast faster motions such as those associated with running and other everyday rapid movements cause no trouble whatsoever. Thus far no physiological evidence has revealed why this frequency dependence is so pronounced.

The susceptibility to motion sickness decreases with increasing age until adulthood is reached. Women are more prone to this problem than men. Of a large number of college students that were questioned on the subject, 20 per cent reported that they had never been motion sick, while 5 per cent of them considered motion sickness to be a personal handicap. There seems to be a difference in the probability of motion sickness for drivers or pilots, as opposed to the passengers. The continual task appears to provide distinct inhibitory factors. Introspective evidence indicates that there are two techniques by which motion sickness may be deferred. The subject must either concentrate upon the task of continual tracking of some steady reference, such as the horizon, or he must choose the opposite extreme, that of complete attention within a narrow frame of reference which is fixed in relation to his own body, particularly his head. This author, on a number of occasions, has unfortunately had opportunity to experiment with motion sickness while in flight under turbulent conditions. Since such weather or night flight makes it impractical to track the horizon, the alternative course had to be taken. If the subject matter being read was interesting enough to completely obliterate concern for the relative position of the fixed reference, then in a short time the feeling of nausea decreased and even vanished. This is not to propose a cure. No doubt there are certain frequencies of movement which would induce motion sickness regardless of what the subject might do. However, any positive course of action to overcome motion sickness is certainly worth trying.

In the recent past, drugs have come upon the market which are effective in both the reduction of probability of motion sickness and its severity, should it be induced. How these drugs prevent sickness is not known and it is hoped that further investigation of the mechanism of body response will provide insight into the nature and immediate cause for motion sickness.

5.6. CONCLUSION

The perception of position and motion results from the integration of a vast amount of information as generated by separate sensors distributed throughout the body. Kinesthetic sensations result from neural messages transmitted to the brain by the proprioceptors within the musculature. These messages furnish evidence of the relative position of various portions of the body. The vestibular sensations are derived from the action of that special sense organ within the labyrinth of the inner ear. The neural message offers unambiguous vector information descriptive of the accelerations imposed upon the head. All of this information is integrated into a single perceptual image of the position and motion of the person with respect to his surroundings. Only on the basis of this "frame of reference" can rational decisions be made with respect to the engagement and/or control of his environment. As such, the sensation of position and motion forms an essential foundation upon which the human operator may build knowledge and achieve a purposeful existence.

BIBLIOGRAPHY

BAHRICK, H. P., P. M. FITTS, and R. SCHNEIDER, "Reproduction of Simple Movements as a Function of Factors Influencing Proprioceptive Feedback," *Journal of Experimental Psychology*, Vol. 49 No. 6 (June 1955), 445–454.

BRIDGES, C. C., and M. E. BITTERMAN, "The Measurement of Autokinetic Movement," *American Journal of Psychology*, Vol. 67 (1954), 525–529.

BROWN, J. L., and M. LECHNER, "Acceleration and Human Performance: A Survey of Research," *Journal of Aviation Medicine*, Vol. 27 No. 1 (1956), 32–49.

CLARK, B., and M. A. NICHOLSON, "Aviator's Vertigo: A Cause of Pilot Error in Naval Aviation Students," *Journal of Aviation Medicine*, Vol. 25 (1954), 171–179.

CLARK, B., and A. GRAYBIEL, "Vertigo as a Cause of Pilot Error in Jet Aircraft," *Journal of Aviation Medicine*, Vol. 28 (October 1957), 469–478.

CLARK, B., and A. GRAYBIEL, "The Breakoff Phenomenon," *Ibid.* (April 1957), 121–126.

COLLINS, W. E., C. H. CRAMPTON, and J. B. POSNER, *The Effect of Mental Set Upon Vestibular Nystagmus and the Electroencephalogram*, US Army Medical Research Laboratory Report No. 439. Fort Knox, Ky., September 12, 1960.

COLLINS, W. E., *Further Studies of the Effects of Mental Set Upon Vestibular Nystagmus*, US Army Medical Research Laboratory Report No. 443. Fort Knox, Ky., December 13, 1960.

DUANE, T. D., E. L. BECKMAN, J. E. ZEIGLER, and H. N. HUNTER, "Some Observations on Human Tolerance to Accelerative Stress: III. Human Studies of 15 Transverse g," *Journal of Aviation Medicine*, Vol. 26 No. 4 (1955), 298–303.

EDWARDS, W., "Autokinetic Movement of Very Large Stimuli," *Journal of Experimental Psychology*, Vol. 48 (November 1954), 493–495.

———. "Two- and Three-Dimensional Autokinetic Movement as a Function of Size and Brightness of Stimuli," *Ibid.* (November 1954), 391–398.

EPPLE, R. G. E., *The Human Pilot* (Vol. III). USN, BuAer Report AE-61-4, Washington, D.C.: Bureau of Aeronautics, August 1954.

FLEISHMAN, E. A., "Perception of Body Position in the Absence of Visual Cues," *Journal of Experimental Psychology*, Vol. 24 (1953), 176–187.

GRAYBIEL, A., W. A. KERR, and S. H. BARTLEY, "Stimulus Thresholds of the Semicircular Canals as a Function of Angular Acceleration," *American Journal of Psychology*, Vol. 61 (1948), 21–36.

GRAYBIEL, A., F. E. GUEDRY, JR., W. JOHNSON, and R. KENNEDY, *Adaptation to Bizarre Stimulation of the Semicircular Canals as Indicated by the Oculogyral Illusion*, US Army Medical Research Laboratory Report No. 464. Fort Knox, Ky., February 23, 1961.

GUEDRY, F. E., JR., and S. J. CERAN, *Derivation of "Subjective Velocity" From Angular Displacement Estimates Made During Prolonged Angular Accelerations: Adaptation Effects*, US Army Medical Research Laboratory Report No. 376. Fort Knox, Ky., February 20, 1959.

GUEDRY, F. E., JR., R. L. CRAMER, and W. P. KOELLA, *Experiments on the Rate of Development and Rate of Recovery of Apparent Adaptation Effects in the Vestibular System*, US Army Medical Research Laboratory Report No. 338. Fort Knox, Ky., June 16, 1958.

GUEDRY, F. E., JR., and L. S. LAUVER, *The Oculomotor and Subjective Aspect of the Vestibular Reaction During Prolonged Constant Angular Acceleration*, US Army Medical Research Laboratory Report No. 438. Fort Knox, Ky., September 8, 1960.

GUEDRY, F. E., JR., and E. K. MONTAGUE, *Relationship Between Magnitudes of Vestibular Reactions and Effective Coriolis Couples in the Semicircular Canal System*, US Army Medical Research Laboratory Report No. 456. Fort Knox, Ky., December 15, 1960.

GUEDRY, F. E., JR., W. E. COLLINS, and L. SHEFFEY, *Perceptual and Oculomotor Reactions to Interacting Visual and Vestibular Stimulation*, US Army Medical Research Laboratory Report No. 462. Fort Knox, Ky., March 15, 1961.

HENRY, F. M., "Dynamic Kinesthetic Perception and Adjustment," *Research Quarterly of the American Association of Health and Physical Education*, Vol. 24 (1953), 176–187.

JOHNSON, W. H., "Head Movement Measurements in Relation to Spatial Disorientation and Vestibular Stimulation," *Journal of Aviation Medicine*, Vol. 27 (April 1956), 148–152.

KRAUS, R. N., "Disorientation in Flight," *Aerospace Medicine*, Vol. 30 No. 9 (1959), 664–673.

LÖWENSTERN, O., and A. SAND, "The Activity of the Horizontal Semicircular Canal of the Dogfish, Scyllium canicula," *Journal of Experimental Biology*, Vol. 13 (1936), 416–428.

LUCHINS, A. S., "The Autokinetic Effect in Central and Peripheral Vision," *Journal of General Psychology*, Vol. 50 (1954), 39–44.

―――. "The Autokinetic Effect and Gradations of Illumination of the Visual Field," *Ibid.* (1954), 29–37.

―――. "The Relation of Size of Light to Autokinetic Effect," *Journal of Psychology*, Vol. 38 (1954), 439–452.

MACCORQUODALE, K., "Effects of Angular Acceleration and Centrifugal Force on Nonvisual Space Orientation During Flight," *Journal of Aviation Medicine*, Vol. 19 (June 1948), 146–157.

MORGAN, C. T., and E. STELLAR, *Physiological Psychology*, 2nd ed. New York: McGraw-Hill Book Company, Inc., 1950.

NUTTALL, J. B., and W. G. SANFORD, *Spatial Disorientation in Operational Flying*, USAF Norton AFB, San Bernardino, Calif., Report No. M-27-56, May 1956.

NUTTALL, J. B., "The Problem of Spatial Disorientation," *Journal of the American Medical Association*, Vol. 166 No. 5 (February 2, 1958), 431–438.

SCHER, S. H., *Pilot's Loss of Orientation in Inverted Spins*. National Advisory Committee for Aeronautics, Tech. Note 3531, Langley Aeronautical Laboratory, Langley Field, Va., October 1955.

VAN SICKLE, N. D., *Modern Airmanship*, 2nd ed. New York: D. Van Nostrand & Co., Inc., 1961.

VINACKE, W. E., "Aviator's Vertigo," *Journal of Aviation Medicine*, Vol. 19 (1948), 158–170.

―――. "Illusions Experienced by Aircraft Pilots," *Journal of Aviation Medicine*, Vol. 18 (1947), 308–325.

Vertigo, Approach Magazine, US Naval Aviation Safety Review, USN, NAVAER-00-75-510, Vol. 4 No. 3 (September 1958), 28–33.

VON BEKESY, G., "Neural Volleys and the Similarity Between Some Sensations Produced by Tones and by Skin Vibrations," *Journal of the Acoustical Society of America*, Vol. 29 No. 10 (October 1957), 1059–1070.

WAPNER, S., and H. A. WITKIN, "The Role of Visual Factors in the Maintenance of Body-Balance," *American Journal of Psychology* (July 1950), 385–408.

WEBSTER, A. P., and H. N. HUNTER, "Acceleration Chart," *Journal of Aviation Medicine*, Vol. 25 (1954), 378–79.

WHITE, W. J., "Acceleration and Vision," *USAF WADC TR 58–333*, Aero Medical Laboratory (November 1958).

WITKIN, H. A., and S. E. ASCH, "Studies in Space Orientation. III. Perception of the Upright in the Absence of a Visual Field," *Journal of Experimental Psychology*, Vol. 38 No. 5 (October 1948), 603–614.

WITKIN, H. A., and S. E. ASCH, "Studies in Space Orientation IV. Further Experiments on Perception of the Upright with Displaced Visual Fields," *Journal of Experimental Psychology*, Vol. 38 No. 6 (December 1948), 762–782.

WITKIN, H. A., "The Nature and Importance of Individual Differences in Perception," *Journal of Personality*, Vol. 18 No. 2 (December 1949), 145–170.

WITKIN, H. A., and S. WAPNER, "Visual Factors in the Maintenance of Upright Posture," *American Journal of Psychology*, Vol. 63 (January 1950), 31–50.

WORCHEL, P., "The Role of the Vestibular Organs in Space Orientation," *Journal of Experimental Psychology*, Vol. 44 (1952), 4–10.

———. "The Vestibular Organs in Space Orientation," *Perceptual and Motor Skills*, Vol. 5 (1955), 164.

YUGANOV, Y. M., and D. M. ZAKHMATOV, "Illusory Perceptions during Flight Under Complex Meteorological Conditions," *Journal of Medical Military* (Moscow), Vol. 4 (1958), 30.

ZIEGENRUECKER, G. H., and E. B. MAGID, "Short Time Human Tolerance to Sinusoidal Vibrations," *USAF WADC TR 59–391*, Aero Medical Laboratory (July 1959).

6

THE SOMATIC CHANNEL

6.1. THE SENSING MECHANISM

It is through the sense of touch that the human operator receives much of the information about his proximal environment. The skin is constantly in contact with the surround and provides a wide range of data through the stimulation of somatic channel receptors.

Ever since 1883, it has been recognized that the skin is not uniformly sensitive to excitation over its entire area. For example, a small probe may be used to explore each square millimeter of a region. If the probe is alternately provided with a blunt end to exert pressure, a thin hair to cause "touch," a warm end or a cold end to excite a thermal sensation, then there are certain spots which are sensitive to each type of probe. On the basis of such exploration, it is possible to map the discrete points of sensitivity with respect to each sensation.

It must not be assumed that each of these sensitive points on the surface of the skin bears some particular internal sensing mechanism while other points do not. The encoding mechanism is much more subtle than that, and only a statistical inference concerning this mechanism would be a valid argument. In general, the sensation received from a particular stimulus is not the result of single excitation of a receptor, or even a single *type* of receptor, thus the subjective information is far from "pure" even under laboratory circumstance. Although the following discussion will separately identify types of receptor mechanisms, these must always be considered in toto with respect to any real world problem. In fact, an experiment was carried out by H. C.

166

Bazett, *et al.* (1932), in which a piece of live human skin was stimulated and then sacrificed to histological examination. Only heat, cold, touch, and pain were subjectively perceived, yet the physical analysis which followed revealed seven distinct types of receptor cells. A one-to-one stimulus-response correspondence would certainly be an oversimplification.

The skin is composed of two layers. The outer layer is called the epidermis, which consists of an outer layer of dead cells and an inner layer which contains many free nerve endings but no blood vessels. The inner layer of the

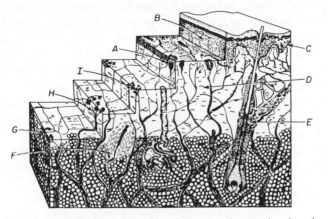

Figure 6.1. Weddell's conception of cutaneous innervation, based on the studies described in his article in *British Medical Bulletin*, Vol. 3 (1945), 167.

skin is called the dermis, a vascular material containing nerve endings and living cells. This layer is not distinctly separate from the inner subcutaneous tissue. Figure 6.1 indicates the physical nature and type of nerve endings in accordance with the work of G. Weddell. Identified by the corresponding letters they are:

(A) groups of Meissner's corpuscles subserving the sensation of touch
(B) beaded nerve nets subserving pain (probably fast pain)
(C) Merkel's discs subserving touch
(D) beaded nerve fibers derived from nerve nets subserving pain and associated with blood vessels (probably slow pain)
(E) nerve terminals around the sheath of a hair subserving touch
(F) a pacinian corpuscle subserving pressure
(G) a group of Ruffini endings subserving warmth
(H), (I) groups of Krause's end-bulb subserving cold (these lie at somewhat variable depths beneath the skin surface).

In every instance, the organized endings are accompanied by fine-beaded nerve fibers subserving pain. The entire tactile sense system is an interlace of complex receptor networks. No single receptor has what might be called a "private line" into the central nervous system. The sensitive points on the surface of the skin, described above, are but evidence of an increased density of the particular type receptor or some greater sensitivity of a large number of cells. The nerve endings over several hundred square millimeters surface area join to form a single nerve fiber.

Thermal Sensing

There is a great deal of uncertainty remaining concerning the exact function of the individual receptor cell types. Certain facts, however, are known which indicate that sensing of cold and warm is accomplished by separate types of receptors. For example, it has been demonstrated that cold sensitivity extends to greater depth in the skin than does warm. Further, some areas, such as the central zone of the cornea, are sensitive only to cold. There are a great many points on the skin surface which respond only to cold, and a fewer number of other points which respond only to warmth. The intervening areas are sensitive to neither. To be specific, on the forearm, cold spots average 13 to 15 per square millimeter, while warm spots average only 1 or 2 per square millimeter. It should be noted, at this point, that the cold spots may also be excited by a warm stimulus (over 45° C) with the resulting sensation called "paradoxical cold." The hot stimulus actually feels cold. The sensation of warmth which accompanies the act of blushing would seem to indicate that the warm receptors are located within a highly vascular domain.

The thermal receptors respond to a change in temperature with an increased electrical impulse discharge rate. A sudden stimulation elicits a characteristic high frequency of discharge which then gradually subsides to a low, almost constant, frequency rate. This constant activity level for, say, the cold receptors delivers continual thermal regulatory information which is required for the body to remain in homeostatic equilibrium. In addition, the cold receptors respond to the thermal rate of change. Rapid cooling causes increased activity over that of slow cooling. Cold receptors are most sensitive in steady state to a particular temperature. Experimental evidence has shown this to be at about 1° C with a corresponding impulse frequency of about 2 per second, which is almost 20 per cent of the maximum discharge rate. If a large number of cold sensitive cells act together, they furnish an almost linear increase in total discharge rate corresponding to temperature over a range from 20° C to 40° C.

The warmth receptors respond to increase in temperature by increase in their discharge rate. These also have some range of maximum sensitivity around 37° C. As shown in Figure 6.2, the warm-receptor sensitivity considerably overlaps that of the cold receptors, so that some additional information used in the encoding for added certainty in mediation may be expected. This additional cue might be that cold receptors fire at a rather steady rate, whereas warm receptors discharge in an irregular sputtering fashion and this at a considerably lower average repetition rate. In addition, the transmission velocity difference corresponds to the difference in the diameter of the connecting nerve fibers. Possibly the most significant cue of them all may be the statistical distribution of the sensitivity threshold of the individual types of receptors. This latter cue is, of course, the most difficult to determine.

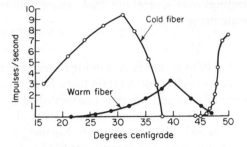

Figure 6.2. Graphs showing to the left the steady discharge of a typical single cold fiber (*open circles*), in the middle a typical single warm fiber (*filled circles*), and to the right the paradoxical cold fiber discharge (*open circles*) as a function of the temperature.

The thermoregulatory system of the body uses the temperature-sensed information from over the entire surface area. The hypothalmus within the brain has recently been shown to be sensitive only to warmth, and this only in a particular region. A slowly responding potential is generated in correspondence with the temperature as shown in Figure 6.3, even to a measured sensitivity of 1 millivolt per 0.1° C. Thus far no cold sensing has been attributed to the hypothalmus. It was suggested by von Euler that this "heat" potential might directly serve to regulate the reflexes of sweating, panting, vasodilatation, and so on.

This independent sensing of temperature at the hypothalmus is a significant finding. There is a relative scarcity of peripheral warmth receptors in comparison to the number of cold receptors. The received information from these cold receptors en masse, might easily lead to an overproduction of heat combined with heat stagnation due to contracted skin vessels. The warmth receptors within the brain respond to blood temperature and thus tend to prevent this from happening. They provide an internally-sensed negative feedback control of the thermoregulatory system. Discovery of a re-representation of a peripheral sensing mechanism internal to the central nervous system may be of profound importance. Similar discoveries have been made about chemoreceptors, and it would not be surprising to see new findings about other automatic mediation control systems.

According to J. D. Hardy and T. W. Oppel, the threshold for the sensing of thermal energy has been measured to be 0.00015 g-calories per square centimeter second. The threshold for the thermal gradient is correspondingly 0.004° C per second for cold receptors and 0.001° C per second for warm receptors, all measured for a three-second time interval over a particular area of the skin. This information is furnished only to indicate an order of magnitude, since the actual quantities are highly dependent upon the specific measuring conditions as well as the physiological status of the person at the time of the experiment.

One of the parameters which affects such measurements as these is the degree of adaptation. Although the skin is a poor conductor of heat, it gradually responds to the thermal control of the central nervous system, and permits adaptation to external temperatures. Once complete adaptation has taken place, the skin may be said to be at "physiological zero." This status

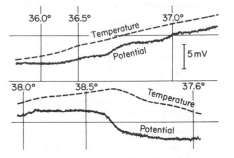

Figure 6.3. From cat under urethane anesthesia. Temperature of the brain stem and temperature potential from a point 0.3 mm in front of the anterior edge of the chiasma, 0.5 mm lateral of ventral III and 1.5 mm dorsal of the ventral boundary of the brain, recorded simultaneously. Upper and lower halves of picture in direct succession. From this electrode site no potential changes could be obtained, owing to changes in blood pressure or respiration. The temperature potential follows the temperature only within a limited region. Records interrupted every 30 seconds. (After Von Euler, *J. Cell. Comp. Physiol.*, 36, 333, 1950.)

may be attained over a range of external temperatures from about 64° to 108° F. There is a dead zone of about 1.8° to 3.6° F around physiological zero in which no temperature is sensed. Each region of the body may simultaneously adapt to its own external temperature. Normal skin temperatures for a subject placed under standard environment ranges from about 90.5° to 92.3° F.

Tactual Sensing

The sense of touch is more accurately described as a measure of the skin deformation gradient. Inserting a subject's finger into a pool of mercury arouses the sensation of touch at the fingertip only as the finger enters the liquid. Deformation in either direction can excite the touch sensation. However, very weak stimuli of pressure and tension are not discriminably different by the average unpracticed subject. As with the thermal receptors, the rate of stimulus is an important factor in determining the degree of excitation. Stimuli so weak that they would not be felt in slow onset or steady application become immediately perceptible if the application rate is made rapid, the threshold being independent of area.

Hairy regions of the skin are more sensitive to touch since the hairs act as levers, effecting a considerable amplification of the applied force on to the nerve endings which are found at the base of the hairs. The touch receptors are directly related to the kinesthetic proprioceptors discussed in Chapter 5; however, these lie *much* nearer the surface. H. H. Woollard showed that the epithelium with its nerve endings could be sliced away without causing sensation other than touch.

The perception of touch is accompanied by negative adaptation. It is common to experience that physical contact of the skin becomes increasingly difficult to perceive as time passes, so long as the contact remains undisturbed. This adaptation does not imply that the receptors have in any way grown less sensitive during the time of steady state adaptation. This is evident by the normal and rapid response to any change in the pressure stimulus. Evidently some homeostatic mechanism tends to return the discharge rate of the receptor to its normal value. The envelope of this normal time response is initiated only by a change of stimulus; in fact, a touch spot may fail to respond after repeated brief stimulations because it is adapted to a larger envelope in time. Such an adaptation is apparently an efficient design, since information is passed only through the channel immediately upon receipt of a new signal and for a short time thereafter. This high-pass filter action prevents bludgeoning the brain with a mass of data which describes nothing new.

Pressure stimuli can be separately resolved in time if the rate of application is less than about 20 pulses per second. Above this frequency the individuality of impulses is lost and a smooth sense of vibration is felt. This sensation bears direct analogy to some aspects of audition. Figure 6.4 indicates the spectral sensitivity as shown by measured data. There is a minimum threshold at about 250 cycles per second, responding to as little as 0.00004 inches double-amplitude of vibration in the frequency range between 100 and 500 cycles per second. Extreme data has indicated the perception of vibration from about 10 cycles per second to about 8,000 cycles per second. Discrimination between frequencies is surprisingly good. For example, with practice a subject may be expected to distinguish 400 cycles per second from 420 cycles per second. The upper limit of tolerance to vibration is roughly 15 to 20 times the threshold amplitude over the frequency spectrum. It is apparent that considerable information can be transmitted to the human operator through coded vibration signals. Reference is made to the section entitled Artificial Somatic Communication, p. 175.

Pain Sensing

The available evidence indicates that there are specific pain receptors just as there are separate sensors for thermal and touch stimuli. Excess mechanical, chemical, thermal, or electrical stimulation can elicit the pain sensation. It is therefore evident that the pain receptors are not specific only to a single form of energy as are the other types of receptors. This is as it should be, since the perception of pain is a protective device in its fundamental intent rather than primarily informative as are the other perceptions. And yet, all degrees of pain are not unpleasant, as witness the degree of pleasure associated with the consumption of certain hot spices.

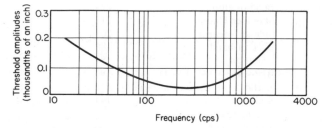

Figure 6.4. The relation between threshold amplitude and frequency for the discrimination threshold of vibration on the surface of the skin.

The normal threshold of pain was found to be 200 grams per square millimeter at the same spot on the skin where the threshold of touch measured from 2 to 3 grams per square millimeter. This numeric value is quoted so as to indicate only an order of magnitude. Obviously the threshold of pain is greatly variable over different regions of the skin and conditions relevant to the experimental situation. It may, however, be stated that, in general, the degree of pain induced by chemical stimulation is proportional to the hydrogen ion concentration, that is, the acidity of the solution in direct contact with the skin. Minimum thermal stimulation to produce pain has been measured at 0.21 gram calories per second per square centimeter. Table 6.1 indicates some data on the density distribution of pain sensing points on the skin of the normal subject.

Each sematic nerve consists of a large number of individual fibers having different diameters. The velocity of propagation of the neural impulse as well as its attenuation is dependent upon the diameter of the nerve fiber which acts to conduct this coded message to the brain. Thus, part of the encoding as to the source of the neural message is embedded in the message *during its transmission from the point of origin at the receptor to its point of reception in the brain*. Specifically, the relative time of arrival and peak voltage reflect the identity of the receptor which was excited to generate the original discharge. Thermal fibers have diameters in the range from 4 to 6 microns, pressure fibers from 8 to about 15 microns. The pain fibers, falling into two separate classes, present a particularly interesting case. The "first" pain sensation which is perceived arrives through fibers which transmit at a rate between 15 and 20 meters per second while the "second" pain (the dull pain) propagates through

Table 6.1. DISTRIBUTION OF PAIN SENSITIVITY

Skin Region	Pain Points per cm^2
Back of knee	232
Neck	228
Bend of elbow	224
Shoulder blade	212
Side of forearm	203
Back of hand	188
Forehead	184
Buttocks	180
Eyelid	172
Scalp	144
Middle finger, radial	95
Ball of thumb	60
Sole of foot	48
Tip of nose	44

(After E. von Skramlik.)

much thinner nerve fibers at a rate of about 2 meters per second. There is a time lag of about 1.9 seconds for the "second" pain to be perceived from stimulation at the toe. Evidently the pain coding is rather unique in that there is little difficulty in distinguishing a pricking sensation as opposed to a burning, scraping, or crushing sensation. The use of cocaine directly affects the thin unsheathed fibers first and, as would be expected, completely removes the "second" pain sensation.

Pain is also accompanied by negative adaptation. Little is known at the present time about the exact portion of the sensory channel which accomplishes adaptation; however, it is clearly evident that this adaptation does exist. It is a common experience for the subject to perceive an increase in pain after an injury. This effect is probably due to a decrease in the pain threshold following the injury, so that the continual normal subliminal stimulation becomes added to pain when it is imposed upon the increased sensitivity pain receptors. The experience of increased pain is certainly real, but this is not to be confused with positive adaptation.

6.2. COMPLEX SOMESTHETIC PERCEPTION

The perception of pattern or form of the stimulus is the result of a vast number of simultaneous signals arriving from various portions of the somatic channel, all integrated into a perceptual totality.

Probably the simplest pattern to discuss is the localization of one or more simultaneous pressure points. Initial work in this regard was done by Weber in 1852. On the back of the hand, for instance, the average error in touch localization is 4.49 millimeters as opposed to 3.81 millimeters for pin pricks (pain). The smallest distance between two points at which the points are still perceived as being separate is called the two-point threshold. Such a threshold can be determined experimentally for all forms of sensation as generated within the somatic channel. Generally a two-point threshold is at a smaller distance for pressure touch than for warmth or cold stimuli. Significant regional differences in the two-point sensibility exist as is shown in Table 6.2. These data are broadly parallel to the accuracy of localization.

Table 6.2. DISTRIBUTION OF TWO-POINT
THRESHOLD

Skin Region	Millimeters
Skin on back part of cheekbone and forehead	23
Tip of tongue	1
Red part of lips	5
Neck and chest	54
Middle of back and upper arm	68
Forearm	40
Back of hand	31
Lower leg	40
Back of foot	54

(After E. von Skramlik.)

Unexpectedly, the two-point threshold is larger than the error of localization of a single point stimulation at a particular spot on the skin. In other words, two points which are close together and excited simultaneously may be placed at the threshold of discrimination, yet if each of these points is sequentially stimulated, the localization error will prove to be less than that expected. This phenomenon is explained in terms of the diffusion within the neural channel so that individual stimulations are no longer independent. The interaction gives an increased stimulation at points between the stimuli points, thus inciting an impression of continuity of the stimulus. To exceed the two-point threshold, the individual excitations must be far enough apart so that the overlap activity remains below the threshold of sensitivity.

It is possible to perceive and recognize simple patterns which are implanted on the skin. If a blunt probe is used to write simple numeric symbols on the palm, then these become recognizable to an average subject within a few trials. The similar excitation of patterns of warmth (without touch) are virtually impossible to recognize. The perception of three-dimensional form, called stereognosis, is the result of the combination of touch and kinesthetic sensations. This is best illustrated by the following example. A cylinder made of solid metal may be placed in the hands of the subject. From the evenness of pressure on the palm he can diagnose a gross contour smoothness. This, combined with the kinesthesis describing the relative degree of opening of the hand, furnishes information that the object is probably cylindrical. Exploration of the surface provides data on two flat smooth ends. The conclusion thus far is that the object is a cylinder. The kinesthetic sensation from the arm muscle indicates its weight. This, taken with the temperature sensing of the skin, yields the decision that the object is a metal cylinder. It is difficult to realize the multitude of separate sensations which must be integrated to achieve even relatively simple form perception. The efficiency of the coding and decoding technique is pointed up by the ordinary subconscious use of the somatic channel in dealing with the three-dimensional environment.

Considerable discussion has prevailed in the past concerning synthesis of various somatic sensations such as tickle, itch, wet, dry, soft, hard, smooth, rough, oily, greasy, blunt, sharp, and so on. For example, it has been shown possible to synthesize a wet sensation through the proper administering of cold and pressure simultaneously. In addition to the large number of surface stimuli which can be diagnosed through the somatic channel, there are also a number of internal sensations which result from similar receptor actions and coding. The sensations of nausea, suffocation, dizziness, hunger, thirst, and so on, are provided by combinations of various types of receptors located at strategic points within the body (including chemoreceptors). The artificial stimulation of a complex sensation through the combination of individual excitations is far from proof that it is these very same factors which always contribute to generating the summary sensation. Synthesis demonstrates sufficiency; however, a complete understanding of the sensory channel mechanism requires both necessary and sufficient demonstrations. It is, of course, impossible to utilize introspective evidence in an effort to partition any complex sensation into its component factors.

6.3. ARTIFICIAL SOMATIC COMMUNICATION

A number of attempts have been made to utilize the somatic channel for purposeful communication to the human operator. One attempt, for example, was based upon the use of electric stimulation of a tactual nerve ending. Due to a number of difficulties, only the crudest of electrocutaneous communication could be achieved. One of the major obstacles was found to be the rapid adaptation to electrical stimulation. It is somewhat surprising that adaptation to both AC and DC nullifies receptor excitation in view of the fact that no energy state transformation is required. Evidently, however, the neural encoding furnishes a series link in the chain of events and as such can accommodate adequately, even to these unusual steady state conditions.

Mechanical vibration was also explored as a practical means for communicating. First attempts at a direct analog of the auditory channel met with failure since intensity and frequency encoded information usually becomes hopelessly confused prior to perception. There are, however, additional dimensions which can be used to furnish discriminable information content. For example, one vibratory communication system was devised which encoded signals into three separate intensity levels, three different time durations, and five alternative loci over the surface of the skin. This choice of the number of "levels" followed an experimental study of the perceptual sensitivity of each of these parameters. The surface of the chest was chosen since it provides a relatively large expanse of tissue of fairly uniform and high sensitivity, ranging between a minimum threshold of about 20 microns to an upper limit of about one-half millimeter displacement for vibration sensing. Empirical results indicated that about 15 separate vibration intensity levels could be subjectively distinguished as just noticeably different. A 60 cycle per second frequency of mechanical vibration was chosen for expediency; at this frequency there were about 25 different distinguishable time durations between the shortest interval which appeared to be of reasonable length (0.1 seconds), and the longest interval which seemed efficient for speed of communication (2 seconds). The practical problem of encoding the locus over the surface of the skin permits a large number of solutions so long as the individual vibration contact points are kept sufficiently far apart to insure separate localization.

The experimental system permitted a total of 45 different combinations of intensity, time duration, and locus, linking each of these elements to a letter of the English alphabet. The vibration signal transmitter was designed to use a standard typewriter keyboard and a number of learning experiments were conducted. Speeds of reception up to 38 words per minute were achieved, this score being well below the maximum possible 67 words per minute transmission-reception speed. The achieved score, however, compares favorably to the conventional use of International Morse Code which is received at about 24 words per minute by a proficient operator. The learning experiments indicated that none of the subjects had reached their psychological limit in the use of the vibratese language. Further, there is no reason to suspect that the system used in the experiment was in any way optimal. It is certainly possible that some other vibration alphabet or codification could achieve greater efficiency. For example, it might prove interesting to explore the use of a phonetic corresponding vibration alphabet in a manner similar to stenotype. The value of vibratory communication system as a prothesis is yet to be assayed.

6.4. CONCLUSION

The skin is in reality a highly variegated surface. It ranges widely in physical characteristics as well as sensitivity to individual types of stimuli. Information relative to temperature, material, and danger provide a continual reference for the human operator. Much investigative effort has been devoted to the measurement and understanding of the sensing, encoding, and transmission of these data from the external source to the perceptive centers within the body.

In general, the sentient skin surface may be regarded as the prototype of all the sense organs. The more highly developed sensory channels may best be understood from the datum plane established by an understanding of the somatic channel. There is an evident analog translation between the sensory surface of the skin and the physical mapping of the related regions of the cortex. The sensing of touch, pressure, and pain provide localized and general messages simultaneously through this analog channel. The macroscopic size of the skin-sensing surface may provide fertile ground for the investigation of this analog property and lead to further insight into its parallel in other sensory systems. These systems are also built up as sentient surfaces but sensitive to specific energy over a microscopic region.

The description above of the somatic channel forms the basis for a mathematical model which can be referenced in various ways. It provides a basis for the exploration of the effect of the proximal environment on the human operator and offers a consistent representation for the investigator of the internal communication system.

BIBLIOGRAPHY

ADRIAN, E. D. (Croonian Lecture), "The Messages in Sensory Nerve Fibres and their Interpretation," *Proceedings of the Royal Society of London*, B109 (1931), 1–18.

———. *The Mechanism of Nervous Action, Electrical Studies of the Neurone*. London: Oxford University Press, 1932.

———. "Afferent Discharges to the Cerebral Cortex from Peripheral Sense Organs," *Journal of Physiology*, Vol. 100 (1941), 159–191.

———. "The Response of Human Sensory Nerves to Currents of Short Duration," *Journal of Physiology* (London), Vol. 53 (1919), 70–85.

ANDERSON, A. B., and W. A. MUNSON, "Electrical Excitation of Nerves in the Skin at Audiofrequencies," *Journal of the Acoustical Society of America*, Vol. 23 (1951), 155–159.

AUSTIN, T. R., and R. B. SLEIGHT, "Accuracy of Tactual Discrimination of Letters, Numerals and Geometric Forms," *Journal of Experimental Psychology*, Vol. 43 (1952), 239–247.

AUSTIN, T. R., and R. B. SLEIGHT, "Factors Related to Speed and Accuracy of Tactual Discrimination," *Journal of Experimental Psychology*, Vol. 44 (1952), 283–287.

BAZETT, H. C., B. McGLONE, R. G. WILLIAMS, and H. M. LUFKIN, "Sensation I. Depth, Distribution and Probable Identification in the Prepuce of Sensory End-Organs Concerned in Sensations of Temperature and Touch; Thermometric Conductivity," *Archives of Neurological Psychiatry*, Vol. 27 (1932), 489–517.

BLISS, J. C., "Kinesthetic-Tactile Communications," *IRE Transactions on Information Theory*, Vol. IT–8 No. 2 (February 1962), 92–99.

DODT, E., "The Behaviour of Thermoceptors at Low and High Temperatures with Special Reference to Ebbecke's Temperature Phenomena," *Acta Physiologica Scandinavica*, Vol. 27 (1952), 295–314.

———. "The Discharge of Specific Cold Fibres at High Temperatures," *Acta Physiologica Scandinavica*, Vol. 26 (1952), 358–365.

DODT, E., A. P. SKOUBY, and Y. ZOTTERMAN, "The Effect of Cholinergic Substances on the Discharges from Thermal Receptors," *Acta Physiologica Scandinavica*, Vol. 28 (1953), 101–114.

DODT, E., and Y. ZOTTERMAN, "Mode of Action of Warm Receptors," *Acta Physiologica Scandinavica*, Vol. 26 (1952), 345–357.

GASSER, H. S., "Pain-Producing Impulses in Peripheral Nerves," *Research Publication of the Association of Nervous Mental Disorders*, Vol. 23 (1943), 44–62.

GASSER, H. S., and H. GRUNDFEST, "Axon Diameters in Relation to Spike Dimensions and the Conduction Velocity in Mammalian A-Fibers," *American Journal of Physiology*, Vol. 127 (1939), 393–414.

GAULT, R. H., "Recent Developments in Vibro-Tactile Research," *Journal of Franklin Institute*, Vol. 221 (1936), 703–719.

GELDARD, F. A., "Adventures in Tactile Literacy," *The American Psychologist*, Vol. 12 No. 3 (March 1957), 115–124.

———. "Hearing Through the Skin," *Research Review* (October 1954), 15–20.

GRANIT, R., and A. LUNDBERG, "Heat- and cold-sensitive Mammalian Nerve Fibres. Some Somatic Reflexes to Thermostimulation," *Acta Physiologica Scandinavica*, Vol. 13 (1947), 334–346.

GRANIT, R., and V. SUURSOET, "Self-Regulation of the Muscle Contraction by Facilitation and Inhibition from its Proprioceptors," *Nature*, Vol. 164 (1949), 270.

HARDY, J. D., and T. W. OPPEL, "Studies in Temperature Sensations. III. The Sensitivity of Body to Heat and the Spacial Summation of the End Organ Responses," *Journal of Clinical Investigation*, Vol. 16 (1937), 533–540.

HENSEL, H., "Physiologie der Thermoreception," *Ergebnisse der Physiologie*, Vol. 47 (1952), 165–368.

HIRSCH, J., "Communication by Vibratory Tactile Stimuli," *IRE Transactions on Medical Electronics*, PGME-7 (December 1956), 29–37.

LEHMANN, A., *Die Hauptgesetze des Menschlichen Gefuhlslebens*, Leipzig: Reisland, 1892.

PAINTAL, A. S., "The Conduction Velocities of Respiratory and Cardiovascular Afferent Fibres in the Vagus Nerve," *Journal of Physiology*, Vol. 121 (1953), 341–359.

RANSON, S. W., and P. R. BILLINGSLEY, "The Conduction of Painful Afferent Impulses in the Spinal Nerves. II," *American Journal of Physiology*, Vol. 40 (1916), 571–584.

SHERRINGTON, C. S., *The Integrative Action of the Nervous System*. Silliman Memorial Lectures, New Haven, Conn.: Yale University Press, 1906.

———. *Man on his Nature*. The Gifford Lectures, Edinburgh, 1937–38, New York: Cambridge University Press, 1941.

SPECTOR, P., "Cutaneous Communication Systems Utilizing Mechanical Vibration," Unpublished Doctorate Thesis, University of Virginia, 1954.

STROM, G., "Influence of Local Thermal Stimulation of the Hypothalamus of the Cat on Cutaneous Blood Flow and the Respiratory Rate," *Acta Physiologica Scandinavica*, Vol. 20 Suppl. 70 (1950), 47–76.

———. "Influence of Skin Temperature on Vasodilator Response to Hypothalamic Heating in Cat," *Acta Physiologica Scandinavica*, Vol. 20 Suppl. 70 (1950), 77–81.

———. "Vasomotor Responses to Thermal and Electrical Stimulation of Frontal Lobe and Hypothalamus," *Acta Physiologica Scandinavica*, Vol. 20 Suppl. 70 (1950), 83–112.

VON EULER, C., "Selective Responses to Thermal Stimulation of Mammalian Nerves," *Acta Physiologica Scandinavica*, Vol. 14 Suppl. 45 (1947).

———. "Slow 'temperature potentials' in the Hypothalamus," *Journal of Cellular and Comparative Physiology*, Vol. 36 (1950), 333–350.

VON FREY, M., "Beitrage zur Physiologie des Schmerzsinns," *Ber. kgl. sachs. Ges Wiss*, Vol. 46 (1894), 185–196.

———. "Physiologie des Sinnesorgame des Menschlichen Haut.," *Ergebnisse der Physiologie*, Vol. 9 (1910), 351–368.

VON SKRAMLIK, E., "Psychophysiologie der Tastsinne," *Asch-ges Ps. Ergbd.*, Vol. 4 (1937), 275–294.

WALL, P. D., and R. MELZACK, "Neural Mechanisms which Discriminate Events on the Skin," *IRE Transactions on Information Theory*, Vol. IT-8 No. 2 (February 1962), 120–125.

WATERSTON, D., "Observations on Sensation. The Sensory Functions of the Skin for Touch and Pain," *Journal of Physiology*, Vol. 77 (1933), 251–257.

WEDDELL, G., "The Anatomy of Cutaneous Sensibility," *British Medical Bulletin*, Vol. 3 (1945), 167–172.

WOOLLARD, H. H., "Anatomy of Peripheral Sensation," *British Medical Journal*, Vol. 2 (1936), 861–862.

———. "Intra-Epidermal Nerve Endings," *Journal of Anatomy*, Vol. 71 (1936–37), 54–60.

WOOLLARD, H. H., G. WEDELL, and J. J. HARPMAN, "Observations on the Neurohistological Basis of Cutaneous Pain," *Journal of Anatomy*, Vol. 74 (1940), 413–440.

ZIGLER, M. J., E. M. MOORE, and M. T. WILSON, "Comparative Accuracy in the Localization of Cutaneous Pressure and Pain," *American Journal of Psychology*, Vol. 46 (1954), 47–58.

ZOTTERMAN, Y., "Special Senses: Thermal Receptors," *Annual Review of Physiology*, (1953), 357–372.

———. "Touch, Pain and Tickling: an Electro-Physiological Investigation on Cutaneous Sensory Nerves," *Journal of Physiology*, Vol. 95 (1939), 1–28.

7

THE TASTE AND SMELL CHANNELS

7.1. INTRODUCTION

Taste and smell have traditionally been coupled in the literature, being termed the "chemical senses," even though there has been no proof that the receptors receive primary stimulation from any chemical reaction with the stimulus. Still, there remains justification in placing these two senses within the same context, since it is usual to find that the same stimulus will activate both sensing systems. The enjoyment of food, for example, is the result of dual stimulation.

7.2. THE TASTE SENSING MECHANISM

The stimulation of taste sensation can result only from direct contact between a liquid and the taste buds. As shown in Figure 7.1, each taste bud occupies a cavity in the outer surface of the skin. The taste bud is composed of *supporting cells* and *gustatory cells*. The supporting cells furnish the body and shape for the taste bud, and the gustatory cells accomplish the sensing. These thin receptor cells protrude through the opening at the surface of the skin in the shape of tiny hairs. The stimulus liquid may come into contact with this opening, called the gustatory pore, and by exciting the gustatory cells provide a taste sensation. The gustatory cells do not end in a long axone. Instead, they remain entirely within the taste bud where they are in electrical contact with many of the dendrites of the nerve cells which pass through the base of the taste bud. One or two gustatory cells may be connected to the same nerve fiber. These nerve fibers extend back from the taste bud, acquire a protective sheath, and terminate in the brain.

The taste buds are distributed over the surface of the tongue and adjacent areas. These areas show a marked difference in sensitivity to the basic tastes. For example, the tip of the tongue senses all tastes but is most sensitive to

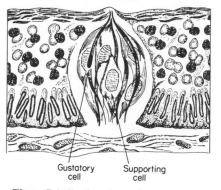

Gustatory   Supporting
cell   cell

Figure 7.1. Section through a taste bud.

sweet and salty. The lateral margins of the tongue are most sensitive to sour stimuli, but may also respond to salty liquids. The underside of the tongue is sensitive to bitter stimuli. The rear portion, particularly in the middle, is relatively insensitive to all tastes.

7.3. TASTE PERCEPTION

There are four basic taste sensations: sour, salty, bitter, and sweet. Any complex taste sensation can presumably be duplicated through the proper synthesis of degrees of each of these four primary tastes. The question of whether or not there are four different types of taste receptors corresponding to each of these apparently basic taste sensations is still unresolved. Physical examination has failed to reveal any significant difference, yet there appears to be functional difference in a number of ways. For example, the topical application of cocaine to the tongue abolishes taste sensitivity in the following order: first bitter, then sweet, then salty, and finally sour. It is also possible to find chemical agents which will selectively eliminate only specific taste sensations. Gymnemic acid selectively eliminates sweet and bitter taste.

C. Pfaffmann recorded neural action potential from single gustatory nerve fibers and was able to isolate three types of single fiber preparations. One provided stimulation only under taste bud contact with a sour solution, another allowed response only to sour and salty, while a third permitted excitation by sour and bitter stimuli. This study was accomplished on the cat, and on this animal no sweet receptors could be found. Note that the single nerve fiber which was monitored might be in contact with several gustatory receptor cells which may individually be sensitive only to a single taste. Obviously much remains to be accomplished in order to reveal the full mechanism for the generation of the taste-sense neural message.

The *sour taste* is a common quality of all but the very weakest of acids. It is well known that acids in solution dissociate into anions and the cation hydrogen, H^+. The strength of the acid is measured by the degree of this dissociation. The intensity of sour taste for certain strong acids appears to correspond to the degree of dissociation or the corresponding hydrogen ion concentration; however, some weak acids, such as acetic acid, provide a sour taste greater than would be expected on this basis. Although the taste intensity of dilute acids rapidly disappears through adaptation, the taste of acid in saliva suspension appears to last as long as the solution is retained in the mouth. The pH value for strong acids (a measure of the degree of dissociation) has been found to increase within the first five seconds after they are placed in the mouth, presumably by action with the saliva. It has been suggested that the saliva may furnish a continual supply of hydrogen ions to maintain the taste sensation.

The *salt taste* is characterized by that of common table salt, sodium chloride in solution. This, incidentally, is the only known agent to elicit a pure salty taste. Some evidence exists which suggests that in this case the anions of the solution furnish the primary excitation. For example, various sodium salts can be arranged in order of decreasing taste sensation as follows:

$$SO_4 > Cl > Br > I > HCO_3 > NO_3$$

However, it is also known that the cation affects the resulting taste sensation. This can be demonstrated by using, say, chlorides of various positive valence elements; in order of decreasing strength of taste:

$$NH > K > Ca > Na > Li$$

This series is probably related to the mobility of the ions.

The *sweet taste* provides a more perplexing problem since the substances which elicit this taste sensation do not appear to have any known physical or chemical property in common. Sweet stimuli include many organic agents which, as a rule, are not ionized. Most of the salts also stimulate some sweetness which poses the hypothesis that there may be a relation between this taste quality and the anion presence. In general, substances with similar physical and chemical properties display a similarity in taste, yet it has been shown that with increasing molecular weight the taste may change from sweet to bitter. Solubility decreases with increase in molecular weight, and thus the concentration available for taste stimulation may be expected to decrease. It has been shown that the sweet taste is related not only to the presence of certain ions or groups of atoms but also to the structural arrangement of the molecules themselves.

The *bitter taste* is similar to the sweet taste in that no single class of chemical agents appears to be characteristic. If salts of increasing molecular weight are provided in solution, it may be expected that the taste will change from salty to bitter. Yet there are situations where bitter appears to be more related to sweet, for instance, when there is a change in the molecular structure, or when certain sweet substances provide a bitter aftertaste. Further, as mentioned above, gymnemic acid depresses both of these taste qualities. Because of this it has been suggested that a single receptor sensing mechanism may be involved for bitter-sweet. Toxic agents frequently have bitter taste and it is generally thought that this is due to their special affinity for the fatty elements in the gustatory cells. Their initial action is frequently excitatory followed by an inhibitory action. Possibly the former may be basic to the sweet sensation while the latter may be associated with the stimulation of the bitter aftertaste.

It is known that the tongue may be affected by the application of electric current passing through monopolar electrodes. A characteristic stinging sour quality is elicited at the anode while a burning alkaline taste occurs at the cathode. A marked sour aftertaste occurs at the cathode once the circuit has been opened. It has been suggested that the sour taste at the anode may be due to hydrogen ions resulting from the electrolysis of saliva. The required gross change in the acidity of the saliva appears to be unlikely. The stimulation latency at the anode is relatively long when compared to that at the cathode. This suggests that the anode may introduce some electrolytic process acting directly upon the receptor cell. And yet, the shorter time lag for cathode response may indicate direct stimulation of a nerve. It has been demonstrated that the same general adaptation rate as that for acids results from anodal stimulation. In general, the time lag for neural response is much less when electrical stimulation is used. This is probably due to the rapid development of strong ionic concentration in the vicinity of the taste cell. There is no time required for the diffusion of the hydrogen ions in an acid to reach the surface of the taste cell. It is interesting to note that the cathode has never been observed to stimulate a single nerve fiber while in a "preparation." It does, however, tend to reduce any spontaneous discharge.

Taste sensitivity may be defined by the threshold of weakest perception. This sensitivity depends, of course, on many concurrent factors including the region of the tongue involved, the stimulation procedure, the individual differences between subjects, the variability from day to day and within the day, just to mention a few. Temperature also affects sensitivity; however, its effect is different for each of the basic tastes. Further, the temperature response is not even the same for all stimuli which yield the same taste. Reference is made to Figure 7.2 for related empirical evidence. The hypothesis that taste sensation is the result of a pure chemical reaction is confounded by such data since most chemical activity increases with temperature. Table 7.1 indicates some data relating to typical subjective judgment of intensity of taste values in terms of the number of grams per 100 cubic centimeters of water.

Table 7.1. Numeric Values in Terms of Grams per 100 Cubic Centimeters of Water

Substance	Typical Subjective Judgment			
	Absolute Threshold	Easily Recognized	Moderately Strong	Very Strong
Sucrose	0.7	4.0	10.0	40.0
Sodium Chloride	0.2	2.5	7.5	15.0
Hydrochloric Acid	0.007			
Citric Acid		1.0	5.0	10.0
Quinine Sulphate	3×10^{-5}			
Quinine Monohydrachloride		0.075	0.5	1.0

(After C. Pfaffman, *The Handbook of Experimental Psychology*, S. S. Stevens, ed.)

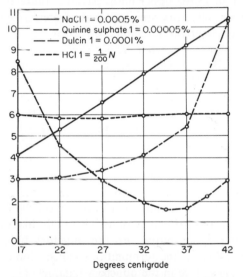

Figure 7.2. The effect of temperature on taste thresholds for sodium chloride, quinine sulphate, dulcin, and hydrochloric acid. The ordinate gives the thresholds in arbitrary units. The value of one unit on the ordinate differs for each of the four substances, as shown by the key in the figure. For example, one unit for NaCl equals 0.0005 per cent.

Loss of body salt may increase the desire for the salt taste sensation; however, physiological examination does not reveal any threshold difference at the taste bud. It is, therefore, reasonable to assume that this homeostatic bias is introduced at a higher point in the central nervous system. It is also possible to affect the sensitivity of the taste sensing channel by the injection of certain chemicals into the blood stream. Injection of insulin apparently leads to a reduced sensitivity for the taste of sugar. Reduction of the blood-sugar level to about 50 miligrams per 100 cubic centimeters of solvent appeared to render the sense of taste specifically less sensitive to sugar, while sensitivity to other substances remains unaffected. A reduction in blood-sugar level may be associated with a decreased sweet taste sensitivity.

Adaptation to taste generally follows the expected exponential curve, the exponent being proportional to the strength of the tasted solution. There are, however, exceptions even to this, and adaptation to complex tastes is not directly predictable from the adaptation characteristics of their basic taste constituents.

7.4. THE SMELL SENSING MECHANISM

The circulation of air in the upper nasal passage conducts odorous particles into contact with the olfactory area in two separate regions on either side of the nasal cavity. Each of these regions, of about 2.5 square centimeters, is covered with a yellowish-brown mucus membrane and is populated with long and thin *olfactory cells* which are supported by the adjacent cells of the outer layer of the skin. The sensing end of each of these receptors terminates in five or six delicate hairs which protrude into the mucus lining of the nose. These sensing cells communicate the stimulated electrical discharge directly to the brain. There are no separate ganglion nerve cells to accomplish the transport task. Such a simple organization is commonly found in the lower animals, but in man only the sense of smell operates in this manner. The bundles of nerve fibers form a plexus in the submucosa and are grouped into about 20 nerves which connect directly with the brain. The axons from the olfactory receptors enter the cranial cavity and meet the frontal lobes of the brain in what is called the olfactory bulb. This bulb, like the retina, is a part of the brain proper. Upon entry into the olfactory bulb, the nerve fibers divide into a profusion of fine terminations called glomeruli. At this point the first synapse takes place in the olfactory channel. This can occur in conjunction with two different types of cells: the large *mitral cells* and the *tufted cells*. Axons from both of these types form the olfactory tract which passes along the base of the frontal lobe. The arrangement of cells within the olfactory bulb provides a convergence of pathways as well as a return signal path back to the glomerulus itself by way of collateral ganglia. It has been suggested that this feedback may account in part for the great sensitivity of smell.

For a long time olfactory reception was thought to be the result of chemical stimulation similar to that affecting the gustatory cells. Recently, however, a number of other theories have been advanced. Notable among these is the infrared absorption theory. It was Faraday who first noted that many odorous materials strongly absorb radiation in the infrared spectrum. The heat radiated by the human body falls in the range of eight to fourteen microns in wavelength. The physical dimensions of the olfactory receptor cells are also within this range so that they may be expected to be more sensitive to certain specific resonant wavelengths. Odorous substances, absorbing specific wavelengths in an infrared spectrum, may selectively cool specific receptors more than others, thus providing a coded excitation which is translated into a neural message. In general, it has not been found possible to determine the particular quality of odor from the chemical constitution of the substance exciting the olfactory channel. As would be expected, an increase in volatility of the stimulus substance increases the odor by placing a greater number of particles in contact with the sensitive olfactory area.

7.5. OLFACTORY PERCEPTION

A great number of attempts have been made to identify "basic" olfactory attributes. H. Henning (1924), who used 400 scents in his investigation, produced what is probably the best known classification. His findings are shown in Figure 7.3 which portrays the basic smells at the vertices of a prism. Since that time, however, a number of other investigations have revealed that this portrayal is only general in nature. Further, the six basic odors have not been shown to correspond in any way to six distinct types of receptor mechanisms.

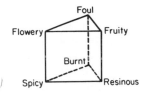

Figure 7.3. The smell prism according to H. Henning.

In 1927, E. C. Crocker and L. F. Henderson devised another conceptual frame of reference based upon four independent odors: fragrant, acrid, burnt, and caprylic. The intensity of each component odor was defined upon a scale from 0 to 8. Any particular odor could then be described in terms of a set of four digits. This system has proved useful in practical applications even with unpracticed subjects, since olfaction is an analytic sense. Practiced subjects can learn to distinguish component smells to a surprising degree. This ability is useful in determining the identity of the chemical components that cause particular characteristics of an odor, as in the synthesis of artificial scents. Of course, the greater the resemblance between the individual component odors, the greater will be the difficulty in discrimination.

Olfactory acuity is remarkable. It has been estimated that the sense of smell is 10,000 times as sensitive as that of taste. Measurement of the threshold of perception, however, is found to be extremely difficult since this metric is affected by a large number of factors including turbulence of the air, inspiration versus expiration, as well as some of the factors which disturb the similar measurement for sensitivity to taste. Table 7.2 indicates some representative results as taken by V. C. Allison and S. H. Katz.

Table 7.2. THRESHOLD CONCENTRATIONS OF VARIOUS ODOROUS MATERIALS

Substance	Boiling Point, degrees C	Milligrams per Liter of Air	Molar Concentration*
Ethyl ether	35	5.83	7.8×10^{-5}
Carbon Tetrachloride	76.7	4.53	3.0×10^{-5}
Chloroform	62	3.30	2.8×10^{-5}
Nitrobenzene	209.4	0.146	1.2×10^{-6}
Valeric acid	186.4	0.029	2.9×10^{-7}
Butyric acid	162.3	0.009	1.0×10^{-7}
Propyl mercaptan	67	0.006	7.9×10^{-8}
Artificial musk	....	0.00004	....

* Computed as the number of gram molecules in a liter of diluent or, more properly, in a liter of solution; but the concentrations are so low that a negligible error results from considering only the diluent.
(After Allison and Katz, 1919.)

Adaptation to odor is a common experience. It has been demonstrated that the time required for adaptation is directly proportional to the vapor pressure exerted by the odorous gas. An increase in vapor pressure introduces a larger number of molecules into the air thus causing increased stimulation. The degree of adaptation, therefore, appears to be inversely proportional to the molecular concentration in the nasal passage.

Early experiments have demonstrated some interesting results. For example, certain odors change during adaptation. The unpleasant odor of mercaptan changes to a pleasant quality as time progresses. In a classical experiment, Nagel (1897) mixed vanillan and cumarine in such proportion that the former completely masked the scent of the latter. As exposure time passed, adaptation to vanillan unmasked the cumarine odor. A large number of experiments have demonstrated cross-adaptation wherein the adaptation to one substance may affect the sensitivity to others.

7.6. CONCLUSION

It is obvious from the discussion above that much work remains to be accomplished toward understanding of these sensing systems. Modern techniques are being developed which offer the possibility of new findings and increased knowledge.

The senses of taste and smell are important to the human operator in that they indicate an essential part of his working environment. Although these senses provide less average information than do others, they remain important since they are often related to the protection of the human being. Without devoting any conscious attention to the matter, the pilot of an aircraft is continually monitoring the ambient odor. His sense of smell furnishes an immediate warning should something begin to "burn" or "leak." In a similar manner, the intake of food or drink is continually monitored by the sense of taste in order to assure that all is well.

There are many more subtle features also connected with taste and smell which help maintain psychological stability in the human operator during times when he may be exposed to otherwise stressful and rigorous environments. Deprivation of these senses may even bear upon personality. It remains important to include these information input channels in the considered design for man-machine systems.

BIBLIOGRAPHY

ADRIAN, E. D., *The Activity of the Mammalian Olfactory Apparatus*, XVII International Physiology Congress, Vol. 1, 1947.

ALLISON, V. C., and S. H. KATZ, "An Investigation of Stenches and Odors for Industrial Purposes," *Journal of Industrial Engineering Chemistry*, Vol. 11 (1919), 336–338.

AREY, L. B., M. J. TREMAINE, and F. L. MONZINGO, "The Numerical and Topographical Relations of Taste Buds to Human Circumyallate Papillae Throughout the Life Span," *Anatomy Record*, Vol. 64 (1935), 9–26.

BECK, L. H., and W. R. MILES, "Some Theoretical and Experimental Relationships Between Infrared Absorption and Olfaction," *Science*, Vol. 106 (1947), 511.

BEEBE-CENTER, J. G., and D. WADDELL, "A General Psychological Scale of Taste," *Journal of Psychology*, Vol. 26 (1948), 517–524.

BEEBE-CENTER, J. G., M. S. ROGERS, and D. N. O'CONNELL, "Transmission of Information About Sucrose and Saline Solutions Through the Sense of Taste," *Journal of Psychology*, Vol. 39 (1955), 157–160.

BEIDLER, L. M., "A Theory of Taste Stimulation," *Journal of General Physiology*, Vol. 38 (1954), 133–139.

BORNSTEIN, W. S., "Cortical Representation of Taste in Man and Monkey. II," *Yale Journal of Biological Medicine*, Vol. 13 (1940), 133–156.

CAUL, J., "Flavor and Odor: A New Frontier," *Industrial Science and Engineering* (April 1955), 9–12.

CLAUSEN, J., A. GJESVIK, and A. URDAL, "Repetition Effect in Pain Threshold Determination," *Journal of Experimental Psychology*, Vol. 51 (1954), 185–192.

CLAUSEN, J., A. URDAL, and A. GJESVIK, "Relation Between Galvanic Skin Resistance and Repetition Effect in Pain Stimulation," *Journal of General Psychology*, Vol. 53 (1955), 29–36.

CROCKER, E. C., and L. F. HENDERSON, "Analysis and Classification of Odors," *American Perfume*, Vol. 22 (1927), 325–326.

CROCKER, E. C., *Flavor*. New York: McGraw-Hill Book Company, Inc., 1945.

DALLENBACH, J. W., and K. M. DALLENBACH, "The Effects of Bitter Adaptation on Sensitivity to the Other Taste Qualities," *American Journal of Psychology*, Vol. 56 (1943), 21–31.

FOX, A. L., "The Relationship Between Chemical Constitution and Taste," *Proceedings of the National Academy of Science*, Vol. 18 (1932), 115–120.

FRINGS, H., "A Contribution to the Comparative Physiology of Contact Chemoreception," *Journal of Comparative Physiological Psychology*, Vol. 41 (1948), 25–34.

GELDARD, F. A., "Somesthesia and the Chemical Sense," *Annual Review of Psychology*, Vol. 1 (1950), 71–86.

GOETZL, F. R., and F. STONE, "Diurnal Variations in Acuity of Olfaction and Food Intake," *Gastroenterology*, Vol. 9 (1947), 444–453.

HENNING, H., *Der Geruch*, 2nd ed. Leipzig: Barth, 1924.

HOAGLAND, H., "Specific Nerve Impulses from Gustatory and Tactile Receptors in Catfish," *Journal of General Physiology*, Vol. 16 (1933), 685–693.

JONES, F. N., and M. H. JONES, "Modern Theories of Olfaction: A Critical Review," *Journal of Psychology*, Vol. 36 (1953), 207–241.

LEWIS, D. R., "Psychological Scales of Taste," *Journal of Psychology*, Vol. 26 (1948), 437–446.

McCORD, C. P., and W. N. WITHERIDGE, *Odors: Physiology and Control*. New York: McGraw-Hill Book Company, Inc., 1949.

MILES, W. R., and L. H. BECK, "Infra-red Absorption in Field Studies of Olfaction in Bees," *Science*, Vol. 106 (1947), 512.

MONCRIEFF, R. W., *The Chemical Senses*. New York: John Wiley & Sons, Inc., 1946.

NAGEL, W. A., "Uber Mischgeruche und die Komponentengliederung des Geruchsinnes," *Z. Psychol. Physio. Sinnesorg.*, Vol. 15 (1897), 82–101.

PFAFFMANN, C., "Gustatory Afferent Impulses," *Journal of Cellular and Comparative Physiology*, Vol. 17 (1941), 243–258.

RANSON, S. W., and S. L. CLARK, *The Anatomy of the Nervous System*. Philadelphia: W. B. Saunders Company, 1947.

ROSS, S., and J. VERSACE, "The Critical Frequency for Taste," *American Journal of Psychology*, Vol. 66 (1953), 496–497.

YOUNG, C. W., D. F. FLETCHER, and N. WRIGHT, "On Olfaction and Infra-red Radiation Theories," *Science*, Vol. 108 (1948), 411–412.

8

SUMMARY OF THE SENSORY
CHANNELS

8.1. INTRODUCTION

It is indeed rare to find situations in which the human operator is stimulated thru only one of his sensory channels. He is commonly exposed to a simultaneous array of energy in various forms which is transduced into informative sensations through his monitoring channels.

The human operator has many more than 5 senses. G. H. Mowbray and J. W. Gebhard have tabulated the results of a general survey of the human sensory capabilities. Table 8.1 presents some of the sensations of the related transducer and the nature of the stimulating energy. Table 8.2 presents a comparison of the intensity ranges and intensity discrimination abilities of some of the senses. Table 8.3 contrasts the extremes of frequency range which can cause sensation and the relative and absolute frequency discrimination capability.

8.2. PROTENSITY, THE SENSING OF TIME

It appears that there is additional sensing of information outside the typical information which is categorized within the previously described channels. Specifically, the human operator senses the passage of time as a separate dimension of his environment. Yet there remains the unresolved question: Is protensity dependent upon the existence of an accompanying sensation

Table 8.1. A SURVEY OF MAN'S SENSES AND THE PHYSICAL ENERGIES THAT
STIMULATE THEM

Sensation	Sense Organ	Stimulated By	Originating
Sight	Eye	Some electromagnetic waves	Externally
		Mechanical pressure	Externally or internally
Hearing	Ear	Some amplitude and frequency variations of the pressure of surrounding media	Externally
Rotation	Semicircular canals	Change of fluid pressures in inner ear	Internally
	Muscle receptors	Muscle stretching	Internally
Falling and rectilinear movement	Semicircular canals	Position changes of small, bony bodies in the inner ear	Internally
Taste	Specialized cells in tongue and mouth	Chemical substances dissolvable in saliva	Externally (contact)
Smell	Specialized cells in mucous membrane at the top of the nasal cavity	Vaporized chemical substances	Externally
Touch	Skin mainly	Surface deformation	On contact
Vibration	None specific	Amplitude and frequency variations of mechanical pressure	On contact
Pressure	Skin and underlying tissue	Deformation	On contact
Temperature	Skin and underlying tissue	Temperature changes of surrounding media or of objects contacted	Externally and on contact
		Mechanical movement	
		Some chemicals	
Cutaneous pain	Unknown, but thought to be free nerve endings in the skin	Intense pressure, heat, cold, shock, and some chemicals	Externally and on contact
Subcutaneous pain	Thought to be free nerve endings	Extreme pressure and heat	Externally and on contact
Position and movement	Muscle nerve endings	Muscle stretching	Internally
	Tendon nerve endings	Muscle contraction	Internally
(kinesthesis)	Joints	Unknown	Internally

From G. H. Mowbray and J. W. Gebhard, "Man's Senses as Information Channels,"
Rept. CM-936 The Johns Hopkins University Applied Physics Lab. (May 1958).

Table 8.2. Man's Senses as Informational Channels: A Comparison of the Intensity Ranges and Intensity Discrimination Abilities of the Senses

Sense	Intensity Range		Intensity Discrimination	
	Smallest Detectable	Largest Practical	Relative	Absolute
Vision	2.2 to 5.7×10^{-10} ergs	Roughly, the brightness of snow in the mid-day sun, or about 10^9 times the threshold intensity	With white light, there are about 570 discriminable intensity differences in a practical range	With white light, 3 to 5 absolutely identifiable intensities in a range of 0.1 to 50 ml.
Audition	1×10^{-9} ergs/cm²	Roughly, the intensity of the sound produced by a jet plane with afterburner or about 10^{14} times the threshold intensity	At a frequency of 2,000 cps, there are approximately 325 discriminable intensity differences	With pure tones about 3 to 5 identifiable steps
Mechanical vibration	For a small stimulator on the fingertip, average amplitudes of 0.00025 mm can be detected	Varies with size of stimulator, portion of body stimulated and individual. Pain is usually encountered about 40 db above threshold	In the chest region a broad contact vibrator with amplitude limits between 0.05 mm and 0.5 mm provides 15 discriminable amplitudes	3 to 5 steps
Touch pressure	Varies considerably with body areas stimulated and the type of stimulator. Some representative values: Ball of thumb—0.026 erg Fingertips—0.037 to 1.090 ergs Arm—0.032 to 0.113 erg	Pain threshold	Varies enormously for area measured, duration of stimulus contact and interval between presentation of standard and comparison stimuli	Unknown
Smell	Widely variant with type of odorous substance.	Largely unknown	No data available	No data available

Table 8.2. (continued)

Sense	Intensity Range		Intensity Discrimination	
	Smallest Detectable	Largest Practical	Relative	Absolute
Smell (continued)	Some representative values: Vanillin— 2×10^{-7} mg/m^3 Mercaptan (C_2H_5SH)— 4×10^{-5} mg/m^3 Diethyl/Ether ($C_2H_5OC_2H_5$) 1.0 mg/m^3	Largely unknown	No data available	No data available
Taste	Widely variant with type and temperature of taste substance. Some representative values: Sugar—0.02 molar concentration Quinine Sulfate— 4×10^{-7} molar concentration	Not known	No data available	No data available
Temperature	Sensation of heat results from a 3-second exposure of 200 cm^2 of skin at rate of 1.5×10^{-4} gm-cal/cm^2/sec	Pain results from a 3-second exposure of 200 cm^2 of skin at a rate of 0.218 gm-cal/cm^2/sec	No data available	No data available
Kinesthesis	Joint movements of 0.2 degree to 0.7 degree at a rate of 10 deg/min can be detected. Generally, the larger joints are the most sensitive	Unknown	No data available	No data available
Angular acceleration	Dependent on the type of indicator used 1. Skin and muscle senses 1 deg/sec^2	Unconsciousness or "blackout" occurs for positive "G" forces of 5 to 8 G lasting 1 second or more	No data available	No data available

Table 8.2. (continued)

Sense	Intensity Range		Intensity Discrimination	
	Smallest Detectable	Largest Practical	Relative	Absolute
Angular acceleration (continued)	2. Nystagmic eye movements 1 deg/sec^2 3. Oculogyral illusion 0.12 deg/sec^2	Negative forces of 3 to 4.5 G cause mental confusion, "red-vision" and extreme headaches lasting some-times for hours following stimulation		
Linear acceleration	In aircraft—0.02 G for accelerative forces and 0.08 G for decelerative forces	For forces acting in the direction of the long axis of the body, the same limitations as for angular acceleration apply	No data available	No data available

From G. H. Mowbray and J. W. Gebhard, "Man's Senses as Information Channels," *Rept. CM-936 The Johns Hopkins University Applied Physics Lab.* (May 1958).

within the traditional sensory channels? A large number of psychological experiments have been carried out in the past in efforts to quantify aspects of human ability in this regard. Probably the simplest of these experiments is intended to determine the accuracy with which a subject can identify the just-noticeable difference (jnd) between two empty time intervals bounded by auditory clicks, or two time intervals filled with either a continuous auditory tone or light stimulus. Results indicate that the greatest accuracy accompanies actual empty intervals of about 0.8 seconds while the filled intervals show greatest accuracy of judgment over the range of about 0.2 to 2 seconds. It has been generally found that shorter intervals are underestimated while longer intervals are overestimated. It is, therefore, reasonable to expect that there is some intermediate length interval which is undistorted, this being called the *indifference interval.* Seldom do various investigators agree upon the particular length of the indifference interval. Estimations generally state that it lies between 0.5 and 0.7 seconds; however, the reported range has extremes from 0.36 to 5.0 seconds. In fact, certain reports indicate that

Table 8.3. A Comparison of the Frequency Ranges and Frequency Discrimination Abilities of Some of the Senses

Sense	Wavelength or Frequency Range		Wavelength or Frequency Discrimination	
	Lowest	Highest	Relative	Absolute
Vision Hue	300 mμ	1,500 mμ	At medium intensities there are about 128 discriminable hues in the spectrum	12 to 13 hues
Interrupted white light	Unlimited	At moderate intensities and with a duty cycle of 0.5, white light fuses at about 50 interruptions per second	At moderate intensities and with a duty cycle of 0.5, it is possible to distinguish 375 separate rates of interruption in the range of 1 to 45 interruptions per second	No greater than 5 or 6 interruption rates can be positively identified on an absolute basis
Audition Pure tones	20 cps	20,000 cps	Between 20 cps and 20,000 cps at 60 db loudness, there are approximately 1,800 discriminable steps	4 to 5 tones
Interrupted white noise	Unlimited	At moderate intensities and with a duty cycle of 0.5, interrupted white noise fuses at about 2,000 interruptions per second	At moderate intensities and with a duty cycle of 0.5, it is possible to distinguish 460 separate interruption rates in the range of 1 to 45 interruptions per second	Unknown
Mechanical vibration	Unlimited	Unknown, but reported to be as high as 10,000 cps with high intensity stimulation	Between 1 and 320 cps, there are 180 discriminable frequency steps	Unknown

From G. H. Mowbray and J. W. Gebhard, "Man's Senses as Information Channels," *Rept. CM-936 The Johns Hopkins University Applied Physics Lab.* (May 1958).

there was no indifference interval in view of the inconsistency of the recorded data.

A number of theories have been advanced to tie the indifference interval to some physiological variable, such as the time between pulse beats, the alleged "wave of attention," the time required to adjust attention for the most effective apprehension of the stimulus, and so on. To date no such correlates have been successfully demonstrated. However, it has been shown that the nature of the time interval bounding signals has a direct effect upon the perception of the time interval length. Further, the effects of learning are always present so that adaptation to a recently perceived length may form a distinct bias upon the judgment of future intervals. There are even more subtle factors involved in terms of subjective techniques used to aid judgment. Does the subject use some rhythm as a base for his time judgment? Does he remember the first time interval in terms of a "picture" or spatial equivalent length? In addition, there must be considered the effect of imposed stress as a result of the experimental situation and the expected individual differences which are always found in phychophysics.

The estimation of longer time intervals may take place through the subjective judgment of some physical quantity such as the number of seconds which pass, the number of breaths, the number of steady counts rather than just a direct judgment of the stimulus time interval. Experimental evidence has shown that almost any time interval may be called "short" or "long" by the subject, this being dependent upon the standard he uses for reference. Even if no obvious "standard" has been furnished, there always remains the unconscious recall of some recently experienced time interval which forms a frame of reference.

An interesting question may be posed: What is the duration of the present? That is, of what physical time duration does the human operator consider that stimuli are simultaneous. For instance, how many clock ticks into the past does a subject recall if unexpectedly asked? Or at the other extreme—what is the minimum threshold of time which can be recognized to have passed?

Obviously this psychological unity of time is vastly different for different subjects. Besides all the usual variability there is the ambiguity of the subjective understanding of the term "unity," that is, of what "simultaneous" really means. Even with a clear logical definition as a basis, the immediate subjective definition can depend to a great extent upon attitude. K. Quasebarth reported an upper limit of about 6 seconds for continuous light and of about 5 seconds for continuous tone stimuli. In other experiments, maximal times of from 2.3 to 12 seconds have been reported. Another approach to the determining of this maximum time interval of the "present" is through the experimental discrimination of the terminating time for achieving identity of a simple rhythmic pattern in, say, audio tones. Such tests result in a time judgment of about 3.5 seconds and, therefore, appear consistent with the above-referenced data.

At the lower extremity of the subjective "present," there is again considerable variability in reported results. G. Durup and A. Fessard report 0.12 second for continuous light duration threshold and from 0.01 to 0.05 seconds for continuous sound. These are the time intervals which were subjectively considered to be of sufficient duration so as *not* to be called simultaneous.

The accuracy of long time judgment is strongly dependent upon the nature of the subjective experience during that time interval. Generally interesting and pleasant activity seems to shorten the time span, while just waiting can "drag the time." In retrospect, however, these judgments are reversed. The memory of empty time periods appears shorter than true, while busy periods appear longer.

Certain tasks may cause the human operator to become completely unaware of the passage of time, as when he is engaged in some all-absorbing or life-and-death struggle. It is also possible to impose the effects of drugs to obliterate, shorten, or lengthen the subjective temporal experience. L. D. Boring and E. G. Boring studied the time judgment of the interval of sleep. The subjects were unexpectedly awakened between 12:15 A.M. and 4:45 A.M. and asked to judge the time. Their low accuracy of 50 minute average error showed no need to assume any psychological time sense mechanism. The great accuracy with which certain people seem to be able to arouse from sleep at prechosen times is yet to be proven by any controlled experiment.

In a manner analogus to the level of activity, artificially imposed noise may decrease the subjective passage of time. H. J. Jerison demonstrated that an increase from 77.5 db to 111.5 db noise field reduced the subject's already short judgment of a true ten-minute interval from an average of 9 minutes down to about 7 minutes. In another experiment he required the subject to track a moving target until it suddenly disappeared, continuing to trace its presumed motion until it would have reached a crosshair. The addition of ambient noise at the time of target disappearance generally caused longer judgment of time intervals relative to those obtained under the quiet control conditions.

8.3. THE SENSING OF PROBABILITY

The real world is a probalistic domain, and it is often of great value for the human operator to estimate the expectation of an event properly (especially in a gambling situation). A number of experiments for measuring the accuracy with which the human operator can judge probability have been performed. However, possibly even more important than these specific results is the fact that a stimulus may occur only in the form of a subjective probability when it exceeds some unspecified threshold value. As William James stated "Perception is of definite and probable things." The subjective estimate of a real world possibility may prove as real as if it already existed.

Further, the informational content of any perceived message is directly related to its uncertainty. It is the subjective uncertainty which must be resolved in order to gain any new information. The informational metric can be of distinct value since it is known that, in a general way, both latency and the accuracy of response are related to the observer's ability to predict in advance the appropriate action to be taken to a given stimulus occurring at any particular point in time. It becomes apparent that the efficiency of the human operator as an information tranducing part of man-machine systems is strongly dependent upon his subjective expectations as these relate to the objective probabilities of his informational environment.

Two methods have been used in the study of the perception of probability. In the first of these the subject is provided with, say, two lights, one activated every tenth of a second in accordance with some predetermined pattern. The true probability associated with each light being on is, therefore, exactly known to the experimenter. The subject is asked to estimate the relative frequency of occurrence for each light, and it is this subjective value which is compared to the actual value over some particular time interval of trial. (The rate of presentation is intentionally made too high for the subject to count the number of times either light is on.) Usually the experimental results follow a sigmoid curve showing that events with very low objective probabilities are overestimated, while those with high objective probabilities are underestimated. It has been shown that even with long experience with any particular objective frequency of occurrence, there is no significant decrease in the discrepancy between subjective and objective values.

In a second method, the subject is requested to predict which of the two lights will illuminate during the next time interval. The experiment is slowed to the point where the subject can make his prediction before the scheduled new light-action takes place. After the next state is reached the subject is again asked to predict and, having done so, the experiment proceeds into the next state, and so on. It was found that initially the subject will equally alternate his predictive choice. However, after about sixty predictions the estimated frequencies of occurrence closely approach the objective frequencies, indicating that the perceived probability has become a close approximation to the actual probability. Similar results have been demonstrated even when the number of alternative events which are possible is made as large as eight.

These two experimental situations are seen to be basically different. In the first, the subject is required to produce an absolute judgment against an unexhibited scale, while in the second, the subject is permitted continual feedback as to the correctness of his prediction. Very soon his predictions approach the objective probabilities (even though he may remain unaware of what this actual probability is). In this latter experimental situation the subject is no longer just accomplishing perception. He may be looked upon as a decision-maker in the most complete sense of the term, and the accuracy of his results reflect his added corrective capacity.

It is interesting to note that the series of events being predicted contains sequential dependencies, and subjects behave as though these have been consciously perceived, even though they may remain unaware that such conditional probabilities exist. H. W. Hake and R. Hyman ran a two-alternative guessing game and found that subjects take advantage of sequential dependencies in choosing their response. Over a large number of experiments general results may be summarized: If the stimulus series has dependencies beyond the immediately previous stimulus, there will be corresponding dependencies in the responses. If there are no dependencies in the stimulus series, the present response will be substantially dependent on the immediately preceding response, perhaps slightly dependent on the one before that, and independent still further back.

In 1948, M. G. Preston and P. Baratta required subjects, using play money, to bid competitively for the privilege of taking a bet. This allowed the assumption that the utility values do not enter as a bias. There resulted the expected sigmoid curve with an *indifference point* (that point where subjective probability equals objective probability) at about 0.2. R. W. Griffith made an analysis of parimutuel betting at race tracks,[1] F. Attneave studied a guessing game, and R. C. Sprowls analyzed lotteries. They all found similar results. F. Mosteller and P. Nogee performed a dice-betting experiment with Harvard undergraduates and National Guardsmen. Although their results were generally in agreement, they found no indifference point for the Harvard students, while the National Guardsmen had an indifference point of about 0.5. They were unable to reconcile these differences.

There are, of course, many variables which enter the subjective judgment of probability, some of which will be discussed in more detail in Chapter 11. Probably the most important thing to remember is that there is always a subjective association of probability with each aspect of the real world, even though these "values" may not be apparent to the human operator. The sensing of information through any one or more sensory channels modifies the probabilistic context within which the subject operates. In forming a basis for decision-making and subsequent actions, his judgment of the frequency of the occurrence may at times prove to be a critical factor in his acceptance of actually perceived information.

8.4. THE PERCEPTION OF INTENSITY

Psychophysics has long been concerned with the problem of relating subjective magnitude[2] of sensation to the physical magnitude of the causal stimulus. Classical experiments measured the *difference threshold*,[3] that is, the amount of stimulus increment which would cause a just-noticeable difference (jnd) in the perceived magnitude. Two particular generalizations

---

[1] Even though it was found that people usually overplayed long shots, this bias was not sufficient to compensate for the track take and breakage on favorites.

[2] The term intensity can be used interchangeably with magnitude in the following discussion.

[3] Also called the "difference limen."

were developed. The first, known as Weber's Law, states that for each sense parameter the ratio between the jnd and the stimulus intensity remains constant. That is to say, there is presumed to be a particular constant which is characteristic of each sense modality, this constant describing the ratio of change in stimulus to the absolute stimulus level which is just perceptible. Actually this ratio remains constant only to a good approximation over about 99.9 per cent of the usual range of sensory perception. The discrepancies which have been noted remain to be included in a refinement of Weber's Law.

Based upon the assumed truth of Weber's Law, the second generalization is reached. Fechner's Law indicates that the subjective magnitude of sensation is proportional to the logarithm of the magnitude of the stimulus. The logarithmic difference of intensity is stated to remain constant, and imposes the constraint that the jnd's remain of equal size over the entire scale of perception. If Fechner's additional postulate were true, then a stimulus, say, 20 jnd's above the threshold would appear twice as great as one of 10 jnd's. Experimental evidence has demonstrated that this is not the case. Specifically jnd's may be unequal in subjective magnitude, and, in fact, this appears to be the case for a number of parameters such as in the subjective judgment of weight, brightness, and so on. On the other hand, subjectively equal jnd's have also been shown in terms of parameters, such as pitch, so that two separate classes of jnd may be identified.

Noting this caused S. S. Stevens to advance an hypothesis in 1939 to the effect that there may be two distinct mechanisms for discrimination. In the case of loudness, for example, neural excitation is added to that excitation level which is already present. This is taken to be distinct from the other mechanism wherein, for example, an increase in pitch occurs upon a change in the distribution of excitation—that is, when some new excitation is substituted for its predecessor. The generalization under the additive mechanism is that the jnd's are subjectively unequal in size, while for the substitutive mechanism they remain equal. In any case, the numbering of jnd's produces the same ordinal scale.

There are two correct methods of experimental attack upon the measurement of the subjective magnitude of sensation. The first of these may be called the method of magnitude production wherein an observer is required to adjust one stimulus to some prescribed apparent fraction of another stimulus. The second method is called the method of magnitude estimation. Subjects are directed to assign numbers proportionate to the subjective magnitude to various stimuli which are offered by the experimenter. Thus far, both of these methods have been applied to about twenty perceptual continua and from none of these has there been obtained data as predicted by Fechner's Law. Rather, the data would tend to support a power law—that is, the subjective magnitude is governed by some exponent of the stimulus magnitude. Exponents ranged from 0.3 in the case of loudness for a thousand-cycle tone, to 3.5 in the case of pain intensity for a sixty-cycle electrical shock applied to the fingers. This means that to double the loudness of a tone the energy has to increase ten-fold; while just doubling the electrical current to the fingers increases the sensation a little more than ten-fold. Exponents between these two extremes were obtained for brightness, heaviness, intensity, and so on.

A particularly interesting experiment was carried out by J. C. and S. S. Stevens. Subjects were presented a pair of lights at different luminance ratios as well as a pair of sounds, in this case noise. Their task was to adjust one of the noises until it formed with the other noise a subjective loudness ratio perceived to be equal to the brightness ratio set between the two lights. In this way no intervening numerics could introduce artificial error into the experimental results. Variability of judgments was rather large, as might be

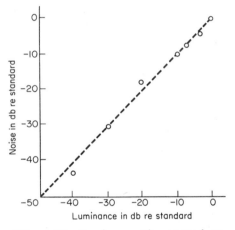

Figure 8.1. Loudness ratio equated to brightness ratio.

expected; however, on the average, the subject set the same ratio of energies between the sounds as the given ratio of luminances between the two lights. Figure 8.1 indicates a plot of the results. If the difference between the two lights was about one logarithmic unit, then the subject, on the average, tended to set the noises about one logarithmic unit apart, thus showing the basic similarity between the two functions. It is important to note once again that these perceptual judgments were accomplished by direct comparison between sensory channels.

It is not altogether surprising to find this additional point of intersensory similarity. In both vision and audition there is about the same range from threshold at the lower bound to discomfort and pain at the upper bound. In both cases the energy ratio over this range is of trillions to one. The strength of this correspondence is emphasized by reference to Figure 8.2.

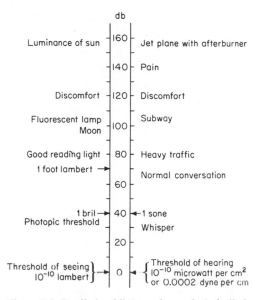

Figure 8.2. Decibels of light and sound. A decibel scale for light and sound showing the approximate levels of luminance and of sound intensity produced by various sources, together with a few important levels. The points indicated by arrows are exact levels fixed by definition, the other levels are approximate only.

8.5. INTERACTIVE EFFECTS OF THE SENSORY CHANNELS

Interaction between sensory channels most often serves to degrade performance. This degradation has often been attributed to intervening variables known as *stress* and *fatigue*. Both of these may be defined in terms of the direct measure of performance degradation of some well-defined task under given environment, or alternatively in terms of indirect measurement of activation of some adaptation syndrome—a behavior pattern which the subject introduces in order to overcome the effects of the sensed disturbance. There is, of course, no situation which can be described as being completely without stress. Similarly, the human operator is never in a zero-fatigue state. Before considering any particular evidence with respect to interaction of sensed modalities, it is probably well to digress for a moment and consider the use of intervening variables, such as stress and fatigue.

The examination of any physical system requires the implicit delineation of boundaries beyond which detailed consideration will not go. Without such tacit assumptions, it would be impossible to present closure to the discussion or offer apparently conclusive reasoning. For example, the aircraft designer considers aerodynamic effects upon wing and fuselage and refers to the structural capabilities of struts and panels as *given data*, that is, beyond requirement for further justification. Actually these structural capabilities are not known with absolute precision, and a complete analysis would have to consider their detailed configuration in terms of rivet patterns, welded joints, honeycomb structure, and so on. Upon this recognition, it is easy to see that the structural capabilities assumed by the aircraft designer are truly intervening variables which exist only as fictions at a particular point within the hierarchical structure of the extremely complex system with which he deals. To complete the illustration, the stress engineer involved in the same aircraft design considers this same hierarchical system but at a lower level. His concern is with the stress patterns set up within the material, and all his calculations are based upon another set of intervening variables. These variables are the specified homogeniety of materials, Brinell hardness, and other physical properties. In a similar manner, the metallurgist is concerned with intervening variables at the molecular level.

It is apparent that reference to intervening variables is a useful tool and, in fact, is such a common practice as to have lost the name of "intervening." In the field of psychophysics, intervening variables of stress, fatigue, emotion, learning, motivation, and so on, are introduced as describing primary properties of the human operator. This practice in itself is not to be frowned upon. There is, however, the distinct problem that in the case of psychophysics these variables are not well known. In fact, in many cases they cannot be separately measured, and, in some instances, they are not even clearly defined. The intuitive properties which these "names" possess serves to inhibit rigorous consideration. Although a large number of papers have been written on the subject of stress, it is difficult to find a concensus except in a most general sense. It is more usual to find that the subject is "the effects of stress" or "experimental techniques for introducing stress." Even when quantitatively expressed, the measure is usually severely dependent upon the particular environmental complex under which the psychophysical evidence was collected. Other intervening variables are found to be in similar circumstance.

This brief digression regarding the assumed basic variables is not intended as a criticism of an accepted technique for dealing with the ultracomplex human operator. Rather, it is intended to clarify the nature of the problem and maintain an awareness of the assumptions which are made so as to allow more effective understanding of the literature and its application.

A wide variety of experimental evidence relates to the interaction of sensed modalities as a result of the experienced environment. Usually the effect is detrimental, and a single illustration should be sufficient. H. Jerison accomplished a number of investigations on the effect of acoustic noise upon performance of visual monitoring tasks. His results support prior conclusions based on other types of monitoring tests to the effect that performance involving vigilance suffers under imposed noise or disturbance. Although the accommodation to noise in the usual range can be effective, there remains the higher level of disturbance which consistently degrades performance. Further, it was shown that the effects of noise upon this visual task were to some extent cumulative, leading to interpretation in terms of a "fatigue" factor. Unfortunately this latter intervening variable is intimately related to the prior considered "stress" factor. Both are extracted from the same data.

In general, it may be expected to find that the interaction among sensory channels is tolerable so long as each modality remains within the normal operating range. Performance deteriorates when any one of these non-task variables reaches a subjective intensity level which is normally considered "high." The exact mechanism by which this interference takes place is as yet unknown. However, it is interesting to hypothesize that degradation results when the incoming information rate exceeds the channel capacity of the subject's conscious processing of information. In other words, diversion of attention may be looked upon as reducing the available channel capacity with respect to the intended task. Of course, this hypothesis is not intended to imply any assumption of linearity in the combined sensory data processing.

It has already been amply demonstrated that the total effect of sensed information is not the simple sum of the individual effects. For example, K. Duncker found that severe pain due to heavy pressure on one arm is noticeably reduced when a painful stimulation is applied to the other arm. Further, it has also been shown that pain (induced by pressure) can be decreased when a loud noise is generated near to the subject.

The interaction of sensory channels may serve a directly useful purpose. Recent work of J. Gardner and J. C. R. Licklider has demonstrated the effective use of *Audio Analgesiac* in dentistry. The dental patient is offered sound introduced through earphones, and the volume control is placed within easy reach and left to his command. The sound itself may be either white noise or music to suit the patient's desire. He is instructed that loud sound will overcome pain. Experimental evidence has shown that of the large number of patients who chose to try the Audio Analgesiac, 63 per cent reported it to be "completely effective," 25 per cent found it "less than effective," and only 12 per cent reported that it was "not considered helpful" toward alleviating pain. Further, 136 extractions were carried out using only Audio Analgesiac. Patients reported their awareness of pressure and pull; however, there was no notice of "severe pain." Only in a few cases was there a report of even moderate pain. In fact, in certain instances, the patient requested the re-use of Audio Analgesiac for a second extraction.

To be effective the sound had to be quite intense (unless of course it could be optimally distributed in both spectrum and time). In general, it was apparent to the patient that pain decreases as the sound intensity increases. Usually the patient found it possible to introduce sufficient sound to mask the dental pain, and this at less than the threshold of auditory pain.

A number of factors may be involved in the positive contribution of

Audio Analgesiac. Specifically, the sound in the earphones serves to mask the sound of the drill and, as such, reduces the level of apprehension. The music or noise diverts attention from the dental action and thereby further reduces anxiety. The value of this factor should not be underestimated. This was dramatically illustrated by soldiers who sustained serious injury during combat without even being aware of their wounds. Similarly, football players experience minor injuries without awareness of pain during the play. The patient is given a task (volume control) and is thereby offered an additional physical point of attention. The manipulated sound level can be monitored by the dentist, and forms worthwhile instruction as to the patient's subjective sensation level in terms of both pain and anxiety. Finally, there must not be discounted the possible effect of sound as a placebo. Belief that the sound can be effective may be a major step toward achieving that goal. All of these factors contribute in various degrees toward making this interaction effect of sensory channels worthwhile for a most practical purpose.

8.6. THE BREAK-OFF PHENOMENON

The advent of high performance, high altitude aircraft has given rise to reports of a psychological phenomenon called *break-off*—the feeling that a pilot gets of a distinct separation from the earth. Of a large number of jet pilots interviewed by B. Clark and A. Graybiel, 35 per cent had experienced the break-off effect. They characterize the sensation as a feeling of isolation and detachment, mixed with the variable quality of either enjoyable exhilaration or lonely insecurity (about 38 per cent of those reporting the break-off phenomena reported the unhappy sensation).

Many factors enter into the onset of the break-off phenomenon, these relating not only to altitude itself, but also the contingent effects relating to such flight. For example, at extremely high altitudes the sky turns from light blue toward black, the aircraft is usually on a non-maneuvering type mission, little if any turbulence is experienced, and the aircraft appears "hung in space" since apparent motion is small. The situation is made even more acute when the pilot is alone or, in a multi-place aircraft, is separated from his companions. It is difficult to predict when the break-off phenomenon will take effect, and its importance in operational flight. The break-off effect is of considerable interest, however, in that future advanced flight will impose just such conditions as have been shown to initiate the effect.

In a more formal sense, the break-off phenomenon has been studied in the field of psychophysics under the title of "sensory deprivation." Pioneer work was accomplished by O. B. Hebb (1951 to 1954) wherein students "were paid to lie on a comfortable bed in a lighted cubicle 24 hours a day" with only brief periods of rest for necessities. During the entire experiment, subjects wore transluscent goggles so as to prevent patterned vision. Special gloves were provided to permit joint movements with but limited tactual perception.

All communication with the subject was kept to a bare minimum. Reoccurring vivid visual "hallucinations" were reported after two or three days, accompanied by a sense of depersonalization and change in the body image. The experience of perceptual isolation impaired performance of intelligence tests. After six days

(1) There was fluctuation, drifting and swirling of objects and surfaces in the visual field.
(2) The position of objects appeared to change with head or eye movements.
(3) Shapes, lines, and edges appeared distorted.
(4) After-images were accentuated.
(5) Colors seemed very bright and saturated, and there seemed to be an exaggeration of contrast phenomena.

It was concluded that "normal visual function is dependent upon an optimum range of patterned visual stimulation."

A number of other experiments were carried out in order to extend these findings in different directions. J. C. Lilly attempted to reduce the absolute intensity of physical stimuli to a minimum in the following manner:

The subject is suspended with the body and all but the top of the head immersed in a tank containing slowly flowing water at 34.5° C, wears a blacked-out mask (enclosing the whole head) for breathing, and wears nothing else. The water temperature is such that the subject feels neither hot nor cold. The experience is such that one tactually feels the supports and the mask, but not much else; a large fraction of the usual pressures on the body caused by gravity are lacking. The sound level is low; one hears only one's own breathing and some faint water sounds from the piping . . . After the initial training period, no observer is present. Immediately after exposure, the subject writes personal notes on his experience.

The experience is described as enjoyable and producing "hallucinations" within a few hours.

Of the number of other experiments which were completed, it appeared that restriction of motility was distinctly correlated with the appearance of hallucinations, this being almost independent of whether the individual field was non-patterned or completely eliminated. The hallucinations take on a wide variety of forms including familiar and unfamiliar objects. It is usual to find some imagery occurring during the transition states between sleeping and waking in everyday life. Almost all subjects sleep for a while during sensory deprivation experiments. The subject finds himself in a condition to sleep with a non-conflicting surround and the conditioned reflex of attitude and position. There is, however, the constant tendency toward wakefulness as induced by the experimental circumstance. These two aspects of the situation tend to maintain an "in between state" which may remain prevalent for hours thus permitting an increase of imagery through normal processes. A number of subjects have reported that they could not tell whether they were asleep or awake. The occurrence of hallucinations may be dependent to some extent upon the subject's normal amount of imagery in both dreams and daydreams.

Initial hallucinations are generally simple, and it was reported that these images gradually tend to increase in complexity as the experimental time draws on. In a recent experiment, S. J. Freedman and M. Greenblatt gave each of 30 normal subjects eight-hour experimental sessions involving non-patterned visual and auditory input combined with social isolation, visual deprivation combined with auditory non-patterning and social isolation, and social isolation alone. It was concluded that "significantly more perceptual distortion occurs with diffuse light stimulation than with the black-out visual field." Rationale for the perceptual distortion was based upon the instability experienced under this unusual environment. This instability forces a regressive tendency in which the subject "desires" to perceive familiar real world items. The subject is driven away from abstractions so that the provided straight line appears to be bent, twisted, or in some other way distorted and in this way becomes more concrete, more "real" than the pure straight line abstraction which would otherwise be named.

The process of perception, viewed as a filtering of all incoming real world data, results in exclusion of all information which falls outside of the known set of ordered patterns. If a new sensation cannot be classified with respect to those already provided, then it is quickly dismissed as "noise." According to William James, the "world" of the infant is a "blooming, buzzing confusion" since the infant has not yet learned which of the incoming stimuli are meaningful and which are not. The subjective view of the real world must remain organized if mental stability is to be preserved.

The isolation problem of future space craft may be further confounded by over-patterning of certain monotonous, repetitive sights, sounds, and other stimuli. The occupant may be *required* to hear engine noise for long periods of time. Computer sounds may become surprisingly apparent in an otherwise "still" environment. A series of experiments was performed by D. Wexler, *et al.*, wherein subjects were placed in a respirator and restricted so that the only sound they could hear was the monotonous drone of a motor. It was reported that in time this over-patterning also yielded perceptual distortion. It appears that the cause of psychological stress is the reduced information content of the sensed real world rather than the reduced sensory stimulation. Under severe environmental constraints the human operator must be provided with an information source which will hold his attention and mean something to him.

Although the problem of isolation has recently been brought to the fore by the advent of aero-space vehicles, it is certainly not a new one. Indeed, there is a long history of empirical findings describing survival under shipwreck conditions, arctic environment, and early ocean explorations. In many of these situations the subject experienced extreme confinement and deprivation, not only of information but also of fundamental requirements for life. The imposed stress of a life-or-death situation certainly modifies behavior over what might be achieved under laboratory simulation.

G. T. Hauty recently described experimental results obtained on test subjects exposed to simulated space-travel environment for 30 hours. Each trial allowed a single man to remain in a sealed chamber with voice communication throughout the experiment. As the test progressed, the occupant of the chamber acted so as to deprive himself of the ambient sensory events which made up his normal sensory environment. As time passed, each occupant reported increased severity of hallucinations, including rhythmic color change in both the instrument panel and clothing of the occupant, visual difficulties in reading instruments because of "melting" of the instrument panel, visual distortion of the wall angles combined with a feeling of falling, and others. In one case, the subject fully believed that the hallucination was real in spite of the fact that he had been precautioned that such hallucinations were possible in the experiment.

The property of sensory deprivation and contingent hallucinations also occurs in normal long-duration flights. Unfortunately, however, most such experiences which have been encountered remain unreported, probably because the crews feel that they may be taken off flight status or be subject to ridicule. The pilot of one jet bomber has recently experienced the distinct impression that "people suddenly appeared to be walking across the nose of his aircraft" while he was flying over the Atlantic Ocean in the course of a long-duration air-refueled mission. In another case, the radar operator of another jet bomber has said that he has seen gremlins and other "strange people" on the face of his radarscope during long missions. Such hallucinations are not related only to flight. They are also prevalent among persons having other arduous long-duration tasks such as long-haul trailer truck drivers.

Future travel times may greatly exceed those of the past. The dangers of mental inactivity must be considered as being of equal importance to the providing of physiologically compatible surroundings.

8.7. CONCLUSION

The sensory channels have been the subject of scientific attention for several hundred years. Although a considerable background of behavioristic evidence has accrued, comparatively little is known regarding the fundamental nature of sensory data processing. In the past, the human operator was viewed as a "black box," describable only in terms of the available input-output relations. It was impossible to ascribe any specific portion of the observed behavior to the sensory mechanism since the measured data included the effect of mediation, implementation, and so on. Even with experiments designed to minimize the effect of these modifying processes, it remained impossible to clearly assess the sensory contribution to the total data processing.

The recent advent of electronics has provided measurement techniques which can extract data from within the living organism. The "black box" is becoming "transparent" as additional internal data is monitored and insight is gained.

The limiting factor has now become the tremendous complexity of the nervous system. Only through a comparable complex measuring apparatus would it be possible to record and assimilate sufficient data to describe the fundamental properties of nervous system behavior. Present equipments are of almost ridiculous simplicity when compared to the subject under their attention. Even "brute force" procedure remains too puny to be attractive.

The only sensible recourse is the intelligent use of mathematical models— models which incorporate representations for optimal mechanisms which could account for the observed stages of data transmission and processing. The validity of such models must prove testable through the prediction of the entire range of sensory experience.

There is, of course, no division between sensing and mediation. The neural encoding of received information is, in itself, a decision process. In fact, the decision process appears as a continuous encoding and re-encoding of the stimulus until the recoded form takes on aspects which are externally observable and, as such, are called response. The frog's eye classifies the observed world with respect to the existence of four fundamental properties as discussed in Chapter 3. It is evident that the brain receives only a fragmentary view of the illuminated real world, and yet, this "limitation" may be a valuable property since the information which is accepted is only that which is pertinent to survival and remains within the decision-making channel capacity. It is not unreasonable to search for similar inherent properties in the human sensory system. There remains the possibility that the neural coding may furnish an absolute upper bound on the directly observable "world."

BIBLIOGRAPHY

ATTNEAVE, F., "Psychological Probability as a Function of Experienced Frequency," *Journal of Experimental Psychology*, Vol. 46 (1953), 81–86.

AX, A. F., *et al.*, "Investigations of Human Reactions to Stress," *National Science Foundation Report 1* (July 1945).

AZIMA, H., and F. J. AZIMA, "Studies on Perceptual Isolation," *Diseases of the Nervous System (Monograph Supplement)*, Vol. 18 No. 8 (1957).

BEXTON, W. H., W. HERON, and T. H. SCOTT, "Effects of Decreased Variation in the Sensory Environment," *Canadian Journal of Psychology*, Vol. 8 (1954), 70–76.

BILLS, A. G., "Blocking: A New Principle of Mental Fatigue," *American Journal of Psychology*, Vol. 43 (January 5, 1931), 230–245.

BILLS, A. G., "Some Causal Factors in Mental Blocking," *Journal of Experimental Psychology*, Vol. 18 (1935), 172–185.

BILODEAU, E. A., "Statistical Versus Intuitive Confidence," *American Journal of Psychology*, Vol. 65 (1952), 271–277.

BLAKELY, W., "The Discrimination of Short Empty Temporal Interval," Ph.D. dissertation, University of Illinois, Urbana, Ill., 1933.

BROADBENT, D. E., "Some Effects of Noise on Visual Performance," *Quarterly Journal of Experimental Psychology*, Vol. 6 (1954), 1–5.

BULBAN, E. J., "Vivid Hallucinations Plague Test Subjects" (taken from experiments of G. T. Hauty), *Aviation Week* (February 1, 1960).

CARTERETTE, E. C., and M. COLE, "Comparison of the Receiver-Operating Characteristics for Messages Received by Ear and by Eye," *Journal of the Acoustical Society of America*, Vol. 34 No. 2 (February 1962), 172–178.

CHEATHAM, P. G., and C. T. WHITE, "Temporal Numerosity: I. Perceived Number as a Function of Flash Number and Rate," *Journal of Experimental Psychology*, Vol. 44 (1952), 447–451.

CHEATHAM, P. G., and C. T. WHITE, "Temporal Numerosity: III. Auditory Perception of Number," *Journal of Experimental Psychology*, Vol. 47 (1954), 425–428.

CLARK, B., M. A. NICHOLSON, and A. GRAYBIEL, " 'Fascination': A Cause of Pilot Error," *Journal of Aviation Medicine*, Vol. 24 (1953), 429–440.

COE, L. A., "Some Notes on the Reaction of Aircraft Pilots to Zero Gravity," *Journal of the British Interplanetary Society*, Vol. 13 (1954), 244.

COHEN, J., and M. HANSEL, *Risk and Gambling. The Study of Subjective Probability*. New York: Philosophical Library, 1956.

COHEN, J., and C. E. M. HANSEL, "Subjective Probability, Gambling and Intelligence," *Nature*, Vol. 181 (1958), 1160.

COHEN, J., E. J. DEARNALEY, and C. E. M. HANSEL, "Measures of Subjective Probability. Estimates of Success in Performance in Relation to Size of Task," *British Journal of Psychology*, Vol. 48 (1957), 271–275.

CONRAD, R., "Adaptation to Time in a Sensorimotor Skill," *Journal of Experimental Psychology*, Vol. 49 (1955), 115–121.

COOPER, F. S., A. M. LIBERMAN, and J. M. BORST, "The Inter-conversion of Audible and Visible Patterns as a Basis for Research in the Perception of Speech," *Proceedings of the National Academy of Science*, Vol. 37 (1951), 318–325.

COWEN, E. L., "The Influence of Varying Degrees of Psychological Stress on Problem-Solving Rigidity," *Journal of Abnormal Soc. Psychology*, Vol. 47 (1952), 512–519.

DEMPSEY, C. A., *et al.*, "Long-term Human Confinement in Space Equivalent Vehicles," *Journal of Astronautics*, Vol. 4 (1957), 52–53 and 59.

DUNCKER, K., "Some Preliminary Experiments on the Mutual Influence of Pains," *Psycholo. Forsch.*, Vol. 21 (1937), 311.

DURUP, G., and A. FESSARD, "Le Seuil de Perciptron de Durée dans l'excitation Visuelle," *Année Psych.*, Vol. 31 (1930), 52–62.

EDWARDS, W., "The Reliability of Probability-Preferences," *American Journal of Psychology*, Vol. 67 (1954), 68–95.

————. "Reward Probability, Amount, and Information as Determiners of Sequential Two-Alternative Decisions," *Journal of Experimental Psychology*, Vol. 52 No. 3 (1956), 177–188.

ERLICK, D. E., "Judgments of the Relative Frequency of Sequential Binary Events: Effects of Frequency Differences," *USAF WADC TR 59–580* (October 1959).

FRASER, D. C., "Relationship of an Environmental Variable to Performance in a Prolonged Visual Task," *Quarterly Journal of Experimental Psychology*, Vol. 5 (1953), 31.

FREEDMAN, S. J., and M. GREENBLATT, "Studies in Human Isolation," *USAF WADC TR 59–266* (September 1959).

GARDNER, W. J., and J. C. R. LICKLIDER, "Auditory Analgesia in Dental Operations," *Journal of American Dental Association*, Vol. 59 No. 6 (1959), 1145–1149.

GILBERT, G. M., "Inter-Sensory Facilitation and Inhibition," *Journal of General Psychology*, Vol. 24 (1941), 381–407.

GRIFFIN, D. R., "Bird Navigation," Chapter 6 in *Recent Studies of Avian Biology*, Albert Wolfson, ed. Urbana, Ill.: University of Illinois Press, 1955.

GRIFFITH, R. M., "Odds Adjustments by American Horse-race Bettors," *American Journal of Psychology*, Vol. 62 (1949), 290–294.

GULLIKSEN, H., "The Influence of Occupation Upon the Perception of Time," *Journal of Experimental Psychology*, Vol. 10 (1927), 52–59.

HAKE, H. W., "The Perception of Frequency of Occurrence and the Development of 'Expectancy'," in *Human Experimental Subjects*, H. Quastler, ed., Information Theory in Psychology, Glencoe, Ill.: The Free Press, 1955.

HAKE, H. W., and R. HYMAN, "Perception of the Statistical Structure of a Random Series of Binary Symbols," *Journal of Experimental Psychology*, Vol. 45 (1953), 64–74.

HARDY, J. D., H. G. WOLFF, and H. GOODELL, *Pain Sensations and Reactions*. Baltimore, Md.: Williams & Wilkins Company, 1952.

HARRIS, J. D., "The Roles of Sensation Level and of Sound Pressure in Producing Reversible Auditory Fatigue," *Laryngoscope*, Vol. 64 (1954), 89–97.

HARRIS, J. D., *Some Relations Between Vision and Audition*. Springfield, Ill.: Charles C. Thomas Co., 1950.

HARETY, G. T., "Human Performance in Space Travel Environment," *Air Univ. Quarterly Review*, Vol. X No. 2 (Summer 1958), 89–107.

HERON, W., R. K. DOANE, and T. H. SCOTT, "Visual Disturbances After Prolonged Perceptual Isolation," *Canadian Journal of Psychology*, Vol. 10 (1956), 13–18.

HERON, W., "The Pathology of Boredom," *Scientific American*, Vol. 196 (1957), 52–56.

HOAGLAND, H., *Pacemakers in Relation to Aspects of Behavior*. New York: Macmillan & Co., 1935.

HORNSETH, J. P., and D. A. GRANT, "The Discrimination of Random Series of Stimulus Frequencies as a Function of Their Relative and Absolute Values," *USAF Research Bulletin AFPTRC-TR 54–76* (1954).

JERISON, H. J., "Effect of a Combination of Noise and Fatigue on a Complex Counting Task," *USAF WADC TR 55–360* (December 1955).

———. "Differential Effects of Noise and Fatigue on a Complex Counting Task," *USAF WADC TR 55–359* (October 1955).

JERISON, H. J., and A. K. SMITH, "Effect of Acoustic Noise on Time Judgment," *USAF WADC TR 55–358* (October 1955).

JERISON, H. J., C. W. CRANNELL, and D. POWNALL, "Acoustic Noise and Repeated Time Judgments in a Visual Movement Projection Task," *USAF WADC TR 57–54* (March 1957).

JERISON, H. J., and S. WING, "Effects of Noise and Fatigue on a Complex Vigilance Task," *USAF WADC TR 57–14* (January 1957).

LEVY, E. Z., *et al.*, "Studies in Human Isolation," *Journal of the American Medical Association*, Vol. 169 (January 17 1959), 236–239.

LILLY, J. C., "Mental Effects of Physical Restraint and of Reduction of Ordinary Levels of Physical Stimuli on Intact, Healthy Persons," *Psychiatric Research Reports*, Vol. 5 (1956), 1–9.

LINCOLN, R. S., "Learning and Retaining a Rate of Movement With the Aid of Kinesthetic and Verbal Cues," *Journal of Experimental Psychology*, Vol, 51 (1956), 199–204.

MARCUS, H. W., "The Role of Hypnosis and Suggestion in Dentistry," *Journal of the American Dental Association*, Vol. 59 No. 6 (December 1959), 1149–1154.

MATHEWS, B. V. T., *Bird Navigation*, Cambridge, England: Cambridge University Press, 1955.

MOWBRAY, G. H., and J. W. GEBHARD, "Man's Senses as Information Channels," reprinted from *Report CM-936, Applied Physics Laboratory*, Johns Hopkins University (May 1958), into *Selected Papers on Human Factors in the Design and Use of Control Systems*, H. W. Sinaiko, ed., New York: Dover Publications Inc., 1961.

214 SUMMARY OF THE SENSORY CHANNELS

MOSTELLER, F., and P. NOGEE, "An Experimental Measurement of Utility," *Journal of Political Economy*, Vol. 59 (1951), 371–404.

NOBLE, C. E., "The Perception of the Vertical: 3. The Visual Vertical as a Function of Centrifugal and Gravitational Forces," *Journal of Experimental Psychology*, Vol. 39 (1949), 839–850.

OMWAKE, K. T., and M. LORANZ, "Study of Ability to Wake at a Specified Time," *Journal of Applied Psychology*, Vol. 17 (1933), 468–474.

POULTON, F. C., and S. S. STEVENS, "On the Halving and Doubling of the Loudness of White Noise," *Journal of the Acoustical Society of America*, Vol. 27 (1955), 329–331.

PRESTON, M. G., and P. BARATTA, "An Experimental Study of the Auction Value of an Uncertain Outcome," *American Journal of Psychology*, Vol. 61 (1948), 183–193.

QUASEBARTH, K., "Zeitschatzung und Zeitauffassung optisch und Akustisch Ausgefullter Intervalle," *Arch. ges. Psychol.*, Vol. 49 (1924), 379–432.

ROSENBLITH, W. A., "Auditory Masking and Fatigue," *Journal of the Acoustical Society of America*, Vol. 22 (1950), 792–800.

RYAN, T. A., "Interrelations of Sensory Systems in Perception," *Psychology Bulletin*, Vol. 37 (1940), 659–698.

SCHAEFER, V. G., and A. R. GILLILAND, "The Relation of Time Estimation to Certain Physiological Changes," *Journal of Experimental Psychology*, Vol. 23 (1938), 545–552.

SCHILLER, P. V., "Interrelations of Different Senses in Perception," *British Journal of Psychology*, Vol. 25 (1935), 465–469.

SOLOMON, P., H. LEIDERMAN, J. MENDELSON, and D. WEXLER, "Sensory Deprivation: A Review," *American Journal of Psychiatry*, Vol. 114 (1957), 357–363.

SPROWLS, R. C., "Psychological-Mathematical Probability in Relationships of Lottery Gambles," *American Journal of Psychology*, Vol. 66 (1953), 126–130.

STEVENS, S. S., "Decibels of Light and Sound," *Physics Today*, Vol. 8 (1955), 12–17.

STEVENS, J. C., and S. S. STEVENS, "The Growth of Subjective Magnitude with Stimulus Intensity," *USN ONR Symposium on Physiological Psychology*, 2nd Report ACR-30, Pensacola, Fla. (March 19–21, 1958).

TYLER, D. B., "The Influence of Placebo, Body Position, and Medication On Motion Sickness," *American Journal of Physiology*, Vol. 146 (1946), 458–567.

VAIL, S., "Alternative Calculi of Subjective Probabilities," Chapter VII of *Decision Process* by R. M. Thrall, C. H. Coombs, and R. L. Davis, New York: John Wiley & Sons, Inc., 1954.

VAN VLECK, J. H., and D. MIDDLETON, "A Theoretical Comparison of the Visual, Aural, and Meter Reception of Pulsed Signals in the Presence of Noise," *Journal of Applied Physiology*, Vol. 17 (1946), 940–971.

VERNON, J., and J. HOFFMAN, "Effects of Sensory Deprivation on Learning Rate in Human Beings," *Science*, Vol. 123 (1956), 1074–1075.

VERNON, J., T. E. McGILL, and H. SCHIFFMAN, "Visual Hallucinations During Perceptual Isolation," *Canadian Journal of Psychology*, Vol. 12 (1958), 31–34.

WHITE, C. T., P. G. CHEATHAM, and J. C. ARMINGTON, "Temporal Numerosity: II. Evidence for Central Factors Influencing Perceived Number," *Journal of Experimental Psychology*, Vol. 46 (1953), 283–287.

WHITE, C. T., and P. G. CHEATHAM, "Temporal Numerosity: IV. A Comparison of the Major Senses," *Journal of Experimental Psychology*, Vol. 58 (1959), 441–444.

WEXLER, D., J. MENDELSON, H. LEIDERMAN, and P. SOLOMON, "Sensory Deprivation," *Arch. Neurology and Psychiatry*, Vol. 79 (1958), 225–233.

WHITE, B. L., and R. M. HELD, "Quantification and Analysis of the Changes in Velocity Perception Following Sensory Deprivation," paper presented to Eastern Psychological Association, April 1959.

WITKIN, H. A., S. WAPNEW, and T. LEVENTHAL, "Sound Localization with Conflicting Visual and Auditory Cues," *Journal of Experimental Psychology*, Vol. 43 (1952), 58–67.

SECTION

C

DECISION-MAKING

In order that the human operator perform in a purposeful manner, he must both receive and process information in such a way that he can effect control of the presented real world situation. Section B has considered the human reception and perception of information. This section proceeds with consideration of the human transduction of information and is specifically concerned with the transformation of sensed information into directives intended to modify the environment. Such transformation may be termed decision-making and includes cognition, memory, apperception, and mediation as the particular situation demands. It is left for Section D to consider separately aspects of the implementation of the results of decision-making onto the surround.

Specifically Chapter 9 is devoted to human tracking. This subject has had a great deal of attention over the years, and yet it is seldom viewed as a particularly simple case of the general human decision-making capability; that is, the application of a short time invariant error criterion intended to minimize some function of the perceived error.

Chapter 10 proceeds to the more general problem of decision-making by automata. An absolute measure for intelligence is described to allow comparison of both animate and inanimate decision-makers as they perform various assignments. Modes of decision logic are indicated in order to distinguish individual characteristics and limitations. With such an overview of decision-making in its widest regard, it is possible to study decision-making as accomplished by the human operator, reference Chapter 11. Some of the features of the human nervous system are described in order to maintain a mechanistic frame of reference for the empirical evidence which is presented. Some theories of learning are indicated together with commentary on their applicability. Both the individual human operator and groups or teams are considered in their ability to accomplish particular types of decision.

Although it is recognized that the acceptance, manipulation, and transmittal of information by a human operator can never be partitioned into truly independent categories, such separate discussion here is considered to be justified in that wherever possible, limiting constraints identifiable with the input and output channels will have been removed. It is felt that only this manner of treatment can best serve the purpose of analysis and improved understanding.

BIBLIOGRAPHY

ALLPORT F. H., *Theories of Perception and the Concept of Structure*. New York: John Wiley & Sons, Inc., 1955.

ASHBY, W. R., *Design for a Brain*. New York: John Wiley & Sons, Inc., 1954.

BLACK, J. W., and W. E. MOORE, *Speech: Code, Meaning and Communication*. New York: McGraw-Hill Book Company, Inc., 1955.

BRILLOUIN, L., *Science and Information Theory*. New York: Academic Press, 1956.

BRUNER, J. S., J. J. GOODNOW, and G. A. AUSTIN, *A Study of Thinking*. New York: John Wiley & Sons, Inc., 1958.

CHERRY, C., *On Human Communication*. New York: John Wiley & Sons, Inc., 1957.

DELATIL, P., *Thinking by Machine*. Boston: Houghton Mifflin Company, 1957.

HARLOW, H. F., and C. N. WOLLSEY, *Biological and Biochemical Bases of Behavior*. Madison: University of Wisconsin Press, 1958.

LYMAN, J., and L. J. FOGEL, *Handbook of Automation, Computation and Control*. Chapter 1 of Volume 3, E. M. Grabbe, S. Ramo, and D. E. Wooldridge, eds., New York: John Wiley & Sons, Inc., 1961.

MILLER, G. A., *Language and Communication*. New York: McGraw-Hill Book Company, Inc., 1951.

SIMON, H. A., *Models of Man; Social and Rational*. New York: John Wiley & Sons, Inc., 1957.

VON NEUMANN, J., *The Computer and the Brain*. New Haven: Yale University Press, 1958.

WIENER, N., *Cybernetics*. New York: John Wiley & Sons, Inc., 1948.

9

MANUAL TRACKING DECISIONS

9.1. INTRODUCTION

Equipment designers have traditionally called upon man to act as part of control systems. They recognized the value of having a human link long before it became possible to describe systems in mathematical terms, a link which could be asked to furnish that particular information transduction needed to overcome unexpected environmental situations and compensate for deficiencies of the equipment system. All this could be accomplished even without explicit knowledge of the nature of the encountered difficulty.

The human operator was provided with some gross instruction as to the goal which the system was intended to fulfill. He was given access to some data relevant to system operation and its present status. With this armament, he was left to muster whatever additional resources were necessary to accomplish the goal through manipulation of a provided set of controls. In part, the human operator was compensated for his efforts by personal satisfaction, prestige, and the sense of power which often accompanies manual control of large or complex physical systems.

Calling upon the human operator generally proved to be good design practice. It was certainly impossible to find any man-made transducer of such unique capability, available in more than adequate supply, and at relatively low cost, which could accomplish a task far too complex even to permit detailed specification.

Today's designers are in somewhat better circumstance. There is a growing awareness of this distinct value as well as the limitations of the human operator. As a result, he may be more sensibly employed with resulting improvement in system performance, and this at lower cost in terms of fatigue and personal jeopardy. Human transduction can be facilitated through proper display-control and immediate environment design, calling upon the human to transduce information only within his natural span of time, channel capacity, and so on. The advent of costly and increasingly complex equipments has focused attention upon the need for detailed knowledge of the human transfer characteristics within normal operating range so as to reduce the great expense and time delays attendant upon modification or redesign of hardware during the development process. Optimal systems synthesis is desired requiring only minimal experimental verification.

Manual tracking decisions remain the same regardless of whether the equipment system under control is a chemical plant, a machine tool, a vehicle,[1] or just the human operator's own body. Information is transduced so as to guide a physical system through a predefined course of action or sequence of states, this being accomplished through a series of decisions similar in that each is intended to minimize or otherwise constrain some function of the perceived error.

The unique ability which makes the human operator particularly suited to control operation is that he can program and reprogram his "computation" while the process is in progress. This programming is the consequence of a hierarchy of decisions which consider the display-control characteristics, as seen within the context of the vehicle, this being viewed as part of an environment which is in turn taken as but one facet of a system within which a goal is to be reached.

It might be possible to establish some convention which would distinguish those lower level decisions which are to be identified with manual tracking; however, such arbitrary cleavage can only serve to obscure the intimate relation of decisions made at various levels. Rather than impose any artificial boundary, the following discussion will examine the tracking decision with increasing scope. Models will be offered which describe single-valued deterministic linear time-invariant decision behavior. These will be generalized so as to introduce some of the many additional features which are characteristic of human behavior. As models become better representations, they also become less tractible and suffer from a lack of quantitative empirical descriptors.

In a very real sense all decisions may be viewed as tracking through a context of available alternatives under the guidance of a metric which is an expression of a set of criteria which support a goal. Consideration of decision-making within this larger frame of reference is left for succeeding chapters.

Any transduction process can be fully described if the probability density function over all possible outputs is specified for each of the possible inputs

---

[1] In the following discussion the term "vehicle" is used to represent any physical system or plant.

(signal and noise). Even if such a general conditional probability matrix were available for the description of a particular process, it would not uniquely identify the *physical* nature of the transductive device. Certainly it is possible to use the input-output probability description to determine an "equivalent circuit," but it must be remembered that such a "circuit" is only one of an extremely large, if not infinite, number of other "circuits" which are also characterized by the same input-output relations. Mathematical models for the human operator must *not* be taken to imply any particular physical, physiological, or psychological functioning. There must be no intent to reify these representations in spite of the temptation to discuss the models in anthropomorphic terms.

If the human operator is said to accomplish an integration, it is certainly not intended to infer that he is performing a truly mathematical integration. He may be using his memory and performing a selection process which might appear as integration to an outside observer. The fact that some human transfer characteristics may correspond, even in a rough way, to certain mathematical operators is indeed fortunate in that it facilitates description and symbolic manipulation.

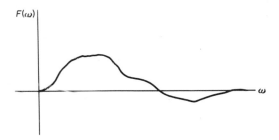

Figure 9.1. Typical human amplitude-frequency transfer characteristic.

It is often said that a system is designed to be most efficient if the human operator is called upon to function in the simplest possible manner. As stated, this is certainly true; however, it is *usual* to find this premise *misinterpreted.* Multiplication is a simpler mathematical operation than differentiation or integration; therefore, it is assumed that that system design which requires only human amplification of the displayed signal into the control signal is superior to one which requires, say, human differentiation. If all human transduction occurred at the conscious level, this might prove true, however, tracking decisions are primarily a result of conditioned reflex.

The experience of system control induces a recall and estimation of the "proper" response to an observed stimulus. The transfer characteristic of such an operation may be viewed as an amplitude function of frequency, $F(\omega)$. In general, this function may be highly irregular, as is illustrated in Figure 9.1. Given different vehicles he will learn to perform with different

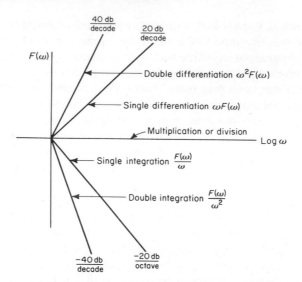

Figure 9.2. Mathematical transfer characteristics.

amplitude-frequency characteristics. Except for extreme circumstances, he may expect to find control of various well-behaved vehicles to be almost equally stressful with respect to the mental aspects of tracking operation, in spite of the fact that the required amplitude-frequency human transfer characteristics may be quite different.

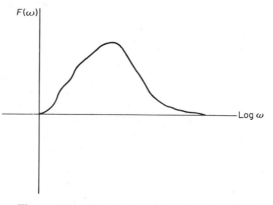

Figure 9.3. Human transfer approximating differentiation.

It would be most unusual to find the human transfer characteristic to be linear, even over a relatively narrow frequency band. Mathematical operations of multiplication, division, differentiation, and integration are perfect linear functions over all frequencies, as shown in Figure 9.2. As such, these are physically unrealizable by human transduction. It would certainly be unrealistic to require that a man act so as to approximate such theoretical functions. If the vehicle control system design induces human display-control differentiation, then the human transfer characteristic may appear as shown in Figure 9.3. The inertial properties of the body limit the human to low frequency response. In summary, there is no reason to believe that it is better to use the human operator to accomplish the function of simple amplification. In fact, if such a system design could be achieved, *there would be no justification for not dispensing with the human operator, replacing him with an amplifier.*

9.2. DETERMINISTIC MODELS OF LINEAR[2] TRANSDUCTION

If the statistical variability of the real world were removed, any transductive process could be exactly specified by stating the relationship between all output signals and their corresponding input signals. It is sometimes possible to find an expression for some significant properties of all inputs and another expression for similar properties of all outputs within the domain of interest. This would be in terms of a single set of algebraic variables common to input and output. In such a case, the transductive process may be described by the ratio of the output to input expressions. For example, mass is defined by the ratio of the acceleration of a body (the output as a function of time) resulting from any applied force to that body (the input as a function of time). Similarly, in the degenerate case, the transduction of a noiseless perfect amplifier is that constant which results from taking the ratio of the output to the input functions of time.

This descriptive ratio need not be confined to the time domain. It may, for instance, prove desirable to express the input and output signals in terms of their spectral properties. This is especially worthwhile when dealing with linear transduction wherein the output signal spectrum is the sum of the spectral components of the individual outputs which would correspond to each of the various frequency components of the input signal.

Repetitive time domain signals of period, T, may be translated into the corresponding spectra by means of the Fourier Series expansion:

$$f(t) = \frac{a_0}{2} + \sum_{n=1}^{\infty} (a_n \cos n\omega t + b_n \sin n\omega t)$$

where

$$a_n = \frac{2}{T} \int_0^T f(t) \cos n\omega t \, dt$$

$$b_n = \frac{2}{T} \int_0^T f(t) \sin n\omega t \, dt$$

---

[2] To be linear, a transducer must satisfy two properties; *homogeneity*—multiplying the input by a constant multiplies the output by the same constant, and *additivity*—the output corresponding to the sum of two inputs is the sum of the outputs corresponding to the separate inputs.

and

$$\omega = \frac{2\pi}{T}$$

Signals which are nonrepetitive require the Fourier Integral,

$$F(\omega) = \frac{1}{\sqrt{2\pi}} \int_{-\infty}^{\infty} f(t)e^{-i\omega t}\, dt$$

the inversion being accomplished by

$$f(t) = \frac{1}{\sqrt{2\pi}} \int_{-\infty}^{\infty} F(\omega)e^{+i\omega t}\, d\omega$$

This generalized form yields a continuous spectrum of sinusoidal components which could be summed to synthesize the original time domain waveform.

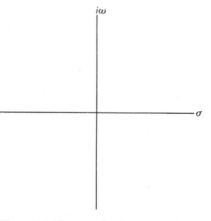

Figure 9.4. The complex frequency plane.

It is often of interest to consider signals which are nonrepetitive and do not asymptotically approach zero amplitude as time approaches infinity. In such a case the Fourier Integral may not be expected to converge to a finite value. This difficulty may be overcome by calling upon the Laplace Transform which is based on the complex frequency, $s = \sigma + i\omega$, where σ is real, being descriptive of the attenuation of the sinusoidal component of radian frequency $\omega(\omega = 2\pi f)$. The imaginary number, i, facilitates graphical representation of signals on Cartesian coordinates as shown in Figure 9.4. Any point on the s-plane describes a complex frequency, that is, an exponentially damped sinusoid in the time domain. Undamped sinusoids (constant amplitude) appear as points on the ordinate, convergent sinusoids appear as points in the right-half plane, while points in the left-half plane indicate exponentially divergent sinusoids.

The Laplace Integral is explicitly stated as,

$$F(s) = \int_0^\infty f(t)e^{-st}\, dt$$

The inverse operation can be accomplished by carrying out the contour integration over a closed path which, for ease of calculation, is the Bromwich path[3] to yield

$$f(t) = \frac{1}{2\pi i} \int_{c-i\infty}^{c+i\infty} F(s)e^{st}\, ds$$

for all t greater than zero, c being an arbitrarily small positive constant. Taken together, these expressions are called the Laplace Transform. Note that application is limited to signals which increase at most at a linear exponential rate over all positive time. Extensive tables of Laplace Transform pairs have been published. Table 9.1 offers a brief indication of their nature.

Table 9.1. SOME USEFUL LAPLACE TRANSFORM PAIRS

Time Domain, $f(t)$	Complex Frequency Domain, $F(s)$
1	$\dfrac{1}{s}$
$\dfrac{t}{\tau}$	$\dfrac{1}{s^2\tau}$
$\dfrac{t^n}{n!}$	$\dfrac{1}{s^{n+1}}$
e^{-at}	$\dfrac{1}{s+a}$
$1-e^{-at}$	$\dfrac{a}{s(s+a)}$
$\sin \omega t$	$\dfrac{\omega}{s^2+\omega^2}$
$\cos \omega t$	$\dfrac{s}{s^2+\omega^2}$

The output signal from a transducer is the result of a convolution of the input signal and the transfer function. That is to say, if $g(t)$ is the response of a transducer, and this transducer is described by an impulse response[4] of $h(t)$ then the input $f(t)$ will yield

$$g(t) = \int_0^t h(u)f(t-u)\, du$$

[3] The Bromwich path is closed over the left-half plane.
[4] The response of the transducer to a single impulse stimulus.

where u is the dummy variable of integration. Here the Laplace Transform finds its greatest value, since convolution in the time domain reduces to simple multiplication in the complex frequency domain, thus

$$G(s) = H(s)F(s)$$

where these functions are the individual Laplace Transforms of the respective time domain functions.

To illustrate, let the transducer in question be accomplishing pure differentiation, that is taking d/dt of the input, $f(t)$. Recalling that integration can be accomplished by parts according to

$$\int u\,dv = uv - \int v\,du$$

the Laplace Integral may be written letting $u = f(t)$ and $dv = e^{-st}\,dt$. Then

$$\int_0^\infty f(t)e^{-st}\,dt = -\frac{1}{s}f(t)e^{-st}\Big|_0^\infty + \frac{1}{s}\int_0^\infty \left(\frac{d}{dt}f(t)\right)e^{-st}\,dt$$

$$= \frac{f(0^+)}{s} + \frac{1}{s}\int_0^\infty \left(\frac{d}{dt}f(t)\right)e^{-st}\,dt$$

The presence of 0^+ indicates the initial condition. Rearranging terms yields,

$$\int_0^\infty \left[\frac{d}{dt}f(t)\right]e^{-st}\,dt = sF(s) - f(0^+)$$

thus, under zero initial conditions, the accomplishment of a time differentiation is equivalent to the multiplication of the complex spectrum of the input signal by s. In a similar manner, the Laplace Transform pairs for other operators can be derived. Table 9.2 furnishes a few of these to indicate their nature.

Taking the Laplace Transform term by term converts a differential equation into a simple algebraic equation. Rather than write transfer functions in the time domain, it is often preferable to express them directly in the complex frequency domain. For example, a closed circuit of resistance, R, inductance, L, can be described by the differential equation

$$\frac{di(t)}{dt} + Ri(t) = v(t)$$

where, in the conventional manner, $i(t)$ is the current time function and $v(t)$ is the voltage time function. Taking the Laplace Transform of the equation yields

$$LsI(s) + RI(s) = V(s)$$

or, in terms of the transfer function,

$$\frac{V(s)}{I(s)} = R + Ls$$

Table 9.2. SOME LAPLACE TRANSFORM PAIRS FOR OPERATIONS

Operation	Time Domain	Complex Frequency Domain
linear	$\begin{bmatrix} af(t) \\ f_1(t) \pm f_2(t) \end{bmatrix}$	$aF(s)$ $F_1(s) \pm F_2(s)$
differentiation	$\dfrac{d}{dt} f(t)$	$sF(s) - f(0^+)$
integration	$\displaystyle\int f(t)\,dt$	$\dfrac{F(s)}{s} + \dfrac{f^{-1}(0^+)}{s}$
scale change	$f\left(\dfrac{t}{a}\right)$	$aF(as)$
translation	$f(t-a)$ if $f(t-a) = 0, \quad 0 < t < a$ $f(t+a)$ if $f(t+a) = 0, \quad -a < t < 0$	$e^{-as}F(s)$ $e^{as}F(s)$
convolution	$\displaystyle\int_0^t f_1(t-\tau)f_2(\tau)\,d\tau$	$F_1(s)F_2(s)$

This furnishes a compact representation which, with a little practice, can be written by inspection for most simple networks. The same holds true for the analyses of mechanical systems, pneumatic systems, accoustic systems, and so on, as long as strict analogical correspondence is maintained.

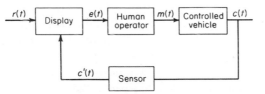

Figure 9.5. A simple control system.

Early attempts toward achieving a useful mathematical representation of the human transfer characteristics proceeded under the assumption that the operator's behavior was time-invariant and linear with respect to a single input-signal stimulus. Under such rather severe (and unrealistic) constraint, there was hope of finding some expression which might prove to be useful in the design of control systems.

Figure 9.5 establishes the notation which will be used in describing a simple control system. $r(t)$ is the reference signal provided to the system, $c(t)$ is the controlled variable which describes the actual performance of the system, $c'(t)$ is the sensed controlled variable (which may include the noise and distortion contributed by the sensor), $e(t)$ is the error signal computed and presented by the display, and $m(t)$ is the manipulated variable which describes the operator's time response. Each of these variables is written in upper case when they are expressed in the complex frequency domain. The human operator transfer function is called $G_p(s)$, the vehicle transfer function is $G_v(s)$, while the sensor in the feedback link is described in the conventional manner as $H(s)$.

Variable gain and response delay are the most obvious human control characteristics. As a first approximation (in the complex frequency domain),

$$G_p(s) = Ke^{-\tau s}$$

where τ is the time lag between the display of the signal and the initial response, and K is the ratio of the output position signal to the input position signal. This gain, K, is dependent upon many factors, including, the controlled vehicle transfer function, the absolute range of display and control displacement, the nature and amount of noise imposed on the system, the physical and emotional status of the man in control, and the nature of the task at hand as seen in terms of a criterion to be measured. In this last regard, the importance weighting of positive and negative errors will probably be the same unless some additional information is provided relative to the "meaning" of the controlled variable. For example, the importance weighting of a negative error is found to be much greater than the same positive error in aircraft altitude during final approach to the runway. In general, the human operator may be expected to behave as if he were minimizing the mean square error of the operator's input signal, so long as the required gain remains well within the range of system stability.

The reaction time, τ, may range from 0.2 to 0.5 seconds for average simple unpredictable signals. Note that this reaction time is strongly dependent upon the nature of the displayed signal. The presentation of a time-patterned and, therefore, more predictable signal is readily recognized by the observer. Upon realization of its regularity (in almost any regard) he may be expected to institute a new tracking procedure wherein that portion of the signal which is predictable will be self-generated in synchronism with the displayed signal. In the case of a perfectly predictable signal, such as a sine wave, a square wave, a series of triangular pulses, and so forth, the human becomes a precognitive signal generator and thus nullifies the time lag. He modifies his behavior from active tracking to what is usually called "monitoring" and thus reduces his work load while accomplishing superior system control.

Completely predictable displayed signals are not commonly found outside the laboratory; however, particular waveshape characteristics may be indigenous to certain vehicle types or system configurations. The human operator may be expected to reflect these in subpatterns of response behavior thus minimizing the amount of new information contained in the displayed signal thereby yielding improved tracking performance with increase of specific experience.

Completely unpredictable displayed signals are generally accompanied by reaction times in excess of 0.5 seconds, this excess being a measure of the interpretability of the display. If n is the number of equiprobable distinguishably different signals which may occur, then, according to W. E. Hick, the average reaction time is approximately $0.27 \ln (n+1)$. Taking a somewhat different point of view, monitoring may be viewed as tracking but with considerably reduced stringency of the error-criteria-function. An output response is only elicited by gross displayed error. These may be expected to occur much less frequently.

The reaction time is a direct function of the minimum quantity of information which must be extracted from the signal in order to identify it. Simple reaction time, where only one stimulus is awaited, averages about 0.2 seconds while in the two-choice situation ($n = 2$) the reaction time is about 0.3 seconds. The usual tracking delay is of the same order, leading Hick to suggest that

> For most of the time, the tracker uses only magnitude of corrective movement, merely choosing whether to employ it and if so in what direction. This is probably an exaggeration, though something approaching it may well be true, since it can be shown that in tracking large errors in the corrective movements would be tolerable if they led to a reduction in time lag.

In 1947, A. Tustin suggested that the human operator also considers the derivative and integral of the presented time dependent data yielding a transfer function of the form

$$G_p(s) = e^{-\tau s}\left[As + B + \frac{C}{s}\right]$$

where the constants A, B, and C indicate separate gains on each derivate. This concept was expanded upon and received a series of careful experimental examinations over the succeeding years. It became possible to identify separately terms of the transfer function which correspond to the physical limitations of human operation. In particular

$$G_p(s) = \frac{Ke^{-\tau s}(T_L s + 1)}{(T_N s + 1)(T_I s + 1)}$$

introduces the neuromuscular time lag, T_N, which is normally between 0.1 and 0.16 seconds; the lead time constant, T_L, usually falling in the range between 0.25 and 2.5 seconds, although these are certainly not limiting values, and the lag time constant, T_I, with observed values between 5 and 20 seconds.

The factor $(T_L s + 1)/(T_I s + 1)$ represents the equalization accomplished by the human operator in order to adjust for characteristics of the input stimulus signal and the controlled vehicle. The linear factor in the numerator, the "lead" term, provides a 6 db per octave rise in the gain characteristic from the breakpoint at a frequency of $1/T_L$. Effectively the operator is placing added importance upon higher frequency components in order to extract anticipatory information. The linear term in the denominator, the "lag" term, provides an integrative smoothing of the input signal so as to fit the displayed signal better to the frequency response capabilities of the controlled vehicle. The more this lag term approaches a pure integration of $1/s$, the greater the relative importance the pilot is attributing to the "drift components" of the displayed signal. A single low frequency lag term has been found in experiments using visual displays in non-moving mockups only when all of the following conditions apply:

(1) When the introduction of a low frequency first order lag would improve the low frequency system response,

(2) When the low frequency system response is important because of the low band width of the input signal,

(3) When the controlled element characteristics are such that the introduction of the low frequency lag will not result in higher frequency destabilizing effects incapable of being overcome by a single first order lead.

For brevity of notation, it is useful to indicate the equalization factor as $\dfrac{\alpha T_I s + 1}{T_I s + 1}$ where α is the ratio of T_L to T_I. Equalization wherein $\alpha > 1$ is called lead-lag while in the case where $\alpha < 1$ the term lag-lead is used.

9.3. DETERMINISTIC MODELS OF NONLINEAR TRANSDUCTION

The human operator does not always attempt to completely eliminate the perceived tracking-error. At times he may feel that the amount of effort required on his part is at greater cost than the value which would be gained through the improved system performance. On the other hand, he may observe that the present error is most probably the direct result of a cyclic disturbance on the system which, if allowed to complete its activity, would leave the primary vehicle trajectory essentially undisturbed. At times the particular observed error may appear to be the result of high frequency noise imposed upon the system. Corrective control action for such high frequency components of the displayed signal may well be considered to be fruitless in view of the low frequency band-pass of the control system, to say nothing of the even lower upper-frequency cutoff usually characteristic of massive vehicles.

In addition to these various logical reasons for the passive acceptance of some error there remain other possibilities. For many reasons the operator may not hold a level of aspiration toward superior system performance over that already being achieved. The nature of the training and/or specific instruction prior to the tracking task may have a significant bearing upon this factor. He may be fatigued, bored, or under the influence of drugs. In any case, the man at the controls just may not care.

These conditions may appear singly or in groups, but whenever they do there exists an indifference threshold, that is, some range around zero error within which perceived error will not elicit an associated control response. Even in the limit of an "all-out" effort the indifference threshold exists. In such a case it may converge to the limit of visual acuity.

The indifference threshold can be included as a term in the transfer function which characterizes the human tracking behavior. Figure 9.6 shows the indifference threshold transfer characteristic. The output control function, $f(x)$, is dependent upon the input error signal, x, for $x > a_T$ and $x < -a_T$ while $f(x) = 0$ over the range $-a_T < x < a_T$.

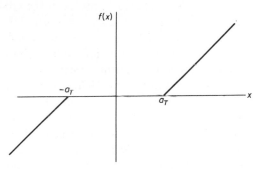

Figure 9.6. The indifference threshold transfer characteristic.

For a particular class of input signals (both the input and output being assumed stationary processes), this non-linear transduction can be described in terms of a linearized component, called the *describing function*, and some usually less significant "remnant" term. The input error signal may appear random to the tracker and yet it is describable in terms of some of its statistical parameters. These, together with the fixed transduction characteristic, furnish the required information to determine the equivalent pure gain, K from

$$K = \frac{\int_{-\infty}^{\infty} x f(x) p(x)\, dx}{\int_{-\infty}^{\infty} x^2 p(x)\, dx}$$

The integral in the numerator may be expressed as the sum of separate integrals covering each of the ranges $-\infty < x < -a_T$, $-a_T < x < a_T$, and $a < x < \infty$, while the integral in the denominator may be recognized as the second moment of the probability density function. In general, the equivalent gain is then a function of both the indifference threshold and the variance (or standard deviation) of the input signal, that is,

$$K\left[\frac{a_T}{\sigma_T}\right]$$

The transfer function for the human operator may then be written as

$$G_p(s) = \frac{Ke^{-\tau s}(T_L s+1)}{(T_N s+1)(T_I s+1)} K\left[\frac{a_T}{\sigma_T}\right]$$

Use of the describing function is but one of a number of techniques which have been developed for the analysis of systems which contain nonlinear elements. It is a natural outgrowth of the frequency response analysis of Nyquist and has proven to be particularly useful in the study of systems of any order. If a linear system is stimulated with a sinusoidal forcing function, the output will also be sinusoidal having some amplitude ratio and phase relation to the input, both being a function of the sinusoidal frequency. Neither of these parameters, the amplitude ratio nor the phase shift, are dependent upon the input amplitude or its time of origin, so that it becomes possible to utilize these parameters to fully describe the linear system in terms of its transfer function. If, however, the same sinusoidal signal were applied to a nonlinear system, the output would not, in general, be sinusoidal. The output can be expanded in a Fourier Series to show its various spectral components. It then becomes possible to use the ratio of the output to the input to define a function which is dependent upon the input amplitude and frequency. This ratio defines the describing function, where conventionally only the first harmonic component of the output is considered for a sinusoidal input. Note that this technique represents a system only for a particular class of inputs. In servoanalysis, these are usually taken to be the sinusoids.

The describing function can be used to examine closed loop system stability. In a simple closed loop system, where the describing function, $N(R_0, \omega)$, and the controlled linear element, $G(\omega)$, are in series the closed loop transfer function is of the form

$$\frac{C}{R}(R_0, \omega) = \frac{N(R_0, \omega)G(\omega)}{1 + N(R_0, \omega)G(\omega)}$$

The poles of the closed loop function occur at points where the denominator goes to zero, that is, where

$$-N(R_0, \omega) = [G(\omega)]^{-1}$$

It is useful to plot $-N(R_0, \omega)$ and $[G(\omega)]^{-1}$ in the complex plane. A point of intersection of these curves (for a prescribed R_0) indicates a point of possible instability. The $[G(\omega)]^{-1}$ function can be looked upon as the locus of a critical point similar to the critical point $-1+j0$ in the Nyquist diagram analysis of linear closed loop systems. The validity of this technique depends upon the degree to which the higher harmonics which are generated by the nonlinearity serve to influence system behavior through their closed loop effect.

Empirical evidence has been gathered in efforts to determine human transfer functions for various types of vehicle characteristics; however, space does not permit adequate description of these experiments. This field has been well summarized by D. McRuer, E. Krendel, and J. Senders who state:

The describing function approach allows the substitution of a linear component and a remnant term for the human operator. The nature of the linear element and of the remnant will vary as a function of the input signal used and the nature of the controlled element dynamics. Tables 9.3, 9.4 and 9.5 show the wide variety of results obtained by different investigators under different experimental conditions. These tables may also provide some insight into the nature of the variation of describing functions for various controlled elements and various inputs.

There are many factors which limit the generality of the describing functions obtained experimentally and listed in the tables. Among these are the following:

(1) The magnitude of the remnant term is large in almost all cases except for the simplest controlled elements and inputs. It may indeed be larger than the linear portion of the describing function. The remnant must be treated as a noise generated by the man as an input to the controlled system. It must, however, be remembered that this "noise" is a result of the method of analysis rather than of the observation of behaviour. The attempt to linearize behaviour gives rise to a large noise component. With more sophisticated techniques of analysis, the noise or uncorrelated part of the behaviour would be reduced in magnitude.

(2) Most of the data on which the conclusions tabulated are based are themselves the result of experimentation on a very few subjects (and for short periods of time). No population data are available, or data about fatigue and learning.

(3) Most of the data apply only to specific aircraft dynamics, rather than to a sample of controlled elements selected for the purpose of exploring the nature of the man's adaptation to different controlled elements.

(4) Most of the data were obtained in experiments in which the subject operated only one channel at a time, or in some cases, two. In most operational situations, the human operator is confronted with many indicators and many controls. He must distribute his attention among all of these rather than concentrate on one. It might be expected that the describing function appropriate to such a sampling system would be different from those found even if the major inputs and controlled elements were the same in the two cases.

(5) In addition to such deficiencies with regard to sampling, there exists also the likelihood of interference and "coupling" among the many channels which a man might be called upon to operate.

In spite of these deficiencies, the describing functions for human operators have considerable utility, both in establishing boundaries for the controlled elements which men are to use, and in estimating the effects of different inputs on behaviour and performance.

Type of Forcing Function	General Control Task	Controlled Element Transfer Function Y_c (gain not shown)	"Best Fit" Human Operator Transfer Function	Frequency Range of Human Operator Measurements	Average Linear Correlation	Investigators and Remarks
① Step functions	Simple following with pencil, stick, or wheel	1	Closed loop transfer function $$\frac{e^{-\tau s}}{\frac{T^2 s^3}{K} + \frac{2\zeta T s^2}{K} + \frac{s}{K} + 1} \doteq \frac{e^{-\tau s}}{T_N s + 1}$$ $\zeta \doteq 0.5$ $K \doteq 6.8 - 7.8\ \mathrm{sec^{-1}}$ $\tau \doteq 0.25\ \mathrm{sec}$ $T \doteq 0.042\ \mathrm{sec}$ $T_N \doteq 1/K$			Goodyear Aircraft Co. (results quoted) Also: L.V. Searle and F.V. Taylor D.C. Cheatham R. Moyne D.G. Ellson and H. Hill
② Sine waves and square waves	Simple following with pencil or wheel	1	"Nonsynchronous" response, closed loop $$\frac{1}{\frac{-2s^3}{K} + \frac{2\zeta Ts}{K} + \frac{s}{K} + 1}$$ with constants as above "Synchronous" response, closed loop $K(\omega)$			Goodyear (R. Moyne) D.G. Ellson and F. Gray D.C. Cheatham
③ Sequence of steps	Simple following with pencil, stick, or wheel	1	Same as for single steps Though τ can approach 0.20 sec as steps get closer together and appear more random			Goodyear (R. Moyne) Small range effect; F.V. Taylor D.G. Ellson and Wheeler C.W. Slack
④ Random appearing white noise through 3rd order binomial filter giving available corner frequencies of 1, 2, and 4 rad/sec	Simple tracker with spring restrained aircraft control stick in aircraft cockpit mockup	1	$$\frac{Ke^{-\tau s}(T_1 s + 1)}{(T_2 s + 1)(T_N s + 1)}$$ Corner freq. / $\frac{1}{T_1}$ / $\frac{1}{T_2}$ / τ / K / α : 1 : 0.04, 1.5, 0.5, 0.15, 100, 0.08 2 : 0.11, 4.55, 2.0, 0.20, 40, 0.055 4 : 0.2, 11.0, 3.0, 0.25, 1.5, 0.067	0.4 to 4.0 rad/sec	0.7 to 0.8	E.S. Krendel and G.H. Barnes These data taken from "aileron" traces; "elevator" was being controlled simultaneously
⑤ Random appearing superposition of 4 sinusoids	Simple tracker handwheel type control with no restraints	1	$$\frac{Ke^{-\tau s}(T_1 s + 1)}{(T_2 s + 1)(T_N s + 1)}$$ $\tau = 0.3$; T_N effect included in τ Forcing function / $\frac{1}{T_1}$ / $\frac{1}{T_2}$ / α / K : Low speed : 0.103, 13.5, 0.0096, 52.5 Medium speed : 0.37, 5.0, 0.074, 11.0 High speed : 0.62, 3.7, 0.167, 2.0	Same frequencies as shown in forcing function		0.9	L. Russell

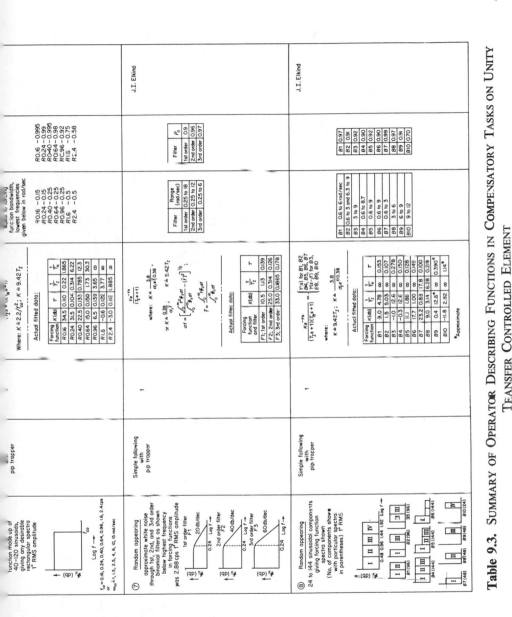

Table 9.3. Summary of Operator Describing Functions in Compensatory Tasks on Unity Transfer Controlled Element

Type of Forcing Function	General Control Task	Controlled Element Transfer Function (gain not shown)	"Best Fit" Human Operator Transfer Function	Frequency Range of Human Operator Measurements	Average Linear Correlation	Investigators and Remarks
⑨ Random appearing superposition of 4 sinusoids ($\Phi_{ii}(\omega)$ vs Log ω; 0.66 1.68 2.87 4.27)	Handwheel type control with no restraints	$\dfrac{1}{(s+1)}$; $\dfrac{1}{(\frac{s}{2}+1)}$; $\dfrac{1}{(\frac{s}{0.2}+1)}$	$\dfrac{Ke^{-\tau s}(T_L s+1)}{(T_I s+1)(\frac{1}{N_w}s+1)}$ — Controlled element / $\frac{1}{\tau_L}$ / $\frac{1}{\tau_I}$ / $\frac{1}{N}$ / α / K : $\frac{1}{s+1}$: 0.68, 0.1, 18, 0.147, 17.7; $\frac{1}{\frac{s}{2}+1}$: 0.9, 0.13, 25, 0.145, 7.55; $\frac{1}{\frac{s}{0.2}+1}$: 2, 3, 14, 1.5, 10	Same frequencies as shown in forcing function		L. Russell
⑩ Random appearing superposition of 4 sinusoids (0.66 1.68 2.87 4.27, Log ω)	Handwheel type control with no restraints	$\dfrac{1}{s}$	$\dfrac{Ke^{-\tau s}(T_L s+1)}{(T_I s+1)}$ — $\frac{1}{\tau_L}$ / $\frac{1}{\tau_I}$ / K / α : 0.19, Very small, 14, 0.123, ≠ 0; where: $\tau = 0.15$	Same frequencies as shown in forcing function		L. Russell
⑪ Random appearing superposition of 3 sinusoids (0.08 0.054 0.08 (1rpm); 0.026 0.078 0.056 (1.5rpm), Log f)	Simulated tank turret tracking with spade grip handwheel; "Displacement-speed control"	$\dfrac{1}{s\left[\left(\frac{s}{\omega}\right)^2 + \frac{2\zeta s}{\omega}+1\right]}$; $\zeta = 0.25$, $\omega = 55$ rad/sec; This is $\cong \frac{1}{s}$ over the frequency range of measurement	$\dfrac{Ke^{-\tau s}(T_L s+1)}{(T_I s+1)(\frac{1}{N_w}s+1)}$ — $\frac{1}{\tau_L}$ / $\frac{1}{\tau_I}$ / $\frac{1}{N}$ / α / K / τ : 0.4, 0.05, 2.5, 0.0125, 220, 0.15	Same frequencies as shown in forcing function	0.94	A. Tustin. Indicated transfer function does not agree exactly with that given by Tustin
⑫ Random appearing superposition of 3 sinusoids (0.08 0.054 0.08 (1rpm); 0.026 0.078 0.056 (1.5rpm), Log f)	Simulated tank turret tracking with spade grip handwheel; "Aided-laying"	$\dfrac{(T_s s+1)}{s\left[\left(\frac{s}{\omega}\right)^2 + \frac{2\zeta s}{\omega}+1\right]}$; $1/T_s = 3.0$, $\zeta = 0.8$, $\omega = 20$; This is $\cong \frac{1}{s}$ over the frequency range of measurement	$\dfrac{Ke^{-\tau s}(T_L s+1)}{(T_I s+1)(\frac{1}{N_w}s+1)}$ — $\frac{1}{\tau_L}$ / $\frac{1}{\tau_I}$ / $\frac{1}{N}$ / α / K / τ : 0.4, 0.07, 1.0, 0.175, 200, 0.2	Same frequencies as shown in forcing function		A. Tustin. Indicated transfer function does not agree exactly with that given by Tustin
⑬ Random appearing superposition of 4 sinusoids (0.277 0.74 1.21 1.80, Log ω)	Handwheel type control with no restraints	$\dfrac{(s+1)}{s}$; $\dfrac{(\frac{s}{2}+1)}{s}$	$\dfrac{Ke^{-\tau s}(T_L s+1)}{(T_I s+1)}$ — Controlled element / $\frac{1}{\tau_L}$ / $\frac{1}{\tau_I}$ / α / K / τ : $\frac{s+1}{s}$: 45, 0.048, 0.0011, 118, 0.2; $\frac{\frac{s}{2}+1}{s}$: 17, 0.3, 0.0177, 250, 0.2	Same frequencies as shown in forcing function		L. Russell
⑭ Random appearing superposition of 4 sinusoids (0.277 0.74 1.21 1.80, Log ω)	Handwheel type control with no restraints	$\dfrac{10\tau_c s+10}{10\tau_c s+1}$ / $\tau_c = 0.5$; $\dfrac{10\tau_c s+10}{10\tau_c s+1}$ / $\tau_c = 2.0$	$\dfrac{Ke^{-\tau s}(T_L s+1)}{(T_I s+1)(\frac{1}{N_w}s+1)}$ — Controlled element τ_c / $\frac{1}{\tau_L}$ / $\frac{1}{\tau_I}$ / $\frac{1}{N}$ / α / K / τ : 0.5: 0.2, 0, 0.6, 0, High, 0.2; 2.0: 0.15, 0, 0.45, 0, High, 0.2	Same frequencies as shown in forcing function	τ_c / ρ_c : 0.5, 0.68; 2.0, 0.87	L. Russell

	Forcing function	Controlled element	Operator describing function	Describing function	Frequency range	Correlation	Remarks / Source
⑮	Random appearing superposition of 4 sinusoids; ω (rad/sec): 0.66 1.68 2.87 4.27	Handwheel type control with no restraints	$\left[\left(\frac{s}{\omega_n}\right)^2 + \frac{2\zeta s}{\omega_n} + 1\right]^{-1}$ Servo n ζ: 1 — 7.8, 0.37; 2 — 16, 0.37	$\dfrac{Ke^{-\tau s}(T_L s+1)}{(T_I s+1)}$ Servo $\frac{1}{T_L}$ $\frac{1}{T_I}$ α K τ: 1 — 6.8, 0.38, 0.056, 5.3, 0.2; 2 — 17, 0.195, 0.015, 16, 0.2	Same frequencies as shown in forcing function	Servo ρ_o: 1 — 0.76; 2 —	L. Russell
⑯	Random appearing superposition of 4 different wave shapes; $\phi_i(t)$ is the sum of: $R_{\phi_i}(\tau) \doteq e^{-0.15\tau}\cos(1.1\tau)$	Simulated aircraft longitudinal control; stick with spring restraints	$\dfrac{(T_I s+1)}{s(T_1 s+1)(T_2 s+1)}$ $1/T_I = 1.37$; $1/T_1 = 1.67$; $1/T_2 = 2.5$	Approximate describing function of analog computer set up: $\dfrac{Ke^{-\tau s}(T_L s+1)}{(T_N s+1)}$ Typical values: $K = 0.425$; $\tau = 0.25$; $1/T_N = 5.3$; $1/T_L = 0.28$			Goodyear Aircraft Co.
⑰	Random appearing	Simulated longitudinal aircraft control in pitching mockup; stick with inertial, spring, and damping restraints	$\doteq \dfrac{(T_I s+1)}{s(T_1 s+1)\left[\left(\frac{s}{\omega_n}\right)^2 + \frac{2\zeta s}{\omega_n}+1\right]}$ $1/T_I = 1.37$; $1/T_1 = 2.4$; $\zeta = 0.523$; $\omega_n = 4.17$	Approximate describing function of analog computer setup: $y_p = K_p e^{-\tau s}\left[\left(\frac{s}{\omega_n}\right)^2 + \frac{2\zeta s}{\omega_n}+1\right]\chi\left(K\left(\frac{\sigma_r}{\sigma_i}\right)\right)$			Goodyear Aircraft Co. Both visual and motion inputs may be involved
⑱	Random appearing white noise through 3rd order binomial filter giving available corner frequencies of 1, 2, and 4 rad/sec	Simulated closed loop control of aircraft lateral axis in tail chase tracking task	$\dfrac{(T_I s+1)(T_4 s+1)(T_6 s+1)}{s^2(T_3 s+1)\left[\left(\frac{s}{\omega_n}\right)^2 + \frac{2\zeta s}{\omega_n}+1\right]}$ $\doteq \dfrac{(T_4 s+1)(T_6 s+1)}{s^2(T_3 s+1)}$ $1/T_1 = 0.242$; $1/T_2 = -2.92$; $1/T_3 = 4.11$; $1/T_4 = 8.32$; $1/T_5 = 0.0017$; $1/T_6 = 5.65$; $\omega_n = 3.88$; $\zeta = 0.084$	$\dfrac{Ke^{-\tau s}(T_L s+1)}{(T_1 s+1)(T_N s+1)}$ ω_{co} $\frac{1}{T_1}$ $\frac{1}{T_L}$ $\frac{1}{T_N}$ α K τ: 1 — 0.8, 2.5, 10, 14, 0.2, 0.15; 2 — 0.3, 3.1, 10, 0.28, 0.15; 4 — 0.9, 1.3, 10, 7, 0.5, 0.15	0.6 to 3.6 rad/sec	$\rho_o \doteq 0.5$	The Franklin Institute. These data taken from "aileron" traces; "elevator" was being controlled simultaneously
⑲	Random appearing white noise through 3rd order binomial filter giving available corner frequencies of 1, 2, and 4 rad/sec	Simulated closed loop control of aircraft longitudinal axis in tail chase tracking task	$\dfrac{(T_I s+1)(T_2 s+1)}{s^2\left[\left(\frac{s}{\omega_n}\right)^2 + \frac{2\zeta s}{\omega_n}+1\right]}$ $1/T_1 = 0.28$; $1/T_2 = 1.58$; $\omega_n = 3.98$; $\zeta = 0.56$	$\dfrac{Ke^{-\tau s}(T_L s+1)}{(T_1 s+1)(T_N s+1)} \doteq K$ ω_{co} $\frac{1}{T_1}$ $\frac{1}{T_L}$ $\frac{1}{T_N}$ α K τ: 1 — 4, 40, 10, 0.63, 0.15; 2 — 6, 20, 10, 5, 0.63, 0.15; 4 — No reasonable fit. Note: A SGN function was at least as good for $\omega_{co}=1$ and 2; and $Ks^{-0.25}s$ was the "best" fit for $\omega_{co}=4$	0.6 to 3.6 rad/sec	$\rho_o \doteq 0.6$	The Franklin Institute. These data taken from "elevator" traces; "aileron" was being controlled simultaneously

Table 9.4. SUMMARY OF OPERATOR DESCRIBING FUNCTIONS IN COMPENSATORY TASKS WITH VARIOUS CONTROLLED ELEMENTS

Table 9.5. Summary of Operator Remnant Characteristics in Compensatory Tasks

Investigator	General Control Task Including Controlled Element Dynamics (gain not shown)	Forcing Function	Average Linear Correlation	Remnant Sources and Best Fit Data			
				All Remnant Assumed to be Due to Noise Injected at the Operator's Input	All Remnant Assumed to be Due to Noise at the Operator's Output	All Remnant Assumed to be Due to Nonsteady Operator Behavior	Nonlinear Operation and Dither
L. Russell	Simple tracker, handwheel type control with no restraints $Y_c = 1$	Random appearing superposition of 4 sinusoids (graph: 0.66, 1.68, 2.87, 4.27)	0.9	$\Phi_{nn_\epsilon} = \dfrac{1}{\lvert H\rvert^2}\dfrac{\Phi_{nn}}{\int_0^\infty \Phi_{ii}\,df}$	$\Phi_{nn_c} = \dfrac{\lvert Y_p\rvert^2}{\lvert H\rvert^2}\dfrac{\Phi_{nn}}{\int_0^\infty \Phi_{ii}\,df}$		$\Phi_{nn_\delta} = A_d^2[\delta(\omega-\omega_d)+\delta(\omega+\omega_d)]$ $\omega_d \doteq 7.73$ rps
J. I. Elkind	Simple following with pip trapper $Y_c = 1$	Random appearing function made up of 40–120 sinusoids, giving any desirable rectangular spectra $f_{co} \doteq 0.16, 0.24, 0.4, 0.64, 0.96, 1.6, 2.4$ cps or $\omega_{co} \doteq 1, 1.5, 2.5, 4, 6, 10, 15$ rad/sec 1 in. rms (graph: f_{co})	R0.16 — 0.995 R0.24 — 0.99 R0.40 — 0.995 R0.64 — 0.98 R0.96 — 0.92 R1.60 — 0.75 R2.40 — 0.58	White noise, $\Phi_{nn_\epsilon}(0) \doteq \dfrac{1}{8}\int_0^\infty \Phi_{ii}\,df$ valid for R0.16 – R0.64 only	$\Phi_{nn_c}(\omega) \doteq 2T\sigma_{n_c}^2\left[\dfrac{\sin\frac{1}{2}\omega T}{\frac{1}{2}\omega T}\right]^2$ or $R_{nn_c}(\tau) = \sigma_{n_c}^2(1-\lvert\tau\rvert/T)$ $T \doteq 0.75/f_{co}$ (All cases) $\dfrac{\sigma_{n_c}^2}{\int_0^\infty \Phi_{ii}\,df} \doteq \dfrac{1.75}{\sqrt{f_{co}}}$ (R0.40 – R2.4)	$R_{\Delta H \Delta H}(\tau) \doteq \sigma_{\Delta H}^2(1-\lvert\tau\rvert/T)$ where: $T_1 \doteq \dfrac{0.5}{\omega_{co}} = 0.25$ sec $\sigma_{\Delta H}^2 = 0.7 f_{co}$ and $R_{\Delta H \Delta H}(\tau) = \lim_{T\to\infty}\dfrac{1}{2T}\int_{-T}^{+T}\Delta H(t)\Delta H(t+\tau)\,d\tau$	No dither observed; Small threshold nonlinearity is possibly present
Goodyear Aircraft Co.	Simulated longitudinal aircraft control in pitching mockup; stick with inertial, spring, and damping restraints $Y_c \doteq \dfrac{T_\zeta s+1}{s(T_A s+1)[(s/\omega_n)^2+2\zeta s/\omega_n+1]}$ $1/T_c \doteq 1.37,\ 1/T_A = 2.4$ $\omega_n = 4.17,\ \zeta = 0.52$	Random appearing (graph: 20 db/sec, 40 db/sec, 0.33, >4, Log ω)					
The Franklin Institute	Simulated F–80 in tail chase; aileron and elevator controlled $Y_{c_A} \doteq \dfrac{(s/0.242)(s/-2.92+1)(s/4.11+1)(s/8.32+1)}{s^2(s/0.0017+1)(s/5.65+1)[(s/3.88)^2+2(0.084)s/3.88+1]}$ $Y_{c_E} = \dfrac{(s/0.28+1)(s/1.58+1)}{s^2[(s/3.98)^2+2(0.56)s/3.98+1]}$	Random appearing white noise through third order binomial filter giving available corner frequencies of 1, 2, and 4 rad/sec (graph: 60 db/sec, 1, 2, or 4, Log ω)	Elevator, $\rho_e \doteq 0.6$ Aileron, $\rho_a \doteq 0.5$ (ρ was a strong function of ω_{co})		$\Phi_{nn_c} \doteq 2T_A(E_A/2)^2\left[\dfrac{\sin\frac{1}{2}\omega T_A}{\frac{1}{2}\omega T_A}\right]^2 + \pi r_d^2[\delta(\omega_d+\omega)+\delta(\omega_d-\omega)]$ $T_A = 2.7$ sec, $\omega_d = 8.8$ rad/sec		Dither (diagram); Computer mechanization
				Although the Franklin F-80 data remnant power is consistent with all of these models, it is not unequivocally assignable to any one source			

Upon the basis of empirical results thus far obtained, a vehicle system should assume deterministic dynamics similar to those shown in Figure 9.7. Locating the lead ahead of the human operator and the lag behind him is based on experimental data which shows that such a filter located behind the

Figure 9.7. Recommended system dynamics based on survey of experimental studies and related data.

pilot can filter enough of his spurious output to help him track. The possibility of modifying the feedback path through the sensors will be described in Chapter 16.

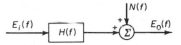

Figure 9.8. Closed-loop block diagram for pursuit and compensatory systems.

Any closed loop system can be described by a single quasi-linear transfer function so long as the noise power remains a small fraction of the total system response power. The term quasi-linear is used to indicate that the particular parameters of this function depend upon the control situation. A

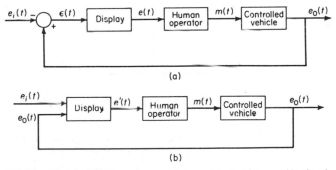

Figure 9.9. (a) Simple compensatory control system, (b) simple pursuit control system.

more complete representation is obtained if the output of the quasi-linear transducer is additively combined with noise which is not linearly coherent with the input of the system, as shown in Figure 9.8.

In the compensatory system, shown in Figure 9.9a, the operator receives only the error. This control system can be represented by the open-loop quasi-linear transfer function $G(f)$ and the noise, as shown in Figure 9.10, thus permitting determination of $G(f)$ in terms of $H(f)$, that is,

$$G(f) = \frac{H(f)}{1 - H(f)}$$

Here the uncorrelated component of the human operator's output is assumed to result from noise $n'(t)$ entering the system at the operator's input. The power spectrum of $n'(t)$, $\Phi_{n'n'}(f)$, can be determined from $\Phi_{nn}(f)$ and $G(f)$, at least over those frequencies where $G(f)$ is measured.

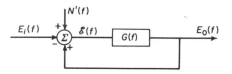

Figure 9.10. Open-loop block diagram for compensatory system.

In the pursuit system, shown in Figure 9.9b, the operator receives separate signals which describe the course to be tracked and the error as functions of time. Such a system can be represented by an open-loop block diagram as shown in Figure 9.11. Here $P_i(f)$ operates directly on the input signal, $G_2(f)$ operates on the error signal, while $G_1(f)$ represents the dynamics of components common to both channels. Each of these are quasi-linear transfer

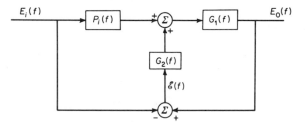

Figure 9.11. Open-loop block diagram for pursuit system. Noise sources are not shown.

functions configured so that their combined effect is equivalent to the closed-loop transfer function $H(f)$. Unfortunately, these three functions cannot be determined uniquely from measurements only on input and output although it should be possible to add a small variable to the error signal, which is statistically independent of the primary input, making it possible to determine the product transfer functions $P_iG_1(f)$ and $G_2G_1(f)$. Published papers by J. I. Elkind contain greater detail on this approach to the problem of constructing mathematical representations for the human operator in continuous tracking behavior, providing both description of the experimental situation and summary of the empirical evidence which was obtained.

The *phase-space* method of analysis, introduced by Poincaré (1881), was first applied in theoretical mechanics. A dynamical system having n degrees of freedom can be represented within a $2n$-dimensional Cartesian hyperspace. These dimensions may be taken to consist of n positional coordinates and n velocity coordinates (the latter being descriptive of momentum), so that for each state of the system there corresponds a particular point within the phase-space. As the system passes through various states, it is possible to trace the trajectory of the corresponding point in the phase-space yielding graphical portrayal.

In a similar manner, it is possible to represent the manipulated variable within a tracking phase-space where each of the Cartesian coordinates is a measure of one of the time-dependent derivates. The tracking error is shown as a trajectory in this hyperspace with time being the implicit variable.

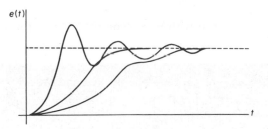

Figure 9.12. Types of corrective response to step displacement error.

To illustrate for the case of a tracking situation, let the phase space be reduced to a *phase plane* showing only the position error, e, (on the abscissa) and the first derivative of this error $\dot{e}$, (on the ordinate). The origin describes the system in steady-state zero error. Sudden shift of the reference signal provides a displacement error. The human operator may offer some corrective response as shown in Figure 9.12. "Proper" corrective action may occur which asymptotically nulls the error through a single ballistic action. However, as indicated, significant "overshoot" or "undershoot" may also occur wherein an additional separate corrective action is taken as the operator perceives that the error will persist for greater time than can be tolerated. These types of corrective responses are clearly distinct when shown in phase plane representation, see Figure 9.13. Note that the trajectory describing the systems state can only proceed in a counter-clockwise direction. In the case of "proper" corrective control a smooth curve is described which spirals to close on the origin. In the case of "undershoot" the second corrective action occurs at a cusp point, while in the case of "overshoot" a distinct inflection point may be noticed. Experimentally it is fairly simple to measure the error function and its derivative and directly display these in phase plane reproduction, as shown in Figure 9.14.

The particular shape of the phase-plane trajectory is severely dependent upon the nature of the system under control. Figures 9.15a and b indicate

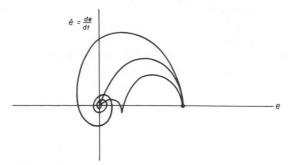

Figure 9.13. The same types of corrective response as shown on the phase-plane.

phase-plane plots obtained with a rate control of the error and an acceleration control of the error, respectively.

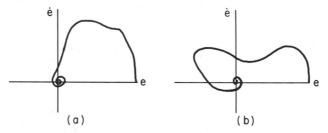

Figure 9.14. Measured phase-plane response to a step-input signal.

The apparent "break points" on the phase-plane trajectory may reasonably be identified with the initiation of separate actions by the human operator.

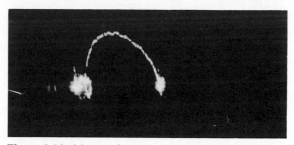

Figure 9.15. (a) Tracking with rate control, (b) tracking with acceleration control.

Using this concept it is possible to unitize the human operation into separate and approximately linear modes of behavior, these being sequentially activated. Such an analytic approach should result in lower order transfer functions for individual modes which, when taken together in sequential operation still reasonably well characterize the tracking behavior. Further, the simpler algebraic form of the transduction components may facilitate design of closed loop man-machine systems and serve to clarify the self-adjusting capability of the human operator.

As a "first-cut," human tracking may be separated into six natural modes of operation, these being described as follows:

Mode 1. Reaction. A mode in which there is no motor output.

Mode 2. Acquisition. A mode which is triggered by any error or error rate outside of the tracking mode domain. The intent is to minimize the error as rapidly as possible. This may cause overshoot and oscillation.

Mode 3. Tracking. This is only triggered by an error within the tracking mode domain and outside of the tremor mode domain. The intent is to zero the error, however, the inertia of the system and physical time constant may prevent attainment and may cause overshoot (with possible oscillation). Any oscillation will have a frequency proportional to the magnitude and/or rate of the error.

Mode 4. Synchronism. It is triggered by perception of some invariant waveform characteristic in the input waveform. The intent is to reproduce the input and as a result of the predictability, the output does not lag the input. The human operator acts as an independent generator driving the tracking mechanisms and monitors the gross characteristics of the input with regard to the particular constant characteristic which identifies it in order to determine when this "generator" should be stopped.

Mode 5. Steady State Tremor. It is only triggered when the error is within the tremor mode domain.

Mode 6. Reassurance. This mode is artificially triggered by the human operator in order to determine the system qualities by feedback. It is most generally used during steady-state tremor mode but can also be used during tracking. The human operator provides a pulse function motor output and then monitors the disturbances in the system so as to allow prediction for anticipated maneuvers and reassurance.

For the sake of mathematical analysis these modes are considered to be mutually exclusive but are not necessarily activated in the order designated above.

Several exploratory experiments have been performed to identify characteristics of the individual mode trajectories and the switching function which separates the modes; however, much work remains undone in this area. For example, it should be worthwhile to determine not only the shape of the switching functions and its extent but also its variability as a function of the nature of the controlled system, the level of training and stress on the operator, the signal-to-noise ratio, and other parameters of the situation. Specifically, the switching function which separates the acquisition from the tracking mode is expected to exist only within some annular ring from an inner radius defined by the tremor mode activity level to an outer radius wherein the momentum of the tracker is of such magnitude that the effect of switching becomes negligible.

In certain situations the human operator is called upon to track an intermittent variable, as in the case of a scanning radar display. At other times he may find that it becomes necessary to monitor a set of instruments while assuming responsibility for tracking of a particular variable. In an even more complex circumstance, the human operator may be required to simultaneously track a number of separate displays with corresponding controls; this latter situation being the general case (which includes the monitoring of an instrument console where the importance weighting of error magnitude has been relaxed in the light of operational automatic control equipment or lowered system performance requirements).

When forced to track with an intermittent display, the operator may not be aware that his performance is degraded as compared to tracking the same function with continuous display. As the per cent of visual reference duration is reduced, his performance suffers in an approximately linear manner regardless of whether the intermittency results from few relatively long looks at the display, with long periods elapsing between looks, or a larger number of relatively short looks at the display. In most cases the latter technique is to be desired so as to increase the likelihood of the operator properly following some sudden perturbation or change of the referent. Flash duration usually affects target brightness, brightness being reduced as the flash duration is abbreviated. This decrease in brightness interacts with the flash rate to further degrade tracking performance.

Multiple display tracking always yields poorer performance than might be expected if exact time sharing were possible. Additional time is taken by eye movement and mental switching of reference, this latter factor being in the order of 0.2 seconds. Normal eye blinks occur about once every three seconds, with each blink obscuring vision for as much as 0.25 seconds. Blinking is, however, of little concern since the operator can inhibit blinks whenever he considers that the tracking task is both important and difficult.

Given a number of displays, the human operator gradually sets up some scanning pattern. At first this pattern is dominated by the display size, shape, color, and physical arrangement, but as experience accrues the pattern begins to reflect the information content of the individual displays, greater total time being devoted to those displays which are most informative. The spectral properties of each of the time functions have an effect upon the frequency with which each display is referenced. Those parameters which show high frequency characteristics of significant amplitude receive more frequent viewing. Empirical evidence has revealed that, given sufficient experience, the human operator erects a most reasonable search and monitoring pattern.

The inertia of the controlled vehicle constrains the system response to the lower portion of the frequency spectrum. Higher frequency components occur with lower and lower amplitude. Recognizing this spectral property allows the operator to intuitively invoke the sampling theorem. *If a time-function contains no frequency higher than* W *cycles per second, it is exactly determined by giving* M *function derivate values at each of a series of equidistant points extending throughout the time domain, the sampling interval* $T = M/2W$ *being the time interval between instantaneous observations.* That is to say, $2WT$ independent sample values are required to specify a function of duration T and bandwidth W.

There are, of course, various ways in which these independent samples can be obtained. For example, the operator may view an analog display which, from the same index, provides simultaneous information about the parameter value and its rate of change. Further discussion of this point is left for Chapter 16. However, here it is important to recognize that although the sampling theorem is of direct interest in judging the maximum time which may elapse between observations of a parameter time-function, it is not to be applied literally. That is to say, in the real world situation the operator does *not* sample instantaneously, periodically, and over all time. He may *not* obtain independent samples either in time or over the various derivatives. His information is noisy with different levels of accuracy for each type of sample value, and so on. Nevertheless, the driver of a car can take his eyes off the tracking task for brief intervals of time safe in the knowledge that at this velocity and within the allowed time duration the car couldn't swerve more than a tolerable amount. In this situation, the driver receives additional data in the form of kinesthetic cues, should there be any sudden deflection of path.

K. J. W. Craik, J. Stroud, and others have suggested that man may only operate on data in discrete segments of time. Under this hypothesis, even a continuous-time function would presumably be acted upon as if it were displayed in value during separate time intervals of about 0.1 seconds each. Thus far, no controlled experiments are on record which conclusively prove that such descrete time functioning is necessarily the case. Empirical evidence taken from human transduction can be equally well explained by continuous or discrete-time transduction.

The human transfer function is strongly dependent upon the transfer characteristics of the other elements which comprise the remainder of the closed loop. Even for a given vehicle it is possible to modify the human transfer characteristics greatly. For example, consider two distinctly different sets of display-control. In the first case, shown in Figure 9.16, the high gain of the display is placed on the higher frequency components of error signal. This display characteristic is compensated for by placing low gain of the control over these same higher frequencies. Using this display-control pair, the human operator will find the tracking task to be highly sensitive requiring his continual active participation. His personal indifference threshold is effectively reduced and he may accomplish superior tracking but at an increased cost in terms of fatigue and the other by-products of stress.

In the second case, shown in Figure 9.17, the spectral properties are reversed in the display and control. Only the drift components of the error signal are emphasized. In this situation the operator reduces his activity level

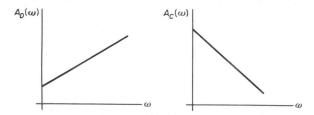

Figure 9.16. Display and control gain or frequency characteristics to emphasize high-frequency human operator transduction.

and, in so doing, modifies the constants of his transfer characteristic. With the same indifference threshold he may allow greater system error without his ever being aware of this condition. He will generally be more relaxed and find it possible to devote greater attention to other aspects of the assigned mission. Obviously there exists a continuum of cases connecting the extreme spectral-property pairs.

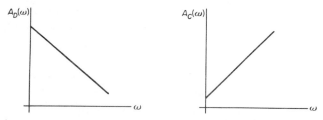

Figure 9.17. Display and control gain as frequency characteristics to emphasize low-frequency human operator transduction.

9.4. A STOCHASTIC MODEL

A next step toward better representation of manual tracking is to include some aspects of the uncertainty which is always associated with real world transduction of information. More specifically, it is intended to include aspects of system behavior which may be called nonsystematic error. But before considering any detailed account of such a model, it is well to recognize that greater specificity in the mathematical model requires a much greater store of knowledge concerning the behavior of the system. It will soon become evident that such a vast body of information is generally not available for any specific manual tracking system. The value of a model, however, does not only lie in its ability to forecast future behavior. Such an analysis may provide greater insight into the functional components which operate within the overall system and may offer direction for the design improvement of future systems. For the sake of simplicity, the following discussion will consider only a single-dimensional tracking task; however, there appears to be no reason why such an analysis cannot be extended to the multivariate situation, even to include parameters which are a composite of others already considered. Obviously, the analysis will be simplified if it is possible to choose a set of parameters which are as near as possible to degrees of freedom of the system. This minimizes the required number of parameters as well as the essential error resulting from incomplete description of the interaction among variables.

Consider the manual control of aircraft altitude. The sensed altitude is furnished to the pilot by means of a display.[5] If the display is compensatory, he reads the altitude error directly. Otherwise, he computes the altitude error from his knowledge of the altitude flight path he intends to follow, this being his reference signal. The pilot provides a corrective control signal which is transformed by the aircraft into a new altitude. While making this transformation, the aircraft is affected by air turbulence and other disturbance, causing noise to be combined with the pilot's corrective control signal. The actual altitude airpath may be looked upon as the message.

At each point in time, there is always some probability distribution associated with the intended altitude path signal. Normally, the human operator tacitly assumes some tolerance around the signal; this, even when his instruction is single-valued. He may assume a rectangular probability density function between the tolerance limits, or, more likely, he may consider the uncertainty to take a form something like a truncated Normal density function. The particular probability distribution the pilot uses is a composite of his immediate instruction, the flight regulations, the nature of the aircraft under his control, and his experience of successful flight with various degrees of error. For "cruise," the signal distribution may be statistically stationary, while for "landing" it is most decidedly nonstationary.

Although the actual airpath is single-valued, the message may be viewed as having some associated probability distribution which would become more and more well-defined through repeated flights under similar circumstance. It is of interest to inquire how the message distribution is related to the signal distribution and the externally introduced noise. Estimation of the reliability of performing a specific mission requires knowledge of the nature and amount of uncertainty associated with the message. Figure 9.18 offers a view of some of the detailed functions performed by the human operator in connection with altitude flight control. At each point in time, the continuous variable, y,

---

[5] The human operator introduces some uncertainty as a result of the error associated with reading the display; however, for the sake of this discussion, this loss of information will be neglected.

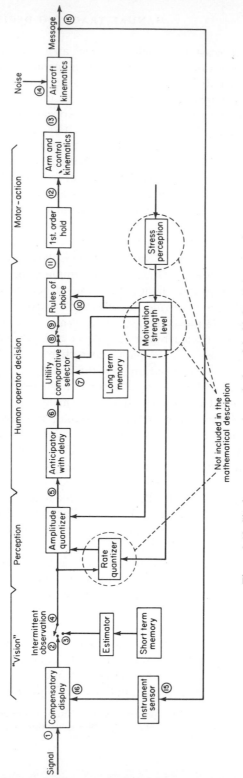

Figure 9.18. Single parameter mathematical model of information transfer system.

is sensed and subtracted from the signal variable, x, so as to furnish the altitude error, z. The moments of z may be written in terms of the moments of x and y,

$$\mu_n(z) = E[z^n] = E[(x-y)^n]$$

Binomial expansion yields

$$\mu_n(z) = E\left[\sum_{j=0}^{n} \binom{n}{j}(-1)^j x^{n-j} y^j\right]$$

$$= \sum_{j=0}^{n} (-1)^j \binom{n}{j}\mu_{n-j,\,j}$$

where $\mu_{n-j,\,j}$ are the cross moments. Expansion yields

$$\mu_0(z) = 1$$

$$\mu_1(z) = \mu_{1,\,0} - \mu_{0,\,1}$$

$$\mu_2(z) = \mu_{2,\,0} - 2\mu_{1,\,1} + \mu_{0,\,2}$$

$$\mu_3(z) = \mu_{3,\,0} - 3\mu_{2,\,1} + 3\mu_{1,\,2} - \mu_{0,\,3}$$

$$\vdots$$

where, following the usual notation, the cross moments are defined as:

$$\mu_{1,\,0} = E[x^1 y^0] = E[x] = \mu_1(x)$$

$$\mu_{0,\,1} = E[x^0 y^1] = E[y] = \mu_1(y)$$

$$\mu_{1,\,1} = E[x^1 y^1] = \overline{xy} = \varphi_{xy}(0)$$

$$\mu_{1,\,2} = E[x^1 y^2] = \overline{xy^2}$$

$$\vdots$$

Note that the first two moments of the error signal only require the mean value of the input signal and the sensed message, and the cross-correlation of zero argument. Of course, higher cross moments require successively higher individual moments.

The pilot must monitor a number of flight parameters; therefore, a switch is shown between points 2 and 4 on Figure 9.18. During the time when he is not in direct contact with the altimeter, he may still use some altitude information as a result of his estimation on the altitude signal extracted from his immediate recall (so long as his attention is not fully occupied with other matters). The result of estimation is increased uncertainty (this process to be described in more detail at a more appropriate point below).

The observed error signal is quantized[6] in both amplitude and rate with

[6] In flying under the most relaxed conditions, an average pilot might quantize altitude to the nearest 1,000 feet. If asked how high he is, he might report 8,000, 9,000, or 10,000 feet but certainly not 8,762 feet. Under greater stress conditions, such as would be encountered under IFR flight or combat conditions, he would quantize more precisely, and, for the same displayed altimeter scale setting, he might read 8,700 feet or 8,760 feet.

some additional increase in uncertainty. Both quantizing operations are strongly affected by the level of motivation and the degree of stress under which the pilot operates. It is, of course, difficult to quantify these relations. Generally, the transfer function which accomplishes rate quantization is of much fewer steps than that used for amplitude quantization. If the error signal remains fairly constant for some time, the rate may remain within the dead zone and be taken to be essentially zero. If, however, the rate quantizer reaches some reasonably high level, or level of activity, it may affect the degree of precision and linearity of the amplitude quantizer. The rate quantization and these interaction effects on the amplitude quantizer are omitted from the following quantitative discussion. Amplitude quantization always occurs and, therefore, demands inclusion.

Let the continuous amplitude input variable, x, be operated upon by a staircase transfer function, thus resulting in the discrete variable, y. If, for simplicity, the staircase is taken to be of equal step length, l, the probability density function of y is defined by

$$p(y) = \int_{C_i - l/2}^{C_i + l/2} p(x)\, dx, \qquad i = 1, 2, 3, \ldots k$$

where C_i are the class interval centers. The moments of $p(y)$ associated with point 5, Figure 9.18, can be determined from the moments of the distribution of the continuous variable, x, through use of Sheppard's Correction under the assumption that the class intervals are equal, individually have rectangular density functions, are closed at the left end, and that the error caused by quantization is independent of the particular value of x. Sheppard's Correction is usually used to convert the moments of an experimentally obtained histogram into the moments of the assumed underlying continuous variable. Here, however, the problem is the inverse. It is desired to yield the moments of the discrete distribution from knowledge of the moments of the continuous distribution and the character of the quantizing transfer function. Sheppard's Correction can then be rewritten to read

$$\mu_1(y) = \mu_1(x)$$

$$\mu_2(y) = \mu_2(x) - \frac{l^2}{12}$$

$$\mu_3(y) = \mu_3(x) + \frac{l^2 \mu_1(y)}{4}$$

Each of the higher moments can be computed in succession. Note that this correction of the moments introduces no error, provided the measure of the class interval and the stated assumptions is fulfilled.

Having accepted a symbol for the present altitude error, the human operator anticipates what this error will be at some point of interest in future time. Some small delay is associated with this anticipation process as noted between points 5 and 6, Figure 9.18. The time interval, Δt, over which the operator anticipates, is of considerable importance. Consider the driver of an automobile which is proceeding at some velocity, v, along a road, as shown in Figure 9.19. Noise, consisting of wind gusts and the transverse effects of road roughness, continuously impinges upon the vehicle. Let the object of the driver be to remain as close as possible to the right side of the white line which marks the center of the road. If the driver fixes his attention upon the white line at some constant distance ahead of the vehicle, his accuracy of tracking will be as shown in Figure 9.19. If he chooses to monitor a point too far ahead

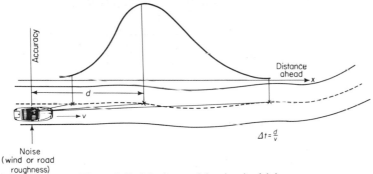

Figure 9.19. Moving anticipation in driving.

of the vehicle, the tortuous nature of the road introduces irrelevant information to the problem of determining immediate control actions. If he monitors too close a point on the white line, the response time of the vehicle becomes a significant factor and his accuracy is again degraded. His performance is best at some intermediate distance which corresponds to an optimal anticipatory time interval. Generally, an increase in the noise level shortens the optimal interval for anticipation, while a decrease in the vehicle responsiveness lengthens it.

Of course, the real driver does not fix his attention at a constant distance ahead of the vehicle. Rather, he scans the road and performs some weighted averaging as a function of velocity and his independent estimates of the character of the noise and the vehicle response. The pilot of an aircraft may not have such flexibility. Consider the final approach of an aircraft to landing. The anticipation time interval is largely dependent upon the distance to touch-down and the approach velocity. Auxiliary information from other approach cues are likely to be much less accurate. As the landing proceeds, the pilot continually foreshortens his anticipatory time interval. This permits the required greater accuracy of the anticipated data. The projected altitude error signal is of decreased uncertainty.

The process of anticipation is recognized to be a special case of the more general process of estimation. A simple model for such an estimation process can be erected upon the following reasonable assumptions:

1. Unless some external bias is introduced (such as the increased danger of a negative altitude error in landing), the mean value of the anticipated variable will remain unchanged.
2. The variance of the anticipated variable will be equal to, or greater than, the variance of the distribution associated with the original information. More specifically, the variance is assumed to be proportional in some simple manner to the time interval of anticipation.
3. The increased uncertainty of anticipation may be looked upon as resulting from the introduction of some noise, N, which has the same moments as the original variable, but a mean of zero value.

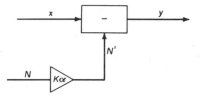

Figure 9.20. Time domain model for the estimator or anticipator element.

These assumptions are realized by the simple circuit shown in Figure 9.20 which produces the anticipated variable by subtracting some amplified noise from the original variable, x; that is,

$$y = x - kN, \qquad k > 0$$

where k is a constant which is proportional to the time interval of anticipation, Δt. In general, the nth moment about the mean of y is expressed by taking the expected value of the expanded binomial. It follows that

$$\mu_1(y) = \mu_1(x)$$
$$\sigma^2(y) = (1+k^2)\sigma^2(x)$$

and

$$\eta(y) = (1+k^3)\eta(x)$$

Higher moments about the mean take on more complicated forms. In accordance with expectation, the uncertainty of the anticipated variable is a direct function of both the time interval of anticipation and the uncertainty associated with the original variable. This model is considered to be equally applicable to the estimation performed by the human operator on his short-term recall at those times when he finds such information to be needed, but does not have immediate access to the appropriate display. Note that the process of estimation takes some finite time so that although the anticipated value is associated with the future, it appears at some delayed time.

The human operator may attempt to increase the certainty of his future through reference to his long-term experience under similar situations. A utility comparative selector is represented by the transformation between points 6 and 8 of Figure 9.18, which only operates if the uncertainty can be reduced by reference to the available experience.

This operation is also keyed to the level of motivation. If the motivation is low, the utility selector approximates a unity transfer. Under high motivation, the pilot will order and reorder his experience so as to find some "corresponding" situation which can be used to reduce some aspect of his uncertainty. In the extreme case, a cocky pilot may remember a similar situation and use this as a substitute for the immediate situation. He discards all uncertainty of the present and, of course, if he is wrong in any regard, he may be dead wrong.

The uncertainty associated with the similar experience in the memory may be described in terms of the character of "learning curves." A reasonable model for the utility comparative selector may take the form of a reduction in the variance and an increase in the third moment about the mean; that is,

$$\mu(y) = \mu(x)$$
$$\sigma^2(y) = \sigma^2(x) - k_1[\sigma^2(x) - \sigma^2(M)],$$
$$0 \leq k_1 \leq \frac{\sigma^2(x)}{\sigma^2(x) - \sigma^2(M)}$$

and

$$\eta(y) = \eta(x) + k_2(\eta(M) - \eta(x)),$$
$$0 \leq k_2 \leq \frac{\eta(x)}{\eta(M) - \eta(x)}$$

so long as

$$\sigma^2(x) > \sigma^2(M) \quad \text{and} \quad \eta(M) > \eta(x)$$

where x, y, and M refer to the input, output, and memory, respectively. k_1 and k_2 are utility factors which depend upon the subjective evaluation of how worthwhile it is to use related experience. If the memory cannot supply information which satisfies these conditions, then the selector is presumably not utilized by a rational human operator. In contrast, even an experienced pilot can fly for pure pleasure and let the utility factors approach zero value, thus reducing the comparative selector to a unity transfer.

At this point, a discrete decision must be made, as represented by the switch shown between points 8 and 9 of Figure 9.18. Closure of this switch passes the probability distribution on to the rules of choice transformation which here take the form of a single-valued conditioned reflex transduction. The error signal distribution at point 9 is transformed into a new distribution at point 11 by

$$p_y(y) = p_x(F^{-1}(y)) \left| \frac{dF^{-1}(y)}{dy} \right|$$

where the output variable, y, is related to the input variable, x, by some monotone function

$$y = F(x)$$

Note that nonmonotone functions can be dealt with by sectionalizing. When $F(x) = \gamma$ if and only if $a \leq x \leq b$, then $P(Y = \gamma) \neq 0$; in fact

$$P(Y = \gamma) = \int_a^b p_x(x)\, dx$$

These rules of choice may be assumed to have some central dead zone and saturate to "hard-over-control" for extreme values of the input variable, these being joined in some smooth manner. The rules of choice may contain many other features. For example, they may be time-weighted as a function of the duration of error, the transduction may be different for different rates of error, and so on. A considerable store of evidence would be needed to identify such aspects of the transduction.

Information is received at point 11 only at discrete points in time; however, the controls act continuously in time so that the pilot may be assumed to perform a first order hold on the variable which results from the rules of choice. That is to say, the human operator forms a continuous output from the decision pulses of the altitude-correction signal by maintaining the last "rate" from the last amplitude value. This appears to be a most reasonable assumption. Having corrected altitude, the pilot turns his attention to some other variable and while performing a decision on that variable, he continues to exercise his last decision on altitude control at a constant rate. Note that lowering the frequency of decision switch closure degrades the average performance of the aircraft, since a greater portion of time is spent under control signals which may be somewhat inappropriate.

The amplitude probability distribution at point 12, Figure 9.18, is a continuous function of time. This distribution must spread as a function of the time from the last pulse, since both altitude-error and error rate are maintained. The connection between pulses Y_1 and Y_2 of the form

$$Y = \gamma Y_2 + (1-\gamma)Y_1, \qquad 0 \leq \gamma \leq 1$$

Given Y_1 and Y_2, each value of γ determines a point on the straight line connecting Y_1 and Y_2, where

$$\gamma = \frac{t-t_1}{t_2-t_1}$$

and $t_2 - t_1$ is the time between the pulses Y_1 and Y_2. Let $f(y_1)$ be the probability density function corresponding to Y_1 and $g(y_2/y_1)$ be the conditional probability density function corresponding to pulse Y_2. Then the joint density function is the product of the marginal and conditional probability density function. It is of interest to find the joint cumulative distribution of specific values y and y_1; that is,

$$P\{Y \leq y, Y_1 \leq y_1\}$$

and the conditional cumulative of y

$$\Psi(y/y_1) = P\{Y \leq y/Y_1 = y_1\}$$

but by substitution

$$\Psi(y/y_1) = P\{\gamma Y_2 + (1-\gamma)Y_1 \leq y/Y_1 = y_1\}$$
$$= P\{\gamma Y_2 + (1-\gamma)y_1 \leq y/Y_1 = y_1\}$$
$$= P\left\{Y_2 \leq \frac{1}{\gamma}[y-(1-\gamma)y_1]/Y_1 = y_1\right\}$$

Now by definition

$$\Psi(y/y_1) = \int_{-\infty}^{1/\gamma[y-(1-\gamma)y_1]} g(u/y_1)\, du$$

Therefore, if $\gamma \neq 0$

$$\psi(y/y_1) = \frac{d}{dy}\, \psi(y/y_1)$$
$$= \frac{1}{\gamma}g\left(\frac{1}{\gamma}[y-(1-\gamma)y_1]/y_1\right)$$

Then, by definition, the joint density function

$$\varphi(y, y_1) = f(y_1)\psi(y/y_1)$$
$$= \frac{1}{\gamma}f(y_1)g\left(\frac{1}{\gamma}[y-(1-\gamma)y_1]/y_1\right)$$

so that

$$p(y) = \int_{-\infty}^{\infty} \varphi(y, y_1)\, dy_1$$

where

$$P\{Y \leq y\} = \int_{-\infty}^{y} p(u)\, du$$

The arm and direct control kinematics are represented between points 12 and 13, Figure 9.18. These are presumed to be nonlinear, but single-valued transduction elements having negligible memory. Without loss of generality, this element may be combined with the aircraft kinematics, which lie between points 13 and 15. The aircraft transduction is assumed to be single-valued, nonlinear, and dynamic. Saturation effects and memory are included but not hysteresis. This transduction can be approximated by two cascade elements as shown in Figure 9.21.[7] Let x be the input at point 12 which enters a linear element, S_L, which includes memory characteristics. Let y be the intermediate variable which enters the nonlinear element, S_{NL}, which is taken to be a point function transformation; that is, it is without memory. The output of the cascade elements is the variable, z.

The intermediate variable y may be expressed as

$$y = \int_{-\infty}^{\infty} x(t-u)S_L(u)\,du$$

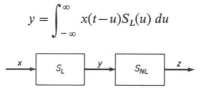

Figure 9.21. Approximate equivalent circuit for kinematics.

where the transfer function vanishes for negative values of the dummy variable, u. In the general case, by k-fold integration,

$$y^k = \int_{-\infty}^{\infty} \cdots \int_{-\infty}^{\infty} x(t-u_1)x(t-u_2)\ldots x(t-u_k)S_L(u_1)S_L(u_2)\ldots$$

$$S_L(u_k)\,du_1\,du_2\ldots du_k$$

The moments of y are found by taking the expected value of the appropriate integral. Thus,

$$\mu_1(y) = E\left[\int_{-\infty}^{\infty} x(t-u)S_L(u)\,du\right]$$

$$= \mu_1(x)\int_{-\infty}^{\infty} S_L(u)\,du$$

This value may be found by passing a step function of amplitude, $\mu_1(x)$, through the linear element, S_L, and measuring the asymptotic value of the output. In the practical case, the impulse response increment reaches a negligible value for any greater time than some finite time into the past, T_M. Using this approximation, the linear system output can be measured time units after an input step is applied, yielding the first moment of y.

The second moment may be expressed as

$$\mu_2(y) = E\left[\int_{-\infty}^{\infty}\int_{-\infty}^{\infty} x(t-u_1)x(t-u_2)S_L(u_1)S_L(u_2)\,du_1\,du_2\right]$$

---

[7] An infinite set of alternating linear set function and nonlinear point function elements would be required to duplicate the kinematic elements.

Consider a stationary process and let $V = t - u_1$ then

$$E[x(t-u_1)x(t-u_2)] = E[x(V)x(V+u_1-u_2)]$$
$$= \phi(u_1-u_2)$$

Substituting and manipulating yields

$$\mu_2(y) = \int_{-\infty}^{\infty} S_L(u_1) \, du_1 \int_{-\infty}^{\infty} S_L(u_2)\phi(u_1-u_2) \, du_2$$

Let the second integral be designated by $\Phi(u_1)$. This function may be generated by passing the correlation function through the linear transfer element, S_L. Letting time of the computer represent u_1,

$$\Phi(t) = \int_{-\infty}^{\infty} S_L(u_2)\phi(t-u_2) \, du_2$$

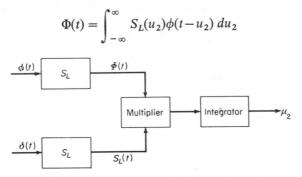

Figure 9.22. An analogue computation for the variance.

The $S_L(u_2)$ or $S_L(t)$ output can be generated by passing an impulse function through the same linear transfer function, S_L. The desired second moment can be obtained by integration of the product.

$$\mu_2(y) = \int_{-\infty}^{\infty} \Phi(t)S_L(t) \, dt$$

Since no precursor can exist for a physically realizable network, the memory is presumed to be time limited to T_M,

$$\mu_2(y) = \int_0^{T_M} \Phi(t)S_L(t) \, dt$$

A suggested block diagram of the computation may be seen in Figure 9.22.
   Higher moments could be computed in a similar manner. However, it would be required that more information concerning the stochastic properties of the input variable be known. Such computations would, of course, require the use of a greater number of operations with the linear function S_L. In an actual computer, these may be accomplished either in simultaneous operation or in sequential order with an appropriate memory storage device.
   Several alternate approaches are possible. For example, it may be noted

that the power spectrum of the output is related to the power spectrum of the input, according to Wiener-Khinchine Theorem, by

$$s_y(\omega) = |\mathscr{F}S_L|^2 s_x(\omega)$$

where $\mathscr{F}$ indicates the Fourier Transformation.
Therefore,

$$\mu_2(y) \cong \int_0^\infty s_y(\omega)\, d\omega$$

if the time series is approximately ergodic.[8] Alternately, an approach to this problem may be based upon the fact that derivatives of the characteristic function at zero are related to the moments. The characteristic function is defined by the Fourier Transform of the probability density function

$$K_y(\theta) = \int_{-\infty}^\infty e^{i\theta y} p(y)\, dy$$

and the moments of a first order process are

$$\mu_n(y) = \int_{-\infty}^\infty y^n p(y)\, dy = \frac{1}{i^n} \frac{d^n K_y(\theta)}{d\theta^n}\bigg|_{\theta=0}$$

This technique can be extended to cover higher order processes.

The nonlinear cascade element, S_{NL}, is presumed to have no memory, that is, to operate as a point function with defined transfer characteristics. The output probability density function could be computed from knowledge of the input distribution and the nonlinear transfer function as indicated in the discussion above related to the transduction through the rules of choice element.

Approximating the transduction by the sum of exponential factors may simplify the numerical computation. Consider

$$y = e^{-Cx}$$

then the expected value can be formed, the expansion of which utilizes the various previously computed moments of the input variable.

$$\mu_1(y) = E[e^{-Cx}] = E\left[1 - Cx + \frac{C^2}{2!}x^2 - \cdots\right]$$

$$= 1 - C\mu_1(x) + \frac{C^2}{2!}\mu_2(x) - \cdots$$

----

[8] A process is ergodic if it is stationary and the probability associated with every stationary subensemble is either zero or unity. If these conditions apply, then the ergodic theorem states that the time average of the functions squared will equal the ensemble average of the function value squared at any particular time for a series of zero mean value. Thus average power equals the variance.

Higher moments only require multiplication of the exponents and thus maintain the simplicity.

A certain amount of amplification may be attributed to any of the transducers within the aircraft information transfer system. Such a point function transduction affects each of the various moments. Those of the output, y, may be related to the input moments of x by

$$E[y^n] = E[(Gx)^n] = E[G^n x^n] = G^n E[x^n]$$

Therefore,

$$\mu_n(y) = G^n \mu_n(x)$$

where G is the gain of the noiseless amplifier.

The aircraft kinematics, represented by the element between points 13 and 15, receives the impact of wind turbulence. This noise is considered to have known statistical properties and be independent of the correction-signal received by the aircraft. Several alternate approaches are feasible; for example, a nonlinear network could be found which would effectively translate the atmospheric noise injected into its equivalent noise on the altitude path, this can then be linearly added at either the input or the output of the kinematic element. A more practical approach would probably utilize previously obtained flight disturbance data, this to be added to the noiseless altitude response of the aircraft. Calculation of moments of the combined variable follows that outlined for the determination of the moments of the original altitude error.

With this accomplished, it is of concern to compute the estimated nonstationary probability density function of the message from the various moments which have been transduced throughout the system. In general, it will probably satisfy the constraints which identify it as belonging to the Pearson Class. That is, it will be continuous over a bounded range with a continuous derivative which has a finite value at the end points and is a solution to a differential equation of the form

$$\frac{p'(x)}{p(x)} = \frac{x+a}{b_0 + b_1 x + b_2 x^2}$$

A Pearson Class distribution can be exactly determined from knowledge of only the first four moments. The actual aircraft message probability density function will usually asymptotically approach zero. It is therefore reasonable to assume that negligible error would result from considering any physically realizable message distribution to be of the Pearson Class.

Cost and time required for the computation of the message through the use of moment techniques is directly dependent upon the number of moments which are traced throughout the model. Consideration should, therefore, also be given to the possibility of using less than four moments for computation of conservative estimates of the various applicable criteria. For example, Tchebycheff's Inequality states

$$p[|x-m| \geq k\sigma] \leq \frac{1}{k^2}$$

which generally yields a conservative measure for criteria such as reliability.

This inequality has been extended to incorporate a measure of the skewness. If Pearson's measure for skewness is utilized, then

$$p[|x-m| \geq k\sigma] \leq \frac{4}{9} \frac{1+s^2}{(k-|s|)^2}$$

where

$$s = \frac{m-x_0}{\sigma}$$

in the unimodal case. It is probably true that the human operator performs only the roughest of operations upon the probability characteristics of the perceived time series. It would then seem unreasonable to consider many moments in the transduction. Certain human operator probability perception qualities can be hypothesized. For example, it may be presumed that the human operator identifies the modal value of the distribution, x_0, the mean value, m, a measure of the "sureness" m/σ, and an asymmetry measure

$$\frac{m-x_0}{\sigma}$$

Each of these would probably be estimated with poorer discrimination in the order presented.

This set of hypothesized perception measures can be algebraically solved for the first two moments. Further information can be obtained about higher moments by reference to the statistical definition for the Pearson Measure for skewness, in exact form,[9]

$$s = \frac{\gamma_1(\gamma_2+6)}{2(5\gamma_2-6\gamma_1^2+6)}$$

where

$$\gamma_1 = \frac{\eta}{\sigma^3}$$

and

$$\gamma_2 = \frac{\mu_4^1}{\sigma^4} - 3$$

Where μ_4^1 is the fourth moment about the mean. If γ_1 and γ_2 are small, then the measure for skewness approximately equals $\gamma_1/2$, or

$$x_0 = m - \tfrac{1}{2}\gamma_1\sigma$$

thus

$$\eta = 2\sigma^2(m-x_0)$$

[9] Using the notation of A. Cramér.

It might also prove of value to estimate the fourth moment from

$$\mu_3^2 < \mu_2 \mu_4$$

however, it is probably true that even such extension in precision to include the fourth moment would introduce considerable additional error over the human operator probability transduction.

Consider the feedback path with respect to moment transduction. The loop can be closed in any one of many ways. If the loop is closed through a linear predictor sensor, it may be presumed that odd moments are unaffected. The effect of prediction on higher even moments than the second is not generally known, but even if these were known, they would probably be of negligible value in aiding the approximation of the mathematical model for human control flight. The amplification increases the various moments of the message as indicated above, and the predictor adds uncertainty as defined by its error curve which is a function of the prediction time interval. Normally this function is empirically determined for a particular device and for independent prediction, the predictor output, σ_y^2, should be the sum of the input variance and the predictor variance of added uncertainty.

Partial prediction in the feedback can be accomplished where the message and the first few derivatives of the message are sensed, weighted, and summed. The differentiation process usually increases the noise due to the increased bandwidth of the output which cannot pass the band-limited physical elements without distortion. The total average power (approximate variance) of the input signal is defined by

$$P_T(x) = \int_0^\infty S(f)\, df$$

The output signal, y, is formed by

$$y = \frac{dx}{dt}$$

then

$$P_T(y) = 4\pi^2 \int_0^\infty f^2 S(f)\, df$$

and, of course, successive differentiations would introduce additional power by the factor of ω^{2n}. This additional energy would be provided by the perfect differentiator.[10] Such a feedback system is considered partial prediction in the sense that it approximates the output message Taylor Series expansion.

The various derivatives may be obtained by tapping the forward channel between any integrations which may take place. Such a loop closure is called quickening, and it appears to be more efficient in actual practice for two

[10] Approximate differentiation is performed by passive networks. However, their degree of best approximation can be determined by comparison of the actual output energy to that of a perfect active differentiator.

reasons. First, the obtained "derivatives" of the output are obtained without the distortion and noise of the forward integrators. Secondly, no additional noise is induced through the practical aspects of differentiation.

It is also possible to consider a predictor included in the forward loop. Here again the variance is increased in a similar manner to that described above.

It may thus be seen that the information transfer loop may be closed in terms of the transformation of the individual moments. The message distribution may be computed as a function of time and the appropriate set of criteria applied. From the weighted set evaluation of a figure of merit, some measure of entire system performance is obtained. For the moment, consider the man to be a unity transfer, then a stationary signal and stationary noise would yield a nonstationary message. Since it is known that the actual man-controlled aircraft has a stationary distribution in the gross sense, it appears valid to attribute much of this to the human operator's time varying nonlinear performance characteristics which are selected so as to "stabilize" the mission performance.

This formulation has been concerned with the transduction of marginal distributions. It should now be extended to the case of joint distributions due to the redundancy essential to the signal as it passes throughout the system. This involves little complication of the formulation, amounting to an increase in the number of variables, but may severely increase the amount and cost of the required computer. The suggested technique of individual moment transduction was only arrived at after careful consideration of actual probability function transduction, characteristic function transduction, and other similar approaches. Each of these was considered to be inefficient with respect to the feasibility and cost of practical computation of actual flight problems. Nevertheless, these previous attempts were not worthless, in that their investigation afforded a new insight into various aspects of the general problem.

At this point, it appears worth repetition to state again that this suggested mathematical model is *not* intended to represent any actual mechanism within the human operator. It is only intended to represent a black box approximation to human operator qualities of flight control. It is recognized that certain very real characteristics have been neglected; however, this seems necessary to reduce the problem to a reasonable level of difficulty.

One of the severest limitations of this model is the neglected interdependency among all the elements. For instance, learning, the accumulation of long- and short-term memory, affects the precision of both amplitude and rate quantization of perception; the stress level sensor affects the accuracy of anticipation as well as the decision rule set which translates the error-signal into a correction-signal; the observation rule which affects the intermittency and fixation period of vision has been neglected from the rules of choice set (in fact, it has been presumed that the rules of choice operate without error).

The variation between human operators has been neglected, and the operator considered represents the average pilot. Undoubtedly, many other features have been neglected in this description for the single parameter information transfer system of human flight control. It is hoped that many of these will be incorporated in future extensions of this model.

9.5. CONCLUSION

Immediate system control, such as vehicle guidance, has traditionally been the assigned task of the human operator. As design techniques advance, it becomes possible to consider the mechanization[11] of a greater portion of this task. The trend toward automation is reflected in successive encroachment upon the lower levels of human supervisory function until it becomes natural to ask: "Can the human operator be entirely eliminated from the system?" This question deserves careful attention.

At the outset it is important to recognize the existence of a continuum over the degrees of automation. At one extreme the human operator remains unaided and completely autonomous with respect to all levels of decision relating to strategy and tactics. In such a system *all* information must be processed by the operator. The reliability with which the system performs the mission he assigns is severely dependent upon the adequacy of personal processing of meaningful data within the limits of human channel capacity.

The first step toward automation is usually in the form of equipment which furnishes sensory extension. The operator finds it wise to place some trust in these devices in order that he have access to a greater portion of the relevant data on system performance. Once such sensing devices become part of the system, it is a natural step to provide some means for their combination and/ or integration so as to assimilate some of the information for the human prior to his acceptance. Such *a priori* data processing removes the operator another step from direct control. The presented variable may prove "easier to handle," but this gain has been purchased at the cost of a loss in system specificity of control. Some of the sensed data may be lost due to the increased coarseness of the classification system through which the operator accepts the displayed information.

It is but a short step from sensing and processing data for human consumption to using some of this data for closing the loop on system control. The use of rate feedback and various configurations of inner loops may improve system stability, but at the same time they constrain system flexibility of response. The complete capability of the system is no longer under the control of the operator. Such mechanism can, however, be of distinct value as illustrated by the extensive use of aircraft autopilots. Even while operating in the

[11] Throughout this discussion, the term "mechanization" or "mechanism" refers to any physical embodiment regardless of whether it be mechanical, electrical, electronic, chemical, and so on.

autopilot mode, the pilot has not been entirely removed from the control system. His function of monitoring is a tracking task, but this under considerably less stringent criteria calls for his intervention only upon the sensing of gross control system error.

The desire for expendable vehicles and the problems associated with new unknown environments bring pressure to bear to remove the human operator from the physical confines of the vehicle. Remote control may make it desirable to furnish additional sensing and telemetry in order to overcome the loss of kinesthetic sensations and other previously unassisted human sensed data. However, relocation of the operator is not in itself a step toward automation.

Lastly, if it is possible for the human operator to completely specify the required mission, and, as part of that specification, the particular task which he would accomplish as part of the control system, then it is conceivable to replace the man by an equivalent mechanization. Only the simplest of vehicle-missions can be so stated at this time.

The extensive search for a mathematical representation of human tracking transfer was initiated to fill a need expressed by design engineers. If an adequate expression were provided, they could design the closed loop system in accordance with stability and other performance criteria. The investigation proceeded in a reasonable manner, analyzing human transfer behavior under successively less constrained experimental conditions. The resulting mathematical expressions revealed terms which could easily be incorporated into the vehicle mechanism. Presumably, such design would remove portions of the operator's task and thereby allow greater efficiency in the human functioning over the remaining, and as yet unknown, portion of the ultimate mathematical representation.

Such logic is deceptive. A mathematical expression of one aspect of the measured transfer characteristic *cannot be taken as a partition of the human functioning*. That which is accomplished by the human operator may have little, if any, correspondence with the operation indicated by the model. Therefore, it does *not* follow that separation of such an equivalent operation will remove it from the human functioning or, indeed, in any way simplify or necessarily facilitate his operation. Certainly, the reduction of time lag in the display of system information brings increased accuracy of tracking performance due to the greater relevance of the data, but this is not the same as removing human "differentiation." Great care must be exercised in the "use" of mathematical models.

There is certainly great cost to the incorporation of a human into a vehicle system. He usually requires sensory extensions, data processing and display, controls for instructing the system, and, when he is placed in the vehicle, there is often considerable expense and weight-cost associated with the necessary life-support equipment. If the vehicle capability is marginal to the intended mission—that is, if there is no significant capability for alternate missions as called for by the exigencies of the operational situation—then the inclusion of the human operator might be unwarranted. If, in contrast, there are a number of possible missions and the cost of the vehicle itself is such as to expand this list even further to include emergency retrieval missions, then the cost of including the human operator is rapidly overcome by the benefits of the saving as measured by the sum of the probability weighted successful missions. The cost of the external uncertainty for using the human operator is essentially fixed, while the savings rise as some direct function of the vehicle capability and cost.

One further point; final production design must be "reliability oriented" while development designs must be "flexibility oriented" in view of the as yet unknown design parameters. Probably the most "flexible" information processor available to the design engineer is the human operator. His tentative inclusion can provide significant on-the-spot analysis of system performance. He furnishes an inherent combination of emergency sensing and performance recording apparatus.

*   *   *

As noted above, all decisions may be viewed as a tracking through a set of alternatives under the constant endeavor to minimize or otherwise constrain some error function as defined by the provided criteria set. At the lowest level of system control, the successive decisions are often governed by a time-consistent criteria-error-function. The observed tracking is then describable in terms of the attributes of this function and its application.

At grosser levels of system control, decisions are usually less frequent and are characterized by significant change of the criteria-error-function in accord with the particular set of alternatives which are being considered by the decision-maker. The usual techniques for describing tracking behavior might prove appropriate for the succession of decisions which occur at any one level, but the overview of system performance covers all levels of decision thereby making tracking analysis exceedingly difficult, if at all possible.

BIBLIOGRAPHY

ADAMS, J. A., "Human Tracking Behavior," *Psychological Bulletin*, Vol. 58 No. 1 (January 1961), 55–79.

———. "Psychomotor Response Acquisition and Transfer as a Function of Control-Indicator Relationships," *Journal of Experimental Psychology*, Vol. 48 (1954), 10–14.

ADAMS, J. A., and L. V. XHIGNESSE, "Some Determinants of Two-Dimensional Visual Tracking Behavior," *Journal of Experimental Psychology*, Vol. 60 No. 6 (December 1960), 391–403.

ADAMS, J. A., and C. E. WEBBER, "The Organization of Component Response Error Events in Two-Dimensional Visual Tracking," *Journal of Experimental Psychology*, Vol. 61 No. 3 (March 1961), 200–212.

ANDERSON, G. W., J. A. ASELTINE, et al., "A Self-Adjusting System for Optimum Dynamic Performance," *IRE National Convention Record*, Part 4 Vol. 6 (1958), 182–190.

ANDERSON, N. H., F. H. DRESSE, and D. A. GRANT, "Effect of Rate of Automatically-Paced Training in a Multidimensional Psychomotor Task," *Journal of Experimental Psychology*, Vol. 49 (1955), 231–236.

ANDREAS, B. G., R. F. GREEN, and S. D. S. SPRAGG, "Transfer Effects Between Performance on a Following Tracking Task and a Compensatory Tracking Test," *Journal of Psychology*, Vol. 37 (1954), 173–183.

ANDREW, G. M., "The Frequency Response and the Transfer Functions of the Human Pilot," *USAF TR 52–28*, Edwards AFB, Calif. (March 1953).

ARCHER, E. J., L. D. WYCKOFF, and F. G. BROWN, "Tracking Performance as Measured by Time Continuously on Target," *USAF WADC TR 54–210* (March 1954).

BAILEY, A. W., "Simplifying the Operator's Task as a Controller," *Ergonomics*, Vol. 1 (1958), 177–181.

BATTIG, W. F., J. F. VOSS, and W. J. BROGDEN, "Effect of Frequency of Target Intermittence upon Tracking," *Journal of Experimental Psychology*, Vol. 49 (1955), 244–248.

BELLMAN, R., and R. KALABA, "On Adaptive Control Processes," *IRE Transactions on Automatic Control*, Vol. AC–4 No. 2 (November 1959), 1–9.

BIRMINGHAM, H. P., and F. V. TAYLOR, "A Human Engineering Approach to the Design of Man Operated Continuous Control Systems," *USN NRL Rep. 4333* (April 1954).

BIRMINGHAM, H. P., A. KAHN, and F. V. TAYLOR, "A Demonstration of the Effects of Quickening in Multiple-Coordinate Control Tasks," *USN NRL Rep. 4380* (June 23, 1954).

BIRMINGHAM, H. P., "The Optimization of Man-Machine Control Systems," *IRE WESCON Convention Record*, Part 4 (1958), 272–276.

BIRMINGHAM, H. P., and F. V. TAYLOR, "A Design Philosophy for Man-Machine Control Systems," *Proceedings of the IRE*, Vol. 42 (1954), 1748–1758.

BOWEN, J. H., and R. CHERNIKOFF, "The Relationship Between Magnification and Course Frequency in Compensatory Aided Tracking," *USN NRL Rep. 4913* (1957).

BOWEN, J. H., and R. CHERNIKOFF, "The Effects of Magnification and Average Course Velocity on Compensatory Tracking," *USN NRL Rep. 5186* (1958).

BRADLEY, J. V., "Desirable Control-Display Relationships for Moving-Scale Instruments," *USAF WADC TR 54–423* (1954).

BUGELSKI, B. R., "Population Stereotypes in Pedal Control of a 'Ball-Bank' Indicator," *Journal of Applied Psychology*, Vol. 39 (1955), 422–424.

BURKE, C. J., R. NARASIMHAN, and O. J. BENEPE, "Some Problems in the Spectral Analysis of Human Behavior Records," *USAF WADC TR 53–27* (July 1953).

CHAPANIS, A., and L. E. LINDENBAUM, "A Reaction Time Study of Four Control-Display Linkages," *Journal of the Human Factors Society,* Vol. 1 No. 4 (November 1959), 8–15.

CHERNIKOFF, R., H. P. BIRMINGHAM, and F. V. TAYLOR, "A Comparison of Pursuit and Compensatory Tracking Under Conditions of Aiding and No Aiding," *Journal of Experimental Psychology,* Vol. 49 (1955), 55–59.

CHERNIKOFF, R., H. P. BIRMINGHAM, and F. V. TAYLOR, "A Comparison of Pursuit and Compensatory Tracking in a Simulated Aircraft Control Loop," *Journal of Applied Psychology,* Vol. 50 (1956), 47–52.

CHERNIKOFF, R., and F. V. TAYLOR, "Effects of Course Frequency and Aided Time Constant on Pursuit and Compensatory Tracking," *Journal of Experimental Psychology,* Vol. 53 No. 5 (1957), 285–292.

CHERNIKOFF, R., J. H. BOWEN, and H. P. BIRMINGHAM, "A Comparison of Zero-Order and Fourth-Order Aided Compensatory Systems as a Function of Course Frequency," *USN NRL Rep. 5262* (1959).

CLUTTON, B. J., "A Comparison Between Combined and Divided Controls and One-Man and Two-Man Aiming," *Great Britain Royal Naval Personnel Research Committee Report 665,* OES 199, Cambridge, England (1951).

CONKLIN, J. E., "Effects of Control Lag on Performance in a Tracking Task," *Journal of Experimental Psychology,* Vol. 53 No. 4 (April 1957), 261–268.

CRAIK, K. J. W., "Theory of the Human Operator in Control Systems: 1. The Operator as an Engineering System," *British Journal of Psychology,* Vol. 38 (1948), 56–61.

———. "Theory of the Human Operator in Control Systems: 2. Man as an Element in a Control System," *British Journal of Psychology,* Vol. 38 (1948), 142–148.

DUEY, J. W., and R. CHERNIKOFF, "The Use of Quickening in One Coordinate of a Two-Dimensional Tracking System," *IRE Transactions on Human Factors in Electronics,* Vol. HFE–1 No. 1 (March 1960), 21–23.

ELKIND, J. I., "Tracking Response Characteristics of the Human Operator," *USAF Human Factors Operation Research Laboratories Report HFORL Memo No. 4* (September 1953).

———. "Characteristics of Simple Manual Control Systems," *MIT Lincoln Laboratory TR No. 111* (April 6, 1956).

ELKIND, J. I., and C. D. FORGIE, "Characteristics of the Human Operator in Simple Manual Control Systems," *IRE Transactions on Automatic Control,* Vol. AC–4 No. 1 (May 1959), 44–55.

ELKIN, J. E., and D. M. GREEN, "Measurement of Time-Varying and Nonlinear Dynamic Characteristics of Human Pilots," *USAF ASD TR 61–225* (December 1961).

ELY, J. H., H. M. BOWEN, and J. ORLANSKY, "Man-Machine Dynamics: Chapter VII of the Joint Services Human Engineering Guide to Equipment Design," *USAF WADC TR 57–582* (November 1957).

EPPLE, R. G. E., "The Human Pilot," *USN BuAer Report AE–61–4111* (August 1954).

FITTS, P. M., and C. M. SEEGER, "S-R Compatibility: Spatial Characteristics of Stimulus and Response Codes," *Journal of Experimental Psychology*, Vol. 46 (1953), 199–210.

FITTS, P. M., and R. L. DEININGER, "S-R Compatibility: Correspondence Among Paired Elements Within Stimulus and Response Codes," *Journal of Experimental Psychology*, Vol. 48 (1954), 483–492.

FITTS, P. M., and C. W. SIMON, "Some Relations Between Stimulus Patterns and Performance in a Continuous Dual-Pursuit Task," *Journal of Experimental Psychology*, Vol. 43 (1952), 428–436.

FOGEL, L. J., "An Analysis for Human Flight Control," *IRE Convention Record*, 1956 National Convention, Part 8, 69–88.

FOGEL, L. J., and M. DWONCZYK, "Anticipatory Display Design Through the Use of an Analog Computer," *IRE Wescon Convention Record*, Part 4 (1958), 67–88.

GARVEY, W. D., and L. L. MITNICK, "An Analysis of Tracking Behavior in Terms of Lead-Lag Errors," *USN NRL Report 4707* (February 16, 1956).

GARVEY, W. D., J. S. SWEENEY, and H. P. BIRMINGHAM, "Differential Effects of 'Display Lags' and 'Control Lags' on the Performance of Manual Tracking Systems," *Journal of Experimental Psychology*, Vol. 56 (1958), 8–10.

GARVEY, W. D., and W. B. KNOWLES, "Response Time Patterns Associated with Various Display-Control Relationships," *Journal of Experimental Psychology*, Vol. 47 (1954), 315–322.

GIBBS, C. B., "The Continuous Regulation of Skilled Response by Kinesthetic Feedback," Great Britain Medical Research Council, *Applied Psychology Unit Report 190*, Cambridge, England (March 1953).

———. "Transfer of Training and Skill Assumptions in Tracking Tasks," *Quarterly Journal of Experimental Psychology*, Vol. 3 (August 1951), 99–110.

GILINSKY, A. S., and J. L. BROWN, "Eye Dominance and Tracking Performance," *USAF WADC TR 52–15* (April 1952).

GOODYEAR AIRCRAFT CORPORATION, "Final Report: Human Dynamics Study," *Report GER–4750*, Akron, Ohio (April 8, 1952).

GOTTSDANKER, R. M., "The Accuracy of Prediction Motion," *Journal of Experimental Psychology*, Vol. 43 (1952), 26–36.

———. "Prediction Motion With and Without Vision," *American Journal of Psychology*, Vol. 65 (1952), 533–543.

GOTTSDANKER, R. M., "Prediction-Span, Speed of Response, Smoothness and Accuracy in Tracking," *USAF AFPTRC, Lab. Note 55–6* (April 1955).

––––––. "A Further Study of Prediction-Motion," *American Journal of Psychology*, Vol. 68 (1955), 432–437.

GRANT, D. A., and N. F. KAESTNER, "Constant Velocity Tracking as a Function of Subjects Handedness and the Rate and Direction of the Target Course," *Journal of Experimental Psychology*, Vol. 49 (1955), 203–208.

HALL, I., "Effects of Controlled Element on the Human Pilot," *USAF WADC TR 57–509* (August 1958).

HARTMAN, B. O., and P. M. FITTS, "Relation of Stimulus and Response Amplitude to Tracking Performance," *Journal of Experimental Psychology*, Vol. 49 (1955), 82–92.

HICK, W. E., "The Discontinuous Functioning of the Human Operator in Pursuit Tasks," *Quarterly Journal of Experimental Psychology*, Vol. 1 (1948), 36–51.

––––––. "Man as an Element in a Control System," *Medical Research Council, Applied Psychology Unit*, APU 150/51 (1951).

HICK, W. E., and J. A. V. BATES, "The Human Operator and Control Mechanisms," *Monograph No. 17.204 Ministry of Supply*, Shell Mex House, London (May 1950).

HIGGINS, T. J., and D. B. HOLLAND, "The Human Being as a Link in an Automatic Control System—Part I," *IRE Transactions on Medical Electronics*, Vol. ME–6 No. 3 (September 1959), 125–133.

HOLLAND, J. G., and J. B. HENSON, "Transfer of Training Between Quickened and Unquickened Tracking Systems," *USN NRL Report 4703* (February 3, 1956).

HOLLAND, J. G., "A Correlation Analysis of Tracking Behavior," *Psychometrika*, Vol. 22 (1957), 275–287.

HUMPHREY, C. E., J. E. THOMPSON, and J. VERSACE, "Time Sharing and the Tracking Task," *Johns Hopkins University, Applied Physics Laboratory Report TG–201* (July 1953).

HUMPHREY, C. E., and J. E. THOMPSON, "Auditory Displays. II. Comparison of Auditory Tracking with Visual Tracking in One Dimension," *Johns Hopkins University, Applied Physics Laboratory Project 20–F–1* (April 1953).

JACKSON, A. S., "Synthesis of a Linear Quasi Transfer Function for the Operator in Man-Machine Systems," *IRE WESCON Convention Record*, Part 4 (1958), 263–272.

JOHNSON, C. W., "Adaptive Servomechanisms," *IRE Transactions on Medical Electronics*, Vol. ME–6 No. 3 (September 1959), 134–140.

KATZ, M. S., and S. D. S. SPRAGG, "Tracking Performance as a Function of Frequency of Course Illumination," *Journal of Psychology*, Vol. 40 (1955), 181–191.

KNOWLES, W. B., W. D. GARVEY, and E. P. NEWLIN, "The Effect of Speed and Load on Display-Control Relationships," *Journal of Experimental Psychology*, Vol. 46 (1953), 65–75.

KOENIG, J. F., "Stability of Nonlinear Feedback Control Systems," *Dept. of Commerce National Bureau of Standards Report 3619* (August 1954).

KRENDEL, E. S., and D. T. McRUER, "Dynamic Responses of the Human Operator," *USAF WADC TR 56–524* (October 1957).

LEVINE, MARVIN, "Transfer of Tracking Performance as a Function of a Delay Between the Control and the Display," *USAF WADC TR 53–237* (November 1953).

LINCOLN, R. S., "Visual Tracking: 3. The Instrumental Dimension of Motion in Relation to Tracking Accuracy," *Journal of Applied Psychology*, Vol. 37 (1953), 489–493.

LINCOLN, R. S., and K. W. SMITH, "Systematic Analysis of Factors Determining Accuracy in Visual Tracking," *Science*, Vol. 116 (1952).

LUCE, R. D., ed., *Developments in Mathematical Psychology*. Glencoe, Illinois: The Free Press, 1960.

MECHLER, E. A., J. B. RUSSELL, and M. G. PRESTON, "The Basis for the Optimum Aided-Tracking Time Constant," *Journal of the Frankling Institute*, Vol. 248 (October 1949), 327–334.

MITCHELL, M. J. H., and M. A. VINCE, "The Direction of Movement of Machine Controls," *Quarterly Journal of Experimental Psychology*, Vol. 3 (1951), 24–35.

NIXON, F. E., *Handbook of Laplace Transformation: Tables and Examples*. Englewood Cliffs, N.J.: Prentice-Hall, Inc., 1960.

NOBLE, M. E., P. M. FITTS, and C. E. WARREN, "The Frequency Response of Skilled Subjects in a Pursuit Tracking Task," *Journal of Experimental Psychology*, Vol. 49 (1955), 249–256.

NORTH, J. D., "The Human Transfer Function in Servo Systems," in *Automatic and Manual Control*, A. Tustin, ed. New York: Academic Press, 1952.

POULTON, E. C., "Perceptual Anticipation in Tracking," *Applied Psychology Unit, Psychological Laboratory APU 118/50*, Cambridge, England (1950).

———. "Speed Anticipation and Course Anticipation in Tracking," *Great Britain Medical Research Council, Pyschological Laboratory Report 123*, Cambridge, England (September 1950).

———. "The Basis of Perceptual Anticipation in Tracking," *British Journal of Psychology*, Vol. 43 (1952), 295.

ROCKWAY, M. R., "The Effect of Variations in Control-Display Ratio and Exponential Time Delay on Tracking Performance," *USAF WADC TR 54–618* (December 1954).

ROIG, R. W., "A Comparison Between Human Operator and Optimum Linear Controller RMS-Error Performance," *IRE Transactions on Human Factors in Electronics*, Vol. HFE–3 No. 1 (March 1962), 18–21.

ROSS, S., B. E. SHEPP, and T. G. ANDREWS, "Response Preferences in Display-Control Relationships," *Journal of Applied Psychology*, Vol. 39 (1955), 425–428.

RUSSELL, L., "Characteristics of the Human as a Linear Servo Element," *S. M. Thesis*, Massachusetts Institute of Technology (1951).

SENDERS, J. W., and M. CRUZEN, "Tracking Performance on Combined Compensatory and Pursuit Tasks," *USAF WADC TR 52–39* (1952).

SENDERS, J. W., "The Influence of Surround on Tracking Performance: 1. Tracking on Combined Pursuit and Compensatory One-Dimensional Tasks With and Without a Structured Surround," *USAF WADC TR 52–229* (February 1953).

———. "Tracking with Intermittently Illuminated Displays," *USAF WADC TR 55–378* (1955).

———. "Survey of Human Dynamics Data and A Sample Application," *USAF WADC TR 59–712* (November 1959).

SIMON, C. W., "The Presence of a Dual Perceptual Set For Certain Perceptual Motor Tasks," *USAF WADC TR 54–286* (June 1954).

SLACK, C. W., "Some Characteristics of the 'Range Effect'," *Journal of Experimental Psychology*, Vol. 46 (1953), 76–80.

SWEENEY, J. S., H. P. BIRMINGHAM, and W. D. GARVEY, "A Study of the Effects of Filtering on the Performance of a Manual Compensatory Tracking Test," *USN NRL Report 5205* (1958).

SWEENEY, J. S., and A. GRAHAM, "The Effect of Loop Characteristics Upon Human Gain," *IRE National Convention Record*, Part 9 (1959), 80–85.

TAYLOR, F. V., and H. P. BIRMINGHAM, "Studies of Tracking Behavior: II. The Acceleration Pattern of Quick Manual Corrective Responses," *Journal of Experimental Psychology*, Vol. 38 (1948), 783–795.

TIPTON, C. L., and H. P. BIRMINGHAM, "The Influence of Control Gain in a First-Order Man-Machine Control System," *Journal of the Human Factors Society*, Vol. 1 No. 3 (August 1959), 69–71.

TRUXAL, J. G., *Automatic Feedback Control Systems Synthesis*. New York: McGraw-Hill Book Company, Inc., 1955.

TUSTIN, A., "The Nature of the Operator's Response in Manual Control and Its Implications for Controller Design," *Journal of the Institution of Electrical Engineers*, Vol. 94 Part IIA No. 2 (1947).

VANHORN, I. H., "Nonlinear Techniques Applied to the Analysis of Pilot Induced Oscillations," *IRE National Convention Record*, Vol. 5 Part 4 (1957), 27–32.

11

HUMAN DECISION-MAKING

11.1. INTRODUCTION

Man likes to distinguish himself from the other animals as being the most intelligent. He claims to possess a sensor-mediator-motor capability which can successfully cope with the challenge of the natural environment, and this with negligible change of his own structural being. To do this, he insulates himself by creating an artificial enclosing environment which can absorb the punishment from nature for him. Surely, no other animal has been so clever in its efforts to maximize the probability of survival with minimal internal structural change.

With increasing ability to sense and modify his surround, the human operator has reduced his primary role to that of a decision-maker. His personal value rests in his ability to translate sensed data into meaningful command signals. Mankind is rapidly becoming an army of generals.

It is certainly of interest to study the nature of human decision-making and to examine the attribute of intellect in some detail.

11.2. THE EVOLUTION OF INTELLECT

Animals which could reasonably be called human have been on earth for a very short time. Through a gradual transition, man first appeared about 100,000 years ago, as shown in Figure 11.1. This time span is only about 1/20,000th of the time during which life has existed on earth. Truly, man is a most recent phenomenon of the natural experiment called evolution.

Over an extended period of time, the evolutionary process which has yielded man has also produced an extremely large number of other organisms which have exhibited widely different degrees of intelligent behavior. In order to see

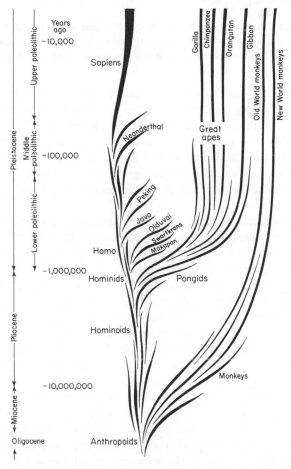

Figure 11.1. Lines of descent that lead to man and his closer living relatives. The hominoid superfamily diverged from the anthropoid line in the Miocene period some 20 million years ago. From the hominoid line came the tool-using hominoids at the beginning of the Pleistocene. The genus *Homo* appeared in the hominoid line during the first inter-glacial; the species *Homo sapiens*, around 50,000 years ago.

human decision-making within a useful frame of reference, it is worthwhile to consider briefly the evolutionary process which has existed on earth for about six billion years. It is important to view the entire process in the large.

The primary problem of science is one of classification. Man proceeds to classify each newly observed process or entity as being like or unlike those he has already experienced. In this manner, he enlarges his knowledge of the world in which he lives. It is important, however, to recognize that the sharp discontinuities of classification *are man-imposed* and not essential to nature. In the words of S. Morgulis,[1]

> The biologist, unlike the layman, knows no line of demarcation separating plant life from animal life, nor for that matter living from nonliving material because such differentiations are purely conceptual and do not correspond to reality.

Evolution is a statistical process. The outcome of any particular portion of the experiment, indeed, the outcome of the entire experiment, is not entirely predictable. Throughout nature the general rule has been "survival of the fittest" with respect to patterns of flow and storage of energy, information, and material. In the Darwinian sense "fittest" is measured in terms of the probability of survival of the species or group of individuals. The governing rule of nature should not be taken to determine the outcome of any particular situation.

In many regards, the outcome of individual events is clouded in uncertainty. Some of this uncertainty is introduced during the lifespan of the individual organism in terms of the stimuli it receives from the larger class of stimuli it could receive. In cases where the organism lives in a restricted environment, this set of stimuli may be a compounding of the uncertainty it introduces as part of its response. Further, there is the uncertainty contributed by perturbations in the reproductive "signal" wherein mutations yield modified genetic properties. Only some of these modified organisms survive.

Somewhere early in the evolution of life an organism existed which was sensitive to its surround and could retain the information derived from its environment from a previous "observation." Its internal state which was sensitive to the surround may be considered as a symbol, the set of these possible symbols defining the language with which the organism modeled its environment. Comparison of the present symbol to that produced by the immediate past observation could yield the elementary decision as to whether or not there had been a change in the environment. All higher forms of rational behavior rest upon there being at least this essential capability. At some higher level in the evolution of life, the organism became sufficiently complex to permit sensory resolution and/or the ability to reference its physical attitude with respect to some orientation. Upon this basis, it became possible for the organism to identify that only a portion of its environment had changed. With specific reference capability, the organism could identify *which* portion of its environment had changed.

Part of the sensed environment is the organism's own response. The comparison of repeated stimuli and similar response provides the organism

---

[1] From the introduction to the second edition of *The Origin of Life*, by A. I. Oparin, Dover Publications, Inc., New York, 1953.

with a model of its own transduction. Its responses serve as stimuli to the environment and the comparison of specific portions of the environment's response to its own actions furnishes a model of the transduction behavior of that portion of the environment. If the comparison of these models shows little difference, then the organism may reach the conclusion that "there is something in the environment like me."

With greater specificity of sensory capability and longer time available for sampling the environment, the organism may be able to discern some differences between the model it has identified within its own environment and the model which represents its own behavior. The discrimination of such a difference within species appears to be a prerequisite to directed sexual behavior. With even greater specificity in the comparison of models, it may be possible for the organism to identify uniqueness of the entity within the environment which behaves grossly like itself and yet shows detailed differences. "That other organism is not only like me, but is different from all other organisms like me that I have yet seen." Having identified uniqueness provides the basis for extended inter-individual relationships and the foundation of family life within the community of organisms.

Those portions of the sensed environment which repeatedly benefit the survival of the organism gradually become more and more positively related to its model of itself, and the concept of "mine" is born. At a higher level in the evolved complexity of organisms, a similar identification of portions of the environment which are repetitively associated with the model of another organism, in a similar manner, can serve to generate the concept of "thine." It appears to be a reasonable step from "mine and thine" to "good and bad" and "like and dislike." Only in the world of abundance does the organism assume the attitude of indifference.

Having a model of the group of organisms to which it belongs and the concept of "good and bad" the structure of moral behavior for the group good is born. At a considerably higher level of evolution, the organism may succeed in holding a model of the entire group of its own kind. Those behavior patterns which are consistently approved by this group are then defined as being "ethical."

Although it is extremely difficult to identify any specific benchmarks in the evolution of life at which these levels of decision capability were attained, it is interesting to note the way in which increasing complexity evolved. The evolutionary tree grows from the complex protein molecules common to all living creatures. The small organisms which are found just above the molecular level in the tree of life comprise the kingdom of Protista. At this level of evolution the distinction between plants and animals does not yet exist. Some of these organisms act like plants part of the time and like animals at other times. They are noncellular and generally highly predictable in their behavior. This kingdom includes the classes Sarcodina, Bacillariales, Bacteria, and Flagellata. This last class is of special interest in that some of its members may be induced to change from plant-like behavior to animal-like behavior but not the reverse.

The kingdoms of Plants and Animals arose from the kingdom of Protista as shown in Figure 11.2. Generally, each newly evolved species was of

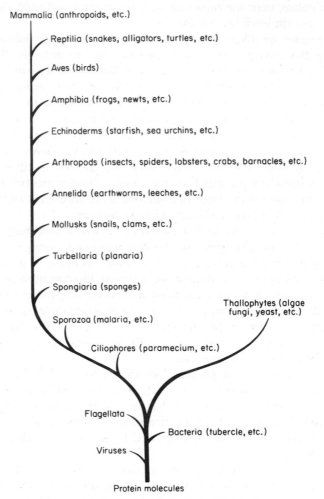

Figure 11.2. A portion of the Tree of Evolution.

greater complexity and revealed increased flexibility in its decision-making behavior thereby increasing the probability of its survival under a changing environment. It is in this sense that intellect gradually evolved. By definition, a decision is reached whenever an organism makes a selection among a set of alternatives. If its behavior is highly predictable, then the organism has contributed little information in making the selection. It survives only so long as its environment remains much the same. Those organisms which behave in a less predictable manner, making selection in a manner consistent with some aspect of their sensed environment, demonstrate greater flexibility and exhibit decision-making behavior which indicates the possibility of a higher level of intellect. Their probability of survival becomes strongly dependent upon the correspondence between the internally held model of their environment and the real world in which they exist.

The recognition by an organism that it can stimulate a portion of its environment to respond in a manner in any way similar to the way it would respond if *it* were so stimulated establishes communication between the organism and that portion of its environment. The specific communicated stimulus and response patterns comprise the external communication language which has some degree of correspondence to the set of symbols internal to the organism with which he has modeled his surroundings. It is most difficult to examine the internal modeling of organisms which occur at lower levels in the evolutionary process. Obviously, something of their internal modeling capability can be determined from the examination of the nature of the language which the organisms use for the purpose of communicating with other similar organisms. The earliest forms of language probably occur through the association of repeated natural disturbance of their own environment. For example, the sound of eating soon becomes meaningful of eating to another similar organism that might only hear the sound. Significantly complex social behavior and well-organized external language first appear in mammalia. This language has properties which relate to the level in the evolutionary cycle as indicated in Figure 11.3.

Seven important properties appear in human language that do not occur in any known non-human communicative system. As indicated by C. Hockett, these are *duality, productivity, arbitrariness, interchangeability, specialization, displacement,* and *cultural transmission,* defined as follows:

Duality. Human language has both sound symbols (phonology) and a grammatical system (morphology). The combination, called duality, is especially useful in a communication system in which large numbers of morphemes must be distinguished from each other, since duality is a means of coding between the message and the symbol. Although most communication between human beings takes place through the vocal-auditory channel, other channels are also used. Therefore, more generalized terms than phonemes (sound symbols) and morphemes (grammatical structure) are needed to explain duality. Hockett suggests the term *cenemes* for phonemes and *pleremes* for morphemes. Thus no matter what the medium of communication, the elements of the communication system have names and functions.

Productivity. Human language is plerematically complex, that is, some of the messages in the communication system consist of two or more pleremes. Combinations of these pleremes, in infinite variety, produce new messages.

Because of this, it is possible for a speaker to make a statement that he has never made before, or for that matter has never heard or read before, and it is just as possible for the listener to understand the statement without

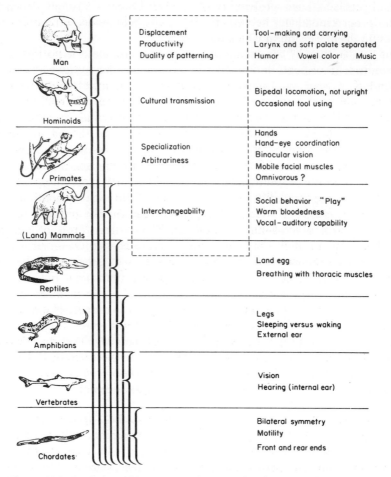

Figure 11.3. Evolution of language and some related characteristics are suggested by this classification of chordates. The lowest form of animal in each classification exhibits the features listed at the right of the class. Brackets indicate that each group possesses or has evolved beyond the characteristics exhibited by all the groups below. The features of language appear in the rectangle. Some, but by no means all of the characteristics associated with communication are presented in the column at the right.

realizing that the message is completely new to the speaker as well as to the listener.

Arbitrariness. If there is some natural reflection of the meaning within the pleremes, then the meaning can be described as iconic. Otherwise the semantic relationship between the plereme and its meaning is arbitrary. Human language is almost entirely arbitrary in its semantic conventions. (The exceptions which reflect iconicity are either wholly or partially onomatopoetic.) Since the complexity of human language is facilitated through the property of arbitrariness, this property has been fortuitous for the development of human language.

Interchangeability. The individual is equipped for both transmission and reception of messages within the same communication system. The speaker can be a listener, the listener can be a speaker, and the speaker can listen to his own messages.

Specialization. An action of one organism triggers behavior in another organism, but the action may also produce direct physical consequences. To gauge the amount of specialization in a communicative system, we analyze the difference between the direct physical consequences of an action and the response triggered in another individual. If there is slight difference, the system is not specialized; if there is great difference, then the system is highly specialized. For example, a shop foreman announces to his men that he will hold a meeting with them in five minutes. The direct physical consequence is simple audible disturbance in the surrounding area, but the response in another individual might be the turning off of machinery and the laying down of tools, acts so divergent from the message that the high degree of specialization in the communicative system is obvious.

Displacement. A message is said to be displaced when its antecedents and its consequences are removed from the time and place of the message transmission. Any message about objects or events of the past or the future, or about objects or events spatially removed from the transmitter or receiver, have the property of displacement.

Cultural Transmission. Cultural transmission is the passing on of the conventions of the communicative system to subsequent organisms. The genetic structure of an individual provides some essential features of the communicative system, but the individual also acquires habit, by means of cultural mechanisms, which provides specific communicative behavior. Thus cultural transmission change makes for efficiency of communication with respect to changing environment. It provides means for a whole group of organisms to find effective communication media and so adapt at a much higher rate than would be achieved through natural selection.

It is interesting to note how various animals communicate. Table 11.1 indicates something of the degree to which these seven properties appear in five species of animals. The advanced complexity of human intellectual behavior is reflected in the strength with which men communicate using all seven properties.

It would be dangerous to assume that the existence of certain common properties in the intercommunication system of various organisms can be

Table 11.1.

	Bee Dancing	Stickleback Courtship	Herring Gull Care of Offspring	Gibbon Calls	Human Language
Duality	no(?)	no	no	no	yes
Productivity	yes	no	no	no	yes
Arbitrariness	slight	...	...	slight	great
Interchangeability	yes	no	no	yes	yes
Specialization	yes	some	?	yes	yes
Displacement	yes	no	no	no	yes
Cultural transmission	no	no	no	no(?)	yes

From C. F. Hockett, *A Course in Modern Linguistics*, New York: Macmillan Company, 1958.

used to relate them in terms of phylogenetic lineage. As Hockett points out, some invertebrates, some reptiles, most birds, and two mammals (bats and men) have independently acquired the ability to fly. Within the history of man it does, however, appear highly probable that certain communicative properties imply the prior existence of others. Of the seven properties, specialization appears to be the earliest, since it is also found in the behavior of birds and fish. Interchangeability is common to both man and gibbon. Cultural transmission may also be common to both of these but to a much lesser extent in the gibbon. It is in this regard that the imitative tendencies of many primates are worthy of attention. It may well be that the seeds for the later development of cultural transmission, displacement, and interchangeability were planted in pre-hominoid times.

Imitation can lead to displacement as a result of situations where the young of a species are taught a habit out of the exact context in which that response would normally be elicited. If the young develop habits through learning rather than through genetically driven maturation, imitation yields interchangeability. Productivity and arbitrariness are only to be found in recent human language. These properties were developed subsequent to the era of the latest common ancestor of all Hominoidea and distinguish man from his lesser rivals. Although it is not yet possible to say whether duality preceded productivity, these must have occurred in close conjunction as an efficient means for erecting a sufficiently large number of discriminably different signals.

The use of language directly affected survival. Natural selection soon filtered out the inefficient genetic strains and ineffective culturally transmitted habits, leading to human language which is about equally efficient for the natural survival of all human communities. The differences which do exist are indigenous to particular environmental situations and the essential statistical variability of the continuing selective process. Indeed, natural languages evolve in a most efficient manner. Empirical data reveal that Zipf's law is generally followed, that is to say, that the frequency of occurrence of each word in the language is inversely proportional to the rank order of the length of that word. This "law" has been shown generally true for other segments of text, including phonemes, syllables, morphemes, Chinese characters, and even the babblings of babies.

It is interesting to note that man has been in biological isolation for the past 30,000 or more years, as the only surviving species of the only surviving genus of the family Hominoidea. His most recent ancestors, common to other survivors, lived ten to fifteen million years ago. This isolation results whenever a number of similar organisms are placed within the same ecological "niche." Soon the group which is most successful at adaptation destroys or interbreeds with the others. In the case of man, genetic changes took place which permitted cultural transmission and the development of social strength through intercommunicative language. Archeological remains indicate that the genetic adaptation which resulted in large brains was common to all the early derivatives of Hominoidea. Only some of these brains may have been functionally structured to allow the development of language and the more efficient codification of the internal model which represented the sensed environment. Indeed, the emergence of this higher communicative ability may well have modified man by its very existence—from an individually oriented organism to one that *needs* to communicate with his fellows as an essential ingredient of life.

11.3. THE RESIDENCE OF INTELLECT

Evolution of the brain is an obvious correlate of the evolution of intelligence, at least during the more recent past. The weight of the brain in contemporary mammals can be related to body weight by

$$w = kW^\beta$$

where w is the brain weight, W is the body weight, and k and β are constants (k being the log w intercept, and β being the slope of a straight regression line in log-log coordinates). A high correlation factor was found between log w and log W for a sample of 115 mammals which revealed $k = 0.18$ and $\beta = 0.66$.

Let it be assumed that β is a mammalian constant. Various values of k then designate members of the family of parallel regression lines on log-log coordinates. The particular value of k which yields a best fit can be used as an index of cephalization, descriptive of the level of evolution of that mammal's brain. This index is, in fact, generally related to human estimates of the intelligence of mammalian orders.

If the assumption made above were completely true, groups of mammals at the same level of evolution should have the same k values. Thus, a plot of k against log W for, say, primates should reveal parallel horizontal lines. Within each group of data points the correlation between k and log W should be zero. Figure 11.4 indicates the empiric inverse relationship between the index of cephalization and the logarithm of the body weight for some primates. The appropriate description of the subgroups of primates shown is clearly in terms of the functional relationship between k and log W, rather than just the mean values of k.

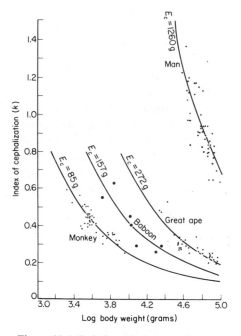

Figure 11.4. Relationship between index of cephalization (k) and log body weight of primates.

It was H. Jerison who indicated that the evolution of mammals, characterized by increasing intelligence, may have involved the differentiation of additional cerebral tissue, the amount being unrelated to body weight (except as the body weight itself may be correlated with the evolution of intelligence). Thus, in a more refined analysis, the total weight of the brain, E, may consist of two parts: w, which varies with body weight as described above, and E_c which is a constant for a group achieving a specific level of cerebral evolution. That is,

$$E = w + E_c \quad \text{and} \quad w = k'W^\beta$$

where log k' is the log w intercept for primative mammals, that is, those for which $E_c = 0$. k' is estimated to be about 0.05 for the opossum, the best contemporary approximation of a primative mammal. From these equations

$$k = \frac{E_c}{W^\beta} + k'$$

which suggests that a large portion of the primate brain weight is independent of body weight. Specific anatomical correlates of intelligence may be found in the development of parts of the brain of monkey, ape, and man as a function of body weight. It may well be that brain weight in primates, and

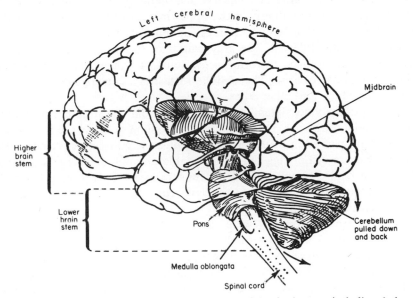

Figure 11.5. The central nervous system of man. The higher brain stem, including thalamus, midbrain, and part of pons are shown within the brain. The lower brain stem composed of pons and medulla emerges below with the cerebellum. (After W. Penfield and L. Roberts, *Speech and Brain Mechanisms*, Princeton University Press, Princeton, N.J., 1959.)

mammals in general, can be accounted for in terms of the development of additional cerebral tissue. More detailed justification of the above argument would require translating brain weight into numbers of neurons and measures of their connectivity.

The adult human brain weighs about 49 ounces in the male and about 44 ounces in the female. It is composed of five fairly distinct but connected parts: the cerebrum, the midbrain, the cerebellum, the pons (Varolii) and the medulla oblongata, as shown in Figure 11.5. The cerebrum is by far the largest of these, filling the upper portion of the skull. The entire surface, called the cortex, is made up of layers of gray matter. Interior to this is white matter, which includes many neural projection fibers (connecting the cerebrum with other parts of the brain and the spinal cord) and association and commissural fibers (connecting various parts of the cerebrum to each other). The midbrain is a relatively short constricted organ which connects the pons and the cerebellum. The cerebellum is situated on the brain stem directly under the cerebrum. Although it constitutes only about ten per cent of the total mass of the brain, it has 75 per cent as much surface area as each of the much larger cerebral hemispheres, since the folds of the outer surface elaborate into subfolds deep within the organ.

The pons is situated in front of the cerebellum between the midbrain and the medulla oblongata. It consists of a mixture of white and gray matter which connects the two halves of the cerebellum and forms a bridge between the medulla and the cerebrum. The medulla oblongata is continuous with the spinal cord, extending almost to the upper margin of the pons. Externally, the medulla resembles the upper part of the spinal cord; however, its internal structure is quite different. The gray matter of the medulla contains nerve cells which are grouped to form *nuclei*, some of which form centers from which cranial nerves arise. The medulla furnishes a control function for the heart, respiratory, and other reflex activities.

The central nervous system is an immensely complex structure containing some 15 billion neurons. Of these, about 10 billion neurons are included in the brain proper. Each neuron is capable of undergoing an electrochemical discharge upon being triggered by a suitable amount of energy impinging upon its extended members (called dendrites). This energy may be in the form of concurrent signals from other neurons or signals received directly from a sensor element.

Neurons are of extremely wide variety of shapes and sizes. Some have a long cylindrical extension of their body which serves to carry the electrochemical discharge as a propagating wavefront to other sections of the human body. For example, a motoneuron originating in the sacral spinal cord transmits its output signal directly to a muscle of the foot. D. P. C. Lloyd draws the following graphic illustration:

> If one were to visualize the cell body of such a motoneuron to be about the size of a tennis ball, then, keeping other parts commensurate, the axon would be a little less than a mile in length and no more than a half inch in diameter. The dendrites of such a motoneuron might be splayed out in a space equivalent to an average living room.

Figure 11.6 shows a reconstruction of part of a single motor nerve cell.

Neurons which are of significant length are termed *fibers*. These carry discharge signals at a rate proportional to their diameter. As a rule of thumb, the velocity of propagation in meters per second is about six times the diameter of the fiber as measured in microns. Nerve fibers usually occur in bundles which include tens of thousands of individual fibers which carry signals to or from the brain at speeds of about 200 miles per hour. Some nerve fibers are insulated from their neighbors by a layer of fatty material which, incidentally, increases the rate of conduction. In the case where a consistent neural signal decoding is used, the total strength of the resulting action depends to some extent upon the number of neurons which are excited.

The electrochemical energy is released as some of the excess of potassium inside the neuron leaks out and some of the excess of sodium outside the body of the neuron is absorbed. This chemical interchange is accompanied by an electrical discharge of about one-tenth of a volt. Classically, the neuron was considered to be either in a state of conduction or not. A more modern view includes the details of the propagating wavefront. Further, graded response mechanisms have recently been identified at either end of the con-

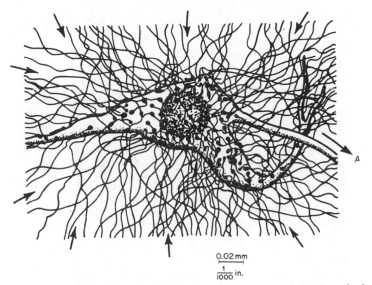

0.02 mm

$\frac{1}{1000}$ in.

Figure 11.6. Reconstruction of a single motor nerve cell from the spinal cord of a cat. Small input fibers bring impulses to the cell and end as knobs attached to its receiving dendrites. When a sufficient number of input fibers work together the cell sends an output of impulses along its axon (*A*). (After J. F. Young, *Doubt and Certainty in Science*, Oxford University Press, London, 1951.)

ducting nerve fiber. This knowledge has greatly increased the comprehension of neuronal function over that provided by the concept of all-or-none activity which was previously confined to the conducting portion of the axon. An interesting comment is furnished by G. H. Bishop. He conceived that graded response is more general as well as more primitive than all-or-none response. Possibly, the latter developed when an early metazoan became too large or underwent separation of related parts to too great a distance for graded responses to be effective as a means of communication between these parts.

Having been excited, the neuron recuperates; that is, the chemical balance gradually returns to its original state. The neuron cannot be triggered during this refractory period. As a result, neural discharge appears in the form of spikes of voltage. The specific information carried by a discharge may well be pulse-time encoded (as a result of the particular interconnection which brings stimulus energy to the neuron). Something of the complexity of this interconnection is revealed in Figures 11.7 and 11.8. The points of interconnection, called synapses, can carry unilateral excitation or inhibition

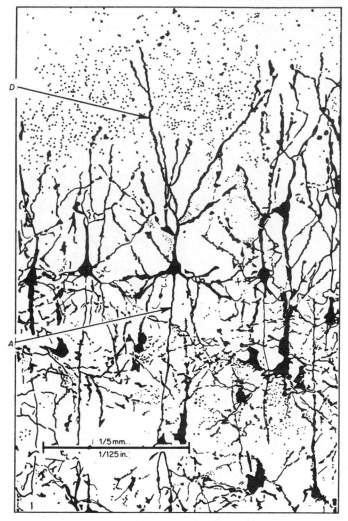

Figure 11.7. Cells of the cerebral cortex of the cat stained to show the receiving dendrites (*D*) and the axons (*A*) along which the output is sent to other regions.

signals, the choice between these being dependent upon the particular physical properties of the contact.

About 90 per cent of cerebral cortex is composed of glia cells and blood vessels. The remaining portion contains nerve fibers which cross and recross each other. In striking contrast to the range of sizes in which neurons occur in different layers and fields of the cortex, this network of interconnecting nerve fibers appears to be of quite consistent density over the entire cortex.

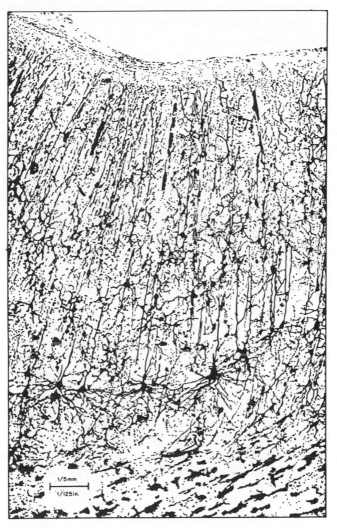

Figure 11.8. Cells of the cerebral cortex of the cat stained but shown with a smaller magnification. The interlacing network of receiving dendrites is well seen towards the inner side of the cortex, but would be 50 times more dense if all the cells were stained. The input fibers are not stained.

In fact, about 200 meters of nerve fiber per cubic milimeter characterize the cortex of a number of animals, including man.

According to S. T. Bok, the cause for this consistent neural density is the tiny cervical vacuoles, each of which are about five microns in diameter. He reports that the cortex appears as a foam-like structure with about one million of these vacuoles per cubic centimeter. The interfibral vacuoles serve to separate the nerve fibers, permitting them to cross at well-spaced intervals. Three close vacuoles form a channel through which a nerve fiber can pass, while four meet to form a junction that is a protoplasm node through which nerve fibers located in the channels can cross, as indicated in Figure 11.9. In such a case, the crossing distance of fibers which remains remarkably consistent over the entire cortex, is about five microns from center to center. It has been theorized that the nerve fibers might follow a screw-like course between vacuoles, bending slightly at each junction, so that they meet other

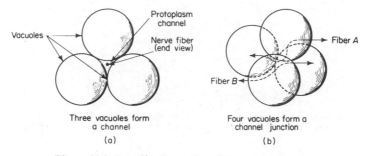

Figure 11.9. Interfibral vacuoles of the cerebral cortex.

fibers in close proximity. On the average, each vacuole is surrounded by about twelve other vacuoles, and about ten fibers pass along any given vacuole. Upon leaving the vacuole, these ten fibers may diverge widely and probably do not meet again. There are about twenty synapses within a very small distance of the vacuole.

The glia cells and the resulting minute structure of the brain may have significant implications with respect to understanding the human information storage and processing capability. In 1886, Nansen suggested that the glia cells act in some unknown manner to organize neurons. In his words "the neuroglia is the seat of intelligence." An outgrowth of this idea will be discussed more fully in the next section.

As a result of a large number of experiments and a great amount of clinical evidence, certain localized areas of the brain are identified as being associated with specific functions. At this point, it is well to caution that in no case is the control of a function limited to a single center within the brain.

Portions of the cerebrum are known as motor areas, others as sensor areas, while still others are identified as association or projection areas. Figure 11.10 indicates the location of some of these cortical functions.

It is the function of the cerebellum to help maintain posture and equilibrium, as well as tone of the voluntary muscles. The neural circuits which connect the cerebrum and muscles are supplemented by feedback signals to the cerebellum. Through these feedback circuits, the cerebellum monitors the direct function, comparing motor signals from the cerebrum to sensory response signals from the muscles. As a result, the cerebellum furnishes the dominant centers with information necessary for the generation of correction signals, or it generates these correction signals itself. As in the cerebrum, the various functions of the cerebellum are distinctly localized in areas of its cortex. Electrical stimulation of the cerebellum permits the identification of corresponding areas of the cerebrum and vice versa.

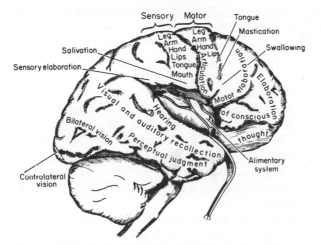

Figure 11.10. Cortical function. This illustration will serve as a summary restatement of conclusions, some hypothetical (for example, the elaboration zones), others firmly established. The suggestion that the anterior portion of the occipital cortex is related to both fields of vision rather than to one alone is derived from the results of stimulation.

Such electrical stimulation of the brain can be used to control certain aspects of behavior. Electrodes implanted in specific areas can cause motor response, arouse aggression or docility, and serve to modify leadership, sexual drive, and social relations. More specifically, artificial stimulation of the cat and monkey have caused actuation of limbs, tail, trunk, head, or ears. When the artificial stimulation was in the same sense as the normal brain function, the behavior response became exaggerated. When these two stimuli were of opposite sense, a counteraction was noted; however, with sufficient artificial stimulation, opposition could be broken down and the animal responded as directed. It is interesting to note that posture compensation appears normal when specific motor response is artificially stimulated. The excitation of a specific area in the brain of the cat caused it to "freeze" and remain motionless during the time of stimulation regardless of the unusual attitude in which it was caught. Upon release from stimulation the cat would resume its normal activities as if unaffected.

Various types of emotional behavior such as anxiety or fear have been artificially stimulated. Repeated electrical excitation of the motor cortex for hours or months did not produce observable modification in the spontaneous behavior of animals. Such modification did occur, however, after experiments in which fear was invoked by direct stimulation of the brain. The tectal area of the brain was found to be responsible for aggressive behavior. Repeated stimulation here could demolish an amicable social relationship between animals. Excitation of another region of the brain would cause a normally fierce animal to become docile. Such artificial stimuli could cause significant modification of social situations.

11.4. THE HUMAN MEMORY

Various estimates have been made of the capacity of human memory. These range from about 43 billion bits (based on a maximum average transduction rate of about 25 bits per second over 16 hours per day of conscious activity and an 80-year life span) to 1.5 million bits (if only 1,000 items of the degree of complexity of a multiplication table were stored). A reasonable estimate for the average amount of information stored in human memory may be a compromise between these two extremes, that is, something in the order of about 100 million bits.

Note that the estimates made above are based on single item information storage. It may well be, however, that human memory does not operate at this level. For example, in a single observation an average person may comprehend 5 to 10 "chunks" of data which he can produce in immediate recall. Each "chunk" may represent approximately 15 bits without significant confusion. This, of course, does not mean that all information which can be retrieved within immediate recall reaches long-term storage.

Further, much data which is retrieved from human memory may actually be the result of associative reconstruction. Possibly, the actual storage is in compressed form of "shortcodes," that is, techniques by which specific data may be reconstructed upon request. Such shortcodes have already found wide usage in the computer field to obviate the need for storing large amounts of information in explicit form.

The naturalness of such shortcodes is evidenced when the human learns to play a new game. For example, consider three-dimensional tic-tac-toe. Each player attempts to place his markers in a straight line of any orientation within a 3 by 3 by 3 rectangular matrix. In the early stages of learning, the player attempts to visualize the three-dimensional figure from a two-dimensional coded response. However, within a relatively short span of time the player learns to recognize that certain coded sequences lead more directly to winning plays; he has derived a set of "rules" which allow him to operate on the data without resort to the original "meaning."

In the game of chess, a player is extremely unlikely ever to experience the exact same middle-game playing situation a second time. Certainly then, the beginner does not learn the game by repetitive conditioning of each successive "move." More likely, he derives a set of rules such as "protect the queen," "use the castle more often," "sacrifice the pawn," and so on. These are ordered in merit by the weighted average of success which resulted from their use. With more experience, the player derives more and more complex rules. These rules are usually more specific and offer greater payoff. Because of their complexity they occur less often. Therefore, it takes longer to accrue a sufficient sample size to justify their worth. The player continues to construct and test new rules and draws from his memory suitable rules for each play, rather than specific remembrance of individual past events.

The important point here is that the memory may well be in terms of a conceptual space rather than the actually perceived real world. A highly evolved organism faces tasks that transcend reductionist models. The organism attends selectively to signals in the face of distractions, extracting relevant information from usually highly redundant and noisy signals. Only a portion of the directly sensed data is used, this forming a less faithful but more useful representation of the real world. Purposeful sensory distortion is permitted for the sake of emphasis. In recognition of this property, it is usually effective teaching to instruct, "Try to state it in your own words." Such a restatement helps by making explicit at least one acceptable shortcode which is compatible with the background of information already stored in the operator's memory. The syntactical structure of language forms such a shortcode that makes it easier to recall word sequences which have meaning rather than those of equivalent length which are meaningless. It is this shortcode property of human memory which prohibits the direct measurement of the redundancy the observer perceives in receiving language (or other signals, for that matter). The amount of contextual redundancy can only be measured if the shortcode storage of symbols were known. Still, human recall is more often limited by message length than by the amount of information. Because of this, it is often of advantage to use low probability symbol coding so that a maximum of information is stored within the same message length. This may be accomplished by enlarging the alphabet.

As yet, no anatomical evidence has been found for the existence of a single storage organ nor for that matter for the existence of any special scanning devices. Yet, the human memory demonstrates unique features in terms of its information storage capacity and access rate. Its address coding is remarkably efficient for use in contextual search. For example, the term "black" can bring to mind an extremely wide variety of other words dependent upon the context within which "black" has been received.

A number of theories have been advanced to offer some explanation for the operation of human memory. These range all the way from highly specific descriptions of suggested "mechanisms" to the general statement that a biological process such as human memory cannot be explained in mechanistic terms. Here it is possible to consider only a few of the more prominent ones.

Memory may exist in the form of structural modification of the protein molecules within the brain tissue, in the way information is stored in the chromosomes. No direct evidence has yet been brought to bear to substantiate this theory of cerebral memory. Another concept presumes the facilitation of transduction in those synapses which have experienced recent electrical closure. In theory at least, repeated use lowers the transfer impedance, thus providing preferred pathways through the neural population. Some observational evidence has favored this theory; however, it is difficult to imagine that the memory "trace" could last for significant periods of time in view of the continual modification of material and metabolism in process. It is well known that the ingestion of even small amounts of alcohol can cause wide variation in the neural threshold level. This may be logically equivalent to a significant change in the synaptic transfer impedance.

Another theory describes memory in terms of reverberating neural impulses. Sense-generated signals might travel in closed loops through the excitation of a large number of neurons. The very existence of such closed circuit signals provides information which might be extracted at some later time. It is difficult, however, to envision such reverberation as extending for those time periods demonstrated by human memory. This dynamic form of memory calls a large number of neurons into simultaneous operation and, of course, a much larger number of synapses. This theory appears consistent with the result of surgical operations and implanted electrodes which seem to indicate that memory is not a localized function within the brain. Yet it is well known that the brain can go through radical changes in its level of electrical activity and not suffer a significant loss of memory.

This concept was amplified by O. B. Hebb. Activity of the closed systems of reverberating association area cells would presumably persist after the stimulation ceased, and, in turn, this might induce permanent changes in the active cells, changes which would increase in depth every time activity occurred. The reverberating activity, Hebb postulated, was the physical manifestation of an "idea," while the permanent changes constituted the "memory traces." Hebb then suggested that those cell assemblies which became active together or in sequence would tend to become associated into larger groups or "phase sequences" and that it was these phase sequences which represented "concepts." Although this model appears inadequate in a number of respects, it does introduce the thought that memory traces were distributed so that the "memory" of a particular concept might involve many thousands of cells. Any cell might participate simultaneously as a member of many different memory traces. Consistent with this concept, removal of brain tissue would not necessarily destroy a memory trace but rather would lead to a gradual general decrease in mental capability as more and more tissue was removed.

S. T. Bok hypothesized that the synapses between nerve fibers in the vicinity of a vacuole may be the organs of memory. When all of the nerve fibers running along the vacuole surface are simultaneously conducting impulses, that vacuole may change from its original indifference state to an activated state which represents stored information. The activated vacuole affects all its immediate synapses so as to lower their threshold values greatly. Now, when any one of the nerve fibers associated with an activated vacuole receives an impulse, the lowered threshold allows that impulse to be transferred immediately to the other nerve fibers. The initial condition which activated the vacuole has been reconstructed, and the stored information is thus retained. The activated vacuole may slowly return to its original indifferent state, thus accounting for the loss of memory. When the vacuole is in an indifferent state, its immediately surrounding synapses have threshold values sufficiently higher so that only some nerve impulses can be transferred across synaptic junctions. Reoccurrence or partial reoccurrence of the original situation would have the effect of restoring the decaying threshold vacuole to its activated level, providing the state of decay has not yet reached a point where the threshold value of the synapse would not be sufficiently high to prevent stimulation across the synapse. Presumably, the degree to which the original situation is re-created determines whether or not this memory is restored. Redundancy in memory storage may occur if some of the ten fibers meet once again. Another form of redundancy may result from allowing two or more nerve fibers to carry impulses from one initial stimulation. It is fully conceivable that just such forms of redundancy exist within the cortex.

In 1912, R. M. Yerkes demonstrated that the earthworm could learn a direction habit in passing through a T maze. The left arm of the maze contained a strip of sandpaper which preceded an electric grill. The other arm of the maze opened to a dark moist environment. Yerkes started his worms at the base of the T several inches from the choice point and found that the habit of turning toward the right arm of the maze appeared in 20 to 100 trials. A three-week rest period yielded no loss of the habit. Surgical removal of the cephalic ganglions (the brain) of the earthworm did not destroy the habit. In fact, these worms performed quite well until segments of the nerves began to regenerate. With the coming of a new brain, the habit degenerated. It is a question where the traces of the habit were during the interval between the first and second brain.

New insight into such problems may be found in the glia-neural theory of brain function advanced by R. Galambos. He suggests that there may be information residing in the glia cells which causes them to organize the neurons in such a way that they sustain the basic life-preserving processes. That is, the glia may contain the program for the information processing by the brain, a program which may well be a model of the genetically experienced environment. If this be true, it might offer some explanation for the previously described behavior of worms as well as why many amphibia and fish will continue to function normally in spite of surgical extraction or dis-arrangement of the brain and spinal cord.

Several other experiments are worth consideration with respect to the glia-neural theory of brain function. It has recently been discovered that the mid-brain reticular formation will continue to demonstrate rhythmical activity that preserves some of the temporal features of the stimulus. For example, if a cat is taught that a light flashing 7 times per second precedes a shock, it is likely that such a 7 per second brain wave will be found even in the dark. It may well be that this information is preserved within a glia-neural complex of cells. A more recent experiment was reported by F. Morrell. A micro-electrode was placed in the visual cortex of a rabbit, isolating a unit that dis-charged with a single burst of impulses to a flash of light. A weak current was passed through the cortex while the eye was stimulated with flashes at 5 per second. Several minutes later, and with the current still flowing, the animal was retested with a single flash of light. The unit now responded not with a single burst, but with a train of bursts at 5 per second. As time passed, the tendency to give this complicated response to a single flash diminished until after a half hour the single flash once again elicited the expected single burst. One reasonable way to explain this phenomenon is to imagine tem-porary alteration in the properties in the glia cells near the electrode.

Experiments have been performed where animals press a key every few seconds for days, barely pausing for food and sleep, when the only result of this key-press action is to cause an electrical shock to be delivered deep inside the brain. The behavior of the animals is insensitive to the frequency, dura-tion, and waveform of the shock; however, over a reasonable range the strength of the response is linearly related to the shock intensity. Possibly the shocks act primarily on the bulk of glia cells surrounding the neural fibers of the limbic-midbrain circuit which in tuin would selectively and appropriately activate the neural complements.

Another interesting series of experiments have been performed on planaria. These flat worms are the lowest creatures in the evolutionary hierarchy which possess a true central nervous system (with bilateral symmetry) and at the same time are the highest ranking among organisms which can reproduce by fission. Upon separation of the head-half from the tail-half, each will grow another half like the one it has lost. In fact, when these worms are cut into as many as six fragments each of these will re-create all the complex organs of the whole individual (including the nervous system). How does each fragment store the knowledge of how to grow the remainder of the individual?

Planaria can be trained, thereby demonstrating nonhereditary memory. A strong flash of light causes no bodily reaction. If this is consistently followed by an electric shock, the animal will soon learn to contract its body upon sensing the flash of light as if it were being shocked. The trained planaria are now cut in two and allowed to regrow the missing half. After a month they are retrained to react reliably. This takes about 40 trials (as compared to the original 150 trials); that is, each new individual shows about 70 per cent retention of the previous conditioning. This is about the same level of retention as is shown by uncut planaria after the same "forgetting" period. In fact, if a trained head-half is allowed to grow a new tail and this tail-half is then separated and allowed to grow a new head, the new individual (which contains none of the original organs) will still retain a significant amount of its learning. Here is evidence that traces of memory acquired during a lifetime can be passed on to the progeny—at least through asexual reproduction.

Planaria need their brains to learn; however, once they have learned, the information is stored outside the nervous system, possibly in the form of some chemical substance. Certainly planaria are a long way from man in the evolution of species, and yet study of their behavior may provide a key to a deeper understanding of human memory.

The search for greater understanding of human brain function may take many paths. For example, the operation of human memory may be viewed in terms of a model based upon the number system of residual classes (described in Chapter 2). Each of the fundamental concept-symbols may appear as a modulus. Newly received data is then classified with respect to the available set of moduli, and a measure of the dissimilarity is taken as the respective residue. Information retrieval may then proceed in a constructive manner. Each residue is used to generate all congruent items, that is, terms which would yield the same residue with respect to the given modulus. If a set of congruent-generated terms appears similar (or identical) a new "concept" is identified. This concept, and other similarly generated concepts (or given concepts), may be taken to form a new set of moduli. This process may be iterated to higher and higher levels of abstraction.

It seems reasonable to expect that these moduli become more and more complex as the successive transformations take place. Could it be that there is no "forgetting," that all information received is fully remembered but stored in terms of successively more complex symbols with only the removal of redundancy? Possibly human recall is limited by man's ability to differentiate among these more difficult to interpret symbols.

This idea is consistent with findings of W. Penfield who has performed over 700 operations on locally anesthetized human brains for the purpose of localizing and removing the causal areas of the cortex with respect to epileptic seizures. These operations have been about 50 per cent successful with some percentage of the remaining being partially successful. During the operations a stimulating electrode was used to explore the cortex until the subject indicated impending seizure. Once the critical area was mapped cutting was performed. In a number of cases highly specific recall was stimulated by voltage excitation. (Recall, similar to reliving the experience, could be regenerated after a few seconds, starting at a "natural" beginning point in the recalled sequence of events.) Stimulation of a particular local area produced a singular context.

(One subject reported "a mother calling a child" in one stimulation position, "a policeman calling a motorist" in a nearby electrode position and "a man calling a secretary" in a third nearby position. "Calling" was the key thought which appeared to localize these recalls.) Restimulation of the same point after a short period of time would not elicit the same memory. No attempt was made to ensure that the electrode was placed at exactly the same position.

These experiments offer an indication that the upper portion of the temporal lobe of the brain is the center for comparative interpretation or recognition, this being the essential decision in recall or memory. This evidence adds strength to the hypothesis of William James; in the words of Penfield, "There is a permanent record of the stream of consciousness within the brain."

11.5. A MEASURE FOR MEANING

There exists a considerable background of attempts toward the qualitative and quantitative description of "meaning." Boole, Russell, Mach, and Wittgenstein are but a few of those who have considered this problem worthy of serious attention. Literature in the fields of philosophy, philology, linguistics, and psychology treats the subject within their own idiom, and, although a number of interesting approaches have developed, the most directly useful and complete is considered to be that recently advanced by D. MacKay. The following discussion is based upon his concepts.

There are two basically different approaches to achieving a measure for the amount of information content in a message. Information theory is based upon the *selective* measure of information. In no way is there an attempt to describe the particular message as distinguished from any other message which might have been sent. For example, if a message consists of a single digit and it is known that all digits are equiprobable, then the information content of the single digit message is about 3.3 bits regardless of which digit it is. In other words, the selective measure of information content is purely a function of the relative probability of the occurrence of this message within the probability weighted ensemble of all possible messages within the delineated system.

To make it clear that the selective measure is insufficient to fully describe the message, consider the following example:

The professor addresses his mathematics class and intends to introduce a significant theorem which he feels "contains a great amount of meaning." In accordance with mathematical formalism he introduces definitions and axioms, theorems and lemmas, and proofs, all in a carefully arranged logical procedure so that the student can follow each step. By the time the lecture is almost over, the students have acquired a considerable background with respect to the subject at hand, and, in fact, from this background, any one of them might be expected to arrive at the final theorem without much difficulty. The professor states the theorem, and, in view of the high expectancy of his statement, there was extremely little *selective* information conveyed by the statement of the theorem.

Contrast the academic situation with that of the comedian who comes before his audience and in a few moments produces some short and unexpected statement provoking gales of laughter. The humor was testimony to the fact that the audience was considerably surprised by the comic's statement. His remark was of low probability and therefore conveyed a great deal of *selective* information. Certainly selective information is far from a measure of the amount of meaning within a message.

It would appear useful to achieve a measure of the amount of *descriptive* information content contained in a message. Such a semantic measure must be related to the number of degrees of freedom which the message contains. In fact, it must be a function of the probability distribution with respect to each of these dimensions. Clearly the multivariate descriptive information measure is far more complex than the selective measure.

Consider a message received by an observer. The meaning of this message results in a change in "psychological set" of the observer. That is to say the reception of this message has to some degree prepared the observer for any future response which he may make. Based upon this concept, a measure for meaning may be tied directly to behavior yielding an operational definition in terms of the change in the conditional probability matrix which describes all possible future responses of the observer.

Note that the conditional probability matrix does not indicate a particular behaviorial pattern. Rather it specifies a change in the state of readiness of the organism with respect to his environment as a result of having received the message. MacKay's example of the railroad switching yard appears to be most appropriate. The particular state of the switching system at any particular time may be looked upon as its state of readiness with respect to its immediate future activity. The switch being in a particular configuration does not imply that trains will actually take the possible paths. In this sense it is a conditional probability matrix in that it sets the stage for the paths the trains might take as they approach the yard from any entrance. By analogy, direct measurement of specific behavior is insufficient to describe the conditional probability matrix which allowed this behavior. It becomes apparent, therefore, that even a complete measurement of behaviorial response cannot provide a complete measurement for the amount of meaning contained within the received message. To summarize thus far, a measure for the amount of meaning may be defined in terms of a multivariate selective function expressed over the range of each of the parameters. These parameters form the degree of modification of the conditional probability matrix which corresponds to the change of readiness of the system.

In the psychological sense, it is impossible to measure the amount of meaning in terms of readily recognized independent variables. In fact, the set of parameters which are of concern are hierarchically organized as a result of the preconditioning experience. There would have to be a great amount of research accomplished to determine uniquely even a small number of these paramount dimensions of human behavior. It might be expected that some factor-analytic technique could be employed to determine independent parameters of the human organism in terms of newly defined qualities. It would certainly be most unlikely if any of these derived "symbols" corresponded to the recognized parameters within the range of common experience.

A received message may prove to be meaningless in two regards. Either the receiver is unequipped to decode the message properly (and as such may not even find it possible to recognize that the message exists), or, in a less probable case, the receiver finds that the message has internal contradictions and as such proves "meaningless *in toto.*" For example, "RUNNING WATER DEFIES WEIGHT AT ACQUEDUCT" proves meaningless to the reader in view of the inconsistency between the individual meanings of these words. The conflict is immediately resolved, and the sentence has meaning, when the reader is told that this example is the headline on the sports page of a newspaper. If a random configuration of letters is offered, no meaning exists (with the exception that a random set of letters is known to exist). As contextual redundancy is increased, the message gradually begins to take on a flavor of English, assuming that the contextual redundancy is in the form of conditional probabilities in agreement with the usual English text. As redundancy is increased, English and near-English words begin to appear, and, although they may have individual meaning, a message, as such, remains meaningless. Only at some particular minimum level of redundancy can decoding take place in order to offer complete meaning to the observer as measured by a consistent change in his conditional probability matrix.

Too often the term meaning is confused with the particular meaning of the message itself. To illustrate, consider the sentence "The lamp is on the table." Although the subjective reaction to this statement is a reflection of the condition of the lamp with respect to the table, the meaning of the statement itself is only *that* the lamp is on the table. There must be careful discrimination between the meaning of the statement itself and a particular story which this message conveyed.

A great deal of meaning can be offered by other than indicative sentences. The asking of a question discloses meaning, and the question itself may take on an indicative form. "I take it that you are going home" is not grammatically a question. Acceptance of this statement as a question by the receiving individual results from his desire to "put right" the transmitting person's states of readiness. Each human operator appears to hold a degree of responsibility in correcting and maintaining the correctness of the conditional probability matrix of those with whom he communicates (neglecting, of course, the case of deceptive jamming wherein the observer will attempt to falsify the conditional probability matrix, and the case of noisy jamming wherein the observer will either reply ambiguously or not at all).

Groups of beings appear to share the burden of maintaining the proper states of readiness for all members within the group. Any utterance becomes a question when it is a token of a defect in the state of readiness of the transmitter. It would appear that one of the essential properties of motivation is the filling of gaps and the correction of the conditional probability matrix for the communicative "public." In one sense at least, this motivational quality corresponds to curiosity. According to MacKay's analogy, "It is as if each individual's track switches (which correspond to his state of readiness) were exposed to those of the other organism with whom he communicates." In order to maintain subjective consistency of the "real world," each individual examines the others' exposed switches and freely offers information to make their switch configuration agree with the subjective belief of the real world situation. The asking of a question depends upon the receiver's state of readiness rather than the question mark. The human operator is motivated by not only "food and sex" but also the drive to ensure that his communication channel with the rest of his world remains properly open.

In review, meaning depends on both the transmitter and the receiver. It may be measured in terms of the range of change of the conditional probability matrix of the receiver. Meaning may be rich or deep relating to a large dimensionality or number of levels in the hierarchy of variables. It may be vague or precise dependent upon the shape of the distribution with respect to the total message vector.

Consider the simplified case of orthogonal coordinates defining behaviorial dimensions as forming a Euclidean space. Each message then corresponds to a particular vector initiating from the origin for each individual observer. The degree of "relevance" of a second message might be measured in terms of the vector difference between the two message vectors. The question "Does it have any *bearing* upon the original message?" may truly refer to an angular measurement. To complete the concept it must be remembered that each vector is formed of the distribution along each coordinate, and, of course, this greatly complicates the picture.

In truth, the dictionary does not offer meanings for words. Rather it furnishes a standard which represents the average receiver within the population of those speaking the language. It provides no measure of meaning but only similar words which might easily be confused by the average observer. The amount of meaning is a relative quantity to the state of the observer and the intent of the transmitter. Its measure is uniquely dependent upon the particular situation.

11.6. HUMAN LEARNING AND INTELLIGENCE

Learning is an extremely complex process. As indicated by O. B. Hebb, it is possible to train both a rat and a chimpanzee to look for food behind a white triangle symbol, shown as the training symbol (a) in Figure 11.11. This learning may take as many as 200, 300, or 400 trials for the monkey, while the rat may demonstrate the learned behavior after only 10 to 20 trials (or for somewhat more difficult discriminations, 50 to 80 trials). Testing of these same animals with other stimuli reveals that their individual perception of the white triangle stimulus was indeed quite different. The rat offers only random response to the stimulus symbols (b), (c), and (d) (shown in Figure 11.11), whereas either symbols (b) or (c) will elicit a positive response from the chimpanzee. It is interesting to note that the two-year-old human child will also recognize the training symbol in stimulus symbols (b), (c), and (d). This evidence emphasizes the importance of distinguishing the difference between

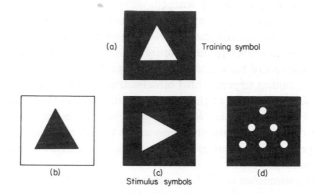

Figure 11.11. Training symbol and stimulus symbols.

what is being learned and what is being taught. Higher animals are capable of generalizing and thus learn far more than the presented information. In the words of Hebb,

> Because a simple task could theoretically be handled by a simple mechanism, does not mean, in fact, that the brain handles it that way. In an uncomplicated nervous system, yes; but in the complex brain of a higher animal other mechanisms may insist on getting into the act and turn the simple task into a complex one.

There have been many attempts to erect a useful theory of human learning. According to Guthrie's Association Theory, it is presumed possible to reduce all learning to a simple associative rule: *Any combination or totality of stimuli which accompanies a movement will be followed by that movement when the same combination occurs again.* It is assumed that learning is complete on the first occasion of each event. In this theory, occurrences are taken at the minute level, so that since no two situations are ever exactly identical, complete learning is not revealed. As a consequence to this ultra-fine detailed view, learning appears to increase gradually through practice as more and more of the possible stimuli-response couples become part of the pattern of experience. These couples are equivalent to the learned pattern for future responses. Such a theory is truly untestable since no subject-situation can ever be completely controlled in the limit. Even the most careful experiments can be challenged as not being careful enough. Although this learning theory has the virtues of simplicity and generality, these are overshadowed by the lack of testability.

Tolman's Sign-Gestalt Theory views the entire organism rather than specific aspects of stimulus-response. According to Tolman, what is learned is not movements or responses but rather "sign-significate expectations." That is to say the organism is presumed to learn "what may lead to what" in some gross sense. It is the time and place contiguity of stimuli which becomes the monitored pattern, the thing which is learned. Obviously, the closer in time and/or place the greater would be the likelihood that expectation will be established. Practice also plays a significant role in strengthening expectations. This entire concept of learning is based upon the cognition of related stimuli in terms of the entire experience of the organism in all situations of its environment. No direct effect of reward for motivation is postulated since, according to the theory, these only form biases which affect performance and, as such, remain separate from the learned experience. The reward does, of course, enter as a stimulus-significate, the presence of which strengthens expectations, but this is quite different from directly effecting learning. It is contended that when automatic responses are available, that pattern of behavior will ensue which is in accordance with the greatest expectancy or likelihood, and, should this primary expectancy be avoided through some immediate experience, then it is the next greatest expectancy which dominates. This theory recognizes the existence of individual differences; however, such a general nonquantitative theory leaves much to be desired in terms of confirmatory evidence.

B. F. Skinner has developed a descriptive account of learning in terms of two separate phenomena: conditioning and instrumental learning. Respondent conditioning, as demonstrated in various Pavlov salivation experiments, is taken to be operative but of little concern in human learning. In instrumental learning, stimulus conditions sufficient to elicit the behavior cannot be specified and are, in fact, considered irrelevant to the understanding of behavior. The important aspect of this model is that *responses are emitted and that these generate consequences.* Skinner calls this "operant" behavior, stressing the role of response. The basic law of operant conditioning states that *if an operant is followed by the presentation of reinforcing stimulus, then its strength is increased and vice versa.* In most situations an operant does become related to the stimulus field. The work of Skinner and others has contributed to the development of teaching machines. These are discussed at a more appropriate point in Chapter 18.

About 22 years of the average man's life are spent in sleep. It is, therefore, no wonder that the notion of sleep-teaching would find a ready audience.

In fact, this proposal has had extensive and recurrent surges of interest dating from the original science fiction publication of Hugh Gernsback in a magazine called *Modern Electrics* published in 1911.

Although it might prove interesting to review some of the many fictional references and publicity stunts which related to sleep-learning, it is considered more worthwhile to review the relatively small number of investigations which have been carried out. L. L. Thurston (1916) attempted to teach Morse code to Navy men during their sleep. He reported that this effort "indicated some gain." L. Le Shan (1942) worked on the fingernail-biting habits of 20 boy campers. Forty per cent of the experimental group and none of the control group stopped biting their nails, and thus the investigator felt that this indicated "the possible theraputic use of suggestion during sleep." In 1943, the same investigator worked with a single subject attempting to teach nonsense syllables. As a result, he had an even more positive attitude toward the possibility of sleep learning. Throughout the studies described above, however, no measure was reported of depth of sleep during the instruction.

In more recent studies, C. R. Elliot used 15 common three-letter words in an effort to increase the subject's anticipation of these words on the following day. Auditory instruction was only provided when the subject's EEG showed no "clear alpha patterns." The experimenter turned off the EEG recording when he believed that the subject would remain asleep. No significant differences between groups were found on the basis of error or the absolute number of trials required to learn the material. T. A. Hedges failed to demonstrate the value of sleep-teaching on the speech defects of 3 aphasic children. In 1952, B. H. Fox and J. S. Robbins attempted to teach 30 college students a list of 25 pairs of English-Chinese vocabulary. Three separate groups were used in order to test for facilitation, interference (through use of mismatched lists), and control for the experiment. The facilitation group required fewer trials, whereas the interference group required more trials to learn the list than the control group. It was concluded that some learning could occur during sleep.

In the same year, C. Leuba and D. Bateman considered that the learning of 3 songs during light sleep was of some success. In a later study, no learning was demonstrated after the use of sedatives. W. G. Hoyt (1953) could detect no learning during sleep on the basis of experimental data taken on 20 subjects using 10 English-Chinese vocabulary pairs. Restlessness on the part of the subjects was taken to indicate too light a sleep level to allow instruction. T. Stampfl attempted to teach 6 college students lists of nonsense syllables during sleep. He concluded that the sleep learning hypothesis was uncertain and improbable. M. Coyne performed a series of experiments with lists of adjectives, pairs of nouns and words, combinations of letters, colors, relative positions, and nonsense syllables. He concluded that the results were generally favorable for sleep-teaching; however, this conclusion was based on the use

Table 11.2. EEG and Psychological Conditions Along the Sleep-Wakefulness Continuum

Level	Electroencephalogram	Psychological Condition
O	Continuous or nearly continuous alpha of maximum amplitude and frequency of not more than 1 cps slower than the S's normal alpha frequency. Frequency and amplitude are slightly less after sleeping than before.	Awake. Relaxed with eyes closed. Response to external stimulation.
A+	More than 50% of the scoring period contains alpha. Also low level, random activity characteristic of an alpha block may be present with alpha disappearing at the onset of stimulation and returning shortly after its cessation.	Drowsy.
A	Less than 50% alpha but scoring period contains at least three cycles of activity having the same frequency as the O level. The alpha amplitude may be of the same or considerably lower amplitude than before.	Attention wanders; reverie. Increased reaction time.
A−	Contains cyclical activity having a frequency more than 1 cps slower than the Level O record. May include waves of mixed duration with periods between 0.12 and 0.08 sec with no one period being dominant. Also includes records showing no alpha rhythm during stimulation, but with alpha occurring within 30 sec prior to stimulation or following but not both.	Partial awareness.
B	Absence of alpha during the stimulus period and the adjacent 30 sec of record. Stimulus effects may occur consisting of low level fast activity or an increase in activity containing both high and low frequency components, with some waves having periods within the alpha range. Low-level delta activity is present in the absence of stimulus effects.	Transition. Dreamlike state. Infrequent responses to external stimulation. Onset of sleep. Easily awakened.
C	Absence of alpha with an increase of delta and the appearance of sleep spindles (14 cps). This state is characterized by stimulus effects such as increases in amplitude of delta waves with the onset of the stimulus. Types of effects vary with individuals.	Light sleep. No behavioral responses to external stimulation (unless stimulus awakens). Dreams sometimes remembered.
D	A further increase in delta amplitude with a reduction in frequency and diminution of stimulus effects and sleep spindles. Amplitude of delta almost at maximum.	Deep sleep. No memory for dreams. Difficult to awaken.
E	Absence of sleep spindles and stimulus effects. Very large delta activity with smooth waves of 0.5- to 1.5-sec duration.	Very deep sleep.

of one-tailed *t* test. A two-tailed *t* test would also have allowed for the possibility of interference.

Probably the weakest aspect in the above-described experiments was their lack of adequate criteria for the depth of sleep during the training exercise. This problem was squarely faced by C. Simon and W. Emmons who developed

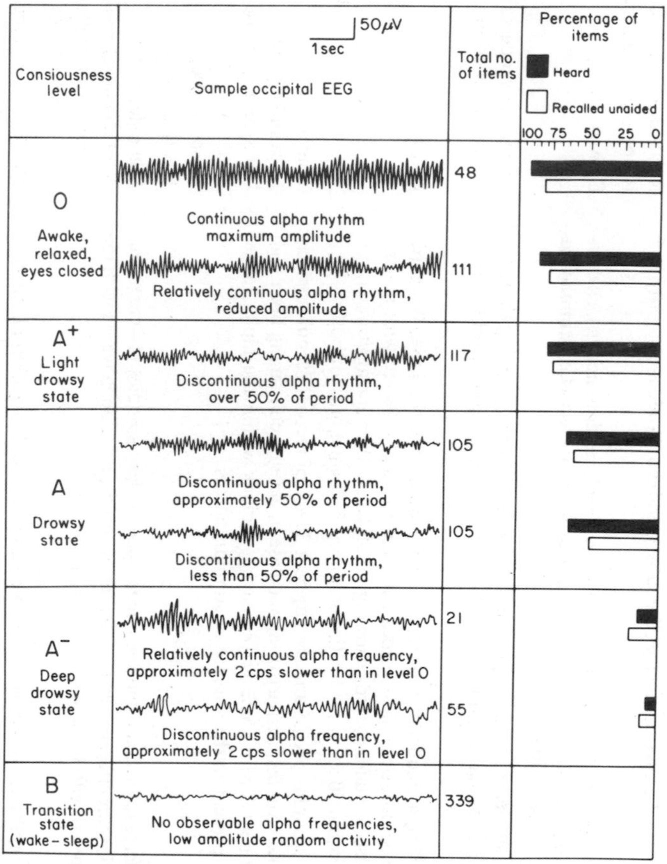
50μV
1 sec
Consiousness level
Sample occipital EEG
Total no. of items
Percentage of items
Heard
Recalled unaided
100 75 50 25 0
O
Awake, relaxed, eyes closed
48
Continuous alpha rhythm maximum amplitude
111
Relatively continuous alpha rhythm, reduced amplitude
A+
Light drowsy state
117
Discontinuous alpha rhythm, over 50% of period
A
Drowsy state
105
Discontinuous alpha rhythm, approximately 50% of period
105
Discontinuous alpha rhythm, less than 50% of period
A−
Deep drowsy state
21
Relatively continuous alpha frequency, approximately 2 cps slower than in level O
55
Discontinuous alpha frequency, approximately 2 cps slower than in level O
B
Transition state (wake – sleep)
339
No observable alpha frequencies, low amplitude random activity

Figure 11.12a. Percentage of items heard and recalled during the appearance of waking electroencephalograms.

a technique which related EEG waveform to various levels of sleep as shown in Table 11.2. Experiments were carried out which, for the first time, revealed that it is unlikely to find learning which takes place during deep sleep. The results shown in Figure 11.12a indicate the degree of learning as a function of the level of sleep. No evidence of increased memory appeared at levels *B* through *E*. In the words of the investigators,

> Since it is generally considered that sleep occurs somewhere during level B, then it appears that learning was slight if any at this point or below. There

appears some basis for assuming that many of these atypical cases (of correct response during inquiry) were artifacts and not the result of true sleep learning.

The important contribution made by this study was the careful quantitative monitoring of the subjects' sleep level during training. The EEG appeared to be more than adequate as a measure for this purpose.

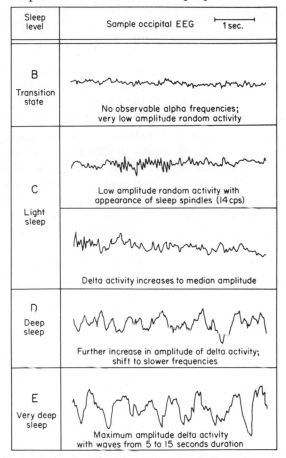

Figure 11.12b. Electroencephalographic patterns during sleep.

Although sleep-learning has now been demonstrated to be most improbable, the possibility of utilizing the drowsy state for training should not be dismissed. As reported by Simon and Emmons, "The results in this study show that approximately 30 per cent of the simple and highly organized material presented in the period just prior to sleep was recalled." *There must be careful compromise between the advantage of limited learning and the possible harmful effects due to loss of sleep.*

*　　　*　　　*

Learning is the process of acquiring a modified behavior pattern to perceived stimuli. It is frequently assumed that the ability to learn is a measure
of intelligence; however, this appears to be an unfortunate oversimplification. Learning is measured in terms of an individual's acceptance and retention of specific information. Intelligence should be a measure of an individual's
capability to utilize information presented to him together with that information which he already holds in such a way as to result in worthwhile judgments
and choice. There is an extensive history of attempts to measure individual
behavior and correlate this behavior with intelligence.

The earliest systematic experimentation on individual differences in behavior arose as a by-product of astronomical research. In 1796, there was the
accidental discovery in differences in the reaction times of various astrono-
mers in making the same observations. In the latter part of the nineteenth
century, it was Galton who first indicated that outstanding intellectual
achievements tended to occur frequently in certain families. Possibly the first
serious attempt toward a measure of intelligence was accomplished by Alfred
Binet, who, in the 1890's, devised experiments intended to measure just how
"bright" and "dull" children differed. Binet was most open-minded in his
approach. He tried many different measures, including the recall of digits,
suggestibility, size of cranium, moral judgment, tactile discrimination, mental
attachment, graphology, and even palmistry. As other investigators had
found before him, his tests of sensed judgment and other simple functions had
little relation to general mental functioning. According to Binet, the essence
of intelligence is "the tendency to take and maintain a definite direction, the
capacity to make adaptations for the purpose of attaining a desired end, and
the power of auto-criticism." In 1905, Binet and Simon published the Binet
scale which was used to identify dull subjects. The Stanford revision of the
Binet scale appeared in 1916, extending the scale to cover both normal and
superior children. The Stanford-Binet test soon became standard and has
remained as a useful tool, even today.

The intelligence quotient, I.Q., in the 1960 revision of the Stanford-Binet
test is nothing more than a standard score with a mean of 100 and standard
deviation of 16. I.Q. score is nearly normally distributed. The subject's
"mental age" is defined as the chronological age at which a normal person
does as well as the subject did. The mental age is converted into an I.Q. score
by referring to appropriate tables.

Originally, I.Q. was a true quotient, being the ratio of the mental age to
the actual age expressed as a percentage. For various reasons, this quotient
was discarded. Originally, the quotient was taken to represent a fixed rate of
development which could be used to predict mental age at subsequent ages.
Later evidence indicated that the rate of mental development is not fixed
and the ratio depends upon technical characteristics of the scale as well as
upon the individual's mental growth. Further, the ratio I.Q. score could not
be applied to persons beyond the age of 13 where mental age units became

arbitrary. The tables for the 1960 revision of the Stanford-Binet test were devised so that whatever mental age fell one standard deviation above the mean for that age was represented by an I.Q. of 116.

It has long been considered dangerous to characterize personnel on the basis of their I.Q. scores, although generally persons with a higher score usually go on to more productive lives. No typical pattern has been found in the periodically sampled I.Q. variation of persons. L. U. Cronbach points out that the Stanford-Binet:

> measures present ability, not neuron capacity;
> is strongly weighted with verbal abilities;
> measures somewhat different mental abilities at different ages;
> does not give a reliable measure of experience aspects of mentality;
> is influenced by the subject's personality and emotional habits;
> requires experiences common to the United States urban culture, and is of dubious value for comparing cultural groups.

Other intelligence scales have been devised to emphasize pattern attributes. These include Atkins object-setting, the Army general classification test (AGCT), and the Wechsler adult intelligence scale. Intelligence is a time dependent multidimensional attribute. Much remains to be done in this area before a truly valid general measure will become available.

11.7. PERSONAL CHOICE

For centuries man has been consciously interested in making wise decisions. In early times, rulers who recognized the responsibility and difficulty associated with decision-making called upon seers to provide advice and guidance. Religious leaders took it upon themselves to create a set of rules which man could use to help him assess whether certain of the alternatives which were open to him were "righteous" with respect to an assumed overriding goal he was instructed to hold. Philosophers studied the world they observed and attempted to reach new understanding by posing problems in the form of dilemmas. Here was a case of intentional construction of difficult problems requiring human decisions for their resolution.

Often the human decision-maker is limited by sheer lack of information relevant to the problem at hand. His ability to select a valuable alternative rests upon his access to pertinent information and an understanding of the goal he wishes to attain through the decision or set of decisions he is about to make. Complete ignorance precludes all but random choice, but this in itself may be of value in that it may serve to mislead an observing adversary. Continued lack of decision soon becomes predictable behavior. The pathological problems associated with severely restricted human access to information (sensory deprivation) are discussed at a more appropriate point in Chapter 8.

Toward the other extreme, the human may be placed under conditions of information overload. So great an amount of information may be furnished to the decision-maker that he no longer can maintain immediate availability of the relevant data. He may have to spend a large portion of his time filtering incoming data or searching the available store of information. Further, there is the danger that such a vast quantity of information may divert him from his original task. He may lose sight of his goal or have this goal modified even without his being aware of the change. Too much information can degrade the decision. Obviously, the "cocktail party" environment is unsuited to decision-making.

Even with a suitable presentation of data, the observer may find it more and more difficult to determine the nature of the displayed information, thus turning his attention away from the decision task of discriminating the desired alternative consistent with the given data. In order to examine this essential human limitation, several experiments were carried out with the subjects under simple read-in and read-out conditions.

H. Hake and W. R. Garner were the first experimenters to use informational analysis of absolute judgments. Subjects were given the task of identifying various positions of a pointer on a linear scale which was divided in one of a number of possible alternative ways. With five alternative segments defined on the scale, the subjects discriminated about 2.3 bits per glance out of the possible 2.32. With ten, twenty, or fifty alternatives, the transmitted information was approximately constant at a value of between 3.0 and 3.2 bits, that is, about the value which would be obtained if nine alternatives were perfectly identified. Hake and Garner concluded that the human observer can absolutely identify only as many as nine different positions along a line. A larger number of alternatives does not increase the amount of information received. In a similar experiment, W. J. McGill found that 2.97 bits were conveyed by a glance observation of a pointer position along a line. This lower information value may have resulted from McGill's use of a scale without end positions, whereas the scale used by Hake and Garner was of limited extent.

A number of studies were conducted to determine the amount of information in absolute judgments of the pitch of pure tones. I. Pollack found that about 2.3 bits were received under optimal conditions, this being equivalent to perfect identification of about five alternatives. In a later experiment, E. B. Hartman studied the effects of prolonged practice on the information content of absolute judgments. Four sets of nine pure tones differing in pitch were employed, these being spaced at 50, 100, 200, or 500 mels, depending upon the subject group. Initially, the separation of tones made relatively little difference. However, after more than seven weeks of practice, during which incorrect judgments were corrected, the efficiency of identification improved until finally tones 300 mels apart were conveying nearly a full bit more information than those only 50 mels apart. Apparently, the opportunity for improvement in precision of identification is limited by the subjective separation of the stimuli. Only about five different pitches could be absolutely identified (up to seven in the case of very good subjects).

C. W. Eriksen and H. Hake found that absolute judgments of various size squares yielded about 2.2 bits under optimal conditions (again, this being equivalent to perfect identification of about five different stimulus values). E. T. Klemmer and F. C. Frick conducted an experiment in which a square containing one or more dots was briefly presented to the subjects, who attempted to reproduce the positions of the dots in a square provided on a response sheet. When the square contained only one dot, 4.4 bits of information were received. This two-dimensional display is converted into a four-dimensional display if the square is allowed to contain either one or two dots, since four coordinates are required to locate the two possible dots. From an eight-dimensional display, that is, a square containing one to four dots, 7.8 bits were received.

Experiments with multidimensional auditory displays confirm that the information received increases with the number of stimulus aspects or dimensions. I. Pollack and L. Ficks studied the judgment of interrupted tones with respect to frequency, loudness, rate of interruption, percentage of time "on," total duration, and direction. With five steps in each of these dimensions, the total information received per stimulus presentation ranged from 6.2 bits to 7.9 bits when interactions among the dimensions were ignored.

J. W. Osborne, H. Quastler, and K. S. Tweedell required subjects to demonstrate their ability to read at a glance the positions of movable red pointers on white circular dials. Analysis of the results allowed an interesting interpretation. The information receiving unit could be viewed as consisting of three parts: (1) a common storage element with an informational capacity of 2.5 bits, easily accessible, and available for storage of information from all elements; (2) four storage elements with informational capacities of 1.7 bits each, available for storage of information concerning single elements only; (3) two storage elements with 1.0 bit capacity, available for single elements only. The unit operates according to the following rule: each information element entering occupies the best available separate storage element, with excess information spilling over into the general compartment; all elements compete for space in the common element in proportion to their information content. According to these investigators,

The specifications of the unit predict the following results: the first information element (scale) can occupy one "special" and all of the "general" compartment, for a total of 4.2 bits. For two scales, the unit provides 1.7 bits separate storage for each and 2.5 bits common storage facility, for a total of 5.9 bits shared equally. For 3 and 4 scales, 7.6 and 9.3 bits, respectively, can be stored, each scale getting an equal share. The 5th scale can place 1 bit in a separate compartment that competes with the other 4 for the 2.5 bits of the common compartment—this gives 2.2 bits for scales no. 1-4, 1.5 for scale no. 5, for a total of

10.3. For 6 scales, the numbers are 2.1 bits for scales 1-4, 1.4 for scales 5 and 6, total 11.3 bits. Additional scales will only compete for the common compartment; for instance, 2 more scales should transmit 2/8 of 2.5 or 0.6 bits, each of the other scales being reduced by 0.1 bit.

Usually, the rate of human transduction of information is limited by the read-out mechanism. Various attempts have been made to measure the maximum average rate at which the human operator can repeatedly perform the simplest of decisions. W. H. Sumby and I. Pollack studied the maximum rate of reproducing verbal material by writing, typing and oral reading. Subjects reached about 35 bits per second in the case of oral reading, which proved to be the most rapid response medium.

H. Quastler and V. J. Wulff conducted an experiment on the typing of sequences of 100 symbols chosen randomly from classes of 4, 8, 16, or 32 alternatives. The rate of transduction increased steadily with the number of alternative symbols from an estimated value of 5 bits per second with four keys to a maximum of about 15 bits per second with thirty-four keys. It was estimated that the maximum rate of impromptu speaking is about 26 bits per second with a mean rate of about 18 bits per second. Silent reading may be as high as 44 bits per second.

In each of the measured performances (playing sequences of notes on the piano, typing letters, and mental arithmetic), the output information rate initially followed the increasing input rate. At a somewhat higher information input rate, a saturation effect was seen and the output rate reached a plateau. At some still higher input rate, the channel capacity was reduced as the subject was placed under information overload. Before reaching the overload point, subjects traded precision for speed and reached rates of between 10 and 14 bits per second when three to five keys of the piano were used; 16 bits per second with nine keys; 19 bits per second with fifteen keys; 23 bits per second with twenty-five keys; and 22 bits per second with thirty-seven keys. With the range extended to sixty-five keys, a few errors occurred even at low speeds and the transduction rate, limited by the distance between keys which had to be played in sequence, peaked at only about 17 bits per second. In general, Quastler found that people can make 5 or 6 successful associations per second, can transduce about 25 bits per second, can operate efficiently over a range of about 30 possible values, and can assimilate some 15 bits at a glance; these measures are taken under optimal input and output information flow situations.

Quastler and Wulff also studied the performance of a famous "lightning calculator," and, using a set of plausible assumptions concerning the specific operations employed for his mental multiplication, they estimated that the maximum rate of information processing (in calculating the product of two 8-digit numbers in 54 seconds) was about 24 bits per second. They indicated that:

What makes a lightning calculator is the ability to carry on in orderly fashion for very long stretches, plus a memory of figures which is several times the ordinary span of 6.6 digits, but not a particularly high rate of handling information. One point of particular interest is that the calculations are performed with little or no conscious control. Thus, we have one situation where the famed rapidity of subconscious thinking can be tested; it turns out to be not too impressive.

As the input information rate is increased beyond that which can be accepted and used, the subjects introduce various protective mechanisms which are intended to overcome the imposed stress. These techniques have been studied by J. G. Miller, who identifies them as:

(a) omission—temporary nonprocessing of information;
(b) error—processing incorrect information, which may enable the system to return to normal processing afterwards;
(c) queuing—delaying the response during a period of high overlap of input information in the expectation that it may be possible to catch up during a lull;
(d) filtering— neglecting to process certain categories of information while processing others;
(e) cutting categories of discrimination—responding in a general way to the input, but with less precision than would be done at lower rates, i.e. instead of reporting "I see yellow," saying "I see a light color" or "I see a color";
(f) employing multiple channels—processing information through two or more parallel channels at the same time; decentralization is a simple case of this; and
(g) escape from the task.

Figure 11.13 indicates data taken by Miller showing the average utilization of some mechanisms of adjustment at various information input rates. There is always a cost for the transduction of information. A measure of this cost is the amount of energy required by the system per bit of information. At very high transduction rates, the cost per bit is probably much greater than at low rates. This is especially true as the information overload point is reached.

It has long been recognized that man is far from an efficient decision-maker. In the words of H. Simon,

The capacity of the human mind for formulating and solving complex problems is very small compared with the size of the problems whose solution is required for objectively rational behavior in the real world—or even for a reasonable approximation to such objective rationality.

Still, a number of efforts toward a normative theory deserve consideration. Such models which describe how decisions ought to be reached are of value, in that they define the domain within which the person should operate.

Hopefully, some of these may be simplified or restricted in some other way to prove useful in predicting actual human decision-making.

Economists have long been concerned with the human being as a decision-maker. They conceived of a hypothetical "economic man" who was presumed to be completely informed, infinitely sensitive to changes in his environment made up of continuous variables, and rational in his behavior (that is, he knows all of the courses of action which are open to him and what the outcome of any particular action will be). Behaving rationally, he can weakly order the states which will result from each presumed action and he acts

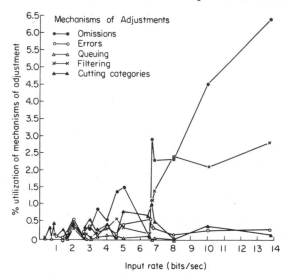

Figure 11.13. Mean utilization of mechanisms of adjustment by both subjects at various input rates.

so as to maximize some function evaluated over these states. Ability to accomplish weak ordering of the possible states implies that his preference is transitive; that is, if he prefers A to B, and B to C, then he also prefers A to C. Certainly, human beings fall far short of the "economic man," yet this fictional concept may prove useful as a reference to which human decision-making may be compared.

Each decision may be viewed as resulting in some degree of subjective value, called utility (positive or negative) to the decision-maker, and he behaves so as to maximize his future utility. If the assumption is made that the utility of any good (product or service) is a monotonically increasing, negatively accelerated function of the amount of the good, then it can be shown that the amounts of most goods which a consumer will buy are decreasing functions of price. These functions become precisely specified once the utility functions are known. Although this result is in agreement with usual experience, it is of limited value since the utilities of various goods are almost never independent. This interdependency forbids the linear combination indicated in classical utility maximization theory. In order to overcome this inadequacy, F. Edgeworth introduced the notion of indifference curves, these being the loci of constant utility, linking various quantities of two or more items.

Another objection was raised by V. Pareto who contended that utility could only be subjectively judged on an ordinal scale. In the language of economics, ordinal utility is contrasted with *cardinal utility*, which is measured on an interval scale. (Measurement scales are defined and discussed in Chapter 1.) Since then, it has been shown that conclusions reached on the basis of cardinal utility measures and marginal utilities can equally well be derived from the concept of indifference curves.

Actual human decision-making introduces inherent variability so that the indifference curves for the human operator are fully described only in terms of probability density functions over the relevant parameter hyperspace. In real situations, the dimensionality of the indifference space is so great as to make experimental determination of these probability functions both difficult and costly. Efforts to simplify the analysis might prove useful; however, it is generally true that as the number of assumptions is increased, the correspondence between theory and empirical results is reduced.

Classical utility theory assumes the existence of interpersonally comparable cardinal utilities. Accordingly, economic policy should be chosen which results in the maximum total utility summed over all members of the economy. Unfortunately, this assumption is not truly representative of real world behavior. A weaker criterion was offered in the form of Pareto's Principle: *Economic change is justified so long as no member of the economy is degraded and at least one member receives benefit from the change.* Still a stronger principle was proposed by N. Kaldor: *If it is possible for those who gain from an economic change to compensate the losers and still benefit from their gains, then the change of policy is desirable.* Under this Compensation Principle, change is presumed to be justified provided the reverse change does not also satisfy the principle. Of course, if the compensation is actually carried out, then this becomes a simple case of Pareto's Principle. It was, however, Kaldor's contention that it need not be paid to evidence an over-all resulting benefit. Here, again, it is important to note that these principles justifying economic policy change are normative and not descriptive of actual human decision-making behavior.

In an economic context, risk and uncertainty are defined as separate concepts. Risk is a measure, derived from a probability distribution, of the likelihood that a proposition is true. Uncertainty exists when the probability density function either is not known or cannot be determined. Under risk, it would seem reasonable to take that decision which will maximize the expected value to the decision-maker, that is, to maximize the sum of the probability-weighted values. However, people do not obey this simple formulation. It was Bernoulli who, in 1738, proposed that people maximize the expected utility rather than the expected value; that is, personal satisfaction may enter into the decision-making process.

The modern period in considering decision-making under risk began in 1944 with the publication of von Neumann and Morgenstern's book *Theory of Games and Economic Behavior*. These authors pointed out that the usual assumption that "economic man" can always say whether he prefers one state to another needs only to be modified to the extent that he can also completely order probability combinations of states in order to imply cardinal utility. Varying the probabilities and using already known utilities, it is possible to determine the utility of any specific quantity of a good (using only two arbitrary points to initially define the utility scale). From an empirical point of view, this means that risky propositions can be ordered in desirability, just as riskless ones can. Further, it means that the concept of expected utility is behaviorally meaningful, and that choices among risky alternatives can be made in such a way as to maximize expected utility. This model may differ from actual human behavior in several ways. The probabilities might well be subjective estimates of the objective probabilities. Further, probabilities and values may not combine linearly. For instance, some positive or negative utility might be given to the process of gambling itself.

On the other hand, it just may be that people do not behave so as to maximize the expected utility. M. Friedman and L. J. Savage raised the interesting question of why it is that a man who willingly buys insurance (that is he pays not to take risks) will also buy lottery tickets (that is he pays in order to take risks). They suggest that this behavior could be explained in terms of a doubly inflected utility function for money, even without the assumption that gambling has any inherent utility. H. Markowitz suggested that the origin of the utility function should be placed at the subject's customary state of wealth, initially concave on each side of the origin, then gradually changing to convex. Markowitz' suggestion means that only a single constant, the scale constant, may be arbitrarily assigned; the zero point is fixed and unchangeable. This is especially true if the zero point is taken as the current rather than the customary position. Consequently, a Markowitzian utility curve is measured on a ratio, not an interval, scale. (If two quantities are measured on the same interval scale, then their difference is measured on a ratio scale, since the origin constant subtracts out.)

Although it is relatively easy to construct situations (large amounts of money and/or small probability differences) in which people do not follow the von Neumann-Morgenstern model, it may still have great value for predicting a wide range of human decision-making behavior. F. Mosteller and P. Nogee carried out betting experiments to apply the von Neumann-Morgenstern model. The indifference curves were found from analysis of the betting procedure of subjects who were either Harvard undergraduates or

National Guardsmen. The utility corresponding to the amount of the money involved in the indifference offer was found from the probabilities involved after defining the utility of zero dollars as zero units of utility (utiles) and the utility of losing a specific sum of money (a nickel) as -1 utile. The results showed that Harvard undergraduates had diminishing marginal utilities, whereas National Guardsmen had increasing marginal utilities. An auxiliary paired-comparisons experiment indicated that it was more likely that the subjects maximized expected utility rather than maximized expected money value. The investigators indicated that the amount of money possessed by the subjects was not seriously important to their betting choice, which showed that their utility curves were of the Markowitz type, that is, descriptive of the utility of the dollar increment and independent of the absolute amounts on hand.

W. Edwards performed a number of experiments which showed that subjects preferred some probabilities to others and that these preferences cannot be accounted for solely by utility considerations. There appears to be a significant interaction between utilities and subjective probabilities. For example, subjects prefer positive expected value bets with objective probability of 0.5 to all other bets with the same expected value. In other words, people usually think they can beat a 50/50 bet. To choose a "best" course of action, one might list the alternatives in decreasing order of the probability with which they are expected, if there is influence by the decision-maker. A preference order rating can then be associated with each of these alternatives and the rule might simply be: Take that course of action which will maximize the magnitude of the difference between probability and preference. That is, if a certain future state is likely to occur and is preferred—do nothing about it. If another future state is unlikely to occur and is undesirable—do nothing about it. Action should be directed to aid those future states which are of low probability but are desirable and to discourage those future states which are likely to occur but are undesirable. This procedure may prove to be simple and worthwhile so long as caution is exercised to ensure against undue interactive influence between probabilities and preferences.

The publication in 1950 of *Statistical Decision Functions* by A. Wald furnished a foundation for various models of decision processes. W. W. Peterson and T. G. Birdsall developed a theory of visual detection. This was broadened by W. P. Tanner, J. A. Swets, and others to cover the general decision problem of detecting the existence of a signal in noise.

The decision may be looked upon as the choice between two random variables (usually taken to be normally distributed). One of these variables is associated with the noise alone, this having a mean value of zero. The other is associated with a signal plus noise and has a mean value other than zero. The observer must decide which of the two alternatives existed during the observation interval. His choice depends upon whether or not a measure of the observation exceeds a criterion value, and the different criterion in turn depends upon the observer's detection goal and upon the information he holds about relevant parameters of the situation. The accuracy with which such decision is made is a function of the mean value of the signal plus noise, this being monotonically related to the signal strength.

Tanner proposes that the human observer be viewed as a noisy receiver of signals. The decision which he makes about the presence or absence of the signal is based upon noisy information, the noise coming from random neural activity in the sensory system. To reach a decision, he must test a statistical hypothesis that the observation which appears to have come from a signal might actually have come from noise alone.

Two probability density functions are defined. One of these, $f_N(x)$, describes the probability density function of the observation under conditions of noise alone. The other, $f_{SN}(x)$, describes the probability density function of x when there is signal plus noise. Clearly, if the probability were high that the observation x came from the signal plus noise, compared with the probability that it came from a noise alone, it would be proper to decide that a signal existed. If the converse were true, then the decision would be that a signal was not present and that noise alone was observed. An ideal observer can make this decision by using the likelihood ratio,

$$\frac{f_{SN}(x)}{f_N(x)}$$

The problem of detection has thus been converted to one of finding the smallest likelihood ratio which the decision-maker will accept and still claim the existence of a signal. All observations with likelihood ratio greater than this critical value will be taken to indicate the existence of a signal, while all those with likelihood less than this will indicate noise without signal. This cut-off can be defined in terms of the ratio of the *a priori* probabilities of no signal and signal, respectively, and the value of correct detection that a signal is present (V_D), the value of rejection (V_R) (the proper diagnosis that no signal is present), the cost of a missed signal (k_M), and the cost of a false alarm (k_F) (calling a signal present when it was not there). It can be shown that the cut-off value which maximizes the expected gain requires that $p(SN) - \beta p(N)$ be a maximum, where

$$\beta = \frac{p(N)}{p(SN)} \cdot \frac{(V_B + k_F)}{(V_D + k_M)}$$

where $p(N)$ and $p(SN)$ are the *a priori* probabilities of no signal and signal respectively.

The importance of the model for human decision-making rests upon the fact that it includes more than sensory information in making the choice. A large share of the nonsensory factors are combined into a single variable, the criterion, while the mean value of signal plus noise becomes a useful measure of the sensitivity of the detection situation. It is this separation of those factors that influence the observer's attitudes from those that influence his sensitivity which is a major contribution of the psychophysical application of statistical decision theory.

Human decision-making can be studied in terms of various personality factors. J. W. Atkinson examined the motive to achieve success and the motive to avoid failure as these relate to the subjective probability of achieving success and of failing (making the crucial assumption that the incentive value of achieving success is inversely related to the subjective probability of succeeding and that the incentive value of avoiding failure is the negative of the subjective probability of succeeding). As a result of his study, Atkinson proposes that two kinds of people can be distinguished: those in whom the motivation to achieve success is greater than that to avoid failure, and those in whom the reverse relation is true. He predicts that subjects of the first category will prefer bets of intermediate probability of success (and consequently relatively high variance), while subjects of the second category will prefer bets with probability success near either one or zero (and consequently relatively low variance).

In static decision theory, the decision-maker presumably never has the opportunity to make a second choice or demonstrate that he may have learned as a consequence of his previous decisions. In an excellent survey paper (1961), Edwards points to the need for a dynamic decision theory in which the decision-maker is conceived of as making a sequence of decisions. Each sequential decision produces some payoff and information which may or may not be relevant to the improvement of later decisions. The decision-maker's objective may be taken to be the maximization of total profit over the long run or some other weighted function of the future profit For example, it might prove to be desirable to forsake a short term profit in order to gain more information and lead to greater profit in the long run. In dynamic situations, the environment may also be a function of the sequence of decisions. Although this model should prove to be a more valid description of real situations, the associated mathematical problems may become extremely difficult.

In real situations, decisions are made in sequence, and each decision is influenced to some extent by information about the nature and consequences of earlier decisions. The problem is complicated, since the stochastic environment may be influenced by the decisions which are made so that the decision-maker operates as part of a closed loop. Further, the information he gathers from the environment may well reflect dependence upon the time of observation in relation to the decision sequence. These factors and many more interact in a most complex manner. Although the human operator is fairly good at estimating the mean of a random variable, he may well introduce significant amounts of error when required to estimate variances and other statistical parameters of interacting variables.

Frequently, the suggestion is made that human choice is always rational; in fact, it is proposed to be optimal with respect to some subjectively held goal. This point of view shifts the problem from one of finding subjective values and probabilities as the individual attempts to maximize the expected value to be gained, to one of finding a single factor (the subjective goal) which will fully explain the observed choice. In theory, at least, it is always possible to construct a goal which would rationalize observed behavior. However, it is doubtful whether subjective goals can ever be predicted as a function of the given situation so as to provide a better prediction and understanding of human decision-making.

Psychology is the study of thinking. Thought may be looked upon as a process of decision-making at various levels of organization. Overt actions reveal the cumulative effect of a vast amount of lower level decisions. Present knowledge remains far short of an essential understanding of this human decision-making process.

11.8. GROUP DECISION-MAKING

Technology has produced systems which can fulfill their intended mission only when they are properly used. Often a number of men are required to perform separate functions which are interlinked through equipments. These men form a team. The team may be a business firm, a military task force, a group engaged in competitive sport, or, indeed, any collection of cooperating individuals. Each member of the team may make decisions about different things and operate quite separately, and yet, these men are unified by the equipment system and the fact that all receive a common reward as a result of the joint success of the mission resulting from the group of decision functions. Obviously, proper design of the personnel subsystem can be every bit as important as the design of the equipment subsystem. Unfortunately, however, relatively little is known about how to design teams so that they will produce the greatest benefit from the systems they operate.

It is easy to see the importance of proper communication among the team members and their equipment since the "right" decision cannot be made in the light of "wrong" or inadequate information. Although it is clear that people can be expected to make better decisions as they know more about the external situation, the cost of providing such knowledge cannot be overlooked. If each member of the team is to know all information which can be known, it is likely that a complex and costly communication network devoted to just that purpose would be required. Even if this cost could be borne, it may be that the time each member spends in becoming fully informed may absorb so much of his time that his decision-making function may well suffer. To some extent, specialization of tasks overcomes this problem. In such cases, only certain information must be supplied to each member of the team. But specialization raises new problems and the relative importance that the proper communication paths be utilized has been considerably increased. The more specialized the function, the greater the over-all cost of misdirected (or undirected) communication.

Other problems must also be recognized. The relative cost of garbled information depends upon the team configuration and the relative importance of each decision-making function. Certain configurations may be particularly susceptible to certain kinds of imposed "jamming." Others may be more sensitive to the time lag associated with individual decisions or the delay imposed by the intercommunication links. The object is to find an optimal decision-making assignment and communication configuration in the light of the nature of the available decision-makers, the equipment to be utilized, the anticipated external situation, and the relative importance of the mission. More precisely stated, the designer endeavors to structure the system so as to maximize the gross success score of the team in terms of the cost of the information to be supplied and the value of the information resulting from the network which joins the decision-makers.

Information upon which decisions are based can be partitioned into invariant data and data descriptive of the varying aspects of the external situation. Let it be presumed that all invariant information is supplied to the decision-makers. The time varying properties of the environment may be characterized by probability density functions. Under the assumption that there is no interaction between individual decisions, each of the possible actions can then be evaluated in terms of the corresponding gross score. This matrix of possible values can be converted into an expected gross score matrix by multiplying by the probability that each value will be realized. Further, the cost of conveying those specified "chunks" of information (which may depend upon the external situation) can be subtracted, leaving a matrix of expected net scores. To be realistic, it is necessary to adjust these data to reflect the effect of interaction between decisions. Obviously, the coordination and direct cooperation among team members can greatly influence the gross score resulting from individual decisions. Interaction strongly affects the optimal configuration of the communication network. As the role of cooperative communication is increased, the value to each member of direct observation of the external environment is diminished.

All too frequently, it is assumed that decisions made by groups are, in general, superior to those made by individuals. This is, of course, a gross oversimplification. The superiority of groups versus individuals depends upon many parameters of the individual situation.

Experiments were carried out by L. S. Christie, R. D. Luce, and J. Macy, Jr., to explore the relative effect of various specific communication configurations. Each of the team members was required to send only single-address messages to other team members at prescribed times, to include in their messages all problem information known to them at the time, and to send nothing other than problem information. Decision-making was restricted to the choice of to whom the message should be sent. The task of the team was considered complete when all five team members possessed all five numbers. The communication networks are shown in Figure 11.14. With the exception of the star, these were evaluated in terms of the number of transmission acts required before the task was completed. This score was compared to the expected number of acts required under completely random link selection by each member, and, at the other extreme, to the most efficient possible choice of link selection.

Each configuration possessed particularly interesting properties. In the totally connected network, each man can send information to every other man. This network includes the other networks as special cases, and thus any pattern of usage of the links that can be developed in other networks can

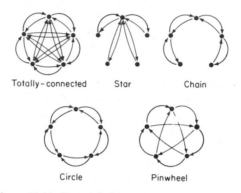

Totally-connected   Star   Chain

Circle   Pinwheel

Figure 11.14. Group decision communication networks.

also be developed in the "totally-connected" network. In contrast, this very richness of possibilities may be a weakness, since so many inefficient usages must be rejected in order to arrive at efficient usage.

The star is the most centralized network possible for a group of five members. The severely restricted communication possibilities nullified the value of experimental study of this network. The chain was taken to represent centralized communication. Connecting the "end men" converts the chain into the circle. Here, each man has the same freedom as every other man. The pinwheel does the most that any network can do to ensure the rapid spread of information in spite of undiscriminating behavior on the part of the men using it.

The totally-connected, circle, and pinwheel require a minimum of three acts. The chain (and star) required five. As reported by Christie, it was also shown that certain configurations helped to influence "locally rational" behavior wherein the member used the pattern of his own previous successes as a basis for further improved decision behavior. Both in the circle and the pinwheel there is a similar tendency toward locally rational individual behavior. When operating in the pinwheel configuration, group results are not favorable. The chain, however, behaves rationally and learns well. Its poor record is dependent upon the inadequacy of its own structure rather than the failure of the individual members to "do well." Totally-connected fails to do as well as circle, because the relation of message-destination choice to information distribution is too complicated.

The star network is an example of the conventional hierarchical system. Eliminating any decision on the part of the subordinate (peripheral) members as to where to send messages tends to enforce behavior near its optimum, provided no information overload occurs. For some tasks, the circle network also has the property that locally optimal decisions tend to lead to optimal group performance. The cost for this better average performance is the increased probability of an occasional bad performance.

Clearly, in the relatively simple case where decisions are made by team members who can communicate in a noiseless field, the configuration of the possible network is an important factor in determining the effectiveness of carrying out full information disclosure. It is important to remember that this is a very restricted team purpose and that the reported results were obtained under severely restricted "laboratory" conditions, which do not generally correspond to the complex situations found in the real world where team members must also decode, store, mediate, and encode the messages, each with a somewhat different purpose in mind.

Generally, the time to learn appropriate behavior in a less rigid system appears to be longer. The conventional hierarchical system is widely applicable with little change of reliability to differing requirements and tasks. (This may not be as true for other organizations.) For each purpose there is likely to be some particular most suitable organization. The particular configuration which is optimal may well depend on the amount and nature of individual errors expected, the nature of the communication channel noise and its effect on message ambiguity, the level of redundancy used or permitted in encoding the data, and the amount of information which must be transduced through individual decisions.

It is usually true that in a highly structured situation, most personnel in the system have an incomplete and often inaccurate concept of the organization and communication links. The exceptional individual is characterized by his additional efforts to represent the over-all system on the basis of the information available to him. Hopefully, this may allow more intelligent decision-making than would otherwise be possible. Certain structural properties can be instituted which bring together diverse information in order to encourage, even force, a specific individual to remain aware of the over-all system function. Of course, this device has its price, since there is always the possibility of creating an information overload situation or separating the individual from having data about any specific function.

There may well be network configurations such that if the individuals operate on some basis of locally optimal decisions, the outcome is optimal or near optimal group performance for the network to achieve a specific purpose. Certainly, two different networks of the same number of individuals may have widely different optimal group performances; however, the efficiency of any organization is limited so long as the system must be constructed from components that react almost entirely to local features.

I. Lorge performed a series of experiments in which complex realistic rational management decision problems were carried out by individuals and *ad hoc* six-member conference teams. Each decision period was of fifty minutes duration, and a unique scoring technique was employed to evaluate the results of decision. In his words:

> The averages of individual second decisions was significantly superior to average of the group first decisions. Conversely, however, there is no significant difference between the quality of individual first and group second decisions, written by the same subjects. While the average of individual decisions written after a group meeting is superior to the average of group decisions made by these same individuals, there is no significant difference between the average of individual decisions written during the first period and the average of the group decision written by the same subjects during the second period. Individuals who write decisions after meeting in groups with this problem make superior decisions than the groups in which they were members. If individual decisions are written first, however, the groups do not make decisions superior to those of the individuals who comprise the group.
>
> The data are incontrovertible in showing for individuals and *ad hoc* groups, relatively naive in group interaction and problem solving techniques, deciding realistic, complex problems in a short period of time, that the average quality of the individual decisions will be superior to the quality of the average group decisions. After fifty minutes of experience with the same problem, however, there is no significant difference between the quality of the average individual and group decision. If members of a group write individual decisions after making a group decision about the same problem, in general, those individual decisions of the group members are superior to the initial group decision. On the other hand, if subjects first write individual decisions and then meet to write a group decision, despite the additional time, in general these group decisions are not superior to those written initially by the individual group members.

In an ideal organization, every individual can perform any task at any time. Even if such fully capable personnel were available, restricted time requirements usually necessitate the formation of a team of individuals (as opposed to a single individual functioning on a sequence of tasks with the successive storage of information between tasks). In some situations, time itself becomes a direct measure of the worth of the group while in other instances time is an indirect measure (as in economic situations). It is also clear that the error rate of a group is related to the operational time requirement, at least indirectly, since in the limit where there is no time pressure inspection and checking procedures can be introduced which ensure arbitrarily good performance. The design of such groups should reflect the relation between error and time.

Various other experiments have demonstrated that individual members significantly affect the decision-making characteristics of small groups. For example, the inclusion of the individual who strives for pre-eminence reduces group cohesiveness and the friendliness of the communications. Generally, the designated leader is expected to be the sole major behavioral leader. However, the sharing of leadership may be accepted in groups which face current problems. The pressure toward group agreement is greatest when the members of the group are dependent on group success for their individual satisfaction. In one experiment, supervisors reached valid decisions more readily when instructed that their status would be affected if they did not do so. The quality of group decisions increases with greater available time. In an experiment by D. Fox, it was shown that individual decisions may be made more rapidly, but these did not attain the quality of the group decision, even if more time was allowed. The good quality which arose in discussion was not readily transmitted to paper by an *ad hoc* group.

It appears that the benefit of group participation is greatest in problems requiring definite originality and insight and least in routine tasks. Predictions made by groups are more apt to be correct than those made by the same individuals working separately. The reliability of these predictions can be appraised to some extent by examining the character of the justifications given for them. However, confidence in prediction is not necessarily correlated with the degree of success. D. Taylor performed experiments on the game of "Twenty Questions." He showed that rapid improvement occurred in the performance of both individuals and groups as measured by the number of questions asked. Group performance was superior to individual performance in terms of number of questions, the number of failures, and the elapsed time per problem, but the performance of groups of four individuals was not superior to that of groups of two. With the exception of the number of failures to reach solution, improvement in individual performance occurred as rapidly with individual practice as with practice as a member of a group.

In recent years, a significant trend toward "management by analysis" has developed in industry and commerce. An attempt is made to delineate the specific goal of the organization, gather relevant information, use these data to estimate the most likely future state of the organization under the influence of the predicted environment, compare this state to the desired state, and choose that course of action which will minimize the difference. At each point in time, decisions are made to select a "best" program under some stated policy of maximizing a payoff (often profit) while minimizing the risk.

Note that there are certain inherent costs of management by analysis. The choice of a specific goal excludes other possible goals over the time interval during which the stated goal provides the basis for operation. It may well be that other goals are of some positive value. This additional value is completely lost when there is only a single goal. Further, the value of each goal may be a function of time, so that even if the most suitable goal had been originally chosen, this goal may no longer be of greatest value. The cost of collecting data may prove to be extremely high, especially in the case of large organizations which strongly affect a widely diversified group of other organizations. Collecting data takes time, so that the "situation" which is synthesized from the data may no longer represent the "present" conditions. In fact, the composite may be composed of fragments measured over a significant span of time. All empirical evidence is to some extent in error and this error is almost always amplified in projecting future conditions. The direct cost of such error may be inappropriate commitments which result in waste or even more detrimental actions. Clearly, management by analysis can be costly.

In contrast to management by analysis, there is the more traditional approach. M. Flood calls this "management by adaptation." Under this policy, the organization responds to its stimuli in accordance with value-weighted experience. Each event is classified with respect to its degree of similarity to previous events. Actions are taken which are as similar as possible to those previous actions which were taken under similar situations and resulted in "a happy outcome." The organization is viewed *in toto* with the state of its "happiness" resulting from each sequence of actions being judged with respect to the goal of that moment. In management by adaptation, the goal remains an implicit property which may be continually modified as a function of time. No specific goal statement is required, and, in fact, the organization may not even recognize in any formal manner that a goal exists.

The costs of "management by adaptation" are somewhat harder to measure than those associated with "management by analysis." The organization is a dynamic entity operating under a continually changing environment, so that situations which might be classified as "happy" at a particular time in the past, might no longer be considered as such. Situations are multidimensional, but even if a single measure could be found, there would be many degrees of similarity between the presently sensed situation and that of any particular point in the past. Gross classification of "similar" or not introduces a significant error of judgment. Usually, the number of similar experiences are few. The statistician would be appalled at the confidence level with which decisions are reached upon the basis of only one or two "similar" experiences. Throughout this procedure, the tacit assumption is made that the preceding sequence of actions taken by the organization were causal to the succeeding state of "happiness." For example, a singular rise in the value of corporate stock might result from a change in the international climate. It might have had little to do with the preceding sequence of actions taken by the management. In "management by adaptation" a course of action is determined on the basis of nonquantitative information. This kind of evidence precludes further assessment of the validity with which control decisions have been reached. The organization becomes more and more dependent upon the particular individuals in charge. Detailed records are nonexistent. The loss of the individual can often mean the demise of the organization.

There appears to be no essential reason why the attributes of management by analysis and management by adaptation cannot be used to compliment each other. It might be possible to find some compromise which optimizes the management function through wise identification of the most significant classes of information which are worthy of collection, reduction, and interpretation. At the same time, a hierarchy of goals can be defined. A modified environment may then be viewed as an opportunity to raise the rank of a subsidiary goal and gain a new benefit for the organization. Nevertheless, the individual decision-maker should be encouraged to remain cognizant of the many diversified minor factors which influence his decision since these, taken together, may constitute sufficient evidence to allow a change in the policy which dictates the nature of the data collected and the formal procedures exercised in management control.

In loose terms, the organization *goal* is used to define a specific statement of *policy*. In turn, this policy results in a set of *procedures*, and the procedures result in some *practice*. Each step attempts to specify the consistencies of the preceding step, thus reducing the number of decisions which must meet unforeseen circumstances at lower levels. In any real world situation there is always some difference between the actual practice and that specified by the procedures. Under the changing situation, the procedures may be somewhat deviant from the policy, and, in a similar manner, the policy may not fully support the goal. Management should extract feedback information from each of these levels and use this data to concurrently minimize these errors at the various levels of specificity of function.

Organizations consist of groups within groups. Each of these groups may have its own goal and loyalties which, when taken together through the configuration of the uniting organization, define the goal for the entire system. Ideally, each group should take only those actions which support both its own goal and the goals of the encompassing groups. There should be no conflicting goals for internal groups at any level. This fortuitous situation is rarely found in the real world, especially in organizations wherein neither the groups nor the purpose of these groups are clearly defined. It is, therefore, considered worthwhile for management to examine the goal implied by the set of actions of each group. Those particular subgoals which appear inconsistent deserve specific attention and suitable corrective action.

An organization comprised of a hierarchy of single decision-makers reacts differently from one wherein each of the decisions is the result of a "round table" discussion. The former organization generally displays the attribute of faster and more concise response to sudden changes of the environment; however, it often suffers from excessive consistency of its fundamental philosophy. The change of outlook by a single individual is often taken as indicative that his previous outlook must have been "wrong." In group decisions the burden of responsibility is diffused. This facilitates change of philosophy and policy.

Much remains to be done before sufficient knowledge will become available to allow the direct planning of organizations. There is, however, every indication of a growing interest in this field of research.

11.9. CONCLUSION

The human decision-maker has protected himself with an artificial envelope of technology. This technology is the direct outgrowth of scientific discovery and the sensed challenge of nature. In an ascending spiral, man has created and is creating new capability to sense needs which he then proceeds to satisfy through more and more complex man-machine systems. Each new scientific discovery furnishes direction and impetus to the machine which *is* technology. Man is no longer the sole guiding agent. He cannot even choose to impede progress. As a result of the struggle among groups of men, he has forfeited the ability to retard and thereby control the rapidity with which his artificial environment changes. It may be that technology has already unleashed destructive agents which may gradually annihilate mankind.

Having lost control of his apprentice, mankind must look to his own flexibility of structure in the hope of surviving a more fearful environment than ever before. Rampant technology is the singular threat which might prove sufficient to anneal mankind into a single cooperative enterprise, provided, of course, that the threat is widely recognized. Hopefully, through proper decision-making and controlled evolution, he can increase his inherent capability to catch up with and overcome the danger created by his own social inadequacy. This race is about to begin in earnest. The next few decades may well require great changes in the organization of mankind, both externally and internally. But living organisms are slow to reproduce and even slower to achieve significant change. It may well be that the outcome of the race has already been determined.

BIBLIOGRAPHY

ABORN, M., and H. RUBENSTEIN, "Information Theory and Immediate Recall," *Journal of Experimental Psychology*, Vol. 45 (1952), 260–266.

ADAMS, J. A., "Psychometer Performance as a Function of Intertrial Rest Interval," *Journal of Experimental Psychology*, Vol. 48 (1954), 131–133.

ADRIAN, E. D., F. BREMER, and H. H. JASPER, eds., *Brain Mechanisms and Consciousness*. Oxford: Blackwell Scientific Publications, 1954.

ATTNEAVE, F., "Symmetry, Information, and Memory for Patterns," *American Journal of Psychology*, Vol. 68 (1955), 209–222.

ATTNEAVE, F., *Applications of Information Theory to Psychology, A Summary of Basic Concepts, Methods, and Results*. New York: Henry Holt & Company, Inc., 1959.

ALLUISI, E. A., P. F. MULLER, JR., and P. M. FITTS, "Rate of Handling Information and the Rate of Information Presentation," *USAF WADC TN 55-745* (December 1955).

BARANKEN, E. W., "Toward an Objectivistic Theory of Probability," *Proceedings of the Third Berkeley Symposium on Mathematical Statistics and Probability*, Vol. V, ed. by J. Neyman, Berkeley: University of California Press, 1956.

BAVELAS, A., "Communication Patterns in Task-Oriented Groups," *Journal of the Acoustical Society of America*, Vol. 22 No. 6 (November 1950), 725–730.

BENDIG, A. A., "Twenty Questions: An Information Analysis," *Journal of Experimental Psychology*, Vol. 46 (1953), 345–348.

BEVAN, W., and P. SAUGSTAD, "Breadth of Experience, Ease of Discrimination and Efficiency of Generalization," *British Journal of Psychology*, Vol. 46 (1955), 13–19.

BILLS, A. G., *The Psychology of Efficiency*. New York: Harper and Brothers, 1943.

BIRKHOFF, G. D., *Aesthetic Measure*. Cambridge, Mass.: Harvard University Press, 1933.

BISHOP, G. H., "Natural History of the Nerve Impulse," *Physiological Reviews*, Vol. 36 (1956), 376–399.

BLANKENSHIP, A. B., "Memory Span: A Review of the Literature," *Psychological Bulletin*, Vol. 35 (1938), 1–25.

BLOOMFIELD, L., *Language*. New York: Henry Holt & Company, Inc., 1948.

BOK, S. T., *The Synapses in the Cerebral Cortex*, Progress in Neurology, J. Ariens Koppers, ed., Elsevier, Amsterdam (1956), 13–25.

———. *Conditioned Synapses*, Recent Neurological Research, A. Biemond, ed., Elsevier, Amsterdam (1959), 22–36.

BRAZIER, M. A., ed., *The Central Nervous System and Behavior* (Trans. of first and second conference). New York: Josiah Macy, Jr., Foundation, 1959.

BROADBENT, D. E., "Effect of Noise on an 'Intellectual' Task," *Journal of the Acoustical Society of America*, Vol. 30 No. 9 (September 1958), 824–827.

BRUNER, J. S., J. J. GOODNOW, and G. A. AUSTIN, *A Study of Thinking*. New York: John Wiley & Sons, Inc., 1956.

BRUNER, J. S., "Neural Mechanisms in Perception," *Psychological Review*, Vol. 64 (1957), 340–358.

BULLOCK, T. H., "Neuron Doctrine and Electrophysiology," *Science*, Vol. 129 (1959), 997–1002.

BUSH, W. R., V. M. DONAHUE, and R. B. KELLY, "Pattern Recognition and Display Characteristics," *IRE Transactions on Human Factors in Electronics*, Vol. HFE-1 No. 1 (March 1960), 11–20.

BUSH, R. R., and F. MOSTELLER, *Stochastic Models for Learning*. New York: John Wiley & Sons, Inc., 1955.

CAMPBELL, D. T., "Systematic Error on the Part of Human Links in Communication Systems," *Information and Control*, Vol. 1 No. 4 (December 1958), 334–369.

CHAPANIS, A., "A Rate of Making Complex Decisions," *American Journal of Psychology*, Vol. 70 (1957), 650–652.

CHERRY, C., ed., *On Human Communication*. New York: John Wiley & Sons, Inc., 1957.

CHRISTIE, L. S., "Organization and Information Handling in Task Groups," *Journal of the Operations Research Society of America*, Vol. 2 No. 2 (May 1954), 188–196.

CHRISTIE, L. S., R. D. LUCE, and J. MACY, "Communication and Learning in Task-Oriented Groups," *Research Laboratory of Electronics TR 231*, Cambridge, Mass.: Massachusetts Institute of Technology, 1952.

COHEN, J., and C. E. M. HANSEL, "The Nature of Decisions in Gambling. Equivalence of Single and Compound Subjective Probabilities," *Acta Phychologica*, Vol. 13 (1958), 357–370.

COHEN, J., E. J. DEARNALEY, and C. E. M. HANSEL, "The Addition of Subjective Probabilities. The Summation of Estimates of Success and Failure," *Acta Psychologica*, Vol. 12 (1956), 371–380.

CONFERENCE OF THE NEW YORK ACADEMY OF SCIENCES, "Mathematical Theories of Biological Phenomena," *Annals of the New York Academy of Sciences*, Vol. 96 Art. 4 (1960), 895–1116.

CROSSMAN, E. R. F. W., "Entropy and Choice Time: The Effect of Frequency Unbalance on Choice-Response," *Quarterly Journal of Experimental Psychology*, Vol. 5 No. 2 (1953), 41–51.

DAVIDSON, D., and P. SUPPES, in collaboration with S. SIEGEL, *Decision Making: An Experimental Approach*. Stanford, Calif.: Stanford University Press, 1957.

DELGADO, J. M. R., "Electronic Command of Movement and Behavior," *Transactions of the New York Academy of Sciences*, Series II Vol. 21 No. 8 (June 1959), 689–699.

ECCLES, J. C., *The Physiology of Nerve Cells*. Baltimore, Md.: The Johns-Hopkins Press, 1957.

———. *The Neurophysiological Basis of Mind*. Oxford: Clarendon Press, 1952.

ECKSTRAND, G. A., and D. D. WICKENS, "Transfer of Perceptual Set.," *Journal of Experimental Psychology*, Vol. 47 (1954), 274–278.

EDWARDS, W., "The Theory of Decision-Making," *Psychological Bulletin*, Vol. 51 No. 4 (July 1954), 380–417.

———. "Behavioral Decision Theory," *Annual Review of Psychology*, Vol. 12 (1961), 473–498.

EDWARDS, W., "Probability-Preferences in Gambling," *American Journal of Psychology*, Vol. 66 (1953), 349–364.

———. "Variance Preferences in Gambling," *American Journal of Psychology*, Vol. 67 (1954), 441–452.

EGAN, J. P., "Human Factors in Detection and in Speech Communication in Noise," *IRE National Convention Record*, Part 4 Vol. 6 (1958), 15

EGAN, J. P., G. Z. GREENBERG, and A. I. SCHULMAN, "Operating Characteristics. Signal Detectability, and the Method of Free Response," *Journal of the Acoustical Society of America*, Vol. 33 No. 8 (August 1961), 993–1007.

ELSASSER, W. M., *The Physical Foundation of Biology*. New York: Pergamon Press, 1958.

ERICKSEN, C. W., and H. W. HAKE, "Absolute Judgments as a Function of Stimulus Range and Number of Stimulus and Response Categories," *Journal of Experimental Psychology*, Vol. 49 (1955), 323–332.

ESTES, W. K., "Of Models and Men," *American Psychologist*, Vol. 12 (1957), 609–617.

FANO, R. M., "The Information Theory Point of View in Speech Communication," *Journal of the Acoustical Society of America*, Vol. 22 (1950), 691–696.

FOGEL, L. J., "The Problems of Engineering Management," *IRE Transactions on Engineering Management*, Vol. EM–3 No. 1 (January 1956), 1–3.

FOX, W. C., "Signal Detectability: A Unified Description of Statistical Methods Employing Fixed and Sequential Observation Processes," *Engineering Research Institute Project M970. Report No. 19*, University of Michigan (December 1953).

FRANK, K., "Basic Mechanism of Synaptic Transmission in the Central Nervous System," *IRE Transactions on Medical Electronics*, Vol. ME–6 No. 2 (June 1959), 85–87.

FRENCH, R. S., "Pattern Recognition in the Presence of Visual Noise," *Journal of Experimental Psychology*, Vol. 47 (1954), 27–31.

FRITZ, E. L., and G. W. GRIER, "Empirical Entropy: A Study of Information Flow in Air Traffic Control," *Control Systems Laboratory Report R–54*, University of Illinois (March 1954).

FULTON, J. F., ed., *A Textbook of Physiology*, 17th ed. Philadelphia: W. B. Saunders Company, 1955.

GARNER, W. R., and H. W. HAKE, "On the Amount of Information in Absolute Judgments," *Psychological Review*, Vol. 58 (1951), 446–459.

GARNER, W. R., "Context Effects and the Validity of Loudness Scales," *Journal of Experimental Psychology*, Vol. 48 (1954), 218–224.

GARVEY, W. D., "Operator Performance as a Function of the Statistical Encoding of Stimuli," *Journal of Experimental Psychology*, Vol. 54 (1957), 109–114.

GOODNOW, J. J., "Determinants of Choice-Distribution in Two-Choice Situations," *American Journal of Psychology*, Vol. 68 (1955), 106–116.

GUILFORD, J. P., "The Structure of Intellect," *Psychological Bulletin*, Vol. 53 (1956), 267–293.

HALSTEAD, W. C., *Brain and Intelligence*. Chicago: University of Chicago Press, 1947.

HARMON, L. D., J. LEVINSON, and W. A. VAN BERGEIJK, "Analog Models of Neural Mechanism," *IRE Transactions on Information Theory*, Vol. IT–8 No. 2 (February 1962), 107–112.

HARLOW, H. F., and C. N. WOOLSEY, eds., *Biological and Biochemical Bases of Behavior*. Madison: University of Winconsin Press, 1958.

HEISE, G. A., and G. A. MILLER, "Problem Solving by Small Groups Using Various Communication Nets," *Journal of Abornal and Social Psychology* Vol. 46 (1951), 327–335.

HERDAN, G., *Language as Choice and Chance*. Groningen, England: P. Noordhoff N.V., 1956.

HERRICK, C. J., *The Evolution of Human Nature*. Austin: University of Texas Press, 1956.

HICK, W. E., "Information Theory in Psychology," *Transaction of the IRE Professional Group on Information Theory*, PGIT–1 (February 1953), 130–133.

———. "On the Rate of Gain of Information," *Quarterly Journal of Experimental Psychology*, Vol. 4 (1952), 11–26.

HOCKETT, C. F., *A Course in Modern Linguistics*. New York: The Macmillan Company, 1958.

HSU, J. C., and W. E. MESERVE, "Decision-Making in Adaptive Control Systems," *IRE Transactions on Automatic Control*, Vol. AC–7 No. 1 (January 1962), 24–32.

HULL, C. L., *A Behavior System: An Introduction to Behavior Theory Concerning the Individual Organism*. New Haven, Conn.: Yale University Press, 1952.

HUSBAND, R. W., "Cooperative versus Solitary Problem Solution," *Journal of Social Psychology*, Vol. 11 (1940), 405–409.

HUXLEY, J., *Evolution in Action*. New York: Harper and Brothers, 1953.

HYMAN, R., and H. W. HAKE, "Form Recognition as a Function of the Number of Forms Which Can Be Presented For Recognition," *USAF WADC TR 54–164* (May 1954).

HYMAN, R., "Stimulus Information as a Determinant of Reaction Time," *Journal of Experimental Psychology*, Vol. 45 (1953), 188–196.

IRWIN, F. W., and W. A. S. Smith, "Value, Cost, and Information as Determiners of Decision," *Journal of Experimental Psychology*, Vol. 54 (1957), 229–232.

JARVIK, M. E., "Probability Learning and a Negative Recency Effect in the Serial Anticipation of Alternative Symbols," *Journal of Experimental Psychology*, Vol. 41 (1951), 291–297.

JEFFRESS, L. A., *Cerebral Mechanisms In Behavior*. New York: John Wiley & Sons, Inc., 1951.

JOOS, M., "Description of Language Design," *Journal of the Acoustical Society of America*, Vol. 22 (1950), 701–708.

KOCHEN, M., and E. H. GALANTER, "The Acquisition and Utilization of Information in Problem Solving and Thinking," *Information and Control*, Vol. 1 No. 3 (September 1958), 267–288.

KOCHEN, M., "A Mathematical Formulation of Influence Distributions in Decision-Making Groups," *Journal of the Society for Industrial and Applied Mathematics*, Vol. 6 No. 3 (September 1958), 199–208.

KRULEE, G. K., "Information Theory and Man-Machine Systems," *Journal of the Operation Research Society of America*, Vol. 2 No. 3 (August 1954), 320–328.

LANZETTA, J. T., and T. B. ROBY, "Group Learning and Communications as a Function of Task and Structure Demands," *Journal of Abnormal and Social Psychology*, Vol. 55 No. 1 (1957), 121–131.

LEAVITT, H. J., "Some Effects of Certain Communication Patterns on Group Performance," *Journal of Abnormal and Social Psychology*, Vol. 46 (1951), 38–50.

LETTVIN, J. Y., H. R. MATURANA, *et al.*, "What the Frog's Eye Tells the Frog's Brain," *Proceedings of the IRE*, Vol. 47 No. 11 (November 1959), 1940–1951.

LICKLIDER, J. C. R., "Man-Computer Symbiosis," *IRE Transactions on Human Factors in Electronics*, Vol. HFE-1 No. 1 (March 1960), 4–10.

LONG, L., "A Study of the Effect of Preceding Stimuli Upon the Judgment of Auditory Intensities," *Archives of Psychology*, Vol. 30 (1937), 209.

LORGE, I., J. TUCKMAN, L. AIKMAN, J. SPIEFEL, and G. Moss, "The Adequacy of Written Reports in Problem Solving by Teams and by Individuals," *Journal of Social Psychology*, Vol. 43 (1956), 65–74.

LUCE, R. D., *et al.*, "Information Flow in Task Oriented Groups," *Research Laboratory of Electronics TR 264*, Massachusetts Institute of Technology (August 1953).

MACKAY, D. M., "On Comparing the Brain with Machines," *American Scientist*, Vol. 42 (1954), 261–268.

MACY, J., JR., L. S. CHRISTIE, and R. D. LUCE, "Coding Noise in a Task-Oriented Group," *Journal of Abnormal and Social Psychology*, Vol. 48 (1953), 401–409.

MAGOUN, H. W., *The Waking Brain*. Springfield, Ill.: Charles C. Thomas, 1958.

MARQUART, D. I., "Group Problem Solving," *Journal of Social Psychology*, Vol. 41 (1955), 103–113.

MARSCHAK, J., "Elements For a Theory of Teams," *Management Science*, Vol. 1 (1955), 127–137.

———. "Norms and Habits of Decision Making Under Certainty," from *Mathematical Models of Human Behavior*, pp. 45–53, Proceedings of a Symposium, Stamford, Conn.: Dunlap & Associates, Inc., 1955.

McCURDY, H. G., and W. E. LAMBERT, "The Efficiency of Small Human Groups in the Solution of Problems Requiring Genuine Cooperation," *Journal of Personality*, Vol. 20 (1952), 478–494.

MacKAY, D. M., "Toward an Information-Flow Model of Human Behavior," *British Journal of Psychology*, Vol. 47 (1956), 30–43.

MILLER, G. A., "Human Memory and the Storage of Information," *IRE Transactions on Information Theory*, Vol. IT–2 No. 3 (September 1956), 129–137.

———. *Language and Communication*. New York: McGraw-Hill Book Company, Inc., 1951.

———. "Language Engineering," *Journal of the Acoustical Society of America*, Vol. 22 No. 6 (November 1950), 720–724.

———. "The Magical Number 7, Plus or Minus 2: Some Limits on our Capacity for Processing Information," *Psychological Review*, Vol. 63 No. 2 (March 1956), 81–97.

MILLER, G. A., and F. C. FRICK, "Statistical Behavioristics and Sequences of Responses," *Psychological Review*, Vol. 56 (1949), 311–324.

MILLER, J. G., "Information Input Overload and Psychopathology," *American Journal of Psychiatry*, Vol. 116 No. 8 (February 1960), 695–704.

MILLER, N. E., "The Effect of Group Size on Decision-Making Discussions," *Speech Monographs*, Vol. 20 (1953), 131–132.

NEWMAN, E. G., "The Pattern of Vowels and Consonants in Various Languages," *American Journal of Psychology*, Vol. 64 (1951), 369–379.

ONCLEY, J. L., ed., *Biophysical Science—A Study Program*. New York: John Wiley & Sons, Inc., 1959.

OWENS, W. A., JR., "Age and Mental Abilities: A Longitudinal Study," *Genetic Psychology Monographs*, Vol. 48 (1953), 3–54.

PENFIELD, W., and L. ROBERTS, *Speech and Brain-Mechanisms*. Princeton, N.J.: Princeton University Press, 1959.

PETERSON, W. W., T. G. BIRDSALL, and W. C. FOX, "The Theory of Signal Detectability," *IRE Transactions on Information Theory*, PGIT–4 (September 1954), 171–212.

PIERCE, J. R., and J. E. KARLIN, "Reading Rates and the Information Rate of a Human Channel," *IRE WESCON Convention Record*, Vol. 1 Part 2—Circuit Theory and Information Theory (1957), 60.

POLLACK, I., "Identification of Elementary Auditory Displays and the Method of Recognition Memory," *Journal of the Acoustical Society of America*, Vol. 31 No. 8 (August 1959), 1126–1128.

———. "Information of Elementary Auditory Displays. II," *Journal of the Acoustical Society of America*, Vol. 25 No. 4 (July 1953), 765–770.

———. "Message Uncertainty and Message Reception," *Journal of the Acoustical Society of America*, Vol. 31 No. 11 (November 1959), 1500–1508.

———. "Message Repetition and Message Reception," *Journal of the Acoustical Society of America*, Vol. 31 No. 11 (November 1959), 1509–1516.

POLLACK, I., and L. FICKS, "Information of Elementary Multidimensional Auditory Displays," *Journal of the Acoustical Society of America*, Vol. 26 No. 2 (March 1954), 155–159.

POULTON, E. C., "Perceptual Anticipation and Reaction Time," *Quarterly Journal of Experimental Psychology*, Vol. 2 (1950), 99–112.

QUASTLER, H., ed., *Information Theory in Psychology*. Glencoe, Ill.: Free Press, 1956.

———. *Information Theory in Psychology. Problems and Methods*. Glencoe, Ill.: Free Press, 1955.

———. "The Complexity of Biological Computers," *IRE Transactions on Electronic Computers*, Vol. EC–6 (1957), 192–194.

QUASTLER, H., and V. J. WULFF, "Human Performance in Information Transmission," *Control System Laboratory Report R–62*, University of Illinois (1955).

RAPOPORT, A., and W. J. HORVATH, "Information Processing in Neurones and Small Nets," *USAF WADD TR–60–652* (December 1960).

RASHEVSKY, N., *Mathematical Biology of Social Behavior*. Chicago: University of Chicago Press, 1951.

RESTLE, F., *Psychology of Judgment and Choice: A Theoretical Essay*. New York: John Wiley & Sons, Inc., 1961.

ROBERTSON, SIR D., "Utility and All What?," *Economic Journal*, Vol. 64 (1954), 665–678.

ROSENBLITH, W. A., "Some Quantifiable Aspects of the Electrical Activity of the Nervous System (with emphasis upon responses to sensory stimuli)," *Review of Modern Physics*, Vol. 31 (1959), 532–545.

SCHEIN, E. H., S. H. WHITE, and W. F. HILL, "The Organization of Communication in Small Problem-Solving Groups," *American Psychologist*, Vol. 10 (August 1955), 357–358.

Second Symposium on Physiological Psychology, USN ONR Symposium Report ACR–30 (March 19–21, 1958).

SHANNON, C. E., "Prediction and Entropy of Printed English," *Bell System Technical Journal*, Vol. 30 (1951), 50–64.

SHAW, M. E., "Group Structure and the Behavior of Individuals in Small Groups," *Journal of Psychology*, Vol. 38 (1954), 139–149.

———. "Some Effects of Problem Complexity Upon Problem Solution Efficiency in Different Communication Nets," *Journal of Experimental Psychology*, Vol. 48 (1954), 211–217.

———. "Random Versus Systematic Distribution of Information in Communication Nets," *Journal of Personality*, Vol. 25 No. 1 (1956), 58–59.

———. "A Comparison of Two Types of Leadership in Various Communication Nets," *Journal of Experimental Psychology*, Vol. 50 (1955), 127–134.

SHAW, M. E., G. H. ROTHSCHILD, and J. F. STRICKLAND, "Decision Process in Communication Nets," *Journal of Abnormal and Social Psychology*, Vol. 54 No. 3 (1957), 323–330.

SHEPARD, R. N., "Stimulus and Response Generalization: A Stochastic Model Relating Generalization to Distance in Psychological Space," *Psychometrika*, Vol. 22 (1957), 325–345.

SHERWIN, C. W., *et al.*, "Detection of Signals in Noise: A Comparison Between the Human Detector and an Electronic Detector," *Journal of the Acoustical Society of America*, Vol. 28 No. 4 (July 1956), 617–622.

SIMON, C. W., and W. H. EMMONS, "EEG, Consciousness, and Sleep," *Science*, Vol. 124 No. 3231 (November 1956), 1066–1969.

———. "Responses to Material Presented During Various Levels of Sleep," *Journal of Experimental Psychiatry*, Vol. 51 No. 2 (February 1956), 89–97.

SIMON, C. W., "Some Immediate Effects of Drowsiness and Sleep on Normal Human Performance," *Journal of the Human Factors Society*, Vol. 3 No. 1 (March 1961), 1–17.

SIMON H. A., "A Behavioral Model of Rational Choice," *Quarterly Journal of Economics*, Vol. 69 (1955), 99–118.

SMITH, W. M., "Past Experience and the Perception of Visual Size," *American Journal of Psychology*, Vol. 65 (July 1952), 389–403.

SOLOMON, H., ed., *Mathematical Thinking in the Measurement of Behavior*. Glencoe, Ill.: Free Press, 1960.

STEVENS, S. S., ed., *Handbook of Experimental Psychology*. New York: John Wiley & Sons, Inc., 1951.

SUMBY, W. H., *et al.*, "Information Transmission with Elementary Auditory Displays," *Journal of the Acoustical Society of America*, Vol. 30 No. 5 (May 1958), 425–430.

SUPPES, P., "The Role of Subjective Probability and Utility in Decision-Making," *Proceedings of the Third Berkeley Symposium on Mathematical Statistics and Probability*, Vol. V, pp. 61–75 (J. Neyman, ed.), Berkeley, Calif.: University of California Press, 1956.

SWETS, J. A., and T. G. BIRDSALL, "The Human Use of Information. III. Decision-Making in Signal Detection and Recognition Situations Involving Multiple Alternatives," *IRE Transactions on Information Theory*, Vol. IT-2 No. 3 (1956), 138–165.

SWETS, J. A., and S. T. SEWALL, "Stimulus vs. Response Uncertainty in Recognition," *Journal of the Acoustical Society of America*, Vol. 33 No. 11 (November 1961), 1586–1592.

SWETS, J. A., "Indices of Signal Detectability Obtained with Various Psychophysical Procedures," *Journal of the Acoustical Society of America*, Vol. 31 No. 4 (April 1959), 511–514.

SZIKLAI, G. C., "Some Studies in the Speed of Visual Perception," *IRE Transactions on Information Theory*, Vol. IT-2 No. 3 (September 1956), 125–128.

TANNER, W. P., JR., and R. Z. NORMAN, "The Human Use of Information. II. Signal Detection Under Uncertainty About Signal Frequency," *IRE Transactions on Information Theory*, Vol. PGIT-4 (September 1954), 222–227.

TANNER, W. P., JR., and J. A. SWETS, "The Human Use of Information. I. Signal Detection for the Case of the Signal Known Exactly," *IRE Transactions on Information Theory*, Vol. PGIT-4 (September 1954), 213–221.

———. "A Decision-Making Theory of Visual Detection," *Psychological Review*, Vol. 61 (1954), 401–409.

TANNER, W. P., JR., "Theory of Recognition," *Journal of the Acoustical Society of America*, Vol. 28 No. 5 (September 1956), 882–888.

———. "Theory of Signal Detectability as an Interpretive Tool for Psychophysical Data," *Journal of the Acoustical Society of America*, Vol. 32 No. 9 (September 1960), 1140–1146.

THRALL, R. M., C. H. COOMBS, and R. L. DAVID, eds., *Decision Processes*. New York: John Wiley & Sons, Inc., 1954.

TOLMAN E. C., and L. J. POSTMAN, "Learning," *Annual Review of Psychology*, Vol. 5 (1954), 27–56.

U.S. DEPARTMENT OF HEALTH, EDUCATION AND WELFARE, PUBLIC HEALTH SERVICE, *The Central Nervous System and Behavior, Selected Translations from the Russian Medical Literature* (December 1, 1959).

VON FOERSTER, H., ed., *Cybernetics, Circular Causal, and Feedback Mechanisms in Biological and Social Systems*, Transactions of the Sixth Conference held March 24–25, 1949. New York: Josiah Macy, Jr., Foundation, 1950.

WASSERMAN, P., with F. S. SILANDER, *Decision-Making: An Annotated Bibliography*. Ithica, N.Y.: Graduate School of Business and Public Administration, Cornell University, 1958.

WEBSTER, J. C., and P. O. THOMPSON, "Responding to Both of Two Overlapping Messages," *Journal of the Acoustical Society of America*, Vol. 26 No. 3 (May 1954), 396–403.

WECHSLER, D., "Intelligence, Quantum Resonance and Thinking Machines," *Transactions of the New York Academy of Sciences*, Series II Vol. 22 No. 4 (February 1960), 259–267.

WILLNER, D., ed., *Decisions, Values and Groups. 1. Reports from the First Interdisciplinary Conference in the Behavioral Science Division*, held at the University of New Mexico. New York: Symposium Publications Division, Pergamon Press, 1960.

YOUNG, J. Z., *Doubt and Certainty in Science*. Oxford: Clarendon Press, 1950.

SECTION

D

THE HUMAN INFORMATION
OUTPUT CHANNELS

Having considered how the human operator receives information through his sensory channels and transduces this information into a desired response, it is important to study how he can communicate the result of this decision to the system under his cognizance. It is worthwhile to consider the case where an overt response is provided. In addition, a great deal of information can be extracted from the human operator while he remains passive, this through the use of physiological monitoring instruments. Each of these human output channels is examined in some detail.

BIBLIOGRAPHY

ELY, J. H., R. M. THOMSON, and J. ORLANSKY, "Design of Controls," Chapter VI of the *Joint Services Human Engineering Guide to Equipment Design*, USAF WADC TR 56–172 (November 1956).

HICK, W. E., and J. A. V. BATES, *The Human Operator & Control Mechanisms*, Monograph No. 17.204, Ministry of Supply, Shell Mex House, London, May 1950.

TUFTS COLLEGE, HANDBOOK STAFF, "Handbook of Human Engineering Data, 2nd ed.," *Institute for Applied Experimental Psychology*, NavExos P–643, Human Engineering Report, SDC 199–1–2a (November 1952).

TUSTIN, A., ed., *Automatic and Manual Control*. London: Butterworth Publications Ltd., 1952.

12

INTENDED HUMAN OUTPUT
INFORMATION

12.1. INTRODUCTION

Having sensed information relative to the behavior of the equipment system over which he is cognizant, the human operator reaches a decision. In order for his decision to be useful, he must communicate the results of this decision to the equipment system through some controls. Controls can take on a wide range of forms including the traditional control stick, various forms of keyboards, knobs and switches, dials, microphones, signal flags, and so on. The particular means chosen for communicating with the equipment depends largely upon the particular circumstance. The design decision should be based upon trade-offs which include consideration of the time alloted to communication, the required accuracy and cost of errors, the availability of certain human motor response capacity, the already available equipments in the system which may be devoted to the purpose of monitoring human commands and other factors. Various experiments on the information transduction rate of the human operator have indicated that it is the coupling between man and the control equipment which often forms the bottleneck. The advent of new electronic equipments which automatically recognize patterns may offer new possibilities for coupling man and machine wherein the machine does the major part of the translation which today rests upon the human. Presumably facility in human communication to the machine would improve the human performance in decision-making and over-all system control.

Great amounts are invested in the design of equipment systems which, in various ways, depend upon man for their control guidance and constraint. It is important that significant attention be focused upon the provided controls which enable the human operator to transfer his desires into machine language and effect suitable equipment behavior. Regardless of whether the equipment system is small and of limited utility or is of wide range and encompasses important objectives, the control problem remains the same: *Intended human output information must be accepted by equipment which mates the human characteristics.*

This chapter presents separate consideration for various types of controls. General principles of design are offered; however, no attempt is made at a complete summary of design data. Such information is more suitably found in appropriate handbooks and the experimental literature.

12.2. THE NEUROMUSCULAR CHANNEL

Every part of the cortex of the brain receives incoming neural messages and gives rise to outgoing messages. The afferent messages come from the sensory channels, and at the same time efferent messages are sent to achieve motor control actions of the various musculature throughout the body. These efferent messages take two different pathways from the cortex to the brain stem and the spinal cord. An uninterrupted pyramidal projection passes directly to the spinal cord while an extrapyramidal motor projection passes from the cerebral cortex to various suprasegmental levels of mediation which include the striatum, thalamus, hypothalamus, and the reticular formation.

Each pathway carries a different type of control information. Interruption of the pyramidal projection will cause the loss of fine volitional movements. The extremities of the body will offer little or no resistance to passive movement. Severing the extrapyramidal pathway may cause varying degrees of paralysis of volitionary movement but does relate to augmented resistance to passive movements.

The motor area of the brain has been mapped in conscious human subjects as shown in Figure 12.1, although such exploration is as yet premature. J. M. R. Delgado, using experimental stimulating electrodes, estimates that more than half of the excitable cortex is buried below the surface, and that precise motor representations exist in hidden areas. It is not expected that there will be a simple mapping, since it is known that stimulation of the same point in the hidden cortex produces different reactions when the experimental conditions are changed. It may be that there are a number of interrelated representations within the brain for the same motor action.

Of the extrapyramidal projections two particular pathways are of interest. The cortico-strio-reticular path is largely concerned with postural adjustments while the cortico-porto-cerebellar path is primarily associated with the control of phasic movements, those connected with speech. Removal of the cerebellum would not be expected to effect sensation or general intelligence. At the same time, decerebellation would seriously effect volitional movements. For example, as more and more of the cerebellum is removed the gait of an animal appears to increasingly imitate the effect of alcoholic intoxication. Exterpations limited to the posterior lobe cause specific error in the rate, range, force and direction of voluntary movement. This is called *terminal tremor*. The tremor increases as the subject brings food closer and closer to his mouth or performs any such convergent task. Complete removal of the cerebellum produces extreme initial incapacitation followed by a gradual restoration of progressive movements.

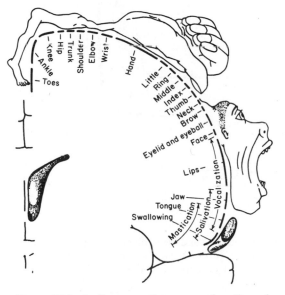

Figure 12.1. A diagrammatic cross-section through half of the cerebrum in the plane of central sulcus showing the motor areas of the cortex. The control of foot and leg movements is at the top of the brain, control of hand, face, and speech mechanism is lower on the side. The designated regions may be taken as a crude indicator of the extent of cortical area devoted to each control function. (After T. Rasmussen and W. Penfield, Fed. Proc. 1947, 6:452–460.)

An excellent summary of the work done on models of muscles has been prepared by J. Pringle. Various attempts have been made to represent the sequence of events which take place in the activation of a muscle. Individual items can be separately considered so long as they are not mutually interacting. Figure 12.2 indicates the type of control sequence. A nerve impulse (1) arrives at the junctional region and causes release of chemical energy (2a) with instantaneous concentration at the site of the muscle cell membrane shown in (2*b*). The many possible nerve fibers affecting the muscle are indicated by the parallel channel in Figure 12.2*b*. The electrical and ionic permeability properties of the muscle cell membrane are represented by (3). There is some coupling process (4) which controls the mechanical properties of the muscle (5) which then affects movement or the load bearing capability of the skeleton. Much remains to be done to provide clearer understanding and quantitative models for each of these blocks.

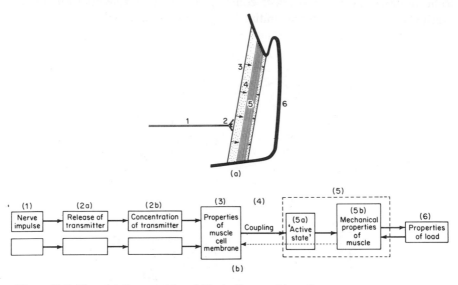

Figure 12.2. Pictorial diagram (a) and block diagram (b) to illustrate the control sequence between nerve and muscle. (From J. W. S. Pringle, "Models of Muscle," *Models and Analogues in Biology*, Society for Experimental Biology Symposium XIV, Academic Press, Inc., New York, 1960.)

Muscle tissue is made up of cells which have special capacity to contract upon proper stimulation. Muscle cells are generally long and are therefore termed *fibers*. Striated muscle tissue is characterized by parallel cross-stripes, which appear in a microscopic view. It is composed of spindle-shaped fibers which may be 1 to 40 millimeters in length and from 0.01 to 0.15 millimeters in diameter. Each fiber consists of a tubular sheath which contains a soft contratile substance. Muscle fibers are closely packed, forming *bundles*. A connective tissue forms a supporting framework, penetrating between the fibers and surrounding small bundles, grouping these into larger bundles, and forming a cover for the entire muscle trunk. It is this connective tissue which carries an intricate network of blood and lymph tubes and nerves so that every muscle fiber is supplied with nerve endings and is surrounded by tissue fluid.

Skelatal muscles are diverse in form and vary in length, extending in some cases to nearly 24 inches. In the trunk of the body they are broad, flattened and expanded, while in the limbs they form more or less elongated spindles or straps. Other types of muscular tissue is located in the visceral sections of the body. The cardiac muscle tissue forms the heart. Here the individual cells are smaller in size, with a nucleus near the center. These cells are roughly quadrangular in shape, connected so as to form a continuous sheet.

Normally muscles are kept in a partial state of contraction, called muscle tone. As a result, posture is maintained and the body remains ready to function in movement if called upon to do so. Muscle tone falls to a minimum during sleep or if the subject should lose consciousness.

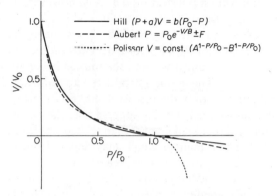

Figure 12.3. The three equations proposed for the force-velocity relationship of muscle. Aubert's equation has a discontinuity at $V=0$. Polissar's equation is similar to the other two for positive values of V and is drawn only for negative values where it diverges widely. (From J. W. S. Pringle, "Models of Muscle," *Models and Analogues in Biology*, Society for Experimental Biology Symposium XIV, Academic Press, Inc., New York, 1960.)

The velocity of muscle shortening, represented by V, and the isotonic load, P, on an excited muscle can be related through three different models. There is the "characteristic equation" of D. K. Hill, which is based on empiric data.

$$(P+a)V = b(P_0-P)$$

where P_0 is the original load (dependent on muscle length) and a and b are empirically determined constants. Another good fit to experimental data was suggested by W. O. Fenn and B. S. Marsh and as modified by X. Aubert,

$$P = P_0 e^{-V/B} \pm F$$

where B and F are constants. Another equation was suggested by M. Polissar,

$$V = c(A^{1-P/P_0} - B^{1-P/P_0})$$

where A, B, and c are constants. All three of these equations are shown in Figure 12.3.

The last two equations were derived from conceptual models. Fenn and Marsh assumed that the drop below the isotonic value in the muscle tension during shortening is due to the limiting velocity of chemical reactions supplying energy and on the need for additional energy during shortening. Polissar based his equation on a generalized physicochemical model in which the contractile elements were assumed to exist in one of two possible states. The elements were either long or short and changed from one state to the other reversibly with velocities of reaction influenced by tension.

Of the three equations, Hill's has found the widest acceptance even though it has no connection with a physical model. It is, however, important to note the limitations in the use of Hill's equation. The isometric tension of an excited muscle varies with the length of the fibers, being maximal near the natural length. The value of P_0, therefore, depends on the muscle length, and the value V must be determined without the muscle being allowed to shorten any significant amount. This alone introduces experimental difficulties.

Although Hill did not study the force-velocity relationship when an active muscle lengthens under load, he did suggest that the same equation might apply. When subjected to a load greater than the isometric tension, an excited muscle elongates but in a manner which may depart from that predicted by Hill's equation. If the load is much greater than P_0, the muscle suffers irreversibly and is not immediately able to develop the same isometric tension. Even at loads slightly greater than P_0, the velocity is significantly less than that indicated by the characteristic equation. Other difficulties arise in connection with the accuracy of the predicted behavior of muscles under the usual wide range of situations.

Heat is liberated when a muscle is excited to contraction. This heat can be divided into three component parts: heat of contraction, heat of relaxation, and heat of recovery. The first of these is most directly concerned with control implementation. The heat of contraction in turn can be viewed as consisting of two components; a heat of activation which accompanies the change from passive to active state and includes the heat of maintenance during isometric contraction, and a heat of shortening which is proportional to the distance shortened but is independent of the load on muscle. Quantitatively, this heat of shortening (per centimeter) is identical with the constant a in the characteristic equation. Hill states that the term $(P+a)V$ identifies the total extra energy liberated when the muscle shortens with velocity V. Since PV is the rate of doing mechanical work, V must be the rate of extra heat production. Much remains to be done before the force velocity relationship of muscles can be well represented by a universal, yet hopefully simple, model.

In 1922, Hill formulated the first clear model of the mechanical properties of muscle in terms of the elasticity and viscosity. According to Hill:

(1) Active muscle contains an undamped elastic element.

(2) Active muscle contains an apparently damped element in series with the undamped one.

Resting muscle contains the elastic element (1) but only to a minor degree the apparently damped element (2).

If the muscle is to be examined over a wide range of lengths, there should also be included a second elastic element in parallel with (1) and (2). Unfortunately the series elastic component, the parallel elastic component, and the contractile component do not appear to be clearly separable when attempts are made to relate them to muscle tissue. In addition, there are properties of active muscles such as the release of energy and the discontinuity of the force velocity relationship of vertebrate muscle which cannot be described by a visco-elastic model.

The activation of musculature allows movements which can be coupled to a control system either through direct mechanical, electrical, or audio devices. These must be designed in a suitable manner so as to minimize the degradation of information transferred while providing for maximum comfort of the human operator.

12.3. MOVABLE CONTROLS

Movable controls can be used to transmit the result of the operator's decision to the equipment system under his cognizance. These controls may assume a wide variety of forms, but they should always be designed with compatibility as the fundamental guiding principle. The designer should attempt to achieve an optimal compromise with respect to a number of often conflicting requirements. There must be physical compatibility. The lever should be easy to grasp and manipulate. If the control requires the operator to exert considerable force, it may contribute to his inaccuracy of performance. Undue exertion results in excessive fatigue and increased error on subsequent operation of the control. In contrast, if the control offers too little resistance, it tends to encourage "over-control" especially in the case where the human operator is under emotional stress.

But physical compatibility is not enough. In almost every case the control is also a display. That is, it furnishes feedback information to the operator regarding his last control action and the signal currently being imposed upon the system. The response of the control to his actuation furnishes evidence that the system has accepted his signal. The operational status of the control as a communication link has been validated. Considered as a display, the controls should clearly define their position and dynamic "feel" in a manner to aid further decision-making.

Since they are also a display, the controls should be compatible with the other displays as well as the nature of the parameters they describe. For example, wherever possible there should be agreement in the direction of motion. The control which affects, say, altitude should move vertically as should the corresponding display, as an analogy in reflection of the fact that altitude is a vertical dimension of the environment. The size, shape, and color of the controls should reflect the nature of the controlled variable. Figure 12.4 indicates certain recommended shapes for use in aircraft cockpits. Adequate illumination should be provided when visual feedback from the control is expected.

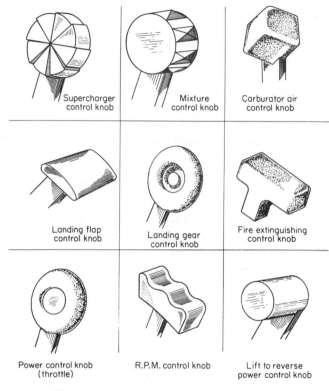

Figure 12.4. Standardized aircraft control shapes.

To illustrate the importance of compatibility between display and control consider the everyday experience of adjusting the water prior to taking a shower. In the usual facility two knobs are provided, these being marked "hot" and "cold." An initial setting produces a spray of some temperature and texture. Since temperature is the primary variable displayed the operator must have patience until the water nearly reaches a constant temperature. The secondary displayed variable is the spray texture. If the temperature is incorrect, an adjustment is made which not only changes the temperature in an appropriate manner but also modifies the spray texture as a result of a change of pressure at the nozzle. An iterative approach is required, with waiting periods between each adjustment until the operator satisfies himself that a better approximation to the desired temperature and texture is not worth the effort. This unfortunate situation results from the set of displayed variables being in other than one-to-one correspondence with the set of controlled variables. Temperature and texture are not in agreement with the control handles marked hot and cold. In contrast, some more modern faciltiies provide a pointer-handle shower control over a scale which goes from the off position through the temperature range. In addition, a secondary control knob adjusts the spray at the nozzle. A single setting of each control provides the desired temperature and texture.

Unfortunately, it is often impossible to attain such ideal one-to-one correspondence of displays and controls in complex vehicles because of the fundamental cross-coupling of parameters. In an aircraft, for example, a turn to the right requires that the aircraft first be placed in a bank which in turn results in a changed heading together with a small change of lift. Suitable rudder control is required to "coordinate" the turn, preventing side slip. It may indeed be possible for space vehicles to have simpler controls than aircraft as a result of a greater degree of independence of position and attitude variables. Design of the controls must take into consideration coupling of position and attitude when the propelling force does not pass through the center of gravity.

The layout of controls should reflect the nature of the task assignment and provide natural priority for the most frequently operated controls and/or for those controls which are of greatest importance to the accomplishment of the assigned mission. Controls should be placed close to the displays which reflect their effect, below or to the left for left handed control operation and below or to the right for right handed operation. Related controls should be grouped so as to emphasize the relation of the associated parameters in the nature of the equipment system. Yet, they must be separated sufficiently to prevent inadvertent actuation as a result of either confusion or blundering. It is helpful if the controls can be placed in order from left to right with respect to the expected sequence of operation. In certain situations, it may be possible to key the controls into a time sequence of operation providing automatic lock so that they become unavailable until the required previous actions have been taken. Control locks should be provided so that their position can be maintained when there is no possibility of requiring immediate control action to avoid a dangerous condition. Such locks are of particular value during periods when full attention should be devoted to some other control function. They preclude inadvertent actuation.

Special consideration should be given to the placement of those controls which are to be used in the event of emergency conditions. These should be within easy access but recessed wherever possible so as to reduce the possibility of accidental activation. If this protection is not possible, they should be equipped with a use guard which requires separate actuation.

As a prerequisite, movable controls should be located within easy access, say within a 24-inch spherical radius of the shoulder pivoting points. An additional 6 inches of radius is available if trunk movement is possible. Most frequently used controls should be located with a 14-inch radius about the elbow pivot points, generally above and inside of a tableline. Here an additional 2 inches can be allowed for elbow movement. Wherever possible manual controls should be positioned between shoulder and waist height within the direct visual field. They should be accessible to both hands, or both feet, in order to provide greater flexibility of operation in the event of unexpected limited disability. Symmetry of motion of the controls is likely to reduce error especially when a number of such controls are to be actuated simultaneously with both hands. The use of standardized controls facilitates operation by personnel having had previous experience on other similar equipments or training apparatus. These controls should reflect the handedness of the using population and agree with other stereotypes of behavior.

The choice of control should take into account the degree of complexity of body movement which must be performed in order to execute the range of possible control actions which are required as seen in the light of their individual probabilities. For example, it may be well to use finger controls if these can fully replace a lever or a crank which requires finger, wrist, forearm and even upper arm motion. Proper selection of controls requires specific definition of their individual purpose and importance in terms of task requirements such as precision, speed of response, required range, available location, space, and so on.

Push buttons are simple controls. Generally, they return to their original position after having been actuated and do not provide definite feedback information by sight or touch. In contrast, toggle switches offer positive clues which identify the nature of the last control action. Of course, when toggle switches can be placed in a number of discrete positions the possibility of confusion once again arises.

A great variety of knob shapes have been studied with respect to discriminability. These have been divided into three classes as shown in Figure 12.5. These may be classified as follows:[1]

> Class A—Multiple Rotation. For controls (1) which require twirling or spinning, (2) for which the adjustment range is one full turn or more, (3) for which the knob position is not a critical item of information in the control operation.
>
> Class B—Frictional Rotation. For controls (1) which do not require spinning or twirling, (2) for which the adjustment range is less than one full turn or, if the adjustment range exceeds one full turn, operating requirements rarely, if ever, call for rapid

[1] J. H. Ely, R. M. Thompson, and J. Orlansky, "Design of Controls," *Joint Services Human Engineering Guide to Equipment Design*, WADC Technical Report 56–172 (November 1956), Chapter VI.

adjustment over a large proportion of the range, and (3) for
which the knob position is not a critical item of information
in the control operation.

Class C—Detent Positioning. For controls (1) which do not require
spinning or twirling, (2) for which the adjustment range is
not more than one full turn, and (3) for which knob position
is a critical item of information in the control operation.

Descrete operating controls should provide definite detent "feel" and,
where possible, specific visual indication of their location as well as an audible

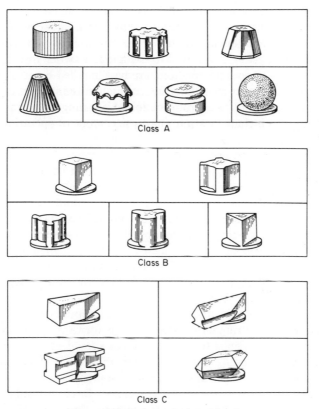

Figure 12.5. Suggested control knobs.

click to indicate the completion of the control action. Circular knobs generally provide little feedback information and require precise positioning
especially when the number of detents is increased. A pointer or bar knob
aids feedback. A serrated or knurled knob provides better finger grip.

Various configurations of cranks can be used wherever a large number of
rotations is expected to be required. Preferably these are mounted on either
side of the operator's center. Empirical studies indicate that the crank should

be about $4\frac{1}{2}$ inches in diameter with a handle of about $\frac{1}{2}$ inch diameter, $1\frac{1}{2}$ inches long, in order to allow ease of wrist and finger movement. If greater force is required, it is well to increase the diameter of both the crank and the handle.

In cases where only small angular motions are expected, handwheels should prove superior. For single hand use the diameter should be between 3 and 5 inches. Larger handwheels are more suitable for two-handed operation, say at least 7 inches in diameter. Provision of a minimum number of spokes furnishes additional feedback as to the setting and facilitates handling.

In general, multi-rotation controls should be used when high precision is required over a wide range of adjustments. Detent controls are most suitable where the adjustment can be satisfied by a limited number of discrete positions. Push buttons or toggle switches serve well for two discrete positions. For three discrete positions, it is well to use a toggle switch or rotary selector switch. From 4 to 24 discrete positions are best handled by a rotary selector switch. A knob or lever is most suitable for small range settings of a continuous variable while a crank is appropriate for a large range continuous variable Control coding can include location, shape, size, mode of operation, labelling, and color.

Various types of hand grips are available. Cylindrical grips should be at least $\frac{7}{8}$ inch in diameter in order to prevent discomfort under heavy load. They should, however, remain less than $1\frac{1}{4}$ inches in diameter in order to ensure security of grip. Ball grips used on levers should be about $1\frac{1}{2}$ inches in diameter. More complex grips can be molded to the hand, furnishing separators between the fingers to assure proper positioning. Several functionally related controls can be combined into a single grip in order to reduce reaching movements and aid in sequential or simultaneous operation and provide an economy of space. There is, however, the ever-present hazard of accidental actuation.

Controls requiring rapid and precise settings should be assigned to the hands while those requiring large or continuous forward application of force should generally be assigned to the feet. Pedals should be designed to utilize the foot and leg as an entire unit. If possible, they should be located so that the angle between the upper and lower leg should be about $107°$ for pedal force under 50 pounds and about $130°$ for greater force. Angle flexion pedals are suitable where only light action is required. Some initial resistance is necessary to prevent inadvertent actuation by the weight of the foot. If the pedal is used in a moving vehicle, this resistance should be great enough to guard against inadvertent actuation resulting from imposed g forces.

The physical range of movement of control sticks and pedals can best be determined through reference to dynamic anthropometric data. Limited range control movement may be used to actuate a variable over a much wider range of amplitude through a nonlinear coupling. Increase of control resistance, as it approaches its end of travel, serves to prevent overshooting and sometimes damage to the equipment. Further, such increased resistance furnishes the operator with an indication that the extreme is being approached. The range of forces recommended for actuation of controls is indicated in Table 12.1. Force setting is equally accurate by either hands or feet.

Table 12.1.

Manual Controls	Pounds of Force
Toggle switches	$\frac{1}{2}$ to 1
Push buttons	1 to 3
Rotating knobs 1 to 2 inch diameter	0 to 2
Smooth-running high-speed small cranks	2 to 5
Handwheels 10 inch diameter and cranks 5 inch radius	0 to 8
Handwheels 18 inch diameter and cranks 9 inch radius	0 to 12
Gear shift type levers	Up to 30
Joy stick sideways	90, max.
Joy stick forward and aft (steady pull)	65, max.
Joy stick forward and aft (momentary)	250, max.
Pedal Controls	
Resistance to overcome resting foot	4 to 7
Hinged pedals (foot throttle, etc.)	10 to 15
Power brakes	Up to 15
Clutches and mechanical brakes	Up to 30
Clutches and brakes	60, max.
Rudder controls	160 to 400
Maximum allowable	500
Maximum force recorded	900

From Henry Dreyfus, *The Measure of Man*, New York: Whitney Library of Design, 1960.

The type and amount of resistance offered by the control affects the operator's force requirements. Resistance can result from static or sliding friction, spring loading, viscous damping, inertia, or combinations of these in proper balance. For example, it might prove desirable to utilize friction or viscous damping in order to counteract some adverse effects of excessive inertia. The physical properties of the control directly affect the precision of control operation, the speed of control action, the "feel" of the control, the smoothness of operation, and the susceptibility of the control to accidental actuation.

Spring loading, the use of elastic control resistance, varies directly with control displacement but is independent of velocity and acceleration. The force thus provided serves to identify the null position and makes for greater precision in small adjustments of the control. In addition, there is the safety feature in that this force returns the control to the null position if the operator loses contact with it. It permits rapid change of direction, allows the operator's limbs to rest upon the control without actuating it (providing there is sufficient pre-loading), reduces the likelihood of undesired actuation, and enhances the sensing of control position by providing a direct feedback "feel."

Static friction decreases rapidly to a constant value when the control starts to move smoothly and continuously. This resistance is independent of displacement and acceleration, tending to hold the control in position. Again such resistance reduces the likelihood of undesired actuation, but at the same time, it increases the difficulty of making precise settings. Sliding friction provides no feedback information in the form of "feel" about control position, but static friction serves to allow the control position to be felt without disturbing it.

Viscous damping resistance varies directly with the control velocity but is independent of displacement and acceleration. It tends to resist sudden movements and reduces the likelihood of inadvertent actuation. Such damping facilitates smooth movements, rapid changes in direction, and small changes in position. It provides the operator with feedback "feel" about the velocity of control movement, although it remains questionable whether he can use this information in any precise sense.

Inertial control resistance varies directly with control acceleration but is independent of displacement and velocity. This property serves to resist sudden changes in velocity thus aiding smooth movements and gradual changes in velocity. It reduces the effects of small vibration and tremor. However, it does require that a larger force be applied in order to stop control movement quickly. Inertial resistance provides feedback "feel" about the acceleration of the control movements, and, as with viscous damping, it is questionable whether the operator finds this information useful. It increases the difficulty of making precise settings quickly, due to the danger of overshooting. High inertia can be used to aid maintaining control movements without requiring the continual application of significant force to the controls. In general, it has been found that control forces in excess of 30 to 40 pounds for the hand and greater than 60 pounds for the feet are fatiguing.

Control dead space can prove useful for the elimination of high frequency tremor. It does, however, provide a small increment in the average times of response, and there has been found to be a systematic decrease in tracking system performance with increase in control dead space. The higher the control gain, the greater the rate of decrease in system performance with increasing control dead space. In general, performance with low and medium control gains is superior to performance with high gain.

The control-display ratio is defined as the linear distance of control displacement to the distance of the resulting display movement under a noiseless situation. The optimum control-display ratio is that which minimizes the total time required to make desired control movements within the specified error range. A number of different factors effect this ratio including the display size, the tolerance requirements, the physical configuration of the control, and the nature of the system under cognizance. Empirical measurements are required to optimize the display-control ratio for a particular design thus taking into account the viewing distance as well as the nature of the time lag characteristics of the controlled equipment system.

It has been experimentally demonstrated that tracking performance in one coordinate is influenced by the dynamics of a second coordinate. Apparently the act of shifting from one transfer function to another consumes some of the human channel capacity. As more and more of this capacity is dissipated with increasing dissimilarity between tasks, less and less remains to be devoted to tracking with the result that performance accuracy drops in both coordinates.

Serious consideration has been devoted to the use of a force-sensing fixed-stick control. Strain gage sensors are placed at the base of the stick and "read" the imposed force transmitting this signal to the equipment system. The stick has negligible displacement. It offers more rapid communication to the equipment system than displacement controls. However, this speed is at a cost in terms of precision of forward, as well as feedback, information. Difficulties may arise in attempts to maintain constant applied force over long periods of time. This is especially true in contrast to the ease with which a movable control stick may be maintained in the same position for extensive periods of time. The force-sensing fixed stick cannot provide as vivid feedback "feel" as the comparative displacement stick. However, it does allow the operator's arm to remain in a fixed position. This latter feature is of special value under high imposed g force conditions. In a similar manner, it is possible to devise a control which is primarily sensitive to the velocity of control stick movement. Each of these, displacement, velocity, and force sensitive controls, have advantages and disadvantages which should be carefully evaluated before any design is finalized.

Equipment systems often require the human operator to control a large number of parameters which are similar in nature. The controls must be arranged in some suitable manner which allows for the efficient use of space and yet provides unique identity or individuality to each of the variables under control and the natural ordering among these parameters. This problem has had an extensive history. For example, the earliest existing representation of a keyed string musical instrument was a primitive clavichord used before 1460 A.D. By 1472, chromatic keyboards were already in use with keys arranged much as in the modern piano keyboard with but a single black key separately identifying each octave. The modern keyboard emerged prior to the time of Bach (who developed the equal temperament tuning which added great flexibility to the use of keyed string instruments). The musical keying problem was also encountered in the design of manual controls for various woodwind instruments. These developed through a natural evolution with gradual improvements extending the range and flexibility of individual finger controls thereby reducing the complexity of manipulation required to produce improved sounding music. Here, feedback is primarily tactual with relative position providing sufficient identity of the notes and their state of actuation. It is not at all unusual to find that an accomplished instrumentalist is uncertain as to the fingering he uses for a particular note until his hands are placed on his instrument.

The problem of arranging a number of similar controls has had an infamous history in the case of a fairly recent car design. A number of push-pull controls of similar shape were placed in a horizontal row on the dashboard. These included the cigarette lighter and the headlights in adjacent position. The danger of inadvertent extinguishing of the lights in place of actuating the desired cigarette lighter was an obvious hazard to the life of the occupants.

Control knobs of different dimensions can be "ganged" by mounting them on concentric shafts. Such placement facilitates particular sequences of control operation and serves to concentrate the controls in a small space. There is, of course, the danger of confusion when more than two knobs are ganged in this manner.

Another means for exhibiting control response to a sensing system is through the use of written materials. Pen and pencil are manual tools which can be manipulated to inscribe the result of decision upon suitable material. The efficiency of the communication may be improved through the use of speed writing and/or short hand techniques which can attain speeds of up to 140 words per minute. Keyboard instruments such as the stenotype machine use phonetic coding and can further increase the channel capacity of the man-machine interface to about 225 words per minute.

The typewriter keyboard furnishes a set of control levers through which the human operator can transmit linguistic signals to the system under control. The typist receives feedback information from the relative position of the fingers in striking the keys and, if desired, visual feedback by direct observation of the impression which is made by the type face. To be most efficient the keys should be selected and arranged in a manner appropriate to the language to be typed, thereby reducing the required expenditure of effort and the error connected with the encoding operation. Keyboards should be as simple and natural as possible.

The keyboard of the modern typewriter was first arranged by Sholes in 1873. Key arrangement of the letters, numerals, and punctuation marks was determined almost entirely by the mechanical problems at hand. Difficulty in the articulation of keys placed an upper limit on the speed with which this instrument could be used. This constraint obviated the value of extensive training. The "hunt and peck" system of typing was then most appropriate. In time, these mechanical problems were resolved which introduced the need for increased training. Even with extensive training, the average typist is still able to achieve somewhat less than one-third of the typing speed possible within the mechanical limits of the standard equipment. Modern electric typewriters, with their increased speed, make it clearly evident that the human operator is the limiting factor.

A number of investigators have attempted to redesign the keyboard to furnish greater compatibility with both the English language and the human hand. The standard keyboard is deficient in that it requires the left hand to do more work than the right, even though this is more likely to be the weaker member. It also places a greater load on the little finger than on the index and second finger as a result of the difference in probability of letters of the English language. This is especially true in view of the fact that the little fingers control the shift keys. There may be considerable room for improvement in the keyboard layout in that a relatively small number of digrams account for 90 per cent of ordinary English written communication.

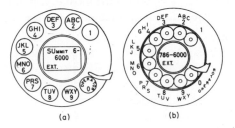

(a)   (b)

Figure 12.6. Original and improved telephone dial. The improved design (b) has letters and numerals outside the holes, so that they will not be covered up when dialing. The dialing circle of design (b) is about the same size as that of design (a).

A detailed analysis of the statistical structure of English was used by A. Dvorák (1932) in rearranging the keyboard so as to minimize the amount of movement and thus maximize speed and efficiency. Considerable reduction of training time was achieved and yet this improved keyboard has not received general acceptance. The large number of standard keyboards in existence and the associated problem of retraining skilled personnel pose strong arguments against any change in the keyboard arrangement. In 1948, Dvorák designed special keyboards for the use of one-hand amputees. Here too the keyboard was arranged so that the most common letters and digrams could be reached by the strongest fingers, with the work distributed in proportion to the finger strength. The right hand keyboard was a mirror image of the left hand one. Amputees were able to reach about 50 nonsense words after only ten weeks of training. This is a speed higher than that achieved by the average typist on the conventional typewriter.

The dial used on standard telephones furnishes another type of keyboard. For the communication of a sequence of symbols to an equipment system, letters should be placed in a manner to minimize error. Originally, the letters were placed under the holes in the dial used on telephones. It was recognized that these letters were obscured by the fingers and the hand as the dial was being used. It was thought that displacement of the letters to the periphery of the dial would increase the efficiency of dialing. Dialing errors increased with this new configuration. An investigation revealed that the removal of the letters and numbers from within the holes had removed a natural target upon which to aim the dialing finger. Putting a dot in each hole, as shown in Figure 12.6, replaced the target. With this improved design, dialing errors were reduced.

12.4. VERBAL CONTROL

Control may be exercised by means of auditory communication. Sounds may be produced in a number of ways, one of the most useful of these being speech. The speech organs encode information intended for the listener. Figure 12.7

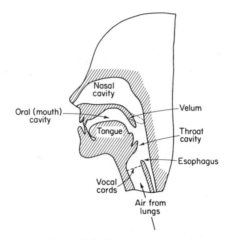

Figure 12.7. The speech organs.

indicates these speech organs: the tongue, the oral cavity, the nasal cavity, the throat cavity, the esophagus, the vocal chords, and the lungs. The air stream, generated by increased pressure in the lungs, passes through the opening between the vocal chords. If the vocal chords are allowed to sustain continuous vibration, the stream of air is amplitude modulated at a periodic rate. The frequency of normal voiced sounds is between 100 and 250 cycles per second.

The shape of the vocal tract can be modified, constricted or blocked by various tongue and lip positions. Further, the entrance to the nasal cavity is controlled by a valve at the rear of the mouth. This variability of configuration enables articulation to take place. Even though these articulators are in constant movement during speech, the listener perceives a succession of descrete sounds. As a result, it becomes possible to transcribe speech phonetically with a notation consisting of about 40 symbols. Although the phonetic sounds may appear the same to the listener, the actual sounds produced are significantly influenced by the particular sequence in which they occur.

Traditionally, the articulatory processes are classified into two groups; those associated with vowels and those associated with consonants. Table 12.2 indicates the elementary sounds which occur in English as identified by the usual phonetic symbols. When a symbol represents a speech sound occurring in a particular context, it is enclosed within square brackets. If, however, the phoneme is represented, diagonals are used. For example, "cool" is phonetically written /kul/. The speech sounds given in conventional spelling are usually in italics.

Table 12.2. TABLE OF ELEMENTARY SOUNDS WHICH OCCUR IN ENGLISH†

Phonetic Symbol	Key Word	Phonetic Symbol	Key Word
vowels		*fricatives*	
i	*eve*	h	*he*
ɪ	*it*	f	*for*
e	*hate*	θ	*thin*
ɛ	*met*	s	*see*
æ	*at*	ʃ	*she*
a	*ask*	ɦ	*ahead*
ɑ	*father*	v	*vote*
ɒ	*not*	ð	*then*
ɔ	*all*	z	*zoo*
o	*obey*	ʒ	*azure*
ʊ	*foot*		
u	*boot*		
ɝ *	*word bird*	*plosives*	
ɜ	*word bird*		
ʌ	*up*	p	*pay*
ə	*about*	t	*to*
		k	*key*
vowel-like		b	*be*
		d	*day*
j	*you*	g	*go*
w	*we*		
l	*let*		
r	*read*	*affricatives*	
m	*me*		
n	*no*	tʃ	*chip*
ŋ	*sing*	dʒ	*juice*

* General American.
† After R. K. Potter, G. A. Kopp, and H. C. Green, *Visible Speech*, New York: D. Van Nostrand Company, Inc., 1957.

Normally the vocal chords are in continuous vibration during the voicing of vowels. The vocal tract is relatively open, and different vowels are characterized by different tongue shape and positions and by the degree of rounding of the lips. The same configurations which would produce the sustained vowel are rarely attained when this vowel appears within connected speech.

Vowels have considerably higher acoustic power than do consonants. As the sound is emitted from the vocal chords, energy is coupled to the vocal cavities causing a change in the sound which is emitted from the speaker. The spectrum of a vowel sound is generally dominant at the fundamental frequency but reflects resonant peaks of energy at the resonant frequency of the excited adjoining vocal cavities. The regions of energy concentration for the particular vowel are called "formants." For example, the sustained vowel [u] has three formants with center frequencies at about 450, 1,050, and 2,250 cycles per second, respectively. Even if the vowel is whispered, these formants will still be present although the resulting energy will be diffused throughout the entire spectrum. Only the relative formant amplitudes will be modified. Certain vowel pairs called diphthongs occur in speech. In such a case, the formant frequency changes smoothly between one vowel and the other of the pair. Obviously diphthongs cannot be sustained. The formant frequency positions of a sustained vowel vary for different speakers and depend upon the speaker's sex. The formant frequencies also change when the speech includes the vowel as a transition between consonants as in the case of normal speech.

Consonants may be classified as vowel-like sounds, fricatives, and plosives. The vocal chords are normally in vibration only for the vowel-like sound. These can be subdivided into glides and semi-vowels. The glides are formed by rapid articulatory changes at the beginning of the vowel with the resonances shifting rapidly over the frequency range dependent upon the speed with which the glide is articulated. To illustrate, four glides are [w] as in we, [j] as in you, [l] as in let, [r] as in read. In contrast to glides, the semi-vowels can be sustained. These are the nasalized sounds which have frequency resonances analogous to vowel formants but, in addition, have a strong resonance in the neighborhood of the fundamental voicing frequency. For example, semi-vowels include [m] as in me, and [n] as in no. In the case of fricatives, the air flow is predominantly turbulent. A sustained stream of air can be passed through the narrow openings in the vocal tract or over the edges of the teeth resulting in sounds like [s] as in see. These can even include voiced sounds such as [z] as in zoo. In general, fricatives are of low acoustic power and wide band frequency spectrum. The plosives are short time duration sounds resulting from air suddenly being released through the vocal channel. [p] and [t] as in pat are unvoiced plosives while the [b] in bit is a voiced plosive.

In general, the probability of interpreting consonants properly is lower than that for vowels. Consonants, therefore, contain more of the speech information, these being concentrated within the higher frequency spectrum of the speech band, while vowels correspond to power which is primarily distributed toward the lower end of the speech spectrum. On the average, the strongest vowel is about 680 times the power of the weakest consonant. Vowels contain much more energy than do consonants. In fact, the frequencies of speech under 1,000 cycles contain about 80 per cent of the power while these frequencies contribute only about 10 per cent of the articulation of speech. This knowledge can be brought to bear through the development of a device which is the auditory equivalent of speedwriting. This electronic device removes the vowel sounds by accomplishing a frequency discrimination permitting transmission only of consonant sounds. The result is a speech signal of much lower transmitted power and is, therefore, of reduced range, which may contribute to secrecy if this is desired. The receiver of this "auditory speedwriting" can decipher the consonants directly or can add a continual pure tone to assist in "visualizing" the proper connective vowels. More detailed discussion of this concept is contained in Patent No. 2,866,848.

It is interesting to examine the information efficiency of speech. The information rate can be estimated from

$$R = BT \log_2 \left(\frac{S}{N} + 1 \right)$$

Using a 5,000 cycles per second bandwidth and a time of one second, and the signal to noise ratio of 30 db, the system is capable of transmitting about 50,000 bits per second. Normal speech communication carries less than 50 bits per second which is less than 0.1 per cent of the possible efficiency of this controlled channel.

The duration of speech sounds ranges from about 150 milliseconds in slow deliberate speech to about 50 milliseconds in rapid conversation. The sound wave in speech is more or less continuous between pauses for breathing. Words are not usually separated by gaps. According to one analysis of written material, a group of 732 words comprise about 75 per cent of those which occur in normal speech. On the average 4 words are spoken per second. Telephone quality speech requires about 3,000 cycles per second bandwidth and a signal to noise ratio of about 30 db, that is, an information rate of about 30,000 bits per second.

The subjective encoding of sound transmits the message in terms of a reference list of symbols having previously agreed upon designation and meaning. Each of the physical characteristics of speech have corresponding subjective sensations. Intensity corresponds to loudness, frequency to pitch, harmonic composition to quality, and time to subjective duration. There is considerable variability of speech intensity between individuals and, in fact, for the same person at different times, remaining largely within the range of from 46 to 86 db. Generally, about 3 db of intensity would be added to the speech signal if the short silent intervals which do occur were eliminated.

The frequency of speech can also have a wide range of difference over individuals and within the same person at different times. In general, women have a fundamental frequency about twice as high as that of men. Each of the

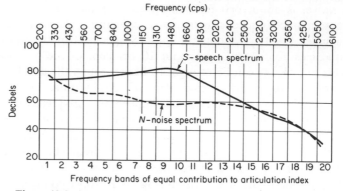

Figure 12.8. Average speech spectrum for men, with superimposed noise spectrum, to illustrate derivation of articulation index.

phonetic sounds has a complex spectrum of harmonics which provides a specific quality to the sound.

It is possible to divide the frequency range from 200 to 6,100 cycles per second into 20 bands that contribute equally to the "articulation index," this

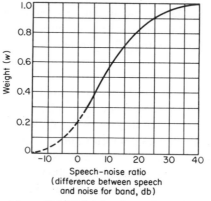

Figure 12.9. Weighting factor for various speech-to-noise ratios for use in deriving articulation index. For each frequency band, the decibel difference between the speech and over-all noise level in that band is multiplied by the weight (w).

being a measure of the intelligibility of speech, short cutting the involved nonsense syllable auditory testing. This frequency deviation allows the representation of the average speech spectrum of loudness in terms of the component frequencies as shown in Figure 12.8. The articulation index can be measured by the following procedure. Determine the difference in db between the speech and noise level and each of the twenty frequency bands using a midpoint of the band, this being taken as the measure of the speech to noise ratio for that band. Derive a weight for each band from Figure 12.9. Multiply the weight for each band by 0.05 and sum these products for all twenty bands to yield the articulation index. Note that this method is most suitable under conditions of steady state noise and where the noise has a rather high spectrum.

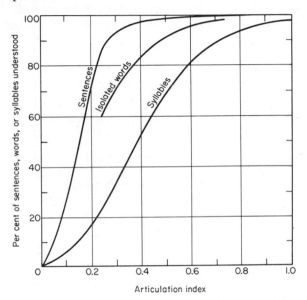

Figure 12.10. Approximate relationship between articulation index and per cent of intelligibility for sentences, isolated words, and syllables.

The articulation index can be converted into the more meaningful value, the intelligibility score, which is an estimate of the percentage of spoken material understood by the listener. Obviously, this intelligibility score is dependent upon the type of material as well as the context in which it is spoken. Figure 12.10 indicates this relationship. The speech interference level is descriptive of how much noise interferes with speech intelligibility under certain conditions. This metric is found by taking the average of the band-levels for the following three octave bands: 600 to 1,200, 1,200 to 2,400, and 2,400 to 4,800 cycles per second. Figure 12.11 indicates the speech interference level as a function of distance for various levels of voice. The db level read from these curves indicates that noise level which would interfere with the reliability of communication of average speech. That is to say, if the communication distance is 12 feet and the average noise level is, say, 60 db, then it would be required to shout in order to have effective verbal communication. The speech interference level metric is most accurate when the noise spectrum is reasonably flat over the 3 octave bands.

Under conditions which are quite different from this ideal, the speech interference level may not prove meaningful. For example, the noise may be intermittent or of particular repetitive waveshape. The intensity may be widely different in the various frequency bands. Further, the speaker may vary the characteristics of his voice in such a way as to enable better or worse communication efficiency. In the judgment of a wide number of people, the use of the currently available telephone system, for example, is adequate under noise levels of less than 60 db, difficult for 60 to 65 db, and impossible

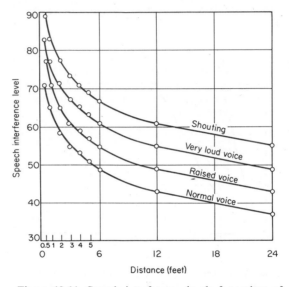

Figure 12.11. Speech interference levels for voices of different levels at various distances. The speech interference level should be less than given in order to have reliable conversation at the distances and voice levels shown.

in noise above 75 db, this being estimated under the presumption of long distance or suburban calling. For local calls about 5 db can be added to each of the above levels.

Intelligibility of normal speech does not depend entirely upon the intelligibility of each and every sound. That is to say, it is possible to reduce and even eliminate some speech sounds and, at the same time, effect the noise in a desirable manner so as to increase the over-all intelligibility of the speech signal. Figure 12.12 shows the syllable intelligibility level for high pass and low pass filtering of speech when operated in quiet under optimal gain. Obviously, the most important range of frequencies of the speech signal lie between 600 and 4,000 cycles per second.

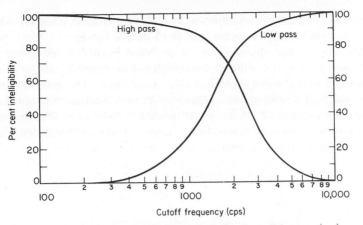

Figure 12.12. Effect on intelligibility of elimination of frequencies by use of filters. A low-pass filter permits frequencies below a given cutoff to pass through the communication system, eliminating frequencies above that cutoff. A high-pass filter, in turn, permits frequencies above the cutoff to pass, eliminating those below.

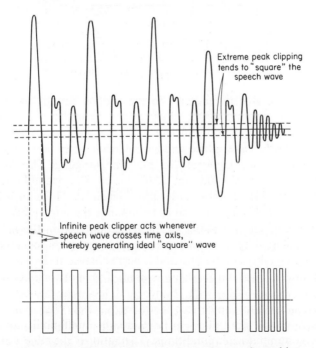

Figure 12.13. Showing how speech may be transformed into rectangular waves by means of a circuit that acts whenever the speech wave crosses the time axis. This transformation may be thought of as infinite peak clipping.

Amplitude selectivity can be brought to bear to improve the intelligibility
of speech signals under increased levels of noise. The speech waveform can
be arbitrarily limited in amplitude, this being termed "peak clipping" as
shown in Figure 12.13. Infinite peak clipping corresponds to reducing the
amplitude level essentially to zero, so that only the zero crossings of the time
waveform are transmitted as changes of sign of a minute bias signal. Under
infinite peak clipping about 70 per cent of the words can be understood from
the remaining rectangular waveform. Figure 12.14 indicates the effect of
peak clipping upon intelligibility.

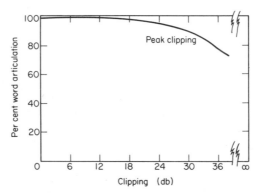

Figure 12.14. The effect of peak clipping upon
intelligibility. When peak clipping is infinite, the
articulation score is approximately 70 per cent.

There is considerable redundancy in the spoken sounds of language, as
described by conditional probabilities. This redundancy is, in effect, a
reduction in communication efficiency in the noiseless case. However,
most communication takes place under somewhat noisy conditions, and the
amount of redundancy incorporated into the language should take into
account the nature and the amount of this noise. For example, the military
services adopt specific alphabet descriptors, such as Alpha or Abel for A,
Bravo or Baker for B, and so on, so as to enhance the intelligibility of speech
under the expected characteristics of noise encountered in the field. A great
deal of the intelligibility of speech is dependent upon the characteristics of
the talker. High quality communication is best achieved if the average syllable
duration is longer, if greater intensity is used, if proportionately more of the
tonal time is spent with speech sounds and less with pauses, and if the
patterns of fundamental voice frequency are varied. With this in mind, it
becomes possible to train talkers to have greater intelligibility under anticipated noisy communication conditions. The ratio of the time during which
the speech sounds are being uttered to the pause time is called the phonation
time ratio. Under noisy conditions this ratio should be increased. Even though
an increase of speech intensity aids intelligibility under noisy conditions, care

must be taken so as not to strain the speaking voice and considerably fore-shorten its time duration of useful communication. The human operator may choose other forms of auditory signal for affecting control. For example, he may actuate a key so as to transmit the auditory or remote auditory sounds of Morse code. The fire alarm bell or siren are useful auditory signals which can be actuated by the human operator. Other forms of nonverbal communication should not be overlooked as control means. These include posture, facial expressions, and other intentional signalling attitudes of the body.

12.5. CONCLUSION

Controls are provided to enable the human operator to communicate with the equipment system under his cognizance. They furnish the communication interface between man and machine. To be most effective, controls should be designed to facilitate this bilateral communication while placing a minimum of constraint upon the human operator with respect to position, the expenditure of force, the requirement for excessive interpretation of the feedback information, and so on. Wherever possible, the controls should provide an affirmative response to actuation revealing to the operator that they have accepted his command. For example, the telephone system provides a side tone so that the operator receives an immediate "confirmation" that his spoken signals are being transmitted through the system.

Controls, in themselves, must be recognized to be displays. As such, they must be made compatible with other displays which reveal the longer time acceptance and response of the control system to the control actuation.

A number of questions are suggested which deserve specific attention in the design of controls.

Are they within easy reach at all times when they might be required by the operator?

Do the controls operate in accordance with the expectations of the operators? Usually this means, "increase to the right, decrease to the left, on or start in the upper position, off or stop in the down position, and so on."

Are rotary switch pointers clearly visible?

Are adjacent positions for rotary switches clearly delineated?

Are the controls spaced so that they are neither difficult to manipulate nor susceptible to accidental activation?

Do the critical controls have mechanical guards or electrical interlocks to prevent inadvertent actuation?

Is the angular displacement of toggle switches sufficient so that the actuated position can be easily recognized?

Are the push buttons large enough to permit ease of actuation without finger slipping off?

Is there a definite feel and/or audible click that indicates actuation?

Does the direction of control movement correspond to the direction of indicator movement?

Are these controls and corresponding displays located in a meaningful spatial relationship?

When operating the controls is it unlikely that the operator will obscure or cover up any significant displays?

Will clothing or other personal equipment modify the control movement by interposing movement limits or other restraints?

Proper design of a control system must be accomplished within the context of system design. The purpose which the system is to fulfill, the results involved in various types of error, the relative importance of individual parameters, should all contribute to providing an effective communication device between man and machine.

BIBLIOGRAPHY

AMMONS, R. B., "Rotary Pursuit Apparatus: I. Survey of Variables," *Psychological Bulletin*, Vol. 52 (1955), 69–75.

———. "Rotary Pursuit Apparatus: II. Effect of Stylus Length on Performance," *Psychological Reports*, Vol. 1 (1955), 103.

ANDERSON, N. H., D. A. GRANT, and C. O. NYSTROM, "Performance on a Repetitive Key Pressing Task as a Function of the Spatial Positioning of the Stimulus and Response Components," *USAF WADC TR 54–76* (1954).

ANDREAS, B. G., and B. WEISS, "Review of Research on Perceptual-Motor Performance Under Varied Display-Control Relationships," *USAF RADC Human Factors Office Scientific Report 2* (1954).

BAHRICK, H. P., W. F. BENNETT, and P. M. FITTS, "Accuracy of Positioning Responses as a Function of Spring Loading in a Control," *Journal of Experimental Psychology*, Vol. 49 (1955), 437–444.

BAHRICK, H. P., P. M. FITTS, and R. SCHNEIDER, "Reproduction of Simple Movements as a Function of Factors Influencing Proprioceptive Feedback," *Journal of Experimental Psychology*, Vol. 49 (1955), 445–454.

BALLARD, J. W., and R. W. HESSINGER, "Human Engineered Electromechanical Tactual Sensory Control System," *Electrical Manufacturing*, Vol. 54 No. 4 (October 1954), 118–121.

BATTIG, W. F., "The Effect of Kinesthetic, Verbal, and Visual Cues on the Acquisition of a Lever-Positioning Skill," *Journal of Experimental Psychology*, Vol. 47 (1954), 371–380.

BENNETT, W. F., P. M. FITTS, and M. NOBLE, "The Learning of Sequential Dependencies," *Journal of Experimental Psychology*, Vol. 48 (1954), 303–312.

BIEL, W. C., G. A. ECKSTRAND, A. D. SWAIN, and A. N. CHAMBERS, "Tactual Discriminability of Two Knob Shapes as a Function of Their Size," *USAF WADC TR 52–57* (1952).

BRADLEY, J. V., "Control-Display Association Preferences for Ganged Controls," *USAF WADC TR 54–379* (1954).

———. "Effect of Knob Arrangement on Consumption of Panel Space," *USAF WADC TR 56–202* (1956).

———. "Control Knob Arrangement Can Save Aircraft Instrument Panel Space," *Journal of Aviation Medicine*, Vol. 28 (1957), 322–327.

———. "Direction-of-Knob Turn Stereotypes," *Journal of Applied Psychology*, Vol. 32 (1959), 21–24.

BRADLEY, J. V., and J. ARGINTEANU, "Optimum Knob Diameter," *USAF WADC TR 56–96* (1956).

BRADLEY, J. V., and N. E. STUMP, "Minimum Allowable Dimensions for Controls Mounted on Concentric Shafts," *USAF WADC TR 55–355* (1955).

BRADLEY, J. V., and N. E. STUMP, "Minimum Allowable Knob Crowding," *USAF WADC TR 55–455* (December 1955).

BRADLEY, J. V., and R. A. WALLIS, "Spacing of On-Off Controls. I. Push-Buttons," *USAF WADC TR 58–2* (1958).

BRADLEY, J. V., and R. A. WALLIS, "Spacing of On-Off Controls. II. Toggle Switches," *USAF WADC TR 58–475* (1959).

BROWN, J. S., and A. T. SLATER-HAMMEL, "Discrete Movements in the Horizontal Plane as a Function of Their Length and Direction," *Journal of Experimental Psychology*, Vol. 39 (1949), 84–95.

BUGELSKI, B. R., "Population Stereotypes in Pedal Control of a 'Ball-Bank' Indicator," *Journal of Applied Psychology*, Vol. 39 (1955), 422–424.

CHAPANIS, A., "Studies of Manual Rotary Positioning Movements: 1. The Precision of Setting an Indicator Knob to Various Angular Positions," *Journal of Psychology*, Vol. 31 (1951), 51–64.

———. "Studies of Manual Rotary Positioning Movements: 2. The Accuracy of Estimating the Position of an Indicator Knob," *Journal of Psychology*, Vol. 31 (1951), 65–71.

CHERRY, C., ed., *On Human Communication*. New York: John Wiley & Sons, Inc., 1957.

CHURCHILL, A. V., "Manipulability of Braille Control Knobs," *Canadian Journal of Psychology*, Vol. 9 (1955), 117–120.

CLARKE, H. H., E. C. ELKINS, G. M. MARTIN, and K. G. WAKIM, "Relationship Between Body Position and the Application of Muscle Power to Movements of the Joint," *Archives of Physical Medicine*, Vol. 31 (1956), 81–89.

CLOS, C., and R. I. WILKINSON, "Dial Habits of Telephone Customers," *Bell System Technical Journal*, Vol. 31 (1952), 32–67.

DAVID, E. E., JR., "Signal Theory in Speech Transmission," *IRE Transactions on Circuit Theory*, Vol. CT–3 No. 4 (December 1956), 232–244.

DAVIS, D. W., "An Evaluation of the Simplified Typewriter Keyboard: Part 4," *Journal of Business Education*, Vol. 11 No. 2 (1935).

DAVIS, L. E., "Human Factors in Design of Manual Machine Controls," *Mechanical Engineering*, Vol. 71 (October 1949), 811–816, 837.

———. "Human Factors in the Design of Manual Machine Controls," *Mechanical World*, Vol. 129 (1951), 601–607.

DEININGER, R. L., "Desirable Push-Button Characteristics," *IRE Transactions on Human Factors in Electronics*, Vol. HFE–1 No. 1 (March 1960), 24–29.

———. "Human Factors Studies of Push-Button Characteristics and Information Processing in Key-Set Operation," *American Psychology*, Vol. 14 No. 7 (1959), 419 (Abstract).

DREHER, J. J., and W. E. EVANS, "Speech Interference Level and Aircraft Acoustical Environment," *Human Factors*, Vol. 2 No. 1 (February 1960).

DVORÁK, A., N. I. MERRICK, W. L. DEALEY, and G. C. FORD, *Typewriting Behavior*. New York: American Publishers, 1936.

DZENDOLET, E., and J. F. RIEVLEY, "Man's Ability to Apply Certain Torques While Weightless," *USAF WADC TR 59–94* (April 1959).

ECKSTRAND, G. A., and R. L. MORGAN, "The Influence of Training on the Discriminability of Knob Shapes," *USAF WADC TR 52–126* (February 1953).

EDWARDS, A. S., "The Relation of Involuntary Movement to Certain Psycho-Motor Activities," *Journal of General Psychology*, Vol. 50 (1954), 111–127.

ELY, J. H., R. M. THOMPSON, and J. ORLANSKY, "Design of Controls. Chapter VI of the Joint Services Human Engineering Guide to Equipment Design," *USAF WADC TR 56–172* (November 1956).

FANO, R. M., "The Information Theory Point of View in Speech Communication," *Journal of the Acoustical Society of America*, Vol. 22 (November 1950), 691–696.

FLANAGAN, J. L., "Evaluation of Two Formant-Extracting Devices," *Journal of the Acoustical Society of America*, Vol. 28 No. 1 (January 1956), 118–125.

———. "Bandwidth and Channel Capacity Necessary to Transmit the Formant Information of Speech," *Journal of the Acoustical Society of America*, Vol. 28 No. 4 (July 1956), 592–596.

FITTS, P. M., "The Information Capacity of the Human Motor System in Controlling the Amplitude of Movement," *Journal of Experimental Psychology*, Vol. 47 (1954), 381–391.

FITTS, P. M., and C. M. SEEGER, "S-R Compatibility: Spatial Characteristics of Stimulus and Response Codes," *Journal of Experimental Psychology*, Vol. 46 (1953), 199–210.

FLETCHER, H., *Speech and Hearing in Communication*. New York: D. Van Nostrand Company, Inc., 1953.

FORBES, T. W., "Human Factors in Highway Design, Operation and Safety Problems," *Human Factors*, Vol. 2 No. 1 (February 1960), 1–9.

GARVEY, W. D., and W. B. KNOWLES, "Response Time Patterns Associated with Various Display-Control Relationship," *Journal of Experimental Psychology*, Vol. 47 (1954), 315–322.

GARVEY, W. D., and W. B. KNOWLES, "Pointing Accuracy of a Joy Stick Without Visual Feedback," *Journal of Applied Psychology*, Vol. 38 (1954), 191–194.

GARVEY, W. D., and L. L. MITNICK, "Effect of Additional Spatial Reference on Display-Control Efficiency," *Journal of Experimental Psychology*, Vol. 50 (1955), 276–282.

GERALL, A. A., P. B. SAMPSON, and S. D. S. SPRAGG, "Performance on a Tracking Task as a Function of Position, Radius, and Loading of Control Cranks: I. Stationary Targets," *Journal of Psychology*, Vol. 41 (1956), 135–150.

GERALL, A. A., P. B. SAMPSON, and S. D. S. SPRAGG, "Performance on a Tracking Task as a Function of Position, Radius, and Loading of Control Cranks: II. Moving Targets," *Journal of Psychology*, Vol. 41 (1956), 151–156.

GIBBS, C. B., "The Continuous Regulation of Skilled Response by Kinesthetic Feedback," *British Journal of Psychology*, Vol. 45 (1954), 24–39.

GOTTSDANKER, R. M., "The Continuation of Tapping Sequences," *Journal of Psychology*, Vol. 37 (1954), 123–132.

GREEN, B. F., and L. K. ANDERSON, "The Tactual Identification of Shapes for Coding Switch Handles," *Journal of Applied Psychology*, Vol. 39 (1955), 219–226.

GREEN, R. F., D. GOODENAUGH, B. G. ANDREAS, A. A. GERALL, and S. D. S. SPRAGG, "Performance Levels and Transfer Effects in Compensatory and Following Tracking as a Function of the Planes of Rotation of Control Cranks," *Journal of Psychology*, Vol. 41 (1956), 107–118.

HALLE, M., and K. STEVENS, "Speech Recognition: A Model and a Program for Research," *IRE Transactions on Information Theory*, Vol. IT–8 No. 2 (February 1962), 155–159.

HARRIS, C. M., "Study of the Building Blocks in Speech," *Journal of the Acoustical Society of America*, Vol. 25 No. 5 (September 1953), 962–970.

HARRIS, S. J., and K. U. SMITH, "Dimensional Analysis of Motions: VII. Extent and Direction of Manipulative Factors in Defining Motions," *Journal of Applied Psychology*, Vol. 38 (1954), 126–130.

HARTMAN, B. O., "The Effect of Joystick Length on Pursuit Tracking," *USA Med. Research Laboratory Rep. No. 279* (1957).

HEMPEL, W. E., and E. A. FLEISHMAN, "A Factor Analysis of Physical Proficiency and Manipulative Skill," *Journal of Applied Psychology*, Vol. 39 (1955), 12–16.

HICK, W. E., "The Precision of Incremental Muscular Forces with Special Reference to Manual Control Design," Great Britain Medical Research Council, *Applied Psychology Unit Report 23* (August 1945).

HIRSH, I. J., "Pathology in Speech Communication," *Journal of the Acoustical Society of America*, Vol. 22 No. 6 (November 1950), 717–719.

HOCKETT, C. F., "An Approach to the Quantification of Semantic Noise," *Philosophy of Science*, Vol. 19 (1952), 257–261.

HOLDING, D. H., "Direction of Movement Relationships between Controls and Displays Moving in Different Planes," *Journal of Applied Psychology*, Vol. 41 (1957), 93–97.

HOWLAND, D., and M. E. NOBLE, "The Effect of Physical Constants of a Control on Tracking Performance," *Journal of Experimental Psychology*, Vol. 46 (1953), 353–360.

HUMPHRIES, M., "Performance as a Function of Control-Display Relations, Positions of the Operator, and Locations of the Control," *Journal of Applied Psychology*, Vol. 42 (1958), 311–316.

HUNT, D. P., "The Coding of Aircraft Controls," *USAF WADC TR 53–221* (August 1953).

HUNT, D. P., and D. R. CRAIG, "The Relative Discriminability of Thirty-One Differently Shaped Knobs," *USAF WADC TR 54–108* (December 1954).

HUNT, D. P., and M. J. WARRICK, "Accuracy of Blind Positioning a Rotary Control," *USAF WADC TR 52–106* (1952).

JENKINS, W. L., and M. W. OLSON, "The Use of Levers in Making Settings on a Simulated Scope Face," *Journal of Applied Psychology*, Vol. 38 (1954), 457–461.

JENKINS, W. L., L. O. MASS, and M. W. OLSON, "Influence of Inertia in Making Settings on a Linear Scale," *Journal of Applied Psychology*, Vol. 35 (1951), 208–213.

JENKINS, W. L., "The Discrimination and Reproduction of Motor Adjustments with Various Types of Aircraft Controls," *American Journal of Psychology*, Vol. 60 (1947), 397–406.

————. "Design Factors in Knobs and Levers for Making Settings on Scales and Scopes: A Summary Report," *USAF WADC TR 53–2* (February 1953).

JENKINS, W. L., and A. C. KARR, "The Use of a Joy-Stick in Making Settings on a Simulated Scope Face," *USAF WADC TR 53-430* (March 1954).

JENKINS, W. L., and M. W. OLSON, "The Use of Levers in Making Settings on a Linear Scale," *Journal of Applied Psychology*, Vol. 36 (1952), 269–271.

KATCHMAR, L. T., "Physical Force Problems: I. Hand Crank Performance for Various Crank Radii and Torque Load Combinations," USA Aberdeen Proving Ground, *Human Engineering Laboratory TM 3-57* (1957).

KLEMMER, E. T., "Rate of Force Application in a Simple Reaction Time Test," *USAF Cambridge Research Center TR 55-1* (1955).

KLEMMER, E. T., and P. F. MULLER, JR., "The Rate of Handling Information. Key Pressing Responses to Light Patterns," USAF Bolling AFB, Washington, D.C., *Human Factors Operations Research Laboratories Report 34* (1953).

LICKLIDER, J. C. R., "On the Process of Speech Perception," *Journal of the Acoustical Society of America*, Vol. 24 (1952), 590–594.

———. "Intelligibility of Amplitude-Dichotomized, Time-Quantized Speech Waves," *Journal of the Acoustical Society of America*, Vol. 22 No. 6 (November 1950), 820–824.

LINCOLN, R. S., "Learning a Rate of Movement," *Journal of Experimental Psychology*, Vol. 47 (1954), 465–470.

———. "Rate Accuracy in Handwheel Cranking," *Journal of Applied Psychology*, Vol. 38 (1954), 195–201.

LINCOLN, R. S., and L. T. ALEXANDER, "Preferred Patterns of Motor and Verbal Responses," *Journal of Experimental Psychology*, Vol. 50 (1955), 106–112.

LONG, E. R., and W. A. LEE, "The Role of Spatial Cuing as a Response-Limiter for Location Responses," *USAF WADC TR 53-312* (December 1953).

LUTZ, M. C., and A. CHAPANIS, "Expected Locations of Digits and Letters on Ten-Button Keysetts," *Journal of Applied Psychology*, Vol. 39 (1955), 314–317.

LYMAN, J., and H. GROTHE, "Prehension Force as a Measure of Psychomotor Skill for Bare and Gloved Hands," *Journal of Applied Psychology*, Vol. 42 (1958), 18–21.

MENZERATH, P., "Typology of Languages," *Journal of the Acoustical Society of America*, Vol. 22 No. 6 (November 1950), 698–701.

MILLER, G. A., *Language and Communication*. New York: McGraw-Hill Book Company, Inc., 1951.

———. "Decision Units in the Perception of Speech," *IRE Transactions on Information Theory*, Vol. IT-8 No. 2 (February 1962), 81–83.

———. "Language Engineering," *Journal of the Acoustical Society of America*, Vol. 22 No. 6 (November 1950), 720–725.

MILLER, G. A., "Speech and Communication," *Journal of the Acoustical Society of America*, Vol. 30 No. 5 (May 1958), 397–398.

MITCHELL, M. J. H., and M. A. VINCE, "The Direction of Movement of Machine Controls," *Quarterly Journal of Experimental Psychology*, Vol. 3 (1951), 24–35.

MUCKLER, F. A., and W. G. MATHENY, "Transfer of Training as a Function of Control Friction," *Journal of Applied Psychology*, Vol. 38 (1954), 364–367.

MULLER, P. F., "Efficiency of Verbal Versus Motor Responses in Handling Information Encoded by Means of Color and Light Patterns," *USAF WADC TR 55–472* (December 1955).

OLSON, H. F., and H. BELAR, "Phonetic Typewriter III," *Journal of the Acoustica Society of America*, Vol. 33 No. 11 (November 1961), 1160–1615.

OLSON, H. F., and H. BELAR, "Phonetic Typewriter," *Journal of the Acoustical Society of America*, Vol. 28 No. 6 (November 1956), 1072–1081.

ORLANSKY, J., "Psychological Aspects of Stick and Rudder Controls in Aircraft," *Aeronautical Engineering Review*, Vol. 8 (1949), 1–10.

PETERS, G. A., and S. MICHELSON, "Selecting Control Devices for Human Operators," *Control Engineering*, Vol. 6 No. 3 (1959), 127.

PETERS, G. A., "When Choosing Selector-Switch Knobs," *Product Engineering*, Vol. 29 No. 50 (1958), 103.

PETERS, R., et al., "Physiology of Voluntary Muscle," *British Medical Bulletin*, Vol. 12 (1956), 161–235.

PETERSON, G. E., "Applications of Information Theory to Research in Experimental Phonetics," *Journal of Speech Disorders*, Vol. 17 (1952), 175–188.

———. "Design of Visible Speech Devices," *Journal of the Acoustical Society of America*, Vol. 26 (1954), 406–413.

PICKETT, J. M., and I. POLLACK, "Prediction of Speech Intelligibility at High Noise Levels," *Journal of the Acoustical Society of America*, Vol. 30 No. 10 (October 1958), 955–963.

POLLACK, I., and W. H. SUMBY, "Visual Contribution to Speech Intelligibility in Noise," *Journal of the Acoustical Society of America*, Vol. 26 No. 2 (March 1954), 212–215.

POLLACK, I., and J. M. PICKETT, "Intelligibility of Peak-Chipped Speech at High Noise Levels," *Journal of the Acoustical Society of America*, Vol. 31 No. 1 (January 1959), 14–16.

POTTER, R. K., G. A. KOPP, and H. C. GREEN, *Visible Speech*. New York: D. Van Nostrand Company, Inc., 1947.

POTTER, R. K., and J. C. STEINBERG, "Toward the Specification of Speech," *Journal of the Acoustical Society of America*, Vol. 22 No. 6 (November 1950), 807–820.

POULTON, E. C., "Eye-Hand Span in Simple Serial Tasks," Great Britain, *Medical Research Council Applied Psychology Research Unit APU 158/53*, Cambridge (1953).

REES, D. W., and W. N. KAMA, "Size of Tabs: A Factor in Handling of Guides and Checklists," *USAF WADC TR 59–158* (1959).

RITCHIE, M. L., "A Comparison of the Stick and Handwheel in the Control of Aircraft," *USAF WADC TR 58–447* (1959).

———. "Control Transitivity as a Function of 'Hand Used'," *USAF WADC TR 58–447* (1959).

ROLOFF, L. L., "Kinesthesis in Relation to the Learning of Selected Motor Skills," *Research Quarterly of the American Association of Health & Physical Education*, Vol. 24 (1953), 210–217.

ROSS, S., B. E. SHEPP, and T. G. ANDREWS, "Response Preferences in Display-Control Relationships," *Journal of Applied Psychology*, Vol. 39 (1955), 425–428.

RUDORF, S. K., "Design for Safety—How Machine Designers Can Improve Controls and Reduce Cost While Promoting Safe Operation," *Machine Design*, Vol. 22 No. 12 (1950), 112–118.

SAUL, E. V., and J. JAFFE, "The Effects of Clothing on Gross Motor Performance," *USA Quartermaster Research Development Center TR EP–12* (1955).

SEMINAR, J., "Designing for Human Strength," *Machine Design*, Vol. 31 No. 11 (May 28, 1959), 96–99.

SHACKEL, B., "The Human Limbs in Control. 2. Optimum Control-Display Ratios at Different Display Distances," Great Britain Medical Research Council, *Applied Psychology Research Unit, APU 215/54* (April 1954).

SIEGEL, A. I., and F. R. BROWN, "An Experimental Study of Control Console Design," *Ergonomics*, Vol. 1 (1958), 251–257.

SIMON, C. W., "Instrument-Control Configurations Affecting Performance in a Compensatory Pursuit Task," *USAF WADC TR 6015* (February 1952).

SPRAGG, S. D. S., and D. B. DEVOE, "The Accuracy of Control Knob Settings as a Function of the Size of Angle to be Bisected and Type of End-Point Cue," *Perceptual Motor Skills*, Vol. 6 (1956), 25–28.

SPRAGG, S. D. S., "Some Factors Affecting the Setting of Dial Knobs," *American Psychologist*, Vol. 4 (1949), 304.

STUMP, N. E., "Toggle Switches: Activation Time as a Function of Spring Tension," *USAF WADC TN 52–39* (August 1952).

———. "Toggle Switches: Activation Time as a Function of the Plane of Orientation and the Direction of Movement," *USAF Aero Medical Laboratory TN 52–51* (September 1952).

STUMP, N. E., "Manipulability of Rotary Controls as a Function of Knob Diameter and Control Orientation," *USAF WADC TN 53–12* (February 1953).

WEISS, B., and R. F. GREEN, "The Effects of Inertia on the Accuracy of Knob Settings," *USN ONR Special Devices Center TR 241–6–9* (January 1953).

WEISS, B., "The Role of Proprioceptive Feedback in Positioning Responses," *Journal of Experimental Psychology*, Vol. 47 (1954), 215–224.

WHITNEY, R. J., "The Strength of the Lifting Action in Man," *Ergonomics*, Vol. 1 No. 2 (February 1958), 101–128.

13

EXTRACTED HUMAN OUTPUT
INFORMATION

13.1. INTRODUCTION

A great amount of information can be extracted from the human operator even without his overt cooperation. Complex systems which utilize man as a critical component in the information flow must be protected through the direct monitoring of the status of the human operator in order to detect incipient failure and ensure the adequacy of his control actions. Bioelectronics provides the tools which make it possible to obtain, reduce, and interpret the required data. The limitation no longer rests with the state of equipment technology. Once again, the burden falls upon the scientist to develop an understanding from which optimal use of the tools at his disposal can be derived.

It is difficult to distinguish the purpose of bioelectronic instrumentation between the diagnostic monitoring of man and the scientific investigation of his internal functioning. This latter function is considered to be outside the scope of this discussion. It is, however, considered necessary to indicate certain relevant limitations as the commentary proceeds.

More in line with the direct problems of biotechnology is the use of the monitoring instrumentation for the purpose of determining human limitations to be used as design criteria. The investigation of animal behavior under severely stressful environments and human behavior under extreme mission simulation provide direct information which should result in an improvement in the design of future systems, realizing greater effectiveness and the avoidance of needless expenditure of human effort.

13.2. THE GALVANIC SKIN RESPONSE

The galvanic skin response (GSR) has had an extensive history as a measure of mental activity level. In 1888, C. Feré noted that the surface conduction of the skin of the palm changes as a result of being startled, mental stress, or emotional shock. The "Feré Effect," as it was called, is exosomatic; that is, the simple measurement of resistance requires the application of an *external* voltage. The "hot" electrode is placed on the palm of the hand, and resistance is measured with respect to a reference electrode placed on the arm or other insensitive area of the skin. A small voltage is applied, and the current flow (in the order of 50 microamps) is measured, this being translated into skin resistance through the use of Ohm's Law. In general, the basal resistance is found to be in the order of thousands of ohms with response to mental stimuli causing variations as great as 25 per cent.

J. Tarschanoff (1890) noted a similar response even when there was no externally applied voltage between the electrodes. Careful measurement revealed that there is a direct endosomatic effect wherein a potential is generated within the skin as a result of mental activity. Voltages were found to be slightly greater than 200 microvolts, and, as expected, these proved to be difficult to monitor. As a result, most of the experimental studies which followed have utilized the exosomatic measurement technique rather than the Tarschanoff effect. L. A. Jeffress has shown that both the Feré and Tarschanoff effects are closely related to sweat gland activity, these two measures correlating at the 95 per cent level.

A number of possible explanations have been advanced for the GSR. Today, it is known that this autonomic reflex is related to the pre-motor cortex with the final neural half being part of the sympathetic nervous system. In fact, the amplitude of the GSR has been shown to be a direct function of the intensity of sympathetic stimulation and the number of post-ganglionic fibers which are available. The response can only be measured in the region of the palm of the hands or the sole of the feet, the remainder of the skin offering an insensitive voltage reference.

About 80 per cent of the total skin resistance is in the epidermis with the remaining 20 per cent in the corium. The majority of the measured resistance change appears due to some physiological condition within the skin itself, this probably being due to the pre-secretory change in the sweat glands.[1] The GSR cannot be voluntarily inhibited for any adequate stimulus situation, but it may be voluntarily produced. It may even occur with respect to stimuli of which the subject remains completely unaware. There remains much to be learned before the mechanism of the GSR is fully understood.

Various types of electrodes are available for use in the measurement of GSR. The standard bioelectric metal disc electrode can be secured to the

---

[1] The sweat activity on the GSR sensitive area of the skin appears to be almost completely independent of the temperature regulatory action of the body.

skin with adhesive tape after placing a standard electrode paste between the electrode and the skin to assure against spurious changes of contact resistance. It has been found equally adequate to utilize a saline solution as the electrolyte or depend upon the sufficiency of sweat alone to form an efficient conducting medium. In the latter case, it may be required to allow a short passage of time in order to attain good contact. It is sometimes found useful to paint a one-inch diameter circle of colodium on the skin around the electrode area so as to prevent an increase in contact size due to spillage of the electrolyte. Finger electrodes have also proven to be satisfactory, these being formed of two flexible thin sheets of copper bent to form semicylinders—one cylinder placed on the palm-side of the finger and the other completing the circle to form a reference signal. An elastic band holds these tight to the finger but separate

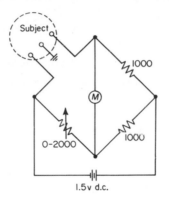

Figure 13.1. GSR bridge circuit.

from each other. Such an electrode can be placed inside of a glove and does little to inhibit mobility. One experiment successfully used a thin lead electrode placed in the instep of the shoe thus providing a completely unencumbered subject.

Consideration has also been given to the possible use of alternating current for the measurement of GSR, this to eliminate artifacts of electrical polarization. Use of the readily available 60 cycle voltage would prevent the simultaneous recording of some of the other body functions and might also pose serious isolation problems. The exploration of higher frequencies might prove worthwhile, although direct current appears to be more than adequate for the task.

Various techniques are available for translating the sensed GSR into a read-out signal. A classical direct current bridge circuit can be used as shown in Figure 13.1. It may prove opportune to have an analog computer available (as part of the simulation equipment or for the purpose of data recording). When this is the case, it is possible to program the spectral filter and feed the directly sensed signal into the computer for display and data reduction.

A current of about 40 microamps can be caused to flow by use of a dry cell. The electrode voltage must be amplified and separated into low-frequency and high-frequency spectra in order to display all information on scale at all times. Figure 13.2 indicates the program for low pass filter which is converted

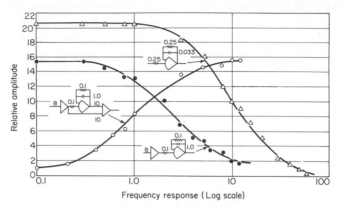

Figure 13.2. Frequency response of component GSR filters.

into a high pass filter by subtracting the filtered voltage from the input. The remaining low pass filter is intended for high frequency noise elimination. Figure 13.3 describes the GSR circuit together with the over-all frequency

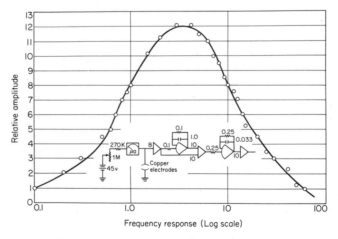

Figure 13.3. GSR circuit and frequency response.

response to sinusoidal input. The low frequency cutoff was chosen to prevent excessive drift during the length of the experimental trials. The circuit effectively attenuated 60 cycle pickup even when operated near fluorescent lighting fixtures. Figure 13.4 shows samples of the recorded high-frequency pass GSR with a simultaneous displayed error and control stick position as taken during one experiment. Note the correspondence of the general activity level, the apparent time lag in GSR, as these relate to control stick movement as well as the causal error. As presented, these three variates describe the input stimulus, something of the transduction mediation, and the output response. The problem of simultaneous recording of the large voltage excursions of full GSR, as taken over long periods of time, can be overcome in a number of ways. One recently successful technique used a self-balancing bridge with separate recording of the balancing signal which corresponded to the basal resistance level.

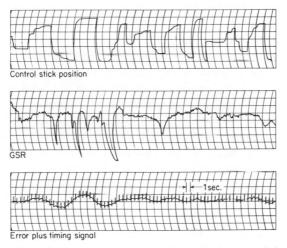

Control stick position

GSR

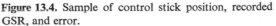

Error plus timing signal

Figure 13.4. Sample of control stick position, recorded GSR, and error.

The GSR has a normal latency of at least one second. Shorter values of time lag are obtained as a result of intense stimulation. The recovery of the GSR to its basal resistance level takes considerably longer, this being in the order of $4\frac{1}{2}$ seconds for, say, allowed stimulus. The time of recovery is highly variable and may be much greater for certain stimuli being in the order of an hour or more when the stimulus has evoked serious emotional shock. It is usual to find the appearance of small oscillations of a few seconds period within the subsiding GSR response. The recovery of GSR is to some degree extended by the time interval required for the evaporation or absorption of the produced sweat.

Experiments have shown that there is little correlation of GSR with a purely physical task or, for that matter, with external temperature over the normally experienced range. A number of mental conditions yield positive and dependable response. Any stimuli which incites emotion, stress, anxiety, degree of arousal, expectancy, and so forth, will cause a sudden decrease in skin resistance corresponding to increased sweat gland activity. Possibly this response could be attributed to a self-protective mechanism which provides sweat to the hands and feet under conditions of jeopardy in order to increase friction and aid the "fighting" ability. Although GSR has been shown to be controlled at the pre-motor cortex of the brain, it is known to be primarily a property of the skin.

Unfortunately, the *specific* quality of the stimulus is totally lost in the GSR records. Certain words, however, may be expected to elicit a response from the normal subject. Words like "mother," "vomit," "adultery," and the like, may be said to be emotionally "loaded." If a list of random words is read aloud to the quiet subject, it may be expected to find a GSR response appearing shortly after the occurrence of an emotionally loaded word. If the subject provides a distinct response during the short rest period after a common word, then it is probably true that this term has some emotional connotation for the subject. The addition of responses which are inappropriate to the experiment may be viewed as an increase in the noise level, and these are but one of the many artifacts encountered in the GSR experiment. The close of a door, the ring of a telephone, even a slight breeze, each may be more than sufficient to cause a GSR response. Even subliminal stimulation can cause a disturbance of the record. In fact, intensive mental attention to private thought can wash out the entire experiment in jamming noise. The existence of these spurious responses makes it necessary to take a most conservative approach in the interpretation of the GSR record.

Various attempts have been made to quantify the GSR. These measures include the absolute resistance level, the absolute conductance level, the relative change in resistance as compared to the basal level, the per cent or frequency of times when the resistance is equal to or greater than some particular change of basal resistance, the logarithm of the resistance, and many others. A. S. Paintal used the ratio of the resistance change to the maximum response resistance. This index was found especially useful in the comparison of conditioned to unconditioned GSR responses. Certainly the last word has not yet been spoken with regard to the determination of the proper measure for general interpretation. Individual quantitative metrics may prove useful for each particular purpose. Recent experiments have examined the derivative of the GSR under the rationale that this signal should prove to be closer to the causal factor for sweat gland activity. Sufficient empirical evidence to validate this hypothesis is as yet unavailable.

Recent experiments have studied the GSR as an indicator of the level of relaxation, drowsiness, or alertness. This bioelectric measure has proven to be sensitive to the level of fatigue and is, therefore, considered as the basis for a possible safety device to indicate to the human operator when he is no longer in satisfactory condition for the control of vehicle or other equipments. Modern electronic techniques may make it possible to provide a compact device which can be used in this regard.

GSR has also been used as a measure of the difficulty experienced by the subject in performing an assigned task. This concept may be extended to furnish a useful technique for the comparison of subjects even when it is impossible to provide the same experimental situation. For example, the piloting skill of two individuals may be compared by taking the ratio of the number of errors that is recognized to the total number of errors committed. This metric overcomes the dissimilarity of the task, available equipment, and many other factors, yet provides some measure of the piloting capability under the assumption that the motivation level for the subjects is the same. It is relatively simple to accomplish an objective measure of the number of errors committed in terms of control reversal, magnitude of deviation, and so on. More sophisticated forms of this technique offer advantages for effective measurement under field conditions.

It is the GSR which forms the foundation for lie-detector work. Although the GSR response can sometimes be voluntarily produced, it, like other autonomic responses, cannot be voluntarily inhibited when adequate stimulus situation is presented.

13.3. THE HEART RESPONSE

The heart has long been recognized as an indicator for both mental and physical stress. Early in this century it was found possible to sense and record the pulse beat mechanically. The normal resting pulse rate is about 72 pulses per minute (within a normal range from 45 to 90). This rate was found to increase significantly as a result of surprise, startle, or expectancy on the part of the subject. Extremely large rate changes can occur. For example, the heart rate of a restrained cat increased by over 82 per cent upon the visual presentation of a dog.

The heart musculature is activated by an electrical wave of energy which descends from the pacemaker onto the auricular and then the ventricular sections.

> The heart cells in the resting state are polarized with positive electric charges on the outside of the cell membrane and negative charges on the inside. The membrane acts more or less like a leaky condenser whose charges are kept intact by an electrochemical mechanism inside the cell. During the resting state, the difference in potential between the inside and outside of the membrane is of the order of 60–80 millivolts. During activation, the cell surface membrane is altered (at the point of "depolarization") so that the inside of the membrane becomes positive and the outside negative. In this way, a potential difference is set up between the active and adjacent areas. The currents now flow from inactive (positive) to active (negative) regions.[2]

As a result of this electrical change, a strong electrical wavefront is conducted through the body tissue spreading until it reaches the surface of the skin. An electrode can be placed directly over the apex of the heart to sense

[2] J. F. Fulton, ed., *Textbook of Physiology*, 17th edition, Philadelphia: W. B. Saunders Company, 1955, p. 635.

a peak to peak voltage of not less than 500 microvolts. Under certain conditions, this voltage has been found to reach as high as 2,000 microvolts. Such a strong signal obviates the necessity for having a shielded room in which to obtain measurements. This sensed voltage traces the electrocardiogram (EKG) requiring only simple electrodes placed on the surface of the skin.

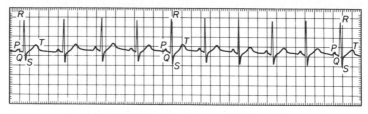

Figure 13.5. The normal electrocardiogram.

A thin metal disc of about one inch diameter, coated with conductive electrode paste, can be secured to the skin with the aid of adhesive tape. Alternately, a thin layer of silver adhesive paint can be applied directly to the cleaned skin, a fine wire mesh placed over the paint, and a second layer of paint placed over and through the mesh wire. An electrical lead is soldered to the wire mesh before it is applied. Such electrodes can be worn for days without removal.

The "signal" electrode may be placed directly over the apex of the heart. This position is best located by pressing the fingers between the ribs. Considerable variation in heart location exists over this population so that this

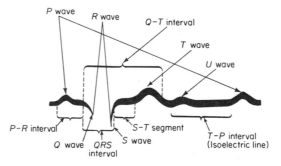

Figure 13.6. The normal EKG Complex.

technique is considered superior to any "rib-counting rule." The "reference" electrode can be placed over the sternum, the bone which lies just below the "V" of the neck.

The normal EKG is shown in Figure 13.5. Each deflection of this waveform (commonly called "waves") has been designated by W. Einthoven and can be directly related to a particular stimulus of the heart musculature. In particular, Figure 13.6 indicates the names for the significant aspects of a normal

EKG waveform. The P wave results from the electrical stimulation of the auricular; the QRS Complex indicates the spread of excitation in the ventricles; the T wave corresponds to the repolarization of the ventricular musculature; and the U wave (which occurs after mechanical systole) indicates continued electrical activity in the ventricles. A large catalog of representative EKG patterns is available in the medical literature to allow comparative diagnosis of normal and abnormal conditions.

The electrical activity of the heart may be viewed as resulting from an equivalent electrical dipole potential source. Determination of its orientation can only be accomplished as a result of the time–phase comparison of a number of voltages sensed at different points on the surface of the torso. Unfortunately, it is not possible to locate truly orthogonal points of "view" for reading the vector voltage components. A rather complex orthogonalization procedure must be used to account for the observed mutual impedance between the 4, 6, 12, or 14 electrodes which are utilized. The computation translates the sensed signals into a vector representation of the heart as a function of its cycle time.

The desire for even greater accuracy and more complete information has required an increase in the number of sensing electrodes. As many as 100 data-taking points have been considered. However, such a large number causes a tedious and costly electrode location and placement task. This difficulty can be overcome by mounting the numerous electrodes inside a straplike harness which can be wrapped around the body of the subject. The large amount of output data makes it greatly desirable to utilize some form of automatic data reduction. Various computer programs have been explored in this regard.

The dipole representation of the heart potential source, first proposed by A. D. Waller (1889), has been recognized to be insufficient in a number of regards. The current flow over the surface is far from concentrated at a single point, and it is the exact nature of the spread of this current which dictates the resulting heart action. In the words of O. H. Schmitt:

> The heart action potential measured at the body surface represents the summed contributions from all the individual muscle fibers of the heart syncytium. The marked variation in pattern obtained at various lead positions reflects primarily the different direction of the leads with respect to the heart fiber directions and secondarily the electrical distance from the fibers to the lead positions. This electrical distance is somewhat dependent upon anatomical form and upon tissue composition, but these factors do not influence the time relationship appreciably. Each fiber can thus be considered to contribute to the total measured potential instant by instant without error due to time of transmission to the electrode.

To portray the heart more fully, O. Schmitt has developed the stereovectorcardiogram which provides a three-dimensional "picture" of the heart voltage pattern created by the visual superposition of the display of two cathode ray tubes. Figure 13.7 indicates the type of spatial representation. There remains much to be accomplished in exploring the usefulness of this device.

A direct read-out of the heart beat rate can be obtained through the use of a cardiotachometer. Early instruments accomplished counting through the use of a magnetic relay which was triggered by the peaks of the EKG. More recent instruments measure the time interval between the last two pulses and display the reciprocal of this interval as the heart rate.

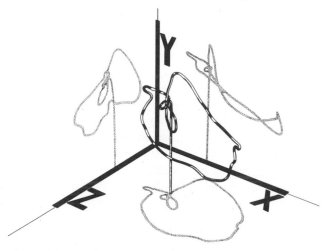

Figure 13.7. Relationship between spatial vector cardiograms and conventional planar vectorcardiogram. A wire model bent to dupli-cate the three-dimensional spatial trace seen directly with the stereovectorelectrocardiograph (SVEC) is arranged to cast pro-jection shadows on each of the principal planes, including the XY, or sagittal, plane. These projections represent the traces seen on a conventional vector cardiography screen. As an exercise it is interesting to attempt reconstruction of the spatial trace from two of the planar projections and to compare this reconstruction with that made from another pair. Any two projections should give an identical result.

Knowledge of the electrical activity of the heart does not tell the complete story. It is also advantageous to obtain a phonocardiac record which can be taken through a stethescope or, even more practically, through the placement of a suitable microphone directly over the chest cavity. Best results can be obtained if external sounds are attenuated through the use of a sound absorbent shield. The sound waveform tells of the mechanical action of the heart musculature and the valves. This can be correlated with the causal EKG waveform often permitting detailed diagnosis of difficulties.

The product of the amplitude of the heart beat and the pulse frequency should provide a measure of the energy rate of the heart. This metric over-comes the fact that certain subjects reflect change of amplitude as a primary response while others show a change of pulse frequency. It has been shown by A. Ford that the product most nearly corresponds to the cardiac energy rate. The energy per pulse can be measured by integrating the EKG or the ballistro-cardiogram (BKG) waveform. The latter indicates the thrust of the blood stream as it is pushed along the general arterial direction in the thigh. To accomplish this mass-inertia measurement, it is required that the subject remain motionless and in a horizontal position on an instrumented bed. In general, the blood pressure will also show some correlation to the heart energy rate.

13.4. THE BRAIN RESPONSE

An electrical potential can be measured on the surface of the scalp as a result of the electrical activity of the brain. The time-history of this voltage, the electroencephalogram (EEG), is commonly called the brain wave. Even though the EEG is obtained after the original signal within the brain has been attenuated and averaged by the skin, the skull, the brain-lining fluid, and even the brain itself, it is remarkably strong, being from 50 to 300 microvolts. Such voltage levels can be measured without severe shielding problems; however, shielding is required in order to obtain noise-free EEG sensing.

The EEG is a direct result of activity within the neural structure of the brain. The complexity of this structure in terms of its interconnections is almost beyond description. The sensed EEG represents the composite behavior of a vast number of neurons acting at the same time, each offering an extremely small contribution to the average signal which is measured. It is important to note that the EEG cannot be related to any single nerve activity. Ford has indicated that the primary EEG potential source is that brain structure which includes "the principal synaptic connection of cerebral spheres located within an outer surface structure less than 1 millimeter deep." Such a mass of almost random connections might be expected to yield only white noise. But such is not the case, however, as is shown in Figure 13.8. Certain low frequency components are immediately apparent. In particular, the alpha rhythm is the name given to that strong sinusoidal component which falls between 8 and 13 cycles per second. It is usual to find this rhythm present in the EEG for the normal subject while he is resting with his eyes closed. The beta rhythm falls between 14 and 30 cycles per second and is likely to occur during periods of mental effort. The delta rhythm of between 0.5 and 3.5 cycles per second may be called the "emergency" rhythm, being associated with extreme physical energy and stress. The theta rhythm of between 4 to 7 cycles per second may also appear during mental stress.

The EEG frequency spectrum is strongly dependent upon the nature of the activity in which the subject is engaged. For example, opening the eyes and allowing visual stimulation directly correlates with loss of the alpha rhythm and the introduction of lower frequency components. In deep sleep, the alpha

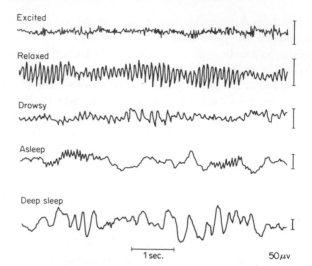

Figure 13.8. Typical EEG records taken during excitement, relaxation, and varying degrees of sleep. Note that excitement is characterized by a rapid frequency and small amplitude and that varying degrees of sleep are marked by increasing irregularity and by appearance of "slow waves."

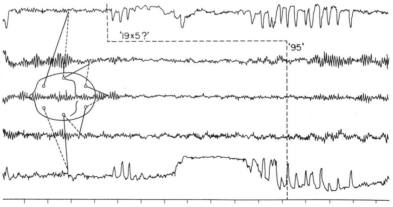

Figure 13.9. EEG of a subject with a "responsive" alpha-rhythm. The record shows a characterized blocking of the alpha-rhythm when the sum is given. The rhythm returns to its previous amplitude once an answer is found. The diagrammatic head shows the positions of the electrodes: each tracing is of the difference in potential between two electrodes, shown by pairs of lines connecting the electrode-positions to the tracing.

rhythm "appears to shift" down to about 3 cycles per second with some components also removed to higher frequencies. It is important to note that these findings are sensitive to the particular location of the EEG electrode on the scalp. Reference is made to Figure 13.9.

D. B. Lindsley (1938) demonstrated that alpha rhythm occurs at particular foci on the surface of the brain. In particular, two occur over the occipital region toward the back of the brain; a third occurs over the anterior (rear) side of the parietal lobe at the middle of the top of the head; a fourth occurs at the temporal region just back of the temples at the side of the head. These foci are connected with the deeper influences of the thalamic connections just about the mid-brain. A frequency component of between 8 and 12 cycles per second was measured from the temporal lobes during strong mental concentration. Although this rhythm lies within the range of the alpha rhythm, it is not correlated with the same mental state, and so it has been termed the kappa rhythm. In general, it can be said that the beta, delta, and theta "waves" do not necessarily represent the same mental condition every time they appear.

Attention has also been focused on the d-c potential as a source of EEG information. Although considerable interest is centered on this data, it is, as yet, only possible to state that if an arm is used as reference, the brain is normally negative by some d-c bias.

A number of measuring techniques have been utilized with respect to EEG. Scalp electrodes are usually only about 4 millimeters in diameter. These may be attached to the cleaned skin by the use of collodion or hard parafin wax. It is important that the electrodes remain fixed in position so that there is no undue change in the resistance of the contact to the skin. J. W. Prast accomplished measurements on moving subjects (pilots in flight) which were improved through the use of a small pre-amplifier strapped close to the head in order to minimize the degrading effect caused by the physical vibration of the leads.

Usually a low frequency amplifier is used, having its lower frequency limit at about one cycle per second. d-c amplifiers offer the advantage of additional information but impose the problem of recording the large drift of basal potential. This information is, of course, lost if a-c amplifiers are used.

Electrode placement is of critical importance with respect to the ensuing interpretation. Because of this, it is usually desirable to monitor the EEG as received from several electrodes simultaneously. This can be accomplished by using multichannel paper tape for recording. Such devices have a maximum frequency response up to 50 cycles per second. As many as 22 electrodes are sometimes used for EEG sensing. In the case of such a large number, W. G. Walter and G. Parr used a two-dimensional display of lights which were individually illuminated in correspondence to each of the electrode voltage signals. This brightness display device was called a "toposcope." Direct extension of this display concept to the cathode ray tube has allowed the monitoring of

EEG over the surface of the brain as the subject receives various experimental stimuli. Some day it may be possible to generalize this descrete display to an analog status which would offer new possibilities for both clinical and interpretative analysis.

Unfortunately, EEG interpretation is as yet an art. Specific diagnosis usually requires the presentation of additional evidence which bears upon the subject. R. H. Blum had the same EEG record given to five neurologists. Correlation among their interpretations was found to be poor. Only the consistent behavior of additional indices can furnish a valuable measure as to the status of the subject with respect to the imposed task. E. C. Lowenberg has used knowledge of the spectral aspects of the EEG to accomplish the synthesis of synthetic EEG's. Such an artificial signal may find utility in studying the statistical aspects of the EEG and for the objective comparative assessment of experimental EEG traces.

A number of experiments have attempted to correlate EEG with the emotional stress. These efforts have shown that there is probably no direct influence of emotional stress on EEG. Any observed change is more probably the result of mental activity resulting from the emotional experience. It was R. S. Schwab who reviewed and carefully described the applications and limitations of EEG.

The EEG has proven useful in the diagnosis of certain psychopathological disorders. In particular, there appears to be a distinct correlation for the identity of epilepsy and certain aspects of brain injury. Although a number of EEG studies have used sinusoidal spectral analysis, there appears to be no reason to believe that the brain function is best described in terms of the sine wave concept. Computer techniques have been explored in the search for patterns in the EEG. Reference is made to the work of B. G. Farley, et al. In particular, parameters were built upon the rhythmic burst recognition process. Mainly, the total activity was measured in bursts, the number of bursts per unit time, and other attributes. The accomplishment of suitable statistical measures on these parameters provides sufficient information to allow the identification of at least certain classes of individuals as taken from the human population. It was recognized that a great amount of additional information would be necessary to furnish anything of a "fingerprint" variety.

N. R. Burch has presented an excellent summary of the various techniques which have been explored for the analysis of EEG. He and others have investigated the use of the autocorrelation function, the time of occurrence of peak amplitude value as well as the zero crossings of the function and its derivative. These measures have been related to states of sleep, alertness, hypoxia, and the mental effects of certain drugs.

Recent work of M. Goldstein indicates a statistical model for interpreting neuro-electric responses which attempts to relate the statistical characteristics of the evoked responses to those of the neuro-elements that contribute to the response. The term "element" is not intended at the neuron level but rather as a gross property of nerve tissue. Indeed, L. Harmon has shown that the interpretation of some measured response of even a few modeled and interconnected neurons is inadequate to allow diagnosis of the particular physical interconnection. The important point here is that response alone remains inadequate for complete meaningful interpretation. Only with detailed knowledge of the stimulus (signal), the environment (noise), and the complete response of the organism can there be intelligent interpretation of the value of bioelectric variables as indicators.

13.5. THE MUSCLE RESPONSE

The electromyogram (EMG) is the result of sensing the electrical potential resulting from the stimulation of a muscle. The voltage sensed is in the order of 25 microvolts or more and thus requires good shielding in order to obtain a valid representation. It would certainly be desirable to operate with a noise level of less than one microvolt. In particular, the rapid polarity reversal of neurons causes spikes of voltage to appear, having harmonic components up to about 1,000 cycles per second. The greatest energy concentration in the EMG appears to lie at about 400 cycles per second with energy ranging down to a d-c potential. Effective EMG sensing should permit the recording of the spectrum between zero and at least 1,000 cycles per second. It is the composite result of this entire spectrum which reveals the tension or stress level which is of interest in biotechnology.

It has been shown by direct measurement that single motor units have a rest frequency of between 3 and 4 pulses per second. Even the thought of using the muscle which includes a specific unit will result in an increase in frequency for that unit to about ten pulses per second.

Two types of electrodes have been used. The needle type are placed under the skin, these being extensively used in early experiments on animals. For monophasic recording, one electrode is placed on neutral tissue. A varnish-coated needle is used with the varnish insulation removed only at the tip in order to sense at a particular point. A concentric needle is used for diphasic pickup, the outer tube forming one electrode and the inner rod forming the other. Insulation is provided between these two electrodes. Sensing occurs only at the embedded exposed tip.

The surface electrode is a flat metal disc which is placed in contact with the skin over the top of a muscle, being secured by adhesive tape. The skin should be clean and coated with a standard electrolyte paste. In the case of EMG, the size of the electrode determines the type of sensed data which is obtained. A large-area electrode can be used to sense total stress on the muscle. In contrast, a small diameter electrode of say 4 millimeters can be used for sensing the activity of particular small segments of the muscles. The resistance between diphasic electrodes should not be less than 2,000 ohms. Skin resistance may be overcome by pricking the skin to bring tissue fluid through the surface. The location of the electrode is of critical importance, and care must be exercised to assure against unwanted pickup of EEG, EKG, GSR, and other effects. One technique for eliminating the major portion of the spurious pickup is to monitor the unwanted signal technically, invert it, amplify, and mix this signal with the original signal at such a level so as to cancel out only the noise component. Reference is made to the literature for detailed discussion regarding the placement of electrodes and techniques for read-out Alternatively the subject can be placed in a rested state for a period of time before the experiment. Measurement of the resting potential should fall to 2 or 3 microvolts. If, at this low level, there are no signs of EKG or other intruding waveforms, then contamination may be said to be at an acceptable level.

The opposite practice of reporting the total sensed voltage is not devoid of merit. In general, bioelectric potentials show positive correlation. It might, therefore, be desirable to analyze some composite voltage as being more correlative with the stress level of the over-all subject. Much study remains to be accomplished in this direction.

Early experiments on the mechanism of voluntary motion depended upon the mechanical measurement of muscle activity. For example, in 1930, R. Dodge and R. C. Travis reported that below a critical level the thickening of a muscle was directly proportional to the force of the exerted pull. By 1932, bioelectric recording became available, and S. R. Hathaway showed a direct measure of the lag from the electrical prime stimulus of a muscle to the "first movement." The first large action potential of a forearm muscle was shown to arrive 0.058 seconds before the first movement of the forearm. This work was followed by that of B. K. Bagchi who demonstrated a latency decrease as movement is more rapid and latency increase for movement under load conditions. It was A. S. Householder who derived a functional relationship between the degree of muscle activity and other measurable parameters as these effect the amount of contraction. His analysis made the essential assumption of parallel muscle fibers acting under stress without movement conditions. Early in the research, it was recognized that the geometry of vector force relations must be considered in the analysis of muscle activity.

As such, the EMG proves to be a more reliable measure of the fatigue cost to the human operator than does the amount of physical work output. The holding of a weight at arms' extension accomplishes zero work in the physical sense (force times the distance moved). However, it is clearly evident that the human operator is rapidly becoming fatigued. Final verification of the proportionality of the EMG index to muscular force measurement has been made by V. T. Inman, et al., who recorded EMG potentials in cineplastic amputees while connecting the muscle directly with the strain gauge dynamometer.

The majority of human movements involve two or more muscles. There is the usual relationship of the flexor-extensor mechanism on opposite sides of a typical joint. Although these muscles can be called antagonistic, it must not be inferred that both muscles are always operational. The particular muscle action involved depends strongly upon the particular task involved. C. S. Sherrington suggested the antagonistic action as but one of the possible modes of operation, and his conjecture has been demonstrated to be true.

The many studies which have investigated the muscular relationship have made it obvious that least fatigue will be imposed on the human operator if he calls upon ballistic movements. Such movements take on dimensions related to the natural inertial properties of the mass. The design of tasks for human operation might take this into account. Reference is made to L. D. Hartson for a general description of the analysis of skilled motions and the consideration of ballistic trajectories in human movement. The EMG can be called upon as a design tool in order to monitor the amount of effort expended thus offering a measure of efficiency of the actual movements as these relate to optimal ballistic movement.

As an extension of this basic subject of investigation, it has been possible to analyze certain skills. For example, A. T. Slater-Hammel recorded EMG on a tennis player's forehand drive. It was found that various players have different personal patterns, but each player remains consistent in his own pattern. Further, the forehand drive was found to be largely non-ballistic. Dynamometer study indicated that continuous practice of one arm not only improved performance of that arm but also resulted in improved performance for the other arm. At first glance, this result appears to be rather surprising; however, it has been shown that the EMG provides collateral activity at remote parts of the body. One particular study showed that practically the whole body becomes involved when only a hand action is required. This interdependency of separate muscles was demonstrated as early as 1883 by E. Jendrassik in that the amplitude of the knee-jerk reflex developed greater amplitude when the subject clenched his fists. Various similar cooperative and inhibitive associations have been demonstrated.

In general, there is some best tone to the musculature in order to facilitate learning as well as performance. Furnishing the human operator with a subsidiary task, in order to induce the proper muscular tone, can aid performance of the assigned task. However, determination of the desired tone must include a quantitative measure of the amount of induced fatigue over the entire body. Caution must be emphasized since the value of tension with respect to efficiency of performance depends to a great extent on what it is that imposed the tension. Psychological factors cannot be neglected.

It has been possible to measure preparatory set in the musculature through the use of EMG. Even the passive thought of action has been shown to increase appropriate muscle tension, and, in fact, the muscles actually execute the desired action on a miniature scale. It was shown by A. A. Smith and H. Wallerstein that inner-verbal thought without lip motion can be sensed at the appropriate muscle. Such muscle response is termed "minetic."

It was K. J. W. Craig who suggested that a representation of the sensed real world environment is created in the brain, this being used to plan suitable response actions. According to this hypothesis, the brain continues to try out possible actions within the plan, forecasting their outcome. When one is found which appears to give a satisfactory result and does not conflict with any general rule of conduct, the action follows. It might be that "trying out" an action involves making tentative neural connections of all those which would be required to effect the task. Many of these connections will already exist since they belong to a series of muscular movements which have been previously learned. The brain has then only to select from its "repertory" a group of movements of which it can predict the usual result. This process increases the dependability of reponse and decreases the amount of specific data processing. The minetic actions might be the image of the mental exploration.

Muscle set is not a sudden "all or none" affair. Rather, it has been shown to gradually increase as time to go decreases. The accomplishment of set then prepares the muscle and results in a decrease in observed latency. The knowledge of "set" aids in self-monitoring and learning. The fact that interjection of some other task usually degrades performance of the original task may be explained upon a rationale of interference of set.

Even if the EMG is linearly related to muscular force, except for severely fatigued muscles, it does not follow that the EMG is linearly related to energy exchange. Just as there is some minimum consumption of oxygen as a function of walking speed, so it may be that there is a point of maximal efficiency at which maximum muscle energy output may be achieved at a minimum of cost in terms of fatigue. This field deserves quantitative study.

As early as 1892 J. Jastrow related mental work to muscular tensions. The EMG may be used to show peaks of muscular tension when difficulty is encountered in the mental task. Further, the probability of such surges is somewhat dependent upon the ability, aptitude, and motivation of a subject. It is important to know that the energy store is not a fixed quantity but is rather dependent upon the immediately previous history through the electro-chemical feedback system.

There are large individual differences among subjects with respect to their muscle tension during times of work and rest. Figure 13.10 indicates a set of EMG recordings as taken by A. Ford. The subjects were requested to do mental arithmetic while lying on their backs. In his words:

> The curve at the left, reading from left to right, shows the last few seconds of mental work. The horizontal line near the middle of the oscillogram shows where the apparatus was stopped while the worker gave his answer. The section of the curve at the right is the rest period when the worker was told to relax. In Example A it is obvious that the worker did not relax at all whereas Example B shows a case of partial relaxation. In Example C it is clear that the worker was under severe work tension, but when opportunity for rest was given, his

relaxation was complete, and dropped the EMG potential to less than 3 microvolts. Example D found a worker who could do mental arithmetic with practically no tension at any time.

E. Jacobson accomplished pioneering work on the cultivation of relaxation. Subjects were trained to relax through the use of a feedback signal which offered an indication of their tension level. It was found possible for subjects to reduce their level of tension down to levels of below 2 microvolts. Even difficult subjects achieved notable progress.

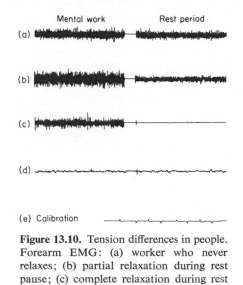

Figure 13.10. Tension differences in people. Forearm EMG: (a) worker who never relaxes; (b) partial relaxation during rest pause; (c) complete relaxation during rest pause; (d) a worker without tension; (e) 5 microvolt calibration signal.

It is usual to find both an increase in speed of work and increase in EMG activity level toward the end of a constantly difficult mental task. A. K. Bartoshuk has shown that this EMG gradient is not the result of the increased speed. It is interesting to hypothesize that the gradient might reflect the motivation of the worker.

The human operator will find peaks of difficulty and encounter points of mental stress as he tackles an assigned task. Knowledge of these increased stress points might make it possible to achieve optimal task design. Further, an EMG measure might prove helpful for the desired numerical assessment with respect to the particular level of skilled performance. Upon this basis, it should be possible to scale the difficulty to the available level of skill and redesign the task in order to smooth out points of severe difficulty. Such redesign should increase the performance level and facilitate learning, adaptation, and habituation of the worker to the climate of his assignment.

In a simple decision situation where the human operator is to determine whether to accomplish a particular action or not, it has been found that the preparatory EMG tension focuses sharply on those muscles related to the action. The more pronounced the resulting EMG tension prior to the decision, the more quickly will be the response as the decision is reached.

The investigations of signal detection in noise pose such questions such as: "Was there a signal?," "Is the signal getting stronger or weaker?," and so on. Einstellung originally performed an experiment in which the subject lifted two weights successfully. The first of these was called the "standard," while the second one was called the "variable." A decision had to be reached as to whether the second weight was heavier or lighter than the standard. The hypothesis was that there was a "trace" left by the first weight (in the mind of the subject), such that it could be used for comparison with the second weight. This trace has been called the Einstellung or mental set preparatory for judgment as the second stimulus arrives.

In view of the fact that no evidence could be presented as to where this trace resided, it was necessary to modify the hypothesis. In 1940, experiments by G. L. Freeman and R. B. Payne showed that when EMG potentials are recorded from the members doing the lifting (in this case the right hand and arm), the lifting and release of the first weight is followed by a cyclical and gradually dropping EMG potential from the arm which has done the lifting. After 4 seconds, this after-potential was still higher than that of the resting potential. If the second weight was presented at this time, there was a preponderance of judgments that it was "lighter." If, however, the second weight was presented 8 seconds or more later, the EMG potential had subsided to a level lower than that of the resting state, and there resulted a shift to "heavier." In a similar manner, R. B. Payne and R. C. Davis demonstrated that high EMG tensions were followed by more frequent "lighter" judgments and low tensions by more frequent "heavier" responses. Evidently the muscle tension formed a distinct bias on the decision-making. The trace of the first weight may have remained in the muscle rather than the mind. Similar experiments were performed in psychoacoustics with the subject requested to judge relative loudness using two tonal signals and arm EMG potentials when right and left keys were pressed to indicate "stronger" or "weaker." Once again the EMG after-affect was demonstrated at least to a partial degree.

Further experiments were carried out by W. A. Livingston who compared simple and multiple reactions. The result suggested that the pattern of EMG potentials governs both the speed and the accuracy of the human operator decision-making in any task where stimuli ought to be compared successively Absolute levels of tension vary greatly as do other individual differences.

As a natural extension of this work, it was possible for R. C. Travis and J. L. Kennedy to devise an "alertness indicator" wherein two small active electrodes and the ground electrode were placed in contact with the skin by a headband around the forehead. Experimental data verified the relation of preparatory set to resulting action time. Gain control was provided directly to the subject in order to normalize-out individual differences. Practical performance in terms of measured readiness for decision was demonstrated.

EMG can also be shown to be correlated with emotional stress. Further, its sensitivity to the emotional personality structure provides a means of separating normal from psychoneurotic patients. R. B. Malmo, *et al.*, presented a loud sharp tone of 3-second duration every 90 seconds to a mixed audience of normal and mentally disturbed subjects. He found that the initial tensional response in less than 0.2 seconds was approximately equal in both groups. However, the normals returned rapidly to the pre-existing tension level, while the patients showed further augmentation of response. This demonstrated emotional instability and proved to be a valid measure for discriminating between these two classes of subjects.

To summarize, it is the EMG which provides insight as to the physical activities involved in the accomplishment of the particular assigned task. The EMG can show the level of muscular stress for each individual muscle which is being used by the human operator. This indicator variable is related to the distribution of force, energy output, and mental step or preparation for a response. In general, it reflects emotional and mental stress factors.

13.6. OTHER BODY RESPONSES

It is possible to monitor the horizontal and vertical movement of the eyes through the use of small electrodes held against the skin at points near to the eyes. This is possible since there is a constant polarity difference between the front of the eye (positive) and the back of the eye (negative). It was W. O. Feen and J. B. Hursh who related the corneal-retinal potentials to the amount of rotational movement of the eye.

Positioning of the electrodes is critical, and it has also been found necessary to employ chlorided silver electrodes and an electrode paste in order to avoid polarization difficulties. It is probably best to determine the desired optimal positions by trial and error calibration and then utilize a plastic mask with embedded electrodes so as to position the pickups accurately during further experiments. The human eye exhibits a distinct potential gradient and thus offers a d-c for amplification. It is almost impossible to prevent incurring EMG potentials related to eyelid blink and the activation of other nearby muscles. These, however, can be easily recognized in the record.

The electrical potential of the human retina can be measured through the use of a corneal contact lens. A small piece of silver is embedded in the edge of the lens forming the active electrode for the electroretinogram (ERG). A very fine wire lead through this electrode is placed in such a way as not to disturb the plastic lens. The reference voltage is taken from any neutral region of the head with care exercised to avoid other bioelectric potentials. The purpose of ERG is the measurement of the response of the retina to light conditions and is thus only useful for the monitoring of certain visual tasks. The motion of the subject is severely restricted.

Skin temperature is a function of the state of capillary constriction-dilation, since this condition directly relates to the transmission of heat from the blood. There is also a significant amount of heat released through cell metabolism, and both of these effects must be considered in the analysis of temperature information. As would be expected, it is usual to find that temperature is a slowly changing variable.

As yet, little is known with certainty regarding the use of skin temperature as a direct indicator. Early work by H. Helson, *et al.*, in 1934, explored the temperature effects of surprise stimuli such as a dash of cold water on the head, loud hammer pounding, anticipation of electrical shock, slapping the face, or getting kissed. It was reported that reliable skin temperature changes occur, some being as high as 4° F. However, the authors stated

> The presence or absence of emotional states cannot be inferred from a temperature response although there is a tendency for large changes to be accompanied by reportable internal changes.

It was their recognition that there may be other causes for changes of skin temperature which are not direct indicators of emotional status.

The ease with which skin temperature can be measured makes it a readily available biological indicator. The use of light-weight thermistors can provide temperature data with a precision of 0.01° F. It must be remembered, however, that temperature is a point function on the surface of the body. Conclusive results might require the monitoring of a large portion of the body surface area in order to provide sufficient indicative data. Further work is required before this variable may prove of consistent value in the monitoring of design efficiency of assigned human tasks.

The rate of breathing may be directly influenced by the emotional state of the subject. The normal respiration rate is about 16 inspirations per minute for the resting individual. Individual differences are found to range from about 12 to 20. The ratio of the inspiration period to the expiration period appears to be a significant indicator of mental work stress level. The number of inspirations per minute also furnishes a general index for the physical stress experienced by the human operator.

Modern measuring techniques include the use of a strain gage placed on a strap around the chest. Breathing may be more accurately and completely monitored by an array of strain gages placed directly in the air-flow within a face mask. Stainless steel cantilever arms are placed so as to flex in one direction during inhalation and in the opposite direction during exhalation. The strain gage wires are connected to these arms and thus change resistance in accord with the displacement. The sensor is placed in a bridge circuit with separate calibration resistors for inhalation and exhalation. Frequency responses of the sensor is essentially constant from d-c up to about 100 cycles per second. Linearity of read-out is better than 1 per cent over a range of 2.5 liters.

Blood pressure forms a well-known index of effort and stress. It is normally measured through the use of a rubber cuff which is strapped around the arm just above the elbow. This cuff is inflated and monitored through a pressure gage (usually in terms of a column of mercury measured in millimeters of height). A stethescope is used to monitor the radial artery just below the elbow. The minimum pressure which eliminates the sound of the pulse beat is called the systolic pressure value. As the pressure is released, the pulse will return. The minimum pressure which will allow "normal" pulse is called the diastolic pressure. Obviously, considerable experience is required for the proper interpretation of the pulse sound and achieving precise measurements.

The traditional technique of examining the blood pressure at a single time is severely limiting and affords too little information for the successful monitoring of the human as he performs a continual operation. A more modern technique has been explored by C. W. Darrow who used two cuffs with different degrees of inflation, one for systolic and the other for diastolic pressure. It would be prohibitive to maintain cuff pressure for any length of time, and so a periodic technique was developed for automatically taking measurements every 20 seconds. A microphone placed on the wrist provides a pulse record. A strain gage is placed on the cuff in order to allow the recording of pressure. Still and all, this equipment is cumbersome and restrictive to the subject.

The oxyhemogram, as measured by an oximeter, furnishes an index for the amount of oxygen carried by the blood. The instrument measures the light absorption characteristic of the red corpuscles within the blood. This is accomplished by placing a small incandescent lamp on one side of the ear lobe and monitoring photocells on the opposite side in order to measure the intensity of light which passes through the pinna and a red filter. The photocell output voltage is fed through an amplifier to allow recording in comparison to the calibrated voltage level of the pressed ear lobe (which contains a minimum of blood). It is not required that the oximeter have a time constant of less than about $\frac{1}{2}$ second since this would be rapid enough to record changes in the oxygen saturation level as quickly as these could ordinarily appear in the vascular bed which is being monitored. Measurement accuracies have been reported in terms of a standard deviation of ± 2 per cent of that level which would be attained if the subject had breathed pure oxygen for a considerable time.

A composite body measure is obtained by the pletheysmograph which records the resistance of a segment of the body, such as the finger. In this case, the measured value is a complex function of the enclosed blood volume, the dilation of the vascular membranes, blood pressure, as well as the GSR.

Many other biological parameters are susceptible to measurement. For example, the digestive movements of the stomach and peristalsis of the

intestines can be measured through the use of a capsule magnet which acti-
vates an external magnetometer. The flow of saliva in the mouth has been
shown to respond to changes in work stress. There is also the possibility of
using certain biochemical indices as measures of stress; however, these
require overcoming more serious difficulties in instrumentation and usually
make it necessary to disturb the subject from his normal assigned task.

13.7. THE CORRELATIVE INTERPRETATION
OF RESPONSES

It was probably Francis Galton (1880) who first carried out experimental
attempts to classify the types of mental imagery. Since then, there have been
a number of interesting and related findings. For example, in 1910, C. W.
Parky showed that there is no clear division between actual seeing and visualizing. He asked subjects to project on a screen a visual image of a banana. At
the same time, he threw a faint picture of a banana on the screen, increasing
its intensity until subjects said they had a good image. The striking confusion
of the mental image and the observed image indicated that there may be
some common physiological mechanism to account for both.

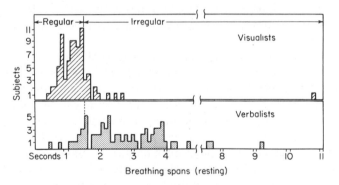

Figure 13.11. Histogram plotting regularity and irregularity of
breathing for all subjects, classed as Visualist or Verbalist from
subjective reports. Horizontal baseline shows the breathing spans
from 0.5 seconds to 10.8 seconds. The number of subjects for each
span (in steps of 0.1 seconds) is plotted vertically.

Since then, many more sophisticated experiments have been performed,
and the advent of bioelectronics has made it possible to identify two primary
modes of imagery: visual and verbal. Figure 13.11 indicates the classification
of subjects as related to the statistical distribution of breathing span (that
time interval between successive breaths). It would appear that the verbalists
tended to breath as if they were speaking their throughts, while the visualists
did not. The data may result from the minetic correlate of the thought process.

The normal breathing habits of the 100 subjects were studied while in a resting state, and a highly significant statistical difference was found between verbalists and visualists.

The EEG was applied as a diagnostic tool using the appearance of the alpha rhythm as an indicator of the lack of a visual-type image. Individual subjects EEG's were studied, and it was shown that the odds against the improper association of alpha rhythm and imagery was more than 10,000 to 1. As a result of the correlation of breathing and EEG data, subjects were placed

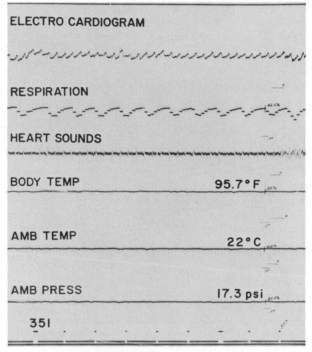

ELECTRO CARDIOGRAM

RESPIRATION

HEART SOUNDS

BODY TEMP   95.7° F

AMB TEMP   22° C

AMB PRESS   17.3 psi

351

Figure 13.12. Composite data record.

into two main categories, visual and verbal. Those subjects which were alpha rhythm "responsive" showed a clearly recognizable predominance of visual over verbal images. The visualists tend always to breath regularly and their alpha rhythms, where present, block whenever they are busy with mental tasks. The verbalists tend to breath irregularly and their alpha rhythms tend to persist whether they are thinking through problems or not. There are, of course, other modes of imagery (including the kinaesthetic). It is not expected to find normal subjects where any of these predominate.

Probably the best known use of multiple response interpretation is for the purpose of lie detection. The polygraph uses the primary GSR response but adds other related variables to allow more complete coverage of the subject and presumably a resulting increase in the validity of interpretation. These data include the respiration variable, the oxygen content of the blood, the pulse intensity, rate, and velocity as measured by comparing the pulse time of arrival at the arm and finger. The polygraph must be used with considerable technique in order to gain maximum utility and guard against loss of information, or even worse, misinterpretation. Generally, an experienced operator can successfully interpret the polygraph on about 90 per cent of the subjects. The same instrument can be used even more effectively if attention is turned upon the subject's knowledge of information related to guilt rather than the direct detection of deception.

Proper interpretation of a set of body response parameters requires additional knowledge of the environmental conditions which prevail during the time of measurement. For example, Figure 13.12 indicates a portion of the graphic record taken on an animal during a rocket flight. The ambient temperature and pressure provide necessary information to allow correlative interpretation of the available body parameters. Often, the number of environmental parameters which can be sensed, transmitted, and recorded is limited by space and weight constraints. In general, however, consideration should be given to the sensing of environmental parameters within the suggested range and accuracy as indicated in Table 13.1.

Table 13.1. PARAMETERS FOR ENVIRONMENTAL MONITORING

Environmental Parameter	Range	Accuracy
3 axes acceleration	0–10 g	5%
Vibration	0–5 g	5%
Noise	140 db	5%
Radiation rate	0–12 rem	5%
Air temperature	0–250° F	3° F
Humidity	20–90%	5%
O_2 reserve	0–3,000 psia	1%
O_2 flow rate	2–12 cft/min	5%
CO_2 partial pressure	0–20 mm Hg	5%
CO_2 filter status	0–100%	10%
Cabin pressure	0–15 psia	1%
Suit pressure	0–15 psia	1%

If possible, it might prove desirable to record aspects of the assigned task performance on the same record in order to provide a more complete description of human transduction. Specifics on these parameters are discussed in Chapter 12.

13.8. CONCLUSION

This chapter presents only a brief survey of some of the techniques available for the extraction of information from the functioning human operator.

There are many other instruments which find specific application in medicine and biology. The discussion has considered only those which are considered to be of direct interest to the man-machine relation. It is hoped that these introductory remarks will furnish a guide to the wealth of references which must be reviewed in order to appreciate fully the many details and intricasies of biological sensing. Further, it is only through extensive practical experience with such devices that it is possible to attain a full understanding of both their capabilities and limitations.

A number of distinct purposes can be approached upon the basis of biological data taken from the functioning human operator. In particular, it is of distinct value to learn the cost of the accomplished performance in terms of both physical and mental fatigue. Such information provides a basis for the optimal allocation of tasks and the design of proper equipment for direct use.

A more subtle purpose lies in furnishing the human operator with some immediate feedback which he can use to benefit his performance in the near future. The provision for such feedback facilitates learning and permits the correction of certain errors before they become of sufficient magnitude to affect system performance seriously. Here is a technique to close the loop and attain very "tight" control.

The human operator is often called a black box. The unknown operational aspects are recognized to be orders of magnitude more efficient in the processing of information than those equipments which have, as yet, resulted from human design. This fact becomes enormously apparent when transduction must occur under the imposed uncertainties, complexities, and difficulties of real situations and environment. It is hoped that the taking of internal measures may provide some insight into techniques through which this biological efficiency is achieved and, as a result, make possible the design of displays and controls of greater compatibility and automata which can be used to remove a major portion of the burden from human shoulders.

There appears to be a natural inclination toward the construction of an "equivalent circuit," that is, some mathematical model which could account for the measured data. The first step toward such a model usually consists of examining the statistical correlation among the various measures. This practice is founded upon the tacit assumption that the coding of these artifacts of human performance is the same (usually correlation is taken on the occurrence of amplitude pulses, and so on). It might easily be that each of these variables may have some different coding as related to their basic information content as it pertains to body operation. Such coding could include frequency, pulse repetition rate, wave shape, phase, and so on. It might even include codes which are as yet completely unknown. Only after the coding of two variables is known, or at least surmised, is it possible to approach the determination of any meaningful correlation of the basic information.

Further, it is possible to construct an infinitude of different models which will all satisfy the same correlation or other input-output measure. *Is it possible to determine exactly which model is most like the operation of the human body?*

Scientific inquiry places a premium upon learning the nature of the "human machine." Man may never rest in his endeavor to understand himself.

BIBLIOGRAPHY

ADAMS, J. A., "Effect of Experimentally Induced Muscular Tension on Psychomotor Performance," *Journal of Experimental Psychology*, Vol. 48 (1954), 127–130.

ADRIAN, E. D., *The Mechanism of Nervous Action*. Philadelphia: University of Pennsylvania Press, 1932.

ARMSTRONG, C. R., "Space Physiology," *Journal of the British Interplanetary Society*, Vol. 12 (1953), 172–175.

BAKER, L. M., and W. M. TAYLOR, "The Relationship Under Stress Between Changes in Skin Temperature, Electrical Skin Resistance, and Pulse Rate," *Journal of Experimental Psychology*, Vol. 48 (1954), 361–366.

BARLOW, J. S., and R. M. BROWN, *An Analog Correlator System for Brain Potentials*, Research Laboratory of Electronics TR 300, Cambridge, Mass.: Massachusetts Institute of Technology, July 14, 1955.

BENDAT, J. S., "Interpretation and Application of Statistical Analysis for Random Physical Phenomena," *IRE Transactions on Bio-Medical Electronics*, Vol. BME–9 No. 1 (January 1962), 31–43.

BILLS, A. G., "Fatigue, Oscillation and Blocks," *Journal of Experimental Psychology*, Vol. 18 (1935), 562–573.

"Blood Flowmeters Symposium," *IRE Transactions on Medical Electronics*, Vol. ME–6 No. 4 (December 1959).

BLUM, R. H., "A Note on the Reliability of EEG Judgments," *Neurology*, Vol. 4 (1954), 143–146.

BOSMA, J. F., and E. GELLHORN, "Electromyographic Studies of Muscular Coordination on Stimulation of Motor Cortex," *Journal of Neurophysiology*, Vol. 9 (1946), 263–274.

BOUSFIELD, W. A., "The Influence of Fatigue on Tremor," *Journal of Experimental Psychology*, Vol. 15 (1932), 104–107.

BROWN, C. H., "The Relation of the Magnitude of the Galvanic Skin Response and Resistance Levels to Rate of Learning," *Journal of Experimental Psychology*, Vol. 20 (1937), 262–277.

BURCH, N. R., and T. H. GREINER, "A Bioelectric Scale of Human Alertness: Concurrent Recordings of the EEG and GSR," *Psychiatric Research Reports Vol. 12, American Psychiatric Association* (January 1960), 183–193.

BURCH, N. R., "Automatic Analysis of the Electroencephalogram: A Review and Classification of Systems," *Electroencephalography and Clinical Neurophysiology Journal*, Vol. 11 No. 4 (November 1959), 827–837.

BURIAN, H. M., "Electrical Responses of the Human Visual System," *American Medical Association Archives of Ophthalmology*, Vol. 51 (1954), 509–524.

BURNS, B. D., "The Respiration-Expiration Ratio During Truth and Falsehood," *Journal of Experimental Psychology*, Vol. 4 (1921), 1–23.

BUTLER, J. A. V., "Pictures in the Mind," *Science News*, Vol. 22, Penguin Books (November 1951), 26–34.

CAMPBELL, P. A., "Medical Aspects of Flight Above the Atmosphere," *Journal of the American Medical Association*, Vol. 150 (1952), 3–6.

CHANG, H. T., T. C. RUCH, and A. A. WARD, JR., "Topographical Representation of Muscles in Motor Cortex of Monkeys," *Journal of Neurophysiology*, Vol. 10 (1947), 39–56.

CLARK, G., and J. W. WARD, "Responses Elicited from the Cortex of Monkeys by Electrical Stimulation Through Fixed Electrodes," *Brain*, Vol. 71 (1948), 332–342.

CLAUSEN, J., A. URDAL, and A. GJESVIK, "Relation Between the Sensitivity for Electrical Stimuli and Adaptation State of the Eye," *Journal of General Psychology*, Vol. 51 (1954), 251–259.

COHN, R., *Electroencephalography*. New York: McGraw-Hill Book Company, Inc., 1949.

CONKLIN, J. E., "Three Factors Affecting the General Level of Electrical Skin Resistance," *American Journal of Psychology*, Vol. 64 (1951), 78–86.

DARROW, C. W., "Sensory, Secretory and Electrical Changes in the Skin Following Bodily Excitation," *Journal of Experimental Psychology*, Vol. 10 (1927), 197–226.

———. "The Electroencephalogram and Psychophysiological Regulation in the Brain," *American Journal of Psychiatry*, Vol. 102 (1946), 791–798.

DARROW, C. W., J. R. GREEN, E. W. DAVIS, and H. W. GAROL, "Parasympathetic Regulation of High Potential in the Electroencephalogram," *Journal of Neurophysiology*, Vol. 7 (1944), 217–226.

DARROW, C. W., J. PATHMAN, and G. KRONENBERG, "Level of Autonomic Activity and Electroencephalogram," *Journal of Experimental Psychology*, Vol. 36 No. 4 (August 1946), 355–365.

DAVIS, F. H., and R. B. MALMO, "Electromyographic Recording During Interview," *American Journal of Psychiatry*, Vol. 107 (1951), 908–916.

DAVIS, H., "Biologic Transducers," *Federation Proceedings*, Vol. 12 (1953), 661–665.

DUSSER DE BARENNE, J. G., H. W. GAROL, and W. S. McCULLOCH, "The 'Motor' Cortex of the Chimpanzee," *Journal of Neurophysiology*, Vol. 4 (1941), 287–303.

ELLINGSON, R. J., "Brain Waves and the Problems of Psychology," *Psychological Bulletin*, Vol. 53 (1956), 1–34.

ELLIOTT, D. N., and E. G. SINGER, "The Paintal Index as an Indicator of Skin-Resistance Changes to Emotional Stimuli," *Journal of Experimental Psychology*, Vol. 45 (1953), 429–430.

FARLEY, B. G., L. S. FRISHKOPF, W. A. CLARK, JR., and J. T. GILMORE, JR., "Computer Techniques for the Study of Patterns in the Electroencephalogram," *Lincoln Laboratory TR 165* (November 6, 1957).

FENNO, R. M., "Man's Milieu in Space; a Summary of the Physiologic Requirements of Man in a Sealed Cabin," *Journal of Aviation Medicine*, Vol. 25 (1954), 612–622.

FERE, C., "Note sur les Modifications de la Resistance Electrique sous l'Influence des Excitations Sensorielles et des Emotions," *Comptes Rendus des Seances de la Societe de Biologie*, Vol. 40 (1888), 217.

FINK, B. R., and M. L. SCHEINER, "The Computation of Muscle Activity from the Integrated Electromyogram," *IRE Transactions on Medical Electronics*, Vol. ME–6 No. 3 (September 1959), 119–120.

FORBES, A., "A Critique of Frequency Analysis in Neurophysiology," *Journal of Electroencephalography and Clinical Neurophysiology*, Vol. 2 (1950), 204.

———. "Localization of Muscle Tone During Severe Mental Effort," *American Psychologist*, Vol. 9 (1954), 369.

FORD, A., "Foundations of Bioelectronics for Human Engineering," USN Electronics Laboratory, San Diego, Calif., *Research Report 761* (April 4, 1957).

FRANK, L. K., G. E. HUTCHINSON, W. K. LIVINGSTON, W. S. McCULLOCH, and N. WIENER, "Teleological Mechanisms," *Annals of the New York Academy of Sciences*, Vol. 50 (1948), 187–277.

FREEMAN, G. L., *Physiological Psychology*. New York: D. Van Nostrand Company, Inc., 1948.

GELDREICH, E. W., "Skin Conductance Changes Occurring During Mental Fatigue and Anoxemia," *Transactions of the Kansas Academy of Science*, Vol. 43 (1940), 343–344.

GIBBS, F. A., and E. L. GIBBS, *Atlas of Electroencephalography*, Vol. 1. Cambridge: Addison-Wesley Press, 1950.

GOLDSTEIN, M. H., JR., "A Statistical Model for Interpreting Neuroelectric Responses," *Information and Control*, Vol. 3 No. 1 (March 1960), 1–17.

HENRY, C. E., and C. W. DARROW, "EEG Relationships to Five Autonomic Variables," *American Psychologist*, Vol. 2 (1947), 421.

HILL, H. E., *A Review of Muscle Activity and Action Potentials as They Are Related to Movement*, Report No. 5, Contract W33–038–ac–13968, USAF Contract with Indiana University (May 1947).

HINES, M., "The 'Motor Cortex'," *Johns Hopkins Hospital Bulletin*, Vol. 60 (1937), 313–366.

HITCHCOCK, F. A., "Some Considerations in Regard to the Physiology of Space Flight," *Astronautica Acta*, Vol. 2 (1956), 20–24.

HOAGLAND, H., "Rhythmic Behavior of the Nervous System," *Science*, Vol. 109 (February 18, 1949), 157–165.

HUSSMAN, T. A., and R. C. HACKMAN, "The Relationship Between Psychogalvanic Activity and Pilot Performance Under Simulated Instrument Flying Conditions," *USN Medical Research Institute, Bethesda, Md., Research Report Project NM 001 056.08.02*, Vol. 13 (September 26, 1955), 581–620.

INMAN, V. T., H. J. RALSTON, J. B. SAUNDERS, B. FEINSTEIN, and E. W. WRIGHT, "Relation of the Human EMG to Muscular Tension," *Electroencephalography and Clinical Neurophysiology Journal*, Vol. 4 (1952), 187–204.

JEFFRESS, L. A., "Galvanic Phenomena of the Skin," *Journal of Experimental Psychology*, Vol. 11 (1928), 130–144.

JENDRASSIK, E., *Beitrage zur Lehre von den Schnenreflexen*, Deutsches Arch. f. klin. Med., Bd. 33, s. 177 (1883).

KLEIN, S. J., "The Summation of Muscle Tensions Due to Stress," *American Psychologist*, Vol. 10 (1955), 451.

KNOTT, J. R., F. A. GIBBS, and C. E. HENRY, "Fourier Transforms of the Electroencephalogram During Sleep," *Journal of Experimental Psychology*, Vol. 31 (1942), 465–477.

KRENDEL, E. S., "The Analysis of Electroencephalograms by the Use of a Cross-Spectrum Analyzer," *IRE Transactions on Medical Electronics*, Vol. ME–6 No. 3 (September 1959), 149–156.

LOWENBERG, E. C., "An Experimental EEG Function Generator," *Electroencephalography and Clinical Neurophysiology Journal*, Vol. 11 No. 2 (May 1959), 355–357.

LYKKEN, D. T., "The GSR in the Detection of Guilt," *Journal of Applied Psychology*, Vol. 43 No. 6 (December 1959), 385–389.

MACKAY, R. S., "Radio Telemetering From Within the Human Body," *IRE Transactions on Medical Electronics*, Vol. ME–6 No. 2 (June 1959), 100–105.

MARTINEK, J., G. C. K. YEH, and R. CARNINE, "A New System for Electrocardiographic Recording, Analysis, and Diagnosis," *IRE Transactions on Medical Electronics*, Vol. ME–6 No. 3 (September 1959), 112–115.

McCULLOCH, W. S., "Models of Functional Organization of the Cerebral Cortex," *Federation Proceedings of the American Society of Experimental Biology*, Vol. 6 (1947), 448–452.

McGUIRE, T. F., "The Normal Human EKG and its Common Variations in Experimental Situations," *USAF WADC TR 56–309* (June 1956).

NIELSEN, F. E., S. P. W. BLACK, and G. G. DRAKE, "Inhibition and Facilitation of Motor Activity by the Anterior Cerebellum," *Federation Proceedings of the American Society of Experimental Biology*, Vol. 7 (1948), 86.

PAUL, W., "An Oximeter for Continuous Absolute Estimation of Oxygen Saturation," *Journal of Scientific Instruments*, Vol. 30 (May 1953), 165–168.

———. "Oximetry," *IRE Transactions on Medical Electronics*, Vol. PGME–11 (July 1958), 34–37.

RHINES, R., and H. W. MAGOUN, "Brain Stem Facilitation of Cortical Motor Responses," *Journal of Neurophysiology*, Vol. 9 (1946), 219–229.

ROSENBLUETH, A., N. WIENER, and J. BIGELOW, "Behavior, Purpose, and Teleology," *Philosophy of Science*, Vol. 10 (1943), 18–24.

ROY, O. Z., "An Electronic Heartbeat Simulator and a Cardiac Tachometer," *IRE Transactions on Medical Electronics*, Vol. PGME–11 (July 1958), 48–52.

SALTZBERG, B., and N. R. BURCH, "A New Approach to Signal Analysis in Electroencephalography," *IRE Transactions on Medical Electronics*, Vol. PGEM–8 (July 1957), 24–30.

SCHMITT, O. H., and E. SIMONSON, "The Present Status of Vectorcardiography," *American Medical Association Archives of Internal Medicine*, Vol. 96 (November 1955), 574–590.

SCHWAB, R. S., "Applications and Limitations of the Electroencephalograph," *Archives of Neurological Psychiatry*, Vol. 62 (1949), 510–511.

SHERRINGTON, C. S., "Further Experimental Note on the Correlation of Action of Antagonistic Muscles," *Proceedings of the Royal Society of London*, Series B53 (1893), 407–420.

SHORT, P. L., "The Measurement of Mental Images," from *Science News*, Vol. 24, Penguin Books (May 1952), 7–21.

SIMONSON, E., O. H. SCHMITT, and R. B. LEVINE, "Comparison of Spatial Instantaneous ECG Vectors, Measured with SVEC, with Mean Vectors Derived from Conventional ECG Leads," *Circulation Research*, Vol. III No. 4 (July 1955), 320–329.

STEINBERG, I. I., "Medical Electronics—Black Bag in Space," *Astronautics*, Vol. 4 No. 6 (June 1959), 26–27.

TRANK, J. W., and O. H. SCHMITT, "Polar Cardioscope," *The Review of Scientific Instruments*, Vol. 25 No. 9 (September 1954), 918–920.

STRUGHOLD, H., "Medical Problems Involved on Orbital Space Flight," *Jet Propulsion*, Vol. 26 (1956), 745–748, 756, 788.

———. "Mechanoreceptors, Gravireceptors," *Journal of Astronautics*, Vol. 4 (1957), 61–63.

WALLACE, J. D., *et al.*, "Intracardiac Acoustics," *Journal of the Acoustical Society of America*, Vol. 31 No. 6 (June 1959), 712–724.

WEISS, H. H., "The Physiology of Simple Tumbling. Part 2. Human Studies," *USAF WADC TR 53–139* (January 1954).

WELCH, W. K., and M. A. KENNARD, "Relation of Cerebral Cortex to Spasticity and Flaccidity," *Journal of Neurophysiology*, Vol. 7 (1944), 255–268.

WOOLSEY, C. N., "Representation in the Motor Cortex of Flexor and Extensor Muscles of the Leg," *American Journal of Physiology*, Vol. 123 (1938), 221–222.

EPILOGUE

Mankind becomes increasingly dependent upon technology. The many conveniences of life are taken for granted, allowing yesterday's luxuries to become today's necessities. This is exemplified by the transition of radio which was first a toy, then an entertainment, and now it provides, among other things, the communication system which permits safety of air travel. The automobile developed from being a curiosity to a means for mass transportation, by virtue of which populated areas have greatly expanded. The result is outlying communities which would be isolated if it were not for the always-available automobile. The list of items is unending, all proving the same point—life in this modern civilization is wrapped around the technological growth thus far attained. It would be difficult for the typical civilian to survive if he were suddenly placed in a jungle environment. He has developed an essential need for modern tools.

It is widely recognized that technological growth increases in an exponential manner. Life in the next century may become so highly integrated with technology that separation from it would result in almost immediate death. The technology, which was initially developed as a benefit, may well become a "monster" which subjugates the population. This danger becomes even more apparent when it is realized that the direction of technological progress is no longer under the control of the scientific investigator. Today, research efforts are directed toward "man in space." What he finds there will dictate what the next subject for investigation *must* be. It is international competition which places the emphasis on the word "must." It is evident that the direction of future research is primarily dictated by nature itself and not by the investigator.

Throughout history, man has been faced with the problem of survival. Thus far, this battle has been won only through continual effort; however, in the winning, man has taken to himself tools which have now become an inherent part of his capability. These tools comprise the technology which opens a new world of threat to his very existence . . . a threat which is a composite of his dependence on the tools coupled with an environment which changes more and more rapidly through the use of these tools. Man has adapted to the natural environment through extension of his own capabilities. The advantage gained by this specialization carries with it the cost of less flexibility with respect to severe changes of the environment which may result from the very existence of these tools.

This threat is compounded through the misuse of technology. Mankind should certainly learn to properly handle the devices through which he communicates with nature. But the application of biotechnology may not be sufficient. Groups of men often behave as entities which are almost independent of the individuals which comprise the group. Structures of men or active machines display properties of hedonistic homeostasis. Current research encourages this development through exploration in the field of information processing and artificial intelligence. Only the intelligent use of machines can preclude the intelligent use of man by machines.

NAME INDEX

A

Aborn, M. 378
Ackerman, W. 58
Ackoff, R. L. 318, 783, 789
Adams, J. A. 265, 378, 454
Adams, O. S. 108, 701, 712
Adler, H. E. 637
Adrian, E. D. 177, 189, 378, 454
Aikman, L. 383
Alexander, H. S. 591
Alexander, L. T. 423
Alexander, M. 533
Allison, V. C. 188, 189
Alluisi, E. A. 108, 379
Alpern, M. 110
Alport, F. H. 62
Altman, J. W. 715
Ames, A. Jr. 106
Ammons, R. B. 418
Anderson, N. 110
Anderson, A. B. 177
Anderson, G. W. 266
Anderson, L. K. 421
Anderson, M. J. 642
Anderson, N. H. 266, 418
Andreas, B. G. 266, 418, 421
Andrew, A. M. 108
Andrew, G. M. 266
Andrews, H. L. 591
Andrews, T. G. 271, 425, 788
Angrist, S. E. 682
Arai, T. 702
Arbuckle, T. 317
Archer, E. J. 108, 266
Archibald, E. R. 596
Arden, G. B. 108

Arey, L. B. 189
Arginteanu, J. 419, 645
Armington, J. C. 108, 215
Armstrong, C. R. 454
Armstrong, H. G. 462, 591
Armstrong, R. C. 546
Arnoff, E. L. 318, 783, 789
Arrow, K. J. 317
Asch, S. E. 165
Aseltine, J. A. 266
Ashby, W. R. 317
Atkinson, J. W. 369
Attneave, F. 108, 200, 210, 378
Aubert, X. 395
Austin, G. A. 379
Austin, T. R. 178
Averbach, E. 641, 643
Ax, A. F. 210
Azima, F. J. 210
Azima, H. 210

B

Babbage, C. 280
Badawy, Y. K. M. 111
Bagchi, B. K. 442
Bahrick, H. P. 162, 418, 788
Bailey, A. W. 266, 645
Baker, C. A. 108, 605, 613, 637, 644, 683
Baker, K. E. 788
Baker, L. M. 454
Baker, R. C. 594
Baker, R. E. 788
Balashek, S. 291, 292, 319
Baldwin, A. W. 637
Ballard, J. W. 418
Ballinger, E. R. 531, 591

Hanes, R. M. 637
Hansel, C. E. M. 380
Hansel, M. 211
Hanson, J. A. 639, 794
Harary, F. 58
Hardy, A. C. 713
Hardy, J. D. 169, 178, 212
Hardy, L. H. 111
Harety, G. T. 213
Harker, G. S. 110, 639
Harlow, H. F. 382
Harmon, L. D. 382, 441
Harpman, J. J. 180
Harriman, M. W. 641
Harris, C. M. 421, 534, 594
Harris, J. D. 142, 212, 534
Harris, L. T. 641
Harris, S. J. 422
Hartline, H. K. 78, 111
Hartman, B. O. 269, 422
Hartman, E. B. 360
Hartridge, H. 111
Hartson, L. D. 443
Hatch, T. F. 534
Hathaway, S. R. 442
Hauty, G. T. 209, 594
Hawkins, J. K. 319
Hebb, D. O. 206, 293, 319, 344, 351
Hecker, C. J. 640
Hedges, T. A. 354
Hefzalla, M. H. 111
Heise, G. A. 142, 382
Heisenberg, W. 1, 21
Held, R. M. 215
Helmholz, H. F. 84, 91, 127, 598
Helson, H. 111, 448
Helstrom, C. W. 319
Hempel, W. E. 422
Henderson, A. 318
Henderson, L. F. 187, 190
Henney, K. 790
Henning, E. 595
Henning, H. 187, 190
Henry, C. E. 456, 457
Henry, E. R. 462, 533
Henry, F. M. 164
Henry, J. P. 593
Hensel, H. 179
Henson, J. B. 269
Herdan, G. 382
Herklotz, H. 641
Heron, W. 210, 213
Herrick, C. J. 382
Herrington, L. P. 537, 598
Hertzbert, H. T. E. 533, 534
Hessinger, R. W. 418

Hiatt, E. P. 541, 544, 595
Hick, W. E. 229, 269, 382, 389, 422, 534, 641, 794
Higgins, T. J. 269
Hilbert, D. 58
Hill, D. K. 395
Hill, H. E. 456
Hill, J. H. 713
Hill, J. J. 794
Hill, W. F. 385
Hillebrand, F. 84, 91
Hines, M. 457
Hirsch, I. J. 422, 534, 641
Hirsch, J. 179
Hirsch, L. J. 142
Hitchcock, F. A. 457, 534, 594
Hoagland, H. 190, 213, 457
Hockett, C. F. 329, 382, 422
Hoehn, A. J. 790
Hoff, E. C. 794
Hoffman, A. C. 639
Hoffman, J. 215
Holding, D. H. 422
Holland, D. B. 269
Holland, J. G. 642
Holmes, G. 642
Hooper, A. 29
Hoover, G. W. 626
Hopkins, C. O. 642, 684, 713
Hopkins, M. 703, 713
Hornseth, J. P. 213
Horowitz, L. P. 319
Horowitz, P. 643
Horvath, W. J. 385
Hosken, B. 794
Householder, A. S. 442
Houston, R. A. 111
Howell, W. D. 593
Howes, D. H. 642
Howland, D. 422
Hoyt, W. G. 354
Hsu, J. C. 382
Huggins, W. H. 142
Hull, C. L. 382
Humphrey, C. E. 269, 642
Humphries, M. 422
Hunt, D. P. 422
Hunt, R. W. G. 111
Hunter, H. N. 163, 165, 542, 597
Hunter, W. S. 110
Hursh, J. B. 447
Hurwicz, L. 276, 320
Husband, R. W. 382, 704, 713
Hussman, T. A. 457
Husson, G. S. 535
Hutchinson, G. E. 456

Swerling, P. 320
Swets, J. A. 323, 367, 387
Sziklai, G. C. 114, 387

T

Taker, A. W. 320
Talbot, G. D. 535
Tall, M. M. 785
Tanner, W. P. 323, 367, 368, 387
Tarjan, R. 323
Tarschanoff, J. 428
Taylor, C. L. 592, 597
Taylor, D. 375
Taylor, F. V. 266, 267, 271, 463, 646, 682, 712, 715
Taylor, M. M. 454
Taylor, W. G. 128
Taylor, W. K. 141
Thiessen, G. J. 536
Thompson, J. E. 269, 642
Thompson, J. M. 646
Thompson, P. O. 388, 597
Thomson, R. M. 389, 400, 420, 593
Thorndike, R. L. 715
Thrall, R. M. 323, 387
Thurston, L. L. 354
Tiffin, J. 114
Tiger, B. 791
Tinker, M. A. 609, 644
Tipton, C. L. 271
Tischer, R. G. 597
Tolman, E. C. 353, 387
Topmiller, D. A. 646
Tower, W. R. 646
Trank, J. W. 458
Travis, R. C. 442, 446
Tremaine, M. J. 189
Trittipoe, W. J. 143
Truxal, J. G. 271
Tsien, H. 715
Tuckman, J. 383
Turing, A. M. 299
Turner, R. D. 791
Tustin, A. 229, 271, 389
Tuttle, A. D. 597
Tweedell, K. S. 361
Tyler, D. B. 214

U

Ulam, S. 320
Unna, P. J. H. 537
Urdal, A. 189, 190, 455
Uttley, A. M. 323

V

Vail, S. 214
Vajda, S. 323

Valle, L. D. 645
van Bergeijk, W. A. 382
Van Cott, H. P. 715
Vanderplas, J. M. 646
van der Velden, H. A. 109
Van Horn, I. H. 271, 323
Van Krevelen, A. 144
Van Liere, E. J. 537
Van Sickle, N. D. 159, 164
Van Vleck, J. H. 214
Veghte, J. H. 537
Venn, J. 32, 281, 284, 311
Vernon, H. M. 701, 715
Vernon, J. 215
Vernon, M. D. 109, 646
Versace, J. 190, 269
Vestine, C. H. 713
Vickers, T. K. 788
Vinacke, W. E. 152, 684
Vince, M. A. 270, 424
Vineber, R. 794
von Beckh, H. J. 543, 558, 597, 684
von Békésy, G. 127, 144, 165
von Buddenbrock, W. 63
von Euler, C. 179
von Foerster, H. 387
von Frey 179
von Gierke, H. E. 571, 594, 597
von Neumann, J. 24, 29, 286, 299, 301, 323, 366
von Skramlik 179
von Wittern, W. W. 594
Vos, J. J. 114
Voss, J. F. 266, 272

W

Waddell, D. 189
Waisman, F. 59
Wakim, K. G. 420
Wald, A. 29, 276, 323, 367
Walden, W. 320
Walker, R. M. 789
Wall, P. D. 179
Wallace, J. D. 459
Waller, A. D. 435
Wallerstein, H. 443
Wallis, P. R. 644
Wallis, R. A. 419
Wallner, L. E. 597
Walston, C. E. 272
Walter, W. G. 439
Wang, H. 318
Wapner, S. 165, 215
Ward, A. A. Jr. 455
Ward, J. E. 597
Ward, J. H. Jr. 699, 715

SUBJECT INDEX

brightness 96
  contrast 94
  discrimination 94
  sensitivity 93

C

canonical variables 135
carbon dioxide 563
cardinal utility 365
cathode-ray tube (CRT) displays 605,
  633, 671
Causality Principle 22
censored reliability test 766
central nervous system 336
cerebellum 336, 393
cerebral cortex 338, 392
cerebrum 336, 341, 393
characteristic values 43
characteristic vectors 43
checkers 296
"chemical senses" 181
chess 10, 296
chromaticity diagram 96
class 31
clo unit 490
clothing 489
  anti-exposure 495
  anti-g 543
  full pressure 502
  gloves 495
  hardware 496
  headgear 503
  helmet visor 523
  partial pressure 514
cochlea 124
COFEC reliability data system 754
cognition 61
cold sweat 161
color 607
color discrimination 93, 95
colorimetry 95
comfort 488
communication networks 372
compensatory control system 239
competitive gaming 275
complementary wave-length 96
cone cells 75
confidence interval 743
confidence level 742
console design 611, 624
consonants 410
constructive model 7
consumer's risk 767
contact lenses 520
control dead-space 404

control display ratio 404
control "feel" 397, 403
controls 391, 674
  cranks 401
  dials 407
  "feel" 397, 403
  force-sensing fixed-stick 405
  grips 402
  keyboard 405
  knobs 400
  movable 397
  push button 400
convection cooling 500
convolution 225
coriolis phenomenon 159
cornea 72
cortex 338, 392
counter display 601
cranks 401
criterion categories 690
critical flicker-fusion frequency 101
critical maneuver display 673
cushion supports 551, 568
cyclic acceleration 553

D

dark-adaptation 93
decibel 116
decision-making 217
  automata 273
  human 324
  tracking 219
decompression 510
degree of symbolism 7
demand type oxygen regulator 505
dendrites 76
depth discrimination 98
derivative 45
descrete-time transduction 245
describing function 231
descriptive information 349
descriptive models 7
design of experiments 759
  analysis of variance 776
  average sample size 768
  confidence interval 743
  confidence level 742
  consumer's risk 767
  factor-analytic 776
  operating characteristic (OC) 767
  producer's risk 767
deterministic error 6
dials 407
difference limen 200
difference threshold 94, 200

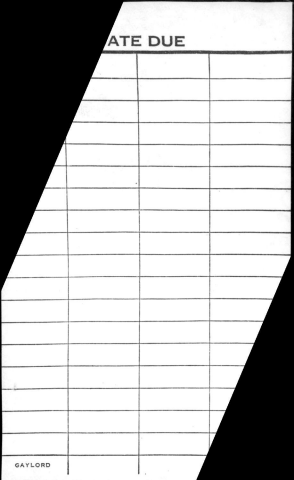

ATE DUE

GAYLORD